A SELECT BIBLIOGRAPHY OF MUSIC IN AFRICA

A select Bibliography of

MUSIC IN AFRICA

compiled at the International African Institute
by L. J. P. Gaskin, F.L.A.

under the direction of Professor K. P. Wachsmann

Institute of Ethnomusicology, African Studies Centre
University of California, Los Angeles

International African Institute

10/11 FETTER LANE, LONDON, EC4

1965

The International African Institute
is grateful to the Ford Foundation for a generous
grant towards the cost of compiling and
publishing this bibliography

Printed in Great Britain by
W. & J. Mackay & Co. Ltd., Chatham, Kent

Contents–List

Introduction

Interest in music in Africa today is directed towards many different aspects of sound. The compilation of a bibliography that is to serve such manifold interests requires much detailed knowledge of the literature on the subject, and involves difficult problems of classification. The use of the words drum and tam-tam in the literature is a case in point: it proved impracticable to distinguish in the bibliography between membrane and slit-drums,[1] and although it is inadmissible from the point of view of the organologist, the two had to be treated together.

In selecting items for inclusion, all known works containing relevant and significant information on music in Africa have been included. But the field of Afro-American music has not been covered except in the case of Cuba, where the work of F. Ortiz is of particular interest to students in the African field; special requests had been received that Ortiz's work should be represented. It is to be hoped that local initiative will lead to the compilation of bibliographies of works on music in African languages. Some of the references in travellers' observations may appear trivial; yet the specifically musical literature often bears witness to the importance of this kind of source material.

The main sections have been geographically subdivided since is was thought most musicologists would approach music and musical instruments primarily from a regional point of view. Some difficulty arose from the nomenclature of the new African states, but it is hoped that this has been overcome by the detailed geographical arrangement of African countries shown in p. ix, and, where necessary, by explanatory notes. Since ethnic and linguistic units do not always fit easily into political boundaries, classification by country proved difficult at times. The literature on the Ewe for instance, contains data collected in the former German Togo, the present-day Togo, in Ghana, or in Dahomey; or, the music of the Tuareg might be described in Niger or in Algeria: to analyze the entries in detail was impracticable. A bibliographical section, not hitherto fully explored, is that concerned with "Musical Instruments", normally classed with music, but here separated wherever possible. It would have been desirable in this section to adopt the Hornbostel-Sachs classification of musical instruments; however, it was found necessary to use a modified and simple classification that provided a compromise between the specialization of the Hornbostel-Sachs system and the nature of the literature. A large section on the Dance has also been included.

Page references to the main headings are given in the Contents-List. References to the numbered entries have been made in the Index of Authors and the Geographical and Ethnic Index. *See also references* in the text refer to the number of the entry. In the case of articles in periodical publications reference is made in the entry to the actual pagination involved, but in the case of books the pagination of the whole work is recorded, and a note of the pages dealing with music is given at the end of the entry when the subject is not mentioned in the Index or Contents-List of the book.

[1] Slit-drum (instead of slit-gong) has been adopted here to conform with Hornbostel and Sachs (No. 117) and Marcuse (No. 1785).

INTRODUCTION

The International African Institute's Card Index provided an initial basis for assembling entries and working out the classification. This was extensively supplemented by further researches made in the Libraries mentioned below to provide, it is hoped, an authoritative and useful survey of the literature on music in Africa.

Grateful thanks are due to all those who helped with advice or criticism, and particularly to those, who, so kindly, sent lists of their works for inclusion in the bibliography. Amongst these may be mentioned Dr. Gilbert Rouget, Professor Marius Schneider, Professor Nketia, and Dr. Applegate. Mrs. Norma Wolff, African specialist in the Michigan State University Library, sent a set of 600 cards for selection. Mr. Thieme of the Library of Congress sent a copy of his thesis afterwards printed in *African Music* under the title "A Selected Bibliography of Periodical Articles on the Music of Sub-Saharan Africa". The Ethnographical Museum at Antwerp sent a list of the catalogues of exhibitions on African Art held in Belgium during the past few years, and Mr. Wassing of the Rotterdam Museum sent a list of books on African Art and Music.

Thanks are also due to the authorities of the undermentioned institutions for the facilities granted to the Compiler for research in their libraries:

BRITISH MUSEUM: General Library
BRITISH MUSEUM: Department of Ethnography Library
COLONIAL OFFICE LIBRARY (London)
FROBENIUS INSTITUTE AND LIBRARY (Frankfurt a M)
MUSEE DE L'HOMME LIBRARY (Paris)
RAUTENSTRAUCH-JOEST-MUSEUM LIBRARY (Cologne)
ROYAL ANTHROPOLOGICAL INSTITUTE LIBRARY (London)
ROYAL COMMONWEALTH SOCIETY LIBRARY (London)
SCHOOL OF ORIENTAL AND AFRICAN STUDIES LIBRARY (London)
TERVUREN CONGO MUSEUM LIBRARY (Brussels)
TROPEN MUSEUM (Amsterdam)
VICTORIA AND ALBERT MUSEUM LIBRARY (London)

Among the bibliographies consulted, special mention should be made of Varley's "African Native Music" of 1936; many of his entries have been incorporated, without, however, including his annotations. Useful too have been J. Kunst's "Ethnomusicology", and A. P. Merriam's "Annotated Bibliography of African and African Derived Music since 1936" (Published in *Africa*, Vol. 21, 1951).

Grateful thanks are due also to the Regents of the University of California for the generous assistance given to Professor Wachsmann; to Mrs. Ann Briegleb, Archivist to the Institute of Ethnomusicology at the University of California; and to Miss Sara Stalder.

List of Countries

(For consistency English versions of the names of all countries have been given)

ALGERIA

ANGOLA

BASUTOLAND

BECHUANALAND

BELGIAN CONGO see CONGOLESE REPUBLIC

BURUNDI (formerly part of Rwanda-Urundi)

CAMEROONS

CANARY ISLANDS

CAPE PROVINCE

CAPE VERDE ISLANDS

CENTRAL AFRICAN REPUBLIC (formerly Oubangui-Shari, A.E.F.)

CHAD

CONGO REPUBLIC (formerly Middle-Congo, A.E.F.)

CONGOLESE REPUBLIC (formerly Belgian Congo)

DAHOMEY

EAST AFRICA (General)

EGYPT

ETHIOPIA

FORMER FRENCH WEST AFRICA (A.O.F.)

GABON

GAMBIA

GHANA

GUINÉE FRANÇAISE see GUINEA

GUINEA (formerly Guinée Française)

IVORY COAST

KENYA

LIBERIA

LIBYA

MADAGASCAR

MALAWI (formerly Nyasaland)

MALI (formerly Soudan Français)

MAURITANIA

MOROCCO

MOZAMBIQUE

NATAL

NIGER

NIGERIA

NORTH AFRICA (General)

NORTH AFRICAN MUSIC IN RELATION TO THAT OF THE IBERIAN PENINSULA

NORTHERN RHODESIA see ZAMBIA

PORTUGUESE GUINEA

RWANDA (formerly part of Rwanda-Urundi)

SÃO TOMÉ

SENEGAL

SIERRA LEONE

SOMALIA (including former British Somaliland)

SOUTH AFRICA

SOUTH-WEST AFRICA

SOUTHERN RHODESIA

SPANISH GUINEA

SPANISH WEST AFRICA

SUDAN (formerly Anglo-Egyptian Sudan)

SWAZILAND

TANGANYIKA (now, with Zanzibar, Tanzania)

TOGO

TRANSVAAL

TUNISIA

UGANDA

VOLTAIC REPUBLIC

WEST AFRICA (General)

ZAMBIA (formerly Northern Rhodesia)

ZANZIBAR

GENERAL

Works not specifically related to Africa, nor otherwise geographically specialised, but of value to the student in the African Field.

1. **Bingham, W. V.** *Five years of progress in comparative musical science.* Psychological bulletin [Lancaster, Pa.], **11**, 1914, 321–33.
2. **Bose, Fritz.** 1953. *Musikalische Völkerkunde.* Pp. 197. Freiburg: Atlantis Verlag (Atlantis Musikbücherei).
3. **Bücher, Karl.** 1902. *Arbeit und Rhythmus.* Pp. 455, ill. Leipzig: B. G. Teubner. [3rd ed.]
4. **Closson, Ernest.** *M. von Hornbostel et l'ethnographie musicale.* Guide musical [Brussels], **60**, 1914, 335.
5. —— *Questionnaire d'ethnographie-musique.* Bull. soc. roy. belge. géog., 1925, 132–44.
6. **Collaer, Paul.** *Cartography and ethnomusicology.* Ethnomusicology, **2**, 1958, 66–68.
7. **Combarieu, J.** 1909. *La musique et la Magie.* Pp. 374. Paris: Picard Fils.
7a. —— 1910. *La musique, ses lois, son évolution.* Pp. 384. Paris: Flammarion.
8. **Comettant, Jean Pierre Oscar.** 1869. *La musique, les musiciens et les instruments de musique chez les différents peuples du Monde.* Pp. v + 737, ill. Paris: Lévy.
9. **Dal, Erik.** *Kongresnotater Isaer om Afrikansk Musik Dansk Musiktidskrift*, **33**, no. 4, 1958, 84– .
10. **Danckert, W.** *Musikethnologische Erschliessung der Kulturkreise.* Mitt. anthrop. Gesell. Wien, **67**, 1937, 53–58.
11. **Gilbert, Will G.** *Ethno-Musicologie.* A.M.E., 1957, 489–94.
12. **Graf, W.** *Musikethnologie und Quellenkritik.* Die Wiener Schule, 1956, 111–24.
13. **Habig, J. M.** *La valeur du rythme dans la musique Bantoue.* Probl. afr. centr. 7, no. 26, 1954, 278–85, ill.
14. **Harrison, F. L., Mantle Hood,** and **C. V. Palisca.** 1964. *Musicology.* P. 337. New York: Prentice-Hall.
15. **Heins, E. L.** *Exotics in music.* Kultuurpatronen, Patterns of Culture. Deel 1, 1959, 112–31, bibl., ill. [Bull. Ethnog. Museum, Delft.]
15a. **Hermann, E.** *Schallsignalsprachen in Melanesien und Afrika.* Nachr. Akad. Wiss. Göttingen: Phil. Hist. Klasse, no. 5, 1943, 127–86.
16. **Hickmann, Hans.** *Fidel 1. Orientalische Vorläufer und Verwandte.* Blume, F. (ed.), Die Musik in Geschichte und Gegenwart, **4**, 1954, 156.
17. —— *Handzeichen I. Altertum und Aussereuropäische Musik.* Blume, F. (ed.), Die Musik in Geschichte und Gegenwart, **5**, 1956, 1443–51, ill.
18. **Hood, Mantle.** *Training and research methods in ethnomusicology.* Ethnomusicology news-letter, no. 11, 1957, 2.
19. **Hornbostel, Erich von.** *Über ein akustisches Kriterium für Kulturzusammenhänge.* Z. f. Ethnol., 1911, 601– .
20. —— *Arbeit und Musik.* Z. Intern. Musikgesell, **13**, 1912, 341.
21. —— *First communication about the theory of the blown fifths.* Anthropos, **14–15**, 1919, 569–70.
22. —— *Translation of A. J. Ellis 'On the musical scales of various nations'.* Sammel. f. vergl. Musikw. [Munich], **1**, 1922, 1.
23. **Howes, Frank.** *Anthropology and music.* Man, **45**, no. 83, 1945, 107.
24. —— 1948. *Man, mind and music.* Pp. viii + 184. London: Secker & Warburg.
25. **Huntington, Mary.** *Man and music.* Nat. hist., **44**, 1939, 111.
26. **Husmann, H.** 1951. *Fünf- und siebenstellige Centstafeln zur Berechnung Musikalischer Intervalle.* Pp. 16. Leiden: E. J. Brill.
27. **Iyeki, J. F.** 1956. *Essai de psychologie du primitif.* Pp. 53, ill. Léopoldville: La Voix du Congolais. [Published from articles in La voix du Congolais, q.v.]
28. —— *Essai de psychologie du primitif.* La voix du Congolais, 1956, 12 ann. Nos. 118, 15–20: 119, 89–93: 121, 251–5: 122, 323–26, ill.
29. **Karpeles, Maud,** and **Arnold, A. Bake.** 1951. *Manual for folk music collectors.* London: I.F.M.C. R. anthrop. inst.
29a. —— *The collecting of folk music and other ethnomusicological material: A manual for field workers.* [Enlarged and partly rewritten version of the above.] 1958. London: I.F.M.C. R. anthrop. inst.
30. **Kirby, P. R.** *Science and music.* S. Afr. J. of science, **51**, 1954, 67.
31. **Kruithof, J.** *Muziekesthetiek.* A.M.E., 1957, 484–6, bibl.
32. **Kunst, Jaap.** 1948. *Around von Hornbostel's theory of the cycle of blown fifths.* Pp. 35. Indisch Instituut, Amsterdam. Koninklijke Vereeniging Indisch Institut Mededeling, No. 76.
33. **Kunz, L.** *Archiv and Phonograph im Dienste einheimischer Musik in den Missionsländern.* Missionswiss. u. Religionswiss., **1**, 1939, 11–18.
34. **Lenoir, Raymond.** *La musique comme institution sociale.* L'anthropologie, **43**, 1933, 47–81.
35. **Lloyd, Ll. S.** *Hornbostel's theory of the blown fifths.* Monthly musical record [London], Jan. and Feb. 1946.
36. —— *The myth of equal-stepped scales in primitive music.* Music and letters, **27**, 1946, 73.
37. **Merriam, Alan P.** *The use of music in the study of a problem of acculturation.* Amer. anthrop., **57**, 1955, 28–34.
37a. —— 1964. *The anthropology of music.* Pp. xi + 358, bibl. Chicago: Northwestern Univ. Press.
38. **Myers, Charles S.** *The beginnings of music.* Essays and studies presented to William Ridgeway, 1913, 560–82.
39. **Nadel, Siegfried.** *The origins of music.* Mus. quart., **16**, 1930, 531.
40. **Reinhard, Kurt.** *Das Berliner Phonogramm-Archiv.* Baessler-Archiv, **9** (1), 1961, 83–94.
41. **Rhodes, Willard.** *Towards a definition of ethnomusicology.* Amer. anthrop., **58**, 1956, 457–63.
42. **Rouget, Gilbert.** *Échelles musicales, facture instrumentale et résonnance.* Actes du colloque sur la résonnance dans les échelles musicales. C.N.R.S. [Paris], 1963, 223–34.
43. **Sachs, Curt.** 1929. *Geist und Werden der Musikinstrumente.* Pp. xii + 282, ill, bibl. Berlin: Reimer.
44. —— 1930. *Vergleichende Musikwissenschaft in ihren Grundzügen.* Pp. 87, bibl. Leipzig: Quelle.
45. —— 1957. *The lore of non-Western music.* Mendel, A. (ed.), Some aspects of musicology, pp. 19–48. New York: The Liberal Arts Press.
46. **Sachs, C.** 1962. *The wellsprings of music.* Pp. xi + 228. The Hague, Nijhoff.
47. **Schaeffner, André.** *Musical ethnology or comparative musicology.* Colloques de Wégimont, **1**, 1954/55.
48. **Schneider, Marius.** *Ethnologische Musikforschung.* Preuss, K. Th. Lehrbuch der Völkerkunde [2nd ed.] 1956.
49. **Seeger, Charles.** *Systematic musicology: viewpoints, orientations and methods.* J. Amer. mus. soc., **4**, 1951, 240–8.
50. —— *Toward a universal music sound writing for musicology.* J. int. folk music council, **9**, 1957, 63.
51. —— and **Others.** 1935. *Music.* Encyclopaedia of the social sciences, vol. 11, pp. 143–65. New York: Macmillan.
52. —— 1950. *Oral tradition in music.* Leach, Maria, ed., Standard dictionary of folklore, mythology, and legend, vols. 1 and 2, pp. 825–9. New York: Funk & Wagnalls.
53. **Simmel, Georg.** *Psychologische und Ethnologische Studien über Musik.* Z. f. Völkerpsychol. u. Sprachwissens, **13**, 1882, 261.

54. **Stumpf, Carl.** 1911. *Die Anfänge der Musik.* Pp. 209, ill. Leipzig: Barth.

54a. **Yale University.** *Human Relations Area Files* (1960–   ).

Encyclopedias and Dictionaries

55. **Algemene Musiek Encyclopedie.** 6 vols. 1957. Algemene Muziek Encyclopedie. Pt. 1 A–B; 2 C–F; 3 G–J; 4 K–M; 5 M–Q; 6 R–Z. Antwerp/Amsterdam: Zuid Nederlandse Uitgeverij.

56. **Apel, Willi.** 1946. *Harvard dictionary of music.* Pp. lx + 831. London: W. & G. Foyle.

57. **Blume, Friedrich** (ed.). *Die Musik in Geschichte und Gegenwart. Allgemeine Enzyklopädie der Musik unter Mitarbeit führender Spezialisten auf allen Gebieten der Musikforschung im In- und Ausland.* 1949–[in continuation]. Kassel: Bärenreiter. London: Novello & Co.

57a. **Collaer, Paul,** and **Others.** 1960. *Bildatlas der Musikgeschichte.* Pp.   , ill. Paris: Elsevier.

58. **Grove, Sir George.** 1954. *Grove's dictionary of music and musicians,* 9 vols. and supplementary vol. to 5th edn. Edited by Eric Blom. London: Macmillan. [5th ed.]

59. **Lavignac, Albert,** and **Lionel de la Laurencie.** *Encyclopédie de la musique et dictionnaire du conservatoire.* Pt. 1 (1913). Histoire de la musique: (*Antiquité–Moyen Age*), pp. viii + 610, ill. Pt. 1 (1913) (*Italie–Allemagne,* pp. viii + 611–1175, ill. Pt. 1 (1913) (*France, Belgique, Angleterre*), pp. ix + 1176–1912, ill. Pt. 1 (1920) (*Espagne–Portugal*), pp. vii + 1913–2484, ill. Pt. 1 (1922) (*Russie, Arabes, Éthiope, Afrique méridionale, Madagascar, Canaries, etc.*), pp. viii + 2485–3401, ill. Pt. 2 (1926) Technique, esthétique, pédagogie. (*Voix-instruments à reservoir d'air*), pp. 761–1400. Pt. 2 (1927) *Technique instrumentale: Instruments à vent, Instruments à percussion, Instruments à cordes automatiques,* pp. 1401–2128, ill. Pt. 2 (1929) (*Orchestration: Musique liturgique des différents cultes*), pp. 2129–2718. Pt. 2 (1930) (*Esthétique*), pp. 2719–3436. Paris: Librairie Delagrave.

60. **Michel, Francois,** and **Others.** 1958–61. *Encyclopédie de la musique,* 3 vols. 1958, vol. 1, pp. 715, ill. 1959, vol. 2, pp. 717, ill. 1961, vol. 3, pp. 1023, ill. Paris: Fasquelle.

61. **Sachs, Curt.** 1913. *Reallexikon der Musikinstrumente.* Pp. xvii + 442, ill. Berlin: J. Bard.

62. **Sohlmans Musiklexikon.** Edited by Gösta Morin. 4 vols. 1948–52. Vol. 1, pp. xv + 1279, ill. Vol. 2, pp. xii + 1294, ill. Vol. 3, pp. xvi + 1375, ill. Vol. 4, pp. xii + 1607, ill. Stockholm: Sohlmans Forlag.

63. **Thompson, Oscar** (ed.). 1956. *The international cyclopedia of music and musicians* (revised by Nicolas Slonimsky). Pp. 2500. London: J. M. Dent. [9th ed.]

History and Prehistory

64. **Dufourcq, Norbert** (ed.). 1946. *La musique: dès origines à nos jours.* Pp. xiv + 592, ill. Paris: Larousse.

65. **Engel, H.** 1962. *Musik der Völker und Zeiten, von den Anfängen bis zur Gegenwart.* Pp. 468, ill.

65a. **Fage, J.** 1964. *Music and history: an historian's essay at the African picture.* Essays on music and history in Africa and Asia. Pt. 2: Africa. [Roy. anthrop. inst.]

66. **Husmann, Heinrich.** 1961. *Grundlagen der Antiken und Orientalischen Musikkultur.* Pp. (6), 213, bibl., ill. Berlin: Walter de Gruyter.

67. **Jeffreys, M. D. W.** *Some historical notes on African tone languages.* Afr. stud., **4**. (3), 1945, 133–45.

67a. —— *Negro influence on Indonesia.* Afr. mus. soc., **2** (4), 1961, 10–16.

67b. **Jones, A. M.** 1964. *Africa and Indonesia: the evidence of the*

xylophone and other musical and cultural factors. Pp. viii + 248, ill. Leiden: E. J. Brill.

68. **Koole, Arend.** *The history, study, aims and problems of comparative musicology.* S. Afr. J. of science, **51** (8), 1955, 227.

69. **Nettl, Bruno.** *Historical aspects of ethnomusicology.* Amer. anthrop., **60**, 1958, 518–32.

70. **Rowbotham, John Frederick.** 1885. *History of music.* Pp. 151. London: Trübner.

71. **Sachs, Curt.** 1924. *Musik des Altertums.* Pp. 84, bibl., ill. Breslau: Ferdinand Hirt. [Jedermanns Bücherei: Abt. Musik.]

72. ——*Anfänge der Musik.* Bull. union musicol., **6**, 1926, 136.

73. —— 1943. *The rise of music in the ancient world.* Pp. 324, ill. New York: Norton.

74. **Wellesz, Egon** (ed.). 1957. *Ancient and oriental music.* Pp. xxiii+530, bibl., ill. London: Oxford Univ. Press. [New Oxford history of music, vol. 1.]

75. **Wiora, Walter.** *La musique à l'époque de la peinture paléolithique.* J. int. folk music council, **15**, 1962, 1–6.

Tribal music (general)

76. **Baglioni, S.** *Contributo alla conoscenza della musica naturale.* Soc. Rom. anthrop., **15**, 1910, 313–60. [Translated into German in Globus, **98**, 1910, 232–6: 249–54: 264–8.]

77. **Emsheimer, E.** *Primitive Musik.* Sohlmans Musiklexikon, vol. 4, 1952, 241–3.

78. **Gilbert, Will G.** *Primitieve Muziek.* A.M.E., 1957, 588–602, ill.

79. **Heinitz, K.** 1931. *Strukturprobleme in Primitiver Musik.* Pp. 258. Hamburg: Friedrichsen.

80. **Herzog, George.** *On primitive music.* Amer. anthrop., **34**, 1932, 546.

81. —— *Recording primitive music in Africa and America.* Bull. folksong soc. of the northeast, no. 8, 1933, 2–3.

81a. ——*Speech-melody and primitive music.* Mus. quart., **20** (4), 1934, 452–6.

82. **Hornbostel, Erich M. von.** *Musik der Naturvölker.* Meyer, Grosses Konversations-Lexikon, vol. 24, 1911/12, pp. 638–43.

83. —— *Musik der Eingeborenen: Musikinstrumente der Eingeborenen.* Schnee, H. (ed.), Deutsches Koloniallexikon, Q.V., vol. **2**, 1920, 602–5.

84. **Kirby, P.** *Primitive music.* Grove, Sir George, Dictionary of music and musicians, vol. 6, 1954, 921–6.

85. **Lachmann, Robert.** *Die Musik der aussereuropäischen Natur- und Kulturvölker.* Bücken, Ernst, 'Handbuch der Musikwissenschaft', 1929, 31, ill. Wildpark-Potsdam: Athenaion.

86. **MacCulloch, J. A.** *Music (Primitive and savage).* Hastings, James, Encyclopaedia of religion and ethics, vol. 9, 1917, 5–10.

87. **Michaelis, C. F.** *Über die Musik wilder und halbcultivierter Völker.* Allg. Musik Zeit., **31**, 1814, 509–15, 524–30.

88. **Myers, Charles S.** *A study of rhythm in primitive music.* Brit. J. of psychol., **1**, 1905, 397.

89. —— 1907. *The ethnological study of music.* Anthropological essays presented to Edward Tylor, pp. 235–54. Oxford: Oxford Univ. Press.

90. —— *The study of primitive music.* Musical antiquary, **3**, 1912, 121.

91. **Nettl, Bruno.** *Notes on musical composition in primitive culture.* Anthrop. quart., **27**, 1954, 81–   .

92. —— *Articles on folk, primitive and oriental music.* Ethnomusicology newsletter, **10**, 1957, 15–22.

93. —— *Change in folk and primitive music: a survey of methods and studies.* J. Amer. mus. soc., **8**, 1955, 101–9.

94. —— *Unifying factors in folk and primitive music.* J. Amer. mus. soc., **9** (3), 1956, 196–201.

95. —— 1956. *Music in primitive culture.* Pp. 182. Music (16 pp.) Cambridge, Mass.: Harvard Univ. Press.

96. **Pastor, Willy.** 1912. *Music of primitive peoples and the beginnings of European music.* Pp. 679–700. Annual report of the Smithsonian Institution for 1912. [Translated from German edn. of 1910.]

97. **Reinhard, Kurt.** *Bedeutung, Wesen und Erforschungsmöglichkeiten primitiver Musik.* Sociologus, Nf., 1 (2), 1951, 81–96.

98. **Roberts, Helen H.** *Primitive music.* Encyclopaedia of the social sciences, 11, 1933, pp. 150–2. [Quelques caractères très généraux de la musique primitive.]

99. **Rouget, Gilbert.** *À propos de la forme dans les musiques de tradition orale.* Les colloques de Wégimont, I, 1956, 132–44.

100. **Sachs, Curt.** *Musik der Naturvölker.* Riemann Musiklexikon, Mainz, 1958. [12th ed.]

101. —— *Primitive and medieval music: a parallel.* J. Amer. mus. soc., 13 (1–3), 1960, 43–49.

102. **Schneider, Marius.** 1934. *Geschichte der Mehrstimmigkeit:* (1) *Die Naturvölker.* Pp. 107 + 47 (Notenbeispiele). Berlin: Julius Bard Verlag.

103. —— *Primitive music.* Wellesz, Egon, Ancient and oriental music, 1957, 1–82, ill.

104. —— 1958. *Die Musik der Naturvölker.* Adam, L. and Trimborn, Lehrbuch der Völkerkunde [3rd ed.], 1958, 82–110.

105. —— *Le rôle de la musique dans la mythologie et les rites des civilisations non-européenes.* Histoire de la musique, 1960, 131–214.

105a. **Tracey, Hugh Travers.** *Primitive music.* Music and dance, 52, 1961, 11– .

106. **Wachsmann, K. P.** *The transplantation of folk music from one social environment to another.* J. int. folk music council, 6, 1954, 41–45.

107. —— *Music primitive.* Encyclopaedia Britannica [New ed.]

108. **Wallaschek, Richard.** 1893. *Primitive music.* Pp. 326, bibl. London: Longmans.

Classification

109. **Balfour, Henry.** Musical section in Notes and queries on anthropology [5th ed.], 1929, 295– . [See also 116.]

110. **Fétis, François-Joseph.** *Sur un nouveau mode de classification des races humaines d'après leurs systèmes musicaux.* Bull. soc. anthrop. [Paris], N.S.2, 1867.

111. **Freeman, Linton C.,** and **Alan P. Merriam.** *Statistical classification in anthropology: an application to ethnomusicology.* Amer. anthrop., 58 (3), 1956, 464–72.

112. **International Folk Music Council.** 195–, *Memorandum on cataloguing and classification of sound recordings of folk music.* Pp. 7, 195.

113. —— 1952. *Notation of folk music: recommendations of the committee of experts convened . . . 1949 and . . . 1950.* Pp. 8.

114. **Kolinski, Mieczyslaw.** *Classification of tonal structures.* I, Studies in ethnomusicology, I, 1961, 38–76.

115. **Norlind, Tobias.** *Musikinstrumentensystematik.* Svensk Tidskrift för Musikforskning, 1–4, 1932, 95–123.

116. **Royal Anthropological Institute, London.** 1951. *Notes and queries on anthropology.* Pp. xii + 403, bibl., ill. London: Routledge. [6th ed.] [Music and dancing, pp. 315–32.]

117. **Sachs, Curt,** and **Erich von Hornbostel.** *Systematik der Musikinstrumente, ein Versuch.* Zeit, f. Ethnol., 46, 1914, 553–90. [English translation in journal of the Galpin society, vol. 14, 1961, 4–29. French summary in Encyclopédie française, vol. 16, 1935, 16 '36–15/16.]

118. **Abt, Ernst.** *Die Musik der Naturvölker unserer Kolonien.* Wissen Berlin, **4**, 1910, 65–68.

119. **Adandé, A.** *L'évolution de la musique africaine.* Notes afr. I.F.A.N., **54**, 1952, 39–44, ill.

120. **Amu, E.** *How to study African rhythm.* Teacher's Journal [Gold Coast], **6**, 1934, 33–34, 121–4.

121. **Anon.** *African music.* Lantern 5, vol. 5 (1), July–Sept. 1955, 35.

122. **Archiv für Musikforschung.** *Über direkte und gestaltmässige Überlieferung wandernder afrikanischer Melodien.* Arch. f. Musik-fors., **4**, 1937.

123. **Ballanta, Nicholas George Julius.** *Music of the African races.* West Afr., **14**, 1930, 752–3.

124. **Bansisa, Y.** *Music in Africa.* Uganda J., **4** (2), 1936, 108–14.

125. **Barat-Pepper, Elaine.** *La musique traditionnelle africaine sera sauvegardée.* Bull. Inform. Haut Commissariat de la République A.E.F., **50**, mars 1950, 1–8.

126. **Basil, Rev. Brother.** *Wandering from pitch.* Afr. mus. soc., **11**, 1958, 54–55.

127. **Berthoud, Gérald.** 1962. *Magie, religion et art africains.* Pp. 23, ill. Geneva: Imp. populaires (Éxtrait de musées de Genève, 25, 28, 29, 1962).

128. **Blacking, John.** *Some notes on a theory of African rhythm advanced by Erich von Hornbostel.* Afr. mus. soc., **1**, 2, 1955, 12–20, ill.

129. **Boateng, Otto A.** 1948. *Infant singing in African schools.* Pp. 29. London: Oxford Univ. Press.

130. **Brandel, Rose.** *The music of African circumcision rituals.* J. Amer. mus. soc., **7**, 1954, 52–62.

131. ——*The African hemiola style.* Ethnomusicology, **3**, 3, Sept. 1959, 106–17.

132. **Calame-Griaule, G.,** and **B. Calame.** *Introduction à l'étude de la musique africaine.* La revue musicale, les carnets critiques, no. [special] 238, 1957, 24 pp., bibl., ill.

133. **Caluza, Reuben Tozakele.** *African native music.* Southern workman, **55**, 1926, 396–7.

134. —— *African music.* Southern workman, **60**, 1931, 152– . [Hampton.]

135. **Chauvet, Stephen.** 1929. *Musique nègre.* Pp. 242, bibl., ill. Paris: Société d'éditions géographiques, maritimes et coloniales.

136. —— *Musique et arts nègres en A.O.F.* Pp. 39. Paris: Apollon.

137. **Colin, Roland.** *Situation de l'art nègre.* Présence africaine, no. 26, 1959, 52–66.

138. **Considine, John J.** 1955. *African world of new men.* Pp. ix + 398, bibl., ill., maps. New York: Dodd, Mead & Co.

139. **Cope, Trevor.** *African music: a lecture given at Natal University.* Afr. mus. soc., **2**, (2), 1959, 33–41.

140. **Courlander, Harold.** 1951. *Negro folk music of Africa and America.* Folkways Records, P500.

141. **Dammann, Ernst.** 1963. *Die Religionen Afrikas.* Pp. xv + 302, bibl., map. Stuttgart: Kohlhammer. [Pp. 238–44.]

142. **Dapper, Olfert.** 1676. *Naukeurige Beschrijvinge der Afrikanische Gewesten.* Sp. Pp. – , ill. Amsterdam: Meurs. [Another edition in French (1686): *Description de l'Afrique.* Pp. 534, ill., maps. Amsterdam: Wolfgang Waesberge, Boom and Van Someren.]

143. **de Bouveignes, Olivier.** *Le rythme dans la musique nègre.* Revue nationale [Brussels], **21**, 1949, 21–193.

144. **de Magalhães, A. A.** *Alguns aspectos da música indígena Africana.* Mensario admin. [Angola], **12**, 1948, 53–54; **13**, 1948, 29–31; **13**, 1949, 20–23, 47–51, 53–56, ill.

145. **Dévigne, Roger.** *Ethnographie sonore. Musiques africaines . . . islamiques,* etc. Rev. psychol. des peuples, **11**, 1956, 425.

146. **Dubois, Henri.** 1932. *Le répertoire africain.* Rome: La Sodalité de St. Pierre Clavier.

147. **Dunbar, Rudolph.** *La musique africaine et son influence dans le Monde.* Présence africaine, nos. 27–28, 1959, 291–302.

148. **Edwards, S. Hylton.** *Music in Africa.* J. roy. soc. arts, **103**, 4958, 1955, 704–11.

149. **Foucart, George.** 1919. *Introductory questions on African ethnology.* Pp. v + 159. Cairo: French Institute of Oriental Archaeology. [Pp. 134–6.] [Sultanieh Geographical Society of Cairo.]

150. **Frobenius, Leo.** *Der Ursprung der afrikanischen Kulturen.* Z. Ges. Erdkunde [Berlin], **33**, 1898, 111–25, map.

151. —— 1928. *Das Sterbende Afrika.* Pp. 502, ill. Frankfurt a.M.: Sozietäts-Druckerei.

152. **Gay, Robert.** *Essai de discographie nègre africaine [catalogue d'enregistrements].* Probl. Afr. centr., **7**, 26, 1954, 345–50.

153. **Gbeho, Phillip.** *Cross rhythm in African music.* W.A.R., **23**, 1952, 11.

154. **Giorgetti, Filiberto.** 1957. *Musica Africana sua tecnica e acustica.* Pp. 128, ill. Bologna: Editrice Nigrizia. [Museum Combonianum no. 10.]

155. **Guernier, Eugene L.** 1952. *L'apport de l'Afrique à la pensée humaine.* Pp. 245. Paris: Payot.

156. **Haberlandt, A.** *Afrika.* Buschan, Georg. (ed.), Illustrierte Völkerkunde, vol. 1, 1922, pp. 428–686, ill., maps.

157. **Habig, J. M.** *La valeur du rythme dans la musique bantoue.* Probl. Afr. centr., no. 26 (4), 1954, 279–85.

158. **Hailey, Lord.** 1957. *An African survey. Revised to 1956.* Pl. xxvi + 1676, bibl., maps. Oxford: Oxford Univ. Press. [Music, pp. 67–72.]

159. **Hambly, Wilfrid D.** 1937. *Source book for African anthropology* [2 vols.]. Vol. 1. Pp. 404, ill., maps. Vol. 2. Pp. 407–953, bibl., ill., maps. Chicago: Field Museum. [Vol. 1. Deformation, ornaments and clothing, pp. 255–75. Vol.. 2. Music and dancing, pp. 446–56, bibl., ill.; Arts and handicrafts, pp. 613–46, bibl., ill. Supplement to source book Bibliog., 1937–49. Publications of the Field Museum anthrop. series.]

160 —— 1945. *Clever hands of the African negro.* Pp. xiii+192, ill. Washington: Associated Publishers Inc. [Music, pp. 59–73.]

162. **Hartmann, Robert.** 1879. *Die Völker Afrikas.* Pp. 94, ill. Leipzig: Brockhaus.

163. **Heilborn, Adolf.** *Die Musik der Naturvölker unserer Kolonien.* Deut. Kol. Zeitg. [Berlin], **21**, 1904, 347–348.

164. **Hichens, William.** *Music: a triumph of African art.* Discovery, **12**, 1931, 192. [Reprinted in 'Art and Archaeology', 1932, 36–41.]

165. **Hickmann, Hans.** *Afrikanische Musik.* Blume, F. (ed.), Die Musik in Geschichte u. Gegenwart, **1**, 1951, col. 123.

166. **Hodeir, Andrè.** *Prolongements de la musique africaine.* Probl. afr. centr., **7**, 1954, 286.

167. **Hornbostel, Erich M. von.** *African negro music.* Africa [London], **1**, 1928, 30–62.

168. —— *African negro music.* Africa, **1**, 1, Jan. 1928, pp. 30–62. Reprint. Memorandum IV. Pp. 35. Oxford Univ. Press for International African Institute.

169. —— 1963. *The demonstration collection of E. M. von Hornbostel and the Berlin Phonogramm-Archiv.* Pp. 40. New York: Ethnic Folkways Library, FE4175.

170. **Hornburg, F.** *Phonographierte Afrikanische Mehrstimmigkeit.* Musik-Forschung, **3**, 1950, 120–42.

171. **Hulskamp, Franciscus.** *Zwarte Muziek.* Het Missiewerk, **23** (Bois-le-Duc), 1942, 18–19.

172. **Hyslop, Graham H.** *Choice of music for festivals in Africa.* Afr, mus. soc., **1**, 2, 1955, 53–55.

173. **Jahn, Janheinz.** 1961. *Muntu.* Pp. 267, bibl., ill., maps. London: Faber & Faber. [Pp. 29–95.]

174. —— and **A. A. Daver.** *Der Blues.* Der Monat, **16**, no. 186, 1964, 55–64.

175. **Jones, A. M.** 1948. *The music makers: suggestions on music teaching for African teachers.* Pp. 28. London, Cape Town: Longmans.

176. —— *African music.* Afr. affairs, **48**, 193, Oct. 1949, 290–7.

177. —— *Folk music in Africa.* J. int. folk music council, **5**, 1953, 36–40.

178. —— *African rhythm.* Africa, **24**, 1, Jan. 1954, 26–47. [Int. Afr. inst. memo. no. 27, 1955.]

179. —— *East and west, north and south [characteristics of African music].* Afr. mus. soc., **1**, 1, 1954, 57–62.

180. —— *On transcribing African music.* Afr. mus. soc., **2**, 1, 1958, 11–14.

180a. —— *African metrical lyrics.* Afr. language stud., **5**, 1964, 52–63.

181. **Kirby, Percival R.** *A study of negro harmony.* Mus. quart., **16**, 1930, 404-14, ill.

182. —— *A musicologist looks at Africa.* S. Afr. archaeol. bull., **16**, 64, 1961, 122–7, bibl.

183. **Kubik, Gerhard.** *Musikgestaltung in Afrika.* Neues Afr., **3**, 5, May 1961, 195–201, ill.

184. —— *Beziehungen zwischen Musik und Sprache in Afrika.* Neues Afr., **4**, 1, Jan. 1962, 33–37.

185. —— *Die Situation der Musik Afrikas.* Neues Afr., **4**, 9, Sept. 1962, 351–2.

186. **Kunst, Jaap.** *A musicological argument for cultural relationship between Indonesia, probably the Isle of Java, and Central Africa.* Proc. mus. assoc., session 62, 1936.

187. —— *Ein musikologischer Beweis für Kulturzusammenhänge zwischen Indonesien- vermutlich Java- und Zentralafrika.* Anthropos [Vienna], **31**, 1936, 131–40, ill.

188. **Lamoral, A.** *Renaissance de la musique bantoue.* Zaire, 1947, 819–25.

189. **Lhoni, Patrice.** *La musique africaine et la morale.* Liaison [Brazzaville], **69**, 1959, 13–24, ill.

190. **Lomax, Alan.** *Song structure and social structure.* Ethnology, **1** (4), 1962, 425–51, bibl.

191. —— *Phonotactique et chants populaires.* Ethnology [4], 1964.

192. **Long, Kenneth R.** *The future of African music.* Nada [Bulawayo], **23**, 1946, 24–28.

193. **Lyle, Watson.** *African primitive instrumental music.* Fanfare [London], 1921, 1, no. 4.

194. —— *Negermusik.* Auftakt [Prague], **5**, 1925, 15–16.

194a. **McGinty, Doris E.** *Africa tribal music: a study of transition.* J. human relations, 8, 3/4, special no., spring and summer 1960, 739–48.

195. **Mackenzie, D. R.** *African music.* Books for Africa, **6**, 1936, pp. 35–37.

196. **Marfurt, Luitfrid.** 1957. *Musik in Africa.* Pp. 110, bibl., ill. München: Nymphenburger Verlagshandlung.

197. **Marques, Belo.** 1943. *Musica negra.* Pp. 121, ill., Lisbon: Edicao da Agência Geral das Colónias.

198. **Maytain, Philémon de Neudaz.** *Le chant et la musique des nègres.* Revue romande, **9**, 1930, 103–7, 126–8, 172–4.

199. **Mbunga, Stephen B. G.** 1963. *Church law and Bantu music.* Pp. xxxi + 211. Schöneck-Beckenried, Schweiz: Neue Zeitschrift für Missionswissenschaft (Supplementa, 13).

200. **Meinhof, Carl.** *Die Geheimsprachen Afrikas.* Globus, **66**, 1894, 117.

201. **Mendes-Corrêa, António.** 1949. *Ultramar Portugues.* (1) Sintese da África. Pp. 400 (36), ill., maps. Lisbon: Agência Geral das Colónias. [Pp. 299–301.]

202. **Merriam, Alan P.** *African music.* Continuity and change in African cultures, ed. W. R. Bascom and M. J. Herskovits, 1958, pp. 49–86.

203. —— *Apports de la musique africaine à la culture mondiale.* Jeune afr., **12**, 31, 1959, 26–34.

204. —— *Characteristics of African music.* J. int. folk music council, **11**, 1959, 13–19.

205. —— *The African idiom in music.* J. Amer. folklore, **75**, 296, 1962, 120–30.

206. —— 1962. *A prologue to the study of the African arts.* Pp. 37, bibl. Yellow Springs, Ohio: Antioch Press.

207. **Milligan, Robert H.** 1912. *The fetish folk of West Africa.* Pp. 328, ill. New York: Revell. [Chap. 5, pp. 72–84, African Music.]

207a. **Murdock, G. P.** 1959. *Africa: its peoples and their culture history.* Pp. xiii + 456, bibl., ill., maps. London: McGraw-Hill. [Useful list of tribal names.]

208. **Nketia, J. H. Kwabena.** *African music,* Pt. 1. Pt. 1, AMSAC newsletter, vol. 3, nos. 5 and 6, Supplement, no. 19. Pt. 2, AMSAC newsletter, vol. 3, nos. 7 and 8. Music in Ghana, no. 2.

209. —— *The music of Africa.* J. of human relations, **8**, nos. 3 and 4, 1960, 730–8.

210. —— *The Hocket-technique in African music.* J. int. folk music council, **14**, 1962, 44–52.

211. —— *The problem of meaning in African music.* Ethnomusicology, **6**, 1, 1962, 1–7, bibl.

212. —— 1962. *Unity and diversity in African music: a problem of synthesis.* Pp. 13. Accra: University of Ghana. [First International Congress of Africanists, 11–18 Dec. 1962, Doc./36.]

213. **Nkhata, A.** *African music clubs.* Afr. mus. soc. newsletter, **1**, 5, June 1952, 17–20.

214. **Norton, W. A.** *African native melodies.* S. Afr. J. of science, **12**, 1916, 619–28.

215. —— *African (Bantu) melodies.* J. Afr. soc., **18**, 1918–19, 122–37.

216. **Obama, Jean Baptiste.** *Musique africaine traditionnelle,* Africa [Rome], **17** (3), 1962, 125–32.

216a. **Olderogge, D. A.,** and **I. I. Potechin.** 1961. *Die Völker Afrikas,* [2 vols.], ill., maps. Berlin: Veb Deutscher, Verlag der Wissenschaften.

217. **Ortiz, Fernando.** 1955–7. *Miscellanea de estudios dedicados a F. Ortiz* [3 vols.]. Vol. 1, pp. 638, ill. Vol. 2, pp. 639–1315, ill. Vol. 3, pp. 1316–1621, ill. Havana: Impresores Úcar Garcia.

218. **Pereverzev, L.** *Muzyka Zapadnoy Afriki.* Sovetskaya Muzyka, **24**, 1960, 182–7, ill. [Popular Music of Africa. Soviet Music.]

219. **Pizzetti, Ildebrando.** *Music (Africa).* Enciclopedia Italiana, vol. 1, 1929, 774–7, ill.

220. **Praetorius, Michael.** 1615. *Syntagma musicum,* 3 tomes. Wölfenbuttel: .... [Tome 3 was never published. The *Theatrum Instrumentorum* forms part of the tome 2 and has a separate t.p. dated 1620. A facsimilie of this work was issued by Breitkopf of Leipzig in 1894.]

221. **Prince, J. Dyneley.** *Music (Muhammadan).* Hastings, James, Encyclopaedia of religion and ethics, vol. 9, 1917, 53–57.

222. **Rhodes, Willard.** *Changing times [new approaches in the study of African music].* Afr. mus. soc., **2**, 2, 1959, 6–9.

223. **Rouget, Gilbert.** *Chroniques musicales.* Présence africaine, **1–2**, 1953, 153–8; **3**, 1955, 71–73; **5**, 1955–6, 108–10.

224. —— *Notes d'ethnographie musicale.* Domaine musical: bulletin intern. de musique contemporaine [Paris], **1**, 1954, 102–6.

225. —— 1956. *Afrique,* vols. 1, 2, 3, 4 (Dahomey, Guinée, Sénégal, Mauritanie) (Jaquettes des EXTP 1026, 1029, 1031, 1032). Paris: Vogue.

226. —— *La musique d'Afrique noire (Histoire de la musique,* 1). Encycl. de la pléiade, 215–37, bibl.

227. —— *Note sur l'ornementation en Afrique noire.* Report of the Eighth Congress, Société Internationale de Musicologie [New York], **1**, 1961, 427–8.

228. —— 1961. *La musique en Afrique noire.* Extraits de l'encyclopédie de la musique. Paris: Fasquelle.

229. —— *Afrique Noire (Musique)*. Michel, Francois, Encyclopédie de la musique, **3**, 1961, 939–40.

230. **Sadji, A.** *Ce que dit la musique africaine*. L'education africaine, **94**, *Bull.* enseign A.O.F., avril–juin 1936, 119–72.

231. **Salmen, Walter.** *Zur sozialen Schichtung des Berufsmusikertums im Mittelalterlichen Eurasien und in Afrika*. Les Colloques de Wégimont, III, 1960, 23–32. [Ethnomusicologie 11.] Paris: Société d'Édition Les Belles Lettres.

232. **Sar Samba Cor.** *Un aspect de la musique africaine*. Etude de la France d'outre-mer, **4**, déc. 1943, 9.

233. **Schaeffner, André.** 1946. *La musique noire d'Afrique*. Dufourq, La Musique dès origines à nos jours. Pp. 460. Paris: Larousse.

234. —— *Musique outre-mer*. France d'outre-mer, **25**, no. 212, 1947, 7– .

235. —— *Situation des musiciens dans trois sociétés africaines*. Colloques de Wégimont, III, 1960, 33–49. [Ethnomusicologie 11.] Société d'Édition Les Belles Lettres.

236. —— *Afrique noire-musique*. Grand Larousse encyclopédique, tome 1, 1960, 146, ill.

237. **Schilde, Willy.** *Die Afrikanischen Hoheitzeichen*. Z. f. Ethnol., **61**, 1929, 117–24, bibl.

238. **Schneider, Marius.** *Über die Verbreitung afrikanischer Chorformen*. Z. f. Ethnol., **69**, 1937, 78–88.

239. —— *Ueber die wörtliche u. gestalmässige Überlieferung wandernder Melodien*. Archiv. f. Musikfors., III, 1938, 363– . [Yoruba, Ewe, Sobo, Shona.]

240. —— *Ist die vokale Mehrstimmigkeit eine Schöpfung der Altrassen?* Acta musicol., 1951, 40– .

241. —— *Die Bedeutung der Stimme in den alten Kulturen*. Tribus (Jahrbuch des Lindenmuseums), **2–3**, 1952–3, 9–29, bibl. [Duala, Bambara.]

242. —— *Die Musik der Naturvölker*. Trimborn, U. Adam, Lehrbuch der Völkerkunde, 1958, 82– .

243. —— *Le rôle de la musique dans la mythologie et les rites des civilisations non-européennes*. Histoire de la musique, 1, Encyclopédie de la pléiade, 1960.

244. —— *Das gestalttypologische Verfahren in der Melodik des Francesco Landino*. Acta musicol, **35**, 1963 (Bezieh. zu Marrokko).

245. **Schuyler, P.** *The music of modern Africa*. Music journal, **18**, 1960, 18– , ill.

246. *Seraphisches Weltapostolat*. 1932. 8. Negermusik, pp. 337–9. Altötting: ......

247. **Spencer, Herbert.** 1930. *Descriptive sociology or groups of sociological facts classified and arranged by H.S.* No. 4, *African races*, ed. by E. Torday. Pp. iv+385, bibl., maps. London: Williams & Norgate.

248. **Tanghe, J.** *Kanttekeningen bij Mr. Kunst's beschouwingen over 'de inheemse kunst en de zending'* [Indisch Instituut, Amsterdam, 1947]. Zaire, **2**, oct. 1948, 909–14.

249. **Thieme, D. L.** *Research in African music: accomplishments and prospects*. Ethnomusicology, **7**, 3, 1963, 266–71, bibl.

250. **Tiersot, Julien.** *La musique dans le continent africain*. Le Ménestrel, **69**, 1903 (7–9), 49–50, 57–58, 65–66: (11–14), 81–82, 89–90, 97–98, 105–6.

251. —— *La musique chez les nègres d'Afrique*. Lavignac, A. and L. de la Laurencie, Encyclopédie de la musique, pt. 1, 1922, 3197–3225, ill.

252. —— 1933. *Chansons nègres*. Pp. 94. Paris: Heugel.

253. **Tracey, Hugh.** *African music—a modern view*. NADA [Bulawayo.], **19**, 1942, 57–60.

254. —— *Organised research in African music*. Human problems, **6**, 1948, 48–52.

255. —— *African folk music*. Man, **32**, 1932, 158–9.

256. —— *African music and dancing*. U. empire, **44**, 1953, 252–4.

257. —— *Short note on the social value of African derived music*. Community development bull., **5**, June 1954, 57–59.

258. —— *The social role of African music*. Afr. affairs, **53**, 212, July 1954, 234–41.

259. —— *Recording African music in the field*. Afr. mus. soc., **1**, 2, 1955, 6–11.

260. —— *Towards an assessment of African scales*. Afr. mus. soc., **2**, 1, 1958, 15–20.

261. —— *African music within its social setting*. Afr. mus. soc., **2**, 1, 1958, 56–58.

262. —— 1962. *The evolution of African music and its function in the present day*. Johannesburg: Institute for the study of man in Africa.

263. —— *The arts in Africa: the visual and the aural* [paper read at S. Afr. Inst. Race Relations, Jan. 1963]. Afr. mus. soc., **3**, 1, 1962, 20–32.

264. —— *The development of music in Africa*. Optima, **14**, 1, Mar. 1964, 42–49, ill.

265. **Turnbull, Colin M.** 1963. *The peoples of Africa*. Pp. 124, ill., maps. Leicester: Brockhampton Press.

266. **Wachsmann, K. P.** *The sociology of recording in Africa south of the Sahara*. Afr. mus. soc., **2** (2), 1959, 77–79. Bull. Brit. Inst. of recorded sound, no. 14, 1959, 24–26.

266a. —— *Africa*. Enciclopedia della musica, **1**, A–C., 1963, pp. 22–26. Milan: Ricordi.

267. **Wängler, Hans Heinrich.** *Über die Beziehungen zwischen gesprochenen und gesungenen Tonhöhen in afrikanischen Tonsprachen*. Bose, Fritz (ed.), Jahrbuch für Musikalische Volks u. Völkerkunde, vol. 1, 1963, 136–45.

268. **Walschap, A.** *Gedachten over Negermuziek*. Aequatoria, **2** (3), 1939, 25–29.

269. **Ward, W. E. F.** 1939. *Music, a Handbook for African Teachers*. Pp. 148. London: Longmans.

270. **Weber, Wolfgang.** *Was ist Negermusik?* Velhagen u. Klasings Monatshefte, **42** (5), 1928, 566–70.

271. **Weman, Henry.** 1960. *African music and the church in Africa*. Pp. 296, bibl., ill. Uppsala: Svenska Institutet for Missionsforskning. [Studia Missionalia Upsaliensia 3.]

272. **Westphal, E.** *Linguistics and the African music research*. Afr. mus. soc., Newsletter, **1**, (1), 1948, 15–21.

273. **Williams, H. C. N.**, and **J. N. Maselwa.** [n.d.] *Choral folksongs of the Bantu for mixed voices*. Pp. vi + 58. London: Chappell.

AFRICAN MUSIC GEOGRAPHICALLY ARRANGED

ALGERIA

274. **Ammár ben Sa'id, dit Boulifa.** 1904. *Recueil de poésies Kabyles (texte Zouaoua). Traduites, annotées et précedées d'une étude sur la femme Kabyle.* Alger: Jourdan. [Pp. lxv–lxxxviii, La musique Kabyle.]

275. **Barbès, L. L.** *La musique musulmane en Algérie.* Information coloniale, no. 33, 1947.

275a. **Bartók, Béla.** *Die Volksmusik der Araber von Biskra und Umgebung.* Z. f. Musikw., **2**, 1920, 489–522.

276. **Certeux, Alphonse,** and **E.-Henry Carnoy.** 1884. *L'Algérie traditionnelle, légendes, contes, chansons, musique, moeurs, coutumes, fêtes, croyances, superstitions . . .* [Contribution au folk-lore des Arabes.] [2 vols.] Paris: Maisonneuve et Leclerc, & Challamel.

277. **El-Boudali Safir.** *La musique arabe en Algérie.* Documents algériens, 1949, 181–9, ill.

278. **Hanoteau, Louis Adolphe.** 1867. *Poésies populaires de la Kabylie du Jurjura: texte Kabyle et traduction francaise, avec des notes.* Pp. xiv + 475. Paris: Impériale.

278a. **Holiday, Geoffrey.** *The Tuareg of the Ahaggar.* Afr. mus. soc., **I** (3), 1956, 48–52.

278b. **Lhote, H.** *La documentation sonore (chant, musique et poésie) établie chez les Touareg du Hoggar en 1948.* Cah. Foucauld [Paris], **3**, 1952, 114–38.

279. **Rouanet, Jules.** *Esquisse pour une histoire de la musique arabe en Algérie.* Mercure musicale, **1**, 1905, 553; **2**, 1906, 128.

280. **Salvador-Daniel, F.** *Notice sur la musique Kabyle.* Hanoteau, Louis Adolphe, Poésies populaires de la Kabylie, 1867, 459–71.

281. **Zerrouki, M.** *Le folklore musical algérien.* Algéria, 3, 1949, 23–27.

ANGOLA

281a. **Angola, Companhia de Diamantes de.** 1961. *Folclore musical de Angola (Coll. de fitas magnéticas e discos).* 1. Povo Quioco (Lóvua)—Lunda. Pp. 296. Lisboa: Serviços Culturais da Companhia de Diamantes.

282. **Bastos, Augusto.** *Traços geraes sobre a ethnografia do districto de Benguella.* Bol. soc. geog., Lisbon, **26**, 1908, 176, 197–200.

283. Separate: Pp. 173–8. Famalicao, 1911.

284. **Baumann, Hermann.** *Die Mannbarkeitsfeiern bei den Tsokwe.* Baessler Archiv, **15**, 1932, 1–52, ill.

285. —— *Lunda.* Pp. 299, 1935, ill., map. Berlin: Würfel Verlag.

286. **Bleek, Dorothea F.** *Buschmänner von Angola.* Archiv. f. Anthrop., **21**, 1927, 53.

287. —— *Bushmen of Central Angola.* Bantu stud., **III**, 1928, 119–22, ill.

288. **Cabrita, Carlos L. Antunes.** 1954. *Em Terras de Luenas.* Pp. 195, ill. Lisbon: Agência Geral do Ultramar. [P. 165.]

289. **Capello, H. C.,** and **R. Ivens.** 1882. *From Benguella to Yacca* [2 vols.]. Vol. 1, pp. lii + 395, ill., maps. Vol. 2, pp. xv + 350, ill., maps. London: Sampson, Low. [Vol. 1, pp. 138–9.]

290. **Cavazzi da Montecuccolo, Antonio.** 1960. *Istorica descrittione de tre regni Congo, Matamba et Angola.* Pp. – , ill. Milan: Angnelli.

291. **Delachaux, Theodor,** and **Ch. E. Thiébaud.** s.d. *Land und Völker von Angola.* 1936. Pp. 143, ill., map. Neuchatel: Verlagsanstalt Viktor Attinger.

292. **de Magalhães, A. A.** *Alguns aspectos da musica indigena Africana.* Mensario admin., **12**, 1948, 53–54; **13**, 1948, 29–31; **13**, 1949, 20–21, 53–56.

293. **Dias de Carvalho, Henrique Augusto.** 1890. *Expedição Portuguesa ao Muatianvua. 1884-1888. Ethnographia e historia tradicional, dos provos da Lunda.* Pp. xv + 731, ill., maps.

Lisbon: Imprensa Nacional. [364–79 (ill.), 427, 478–9] 429.

294. **Diniz, Ferreira.** 1918. *Populações indigenas de Angola.* Pp. 18, 43, 78, 135–6, 175–6, 217, 233, 242, 265, 328, 354–6, 388, 424, 441, 550, ill. Coimbra: Imprensa da Universidade.

294a. **Estermann, Carlos.** 1956-7. *Etnografia do Sudoeste de Angola* [2 vols.] Vol. 1, pp. 265, bibl., ill., maps. Vol. 2, pp. 299, bibl., ill., maps. Lisbon: Ministério do Ultramar.

295. **Hambly, Wilfrid Dyson.** 1934. *The Ovimbundu of Angola.* Pp. 87–362, bibl., ill., map. Chicago: Field Museum. [Field Museum of Natural History, Anthrop. Series, vol. 21 (2).]

296. —— *Occupational ritual, belief and custom among the Ovimbundu.* Amer. anthrop., **36**, 1934, 167, ill. [Plate 4, drum and flute players.]

297. **Herzog, George.** *Remarks on Ovimbundu singing and drumming: transcriptions of four melodies and three drum rhythms.* Hambly, W. D., The Ovimbundu of Angola. [Field Museum of Natural History, Anthrop. Series 21, 1934, 217–19, 223, ill.]

298. **J.** . *Musica indigena da Lunda.* Estudos colóniais, **II**, no. 1, 1950, – .

299. **Jaspert, Fritz und William.** 1930. *Die Völkerstämme Mittel-Angolas.* Pp. xv + 155, bibl., ill., maps. Frankfurt a. M.: Joseph Baer. [Veröff. Städt., Völker-Mus. Frankfurt a.M., vol. 5, pp. 134–9.]

300. **Jessen, O.** 1936. *Reisen und Forschungen in Angola.* Pp. xiv + 398, ill., maps. Berlin: Dietrich Reimer.

301. **Lang, A.,** and **C. Tastevin.** 1937. *Ethnographie: La tribu des Va-Nyaneka.* Pp. x + 219, ill. [Mission Rohan-Chabot-Angola et Rhodésie (1912–14), 5.]

302. **Le Mailloux, E. R. P.** *A música dos Pretos* [Annales des Pères du Saint Esprit de Maio de 1928]. Portugal em Áfr., **3**, 17, Sept.-Oct. 1946, 274–80.

303. **Lux, A. E.** 1880. *Von Loanda nach Kimbundu.* Pp. viii + 219, ill., map. Vienna: Eduard Holzel. [Pp. 120, 122, ill.]

304. **Merolla da Sorrarto, Girolamo.** 1692. *Breve e succinta relatione del viaggio nel regno di Congo.* Pp. 466, ill. Naples: Mollo.

305. —— 1814. *A voyage to Congo.* Pinkerton's Voyages, **10**, 1814, 244–5. [London.]

306. **Monard, A.** *Voyage de la mission Suisse en Angola, 1928–29.* Bull. soc. Neuchât. géog., **39**, 1930, 43–44, ill.

307. —— *Note sur les collections ethnographiques de la mission scientifique Suisse en Angola.* Bull. soc. Neuchât. géog., **39**, 1930, 104–16, ill.

308. **Monteiro, J. J.** 1875. *Angola and the river Congo* [2 vols.]. Vol. 1, pp. viii + 305, ill., map. Vol. 2, pp. iv + 340, ill. London: Macmillan. [Vol. 2, 138–42.]

309. **Redinha, J.** 1953. *Campanha etnografica ao Tchiboco (Alto-Tchicapa).* Pp. 11. Lunda: Museu do Dundo.

310. **Sarmento, Alexandre.** 1945. *O negro de Menongue (notas antropológicas e etnográficas).* Pp. 88, ill., Lisbon: Divisâo de Publicaçoes e Bibliotheca, Agência Geral das Colónias. [Music and dance, pp. 42–45.]

311. **Schachtzabel, Alfred.** 1923. *Im Hochland von Angola.* Pp. 192, ill., maps. Dresden: Deutsche Buchwerkstätten.

312. —— 1926. *Angola.* Pp. 224, ill., map. Berlin: Die Buchgemeinde. [Illustrations of musical instruments.]

313. **Serpa Pinto, Alexandre de.** 1881. *How I crossed Africa* [2 vols.] Vol. 1, pp. 191, 332, ill., maps. Vol. 2, pp. vii + 384, ill., maps. London: Sampson, Low.

314. **Statham, J. C. B.** 1922. *Through Angola.* Pp. xv + 388, ill., map. Edinburgh: Blackwood. [Pp. 221–2, see ill.]

315. **Tönjes, Hermann.** 1911. *Ovamboland.* Pp. viii + 316, ill., map. Berlin: Martin Warneck. [Pp. 81–84.]

316. **Valdez, Francisco Travassos.** 1861. *Six years of a traveller's life in Western Africa* [2 vols.]. Vol. 1, pp. 120, ill. Vol. 2, pp. 220–5, 344, ill. London: Hurst.

317. **Vista, Tula di.** 1933. *Im Lande der Buschneger und Magier.* Pp. 189, ill. Berlin-Schöneberg: P. J. Oestergaard.

BASUTOLAND

320. **Casalis, Eugene.** 1859. *Les Bassoutos.* Pp. 436, ill., map. Paris: Société des Missions Évangeliques. [Pp. 155–8; 360–2.]

321. —— 1861. *The Basutos.* Pp. xix + 355. London: Nisbet. [Pp. 148–50; 344–7.]

322. **How, Marian Walsham.** 1962. *Mountain bushmen of Basutoland.* Pp. 63, bibl., ill. Pretoria: J. L. van Schaik Ltd. [Pp. 43, 60.]

323. **Koole, Arend.** *Report on an inquiry into the music and instruments of the Basutos in Basutoland.* Kongressbericht Intern. Ges. f. Musikwissenschaft, Utrecht, 1952, 1953, 263.

324. **Mabille, H. E.** *The Basutos of Basutoland.* J. Afr. soc., **5**, 1905–6, 241–2.

325. **Martin, Minnie.** 1903. *Basutoland: its legends and customs.* Pp. 174. London: Nichols. (Pp. 48–49.]

326. **Norton, William Alfred.** *Sesuto songs and music.* S. Afr. J. of science, **6** (no. 8), 1910, 314–16.

327. ——*African native melodies.* S. Afr. assoc. adv. science, **12**, 1916, 619–28.

328. **Scully, N.** *Native tunes heard and collected in Basutoland.* Bantu stud., **5** (3), 1931, 247–52.

329. **Tracey, Hugh.** *The future of music in Basutoland.* Afr. mus. soc., **2** (2), 1959, 10–14.

330. —— *Basutoland recording tour,* 19 Nov. to 3 Dec. 1959. Afr. mus. soc., **2** (2), 1959, 69–76.

331. —— *Sotho folk music: report on a recording tour by the International Library of African Music,* 19 Nov. to 3 Dec. 1959. Lesotho, **2**, 1960, 37–48.

BECHUANALAND

331a. **Andersson, Charles John.** 1856. *Lake Ngami.* Pp. xviii + 546, ill., map. London: Hurst & Blackett.

332. **Bleek, D. F.** 1928. *The Naron: a bushman tribe of the Central Kalahari.* Pp. ix + 67, ill. Cambridge: Cambridge Univ. Press.

333. **Bleek, W. H. I.,** and **L. C. Lloyd.** 1911. *Specimens of bushman folklore.* Pp. xl + 468, ill. London: George Allen. [Pp. 321–5, 351–7.]

334. **Burchell, William J.** 1822. *Travels in the interior of Southern Africa.* Vol. 1, pp. viii (iii) + 582, ill., map. Vol. 2, pp. vi + 648, ill. London: Longmans. [Vols. 2, pp. 410–13, 437–8, 578, 598–9.]

335. **Dornan, Samuel S.** *Tati Bushmen (Masarwas) and their language.* J. roy. anthrop. inst., **47**, 1917, 44, 53–55.

336. —— 1925. *Pygmies and bushmen of the Kalahari.* Pp. 318, ill., map. London: Seeley Service. [Chap. 14, pp. 136–9, Music.]

337. **Jones, J. D. R.,** and **C. M. Doke.** 1937. *Bushmen of the Southern Kalahari.* Pp. vii + 283, ill. Johannesburg: Univ. of Witwatersrand Press: [Ex Bantu Studies, vol. 10 (4) and 11 (3). with some additional matter].

338. **Kay, Stephen.** 1834. *Travels and researches in Caffraria.* Pp. ix + 428. London: Mason.

339. **Passarge, S.** *Das Okawangosumpfland und seine Bewohner.* Z. f. Ethnol., **37**, 1905, 684–5, ill.

339a. —— 1907. *Buschmänner der Kalahari.* Pp. 144, ill., map. Berlin: D. Reimer. [Pp. 95–98.]

340. **Schultze, Leonhard.** 1907. *Aus Namaland und Kalahari. Eine Forschungsreise . . . in* 1903–1905. Pp. xiv + 752, ill., map. Jena: Gustav Fischer.

341. **Tracey, Hugh.** *Recording tour of the Tswana tribe, October-November* 1959. Afr. mus. soc., **2**, 2, 1959, 62–68.

BURUNDI
(Formerly part of Rwanda-Urundi)

342. **Belgium: Ministère des Colonies.** 1927. *Rapport sur l'administration belge du Ruanda et de l'Urundi pendant l'année* 1926. Pp. 102. Brussels: . . . . [Note on the manufacture of drums.]

343. **Bourgeois, R.** 1957. *Banyarwanda et Barundi* [tome 1]. Pp. 792, bibl., ill. Brussels: . . . . [Pp. 643–65.]

344. **Brandel, Rose.** *The African hemiola style.* Ethnomusicology, III (3), 1959, 106–17.

345. —— 1961. *The music of Central Africa. Former French Equatorial Africa, the former Belgian Congo, Ruanda-Urundi, Uganda and Tanganyika.* Pp. xii + 272, bibl., ill. The Hague: M. Nijhoff.

346. **Césard, Le R. P. Edmond.** *Le Muhaya (l'Afrique orientale).* Anthropos, **31**, 1936, 489–508, ill.

347. **Collaer, P.** *Notes sur la musique d'Afrique centrale.* Probl. Afr. Centr., no. 26, 1954, 267–71.

348. **Cureau, Adolphe Louis.** 1915. *Savage man in Central Africa.* Pp. 351, ill., map. London: T. F. Unwin. [See chap. 10, pp. 87–93, The aesthetic sense.]

349. **De Geeter, G.** *La question de la musique nègre.* AFER, no. 10, 1937, 2–3.

350. **Gille, A.** *L'Umuganuro ou fête du sorgho en Urundi.* Bull. jurid. indig., **14**, no. 11, 1946, 368.

351. **Marie-Elisabeth, des Dames de Marie (Mère).** *La musique et l'éducation sociale dans l'Urundi.* Louvain: Semaine de Missiologie. [Problèmes sociaux et missions: Le rôle des laïcs dans les missions. Rapports et compte rendu de la 21e semaine . . . 1951–1952. 1953. Pp. 128–41.]

352. **Merriam, A. P.** *Les styles vocaux dans la musique du Ruanda-Urundi.* Jeune Afr., **7**, 19, 1953, 12–16, ill.

353. ——*African music re-examined in the light of new materials from the Belgian Congo and Ruanda Urundi.* Zaire, **7**, 3, mars 1953, 245–53. [Reprint Afr. mus. soc. newsletter, **1**, 6, Spet. 1953, 57–64.]

354. **Meyer, Hans.** 1916. *Die Barundi.* Pp. xiv + 215, 55 plates, maps. Leipzig: Otto Spämer. [Kön. Sächs. Forschungsinstitut in Leipzig, Inst. für Völkerkunde, Band 1.]

355. **Ntakokaja, J.-B.** *La musique des Barundi.* Grands Lacs (Namur), **64**, 4/6, nouv. sér. 116/118, 1949, 45–49.

356. **Sandrart, Georges.** 1953. *Images du Congo: Ruanda-Urundi.* s.p., ill. Brussels: Charles Dessart.

357. **Sartiaux, P.** *Aspects traditionnels de la musique au Ruanda-Urundi.* Jeune Afr., no. 21, 1954, 19–26.

358. **Sebakiga, A.** *La musique indigène et son adaptation au culte religieux.* Brousse [Brussels], no. 1, 1940, 13–16.

359. **van der Burgt, Jean Martin Michel.** 1903. *Un grand peuple de l'Afrique équatoriale.* Pp. 190, ill. Bois le Duc: L'Illustration Catholique. [Pp. 20–21, 91–93.]

360. —— 1903. *Dictionnaire Français-Kirundi.* s.p. Bois le Duc: L'Illustration Catholique. [See under Chant, Musicien, Danse.]

361. **Verwilghen, Leo A.** 1952. *Songs of the Watutsi.* Folkways Records P428.

362. **Zuure, Bernard.** 1932. *L'âme du Murundi.* Pp. 506. Paris: Beauchesne. [Pp. 452–6. Appendix: La musique des Barundi.]

363. —— *Poésies chez les Barundi.* Africa, **5**, 1932, 344–54.

CAMEROONS

364. **Albert, A.** 1943. *In French Cameroons-Bandjoon.* Pp. 340, ill. Ottawa: Les Editions de l'Abre Enregistrée. [Chap. 11, Songs, Music and Art in Bandjoon, pp. 245–57.]

365. **Ankermann, Bernhard.** *Ethnographische Forschungsreise im Grasland von Kamerun.* Z. f. Ethnol., **17**, 1910, 309, ill.

367. **Bufe, Missionary.** *Die Bakundu.* Archiv f. Anthrop., **40**, 1913, 229–30.

368. **Cozzens, Edwin.** 1954. *Bulu songs from the Cameroons.* Folkways Records, P451.

369. **Dugast, Idelette.** 1955–60. *Monographie de la tribu des Ndiki (Banen du Cameroun).* 1955, tome 1, pp. xxiv + 823, ill., maps, bibl. 1960, tome 2, Vie sociale et familiale, pp. xx + 633, ill., bibl. Paris: Travaux et Mémoires de l'Institut d'Ethnologie, 58 and 63. [Annexe (1) Le langage tambouriné ou, sifflé chez les Banen, 567–602.]

370. **Dühring, F. K.** *Die Bevölkerung des Logone Bezirks.* Mitt. Schutz., **33**, 1925, 64–77, ill., map.

371. **Ebding, F.,** and **J. Ittmann.** *Religiöse Gesänge aus dem nördlichen Waldland von Kamerun.* Afr. Übersee, **39**, 1955, 169–77; **40**, 1955–6, 39–44, 125–32.

372. **Fourneau, J.** *Des transmissions acoustiques chez les indigènes du Sud-Cameroun.* Togo-Cameroun, 1930, 387– .

373. **Froelich, J. C.** *Notes sur les Mboum du Nord-Cameroun.* J. soc. africanistes, **29**, 1959, 91–117, ill.

374. **Gardi, R.** 1956. *(Matakam) Mandara: Unbekanntes Bergland in Kamerun.* Pp. 231, ill., map. Zürich: Orell Füssli Verlag. [2nd ed.]

374a. **Gardi, R.** 1954. *Der schwarze Hephastus.* Pp. 22, ill. Bern: Büchler & Co. [Pictures of musical instruments.]

375. **Hagen, Günther von.** *Die Bana.* Baessler Archiv, Band 2, Heft 2, 1911, 77–116, ill., map. [See pl. Anlage 4 for musical instruments.]

375a. **Harttmann, Hermann.** *Ethnographische studie über die Baja.* Z. f. Ethnol., **59** (1–2), 1927, 50–51, ill.

376. **Heinitz, Wilhelm.** *Musikinstrumente und Phonogramme des Ost-Mbamlandes.* Thorbecke, Im Hochland von Mittel-Kamerun, pt. 3, 1919, 121–78 + append. (20 pp.), ill. Abh. Hamburger Kol. Inst., 41.

377. **Hoesemann, Dr.** *Ethnographische Tagebuchnotizen von der Expedition gegen die Esum,* 1901. Ethnol. Notizbl., **3**, 1901, 108–9, 111.

378. —— *Aus dem Schutzgebiete Kamerun: Ethnologisches aus Kamerun.* Mitt. Schutz., **16**, 1903, 150–82, ill. [P. 175.]

379. **Hutter, Franz.** 1902. *Wanderungen und Forschungen im Nord-Hinterland von Kamerun.* Pp. xiii + 578, ill., maps. Brunswick: Vieweg. [Pp. 297–8, 387–8, 404, 433–5.]

380. —— *Explorations dans l'hinterland septentrional de la colonie du Cameroun.* Bull. soc. anthrop. [Paris], **5**, 1903, 524.

381. **Ittman, Johannes.** *Lieder aus dem Kameruner Waldland.* Afr. u. Übersee, **42** (1), 1958, 1–15; **42** (2), 1958, 69–79.

382. **Karsten, Paula.** 1903. *Wer ist mein Nächster: Negertypen aus Deutschwestafrika.* Pp. xxxi + 128, ill. Berlin: Gose.

383. **Lembezat, Bertrand.** 1961. *Les populations paiennes du Nord-Cameroun et de l'Adamaoua.* Pp. 252, bibl., map. Paris: Presses Univ. de France. [Monographies Ethnologiques Africaines: Institut International Africain.] [Pp. 57, 106, 219, 236.]

384. **Lenz, Oskar.** 1879. *Skizzen aus Westafrika.* Pp. 346, map. Berlin: A. Hofmann.

385. **Malcolm, L. W. G.** *Notes on the religious beliefs of the Eghāp, Central Cameroon.* Folklore, **33**, 1922, 354–79.

386. **Malzy, Pierre.** *Les Fali du Tingelin (Nord Cameroun).* Études Cam., **51**, 1956, 1–37, ill., map. [Pp. 32–37, ill.]

387. **Mansfeld, Alfred.** 1908. *Urwald-Documente: vier Jahre unter den Crossflussenegern Kameruns.* Pp. xvi + 309, ill. Berlin: Reimer. [Anhang 6, Drei Lieder.]

388. **Marchesseau, G.** *Quelques elements d'ethnographie sur les Mofu du massif de Durum.* Études Cam., no. 10, 1945, 46–48, ill., map.

389. **Meidhols, Alfred.** 1943. *Bei den Bergheiden in Nord Kamerun.* Pp. viii + 264, ill., map. Vienna: Ostmarken-Verlag.

390. **Meyer, Hans** (ed.). 1909. *Das Deutsche Kolonialreich.* Vol. 1, pp. 490–1, ill. Leipzig: Bibliographisches Institut. [Notes of distribution of musical instruments in Cameroons, with map.]

391. **Morgen, Carl (or Curt?).** 1893. *Durch Kamerun von Süd nach Nord . . . 1889–91.* Pp. x + 390, ill., map. Leipzig: Brockhaus. [Pp. 40, 55, 200, 278.]

392. **Müller, Robert.** *Leben und Treiben in Kamerun.* Ausland, **62**, 1889, 83–84.

393. **Nicol, Yves.** 1929. *La tribu des Bakoko.* Pp. 240, maps. Paris: Larose. [Music and dance, pp. 196–9.]

394. **Passarge, Siegfried.** 1895. *Adamaua . . . Expedition . . . Deutschen-Kamerun-Komitees in . . . 1893–94.* Pp. xvi + 573, ill., map. Berlin: Reimer. [Pp. 68, 104–5, 142, 283 (Marimba), 321, 427, 454, 476–7.]

395. **Rein-Wuhrmann, Anna.** 1925. *Mein Bamumvolk im Grasland von Kamerun.* Pp. 159, ill. Stuttgart: Evang. Missions-Verlag. [Pp. 63–66.]

396. **Salasc, Leon.** *Sur les musiques du Haut Cameroun.* Togo-Cameroun, 1934, 34–45, ill.

397. **Schaeffner, André.** *Notes sur la musique des populations du Cameroun Septentrional.* Minotaure, no. 2, 1933, 65–70, ill.

398. **Schneider, Marius.** *Lieder der Duala.* Deutsches Jahrbuch d. Musikwissenschaft für 1959, Vierter Jahrgang (51 Jahrgang des Jahrbuches der Musik-Bibliothek Peters.) Leipzig: . . . .

399. **Schwarz, Bernard.** 1886. *Kamerun.* Pp. 357, map. Leipzig: Frohberg. [Pp. 159–61.]

400. **Seidel, August.** *Das Bakwirivolk in Kamerun.* Beitr. Kol. Polit., **3**, 1902, 163, 170–1.

401. —— 1906. *Deutsch-Kamerun.* Pp. 16 + 367, ill. Berlin: Meidinger. [Pp. 227–8.]

402. **Tessmann, Günter.** *Die Mbaka-Limba, Mbum and Lakka.* Z. f. Ethnol., **60**, 1928, 315, 328–9, 344.

402a. **Tessmann, Günter.** 1934. *Die Baja: Ein Negerstamm im mittleren Sudan.* Teil, 1. Materielle u. seelische Kultur. Pp. xi + 243, bibl., ill., map. Stuttgart: Strecker u. Schröeder Verlag. [Abschnitt, VII. Bildende Kunst: 187–96: LX Musikinstrumente, 212–19. Anhang 'Tanz'.]

403. —— 1934. *Die Bafia.* Pp. xii + 270, ill., map. Stuttgart: Strecker. [Pp. 161, 169–76.]

404. **Zenker, G.** (On Yaunde music.) Mitt. Schutz., **8**, 1895, 58–60.

405. **Zintgrafe, Eugen.** 1895. *Nord-Kamerun (1886–92.)* Pp. viii + 468, ill., map. Berlin: Paetel.

CANARY ISLANDS

406. **Classe, A.** *The unusual whistle language of the Canary Islanders.* Unesco Courier, 10, 1957, 30.

407. **Knosp, Gaston.** *Les Iles Canaries.* Lavignac, A. and L. de la Laurencie, Encyclopédie de la musique, pt. 1, 1922, 3234–44.

408. **Ricard, Robert.** *À propos du langage sifflé des Canaris.* Hespéris, **15**, 1932, 140–2.

CAPE PROVINCE

409. **Arbousset, J. T.,** and **F. Daumas.** 1842. *Relation d'un voyage d'exploration au nord-est de la colonie du Cap de Bonne-Espérance.* Pp. 400: 490–1. Paris: Bertrand.

410. **Borcherds, Petrus Borchardus.** 1861. *Autobiographical memoir.* Pp. xxv + 500. Cape Town: Robertson. [Pp. 114, 178.]

411. **Engelbrecht, J. A.** 1936. *The Korana.* Pp. xii + 240, bibl., ill. Cape Town: Maskew Miller. [Pp. 170–4.]

412. **F.W. South Africa.** 1851. *Sketches of . . . various classes and tribes . . . of the Cape of Good Hope and . . . interior of South Africa with a brief account descriptive of the manners and customs of each.* + S.P. 42 plates with descriptive text. London: W. R. & Lowes Dickinson. [Pl. 35, A Hottentot musician (with text) shows musical bow, plectrum (feather) and gourd resonator: leather rings at ankles.]

413. **Kolbe, Peter.** 1731. *The present state of the Cape of Good Hope.* Pp. xviii + (8), 365. London: W. Innys. [Pp. 155, 239, 271–81.]

414. **Le Vaillant, Francois.** 1790. *Voyage . . . dans l'interieur de l'Afrique par le Cap de Bonne-Espérance . . . 1780–85* [2 vols.]. Vol. 1, xxii + 274, ill. Vol. 2, (i) + 292, ill. Paris: Leroy. [Vol. 2, pp. 247–9, 343.]

415. **Lichtenstein, Martin Heinrich Karl.** 1811–12. *Reisen im Südlichen Afrika . . . 1803–06* [2 vols.]. Vol. 1, x + 685, ill., map. Vol. 2, 7 + 661, ill. Berlin: C. Salfeld. [Vol. 1, 44–45, 150, 247–8. Vol. 2, 379–80, 549–50.]

416. —— 1812–15. *Travels in Southern Africa . . . 1803–06* (2 vols.]. Vol. 1, xii + 383 (32). Vol. 2, xiv + 368, 24, ill., map. London: English & Foreign Library. [Vol. 1, pp. 28, 94, 153–4. Vol. 2, pp. 232, 337–8.]

417. **Moodie, John Wedderburn Dunbar.** 1835. *Ten Years in South Africa* [2 vols.]. Vol. 1, xii + 347, ill. Vol. 2, viii + 352, ill. London: Bentley. [Vol. 1, pp. 224–9.]

418. **Schapera, I.** (*ed.*). 1933. *The early Cape Hottentots described in the writings of O. Dapper* (1668), *W. Ten Rhyne* (1686). *J. G. de Grevenbroek* (1695). Pp. xv, 309 x, bibl., ill. Cape Town: Van Riebeeck Society.

419. **Sparrman, André.** 1786. *A voyage to the Cape of Good Hope . . . 1772–1776* [2 vols.]. Vol. 1, xxiii + 368, ill., map. Vol. 2, viii + 365, ill. London: Robinson. [2nd ed.]

420. **Thompson, George.** 1827. *Travels and adventures in Southern Africa* [2 vols.]. Vol. 1, xxi + 450, ill. Vol. 2, vi + 430, ill., map. London: Colburn. [Vol. 1, pp. 339, 422.]

421. **Thunberg, Karl Peter.** 1795. *Travels in . . . Africa . . . 1770–1779* [4 vols.]. Vol. 1, xii + 317, ill. Voyage to Cape. Vol. 2, xiv + 316 (xv), ill. Vol. 3, xiii + 285, 31. Vol. 4, xix + 293 (xvi), ill. London: Richardson. [Vol. 1, pp. 218, 233. Vol. 2, pp. 43–44, 78.]

See also 2339, 2341, 2479.

CAPE VERDE ISLANDS

421a. **Mendes Correa, Antonio.** 1954. *Ultramar Português* (2) *Ilhas de Cabo Verde.* Pp. 262 + (24), ill., maps. Lisbon: Agência Geral do Ultramar.

See also 2566b, 2566c.

CENTRAL AFRICAN REPUBLIC
(Formerly Oubangui-Shari A.E.F.)

422. **Barat-Pepper, Elaine.** 1950. *Choeurs de l'Afrique équatoriale; chants de piroguiers, féticheurs, etc.* Pp. 24, ill. Paris: Henri Lemoine.

423. **Blanc, F.** *En mission dans l'Oubangui-Chari.* La terre et la vie, 1932, 699–712.

424. **Brandel, Rose.** 1961. *The music of Central Africa: former French Equatorial Africa, the Former Belgian Congo, Ruanda-Urundi, Uganda, Tanganyika.* Pp. xii + 272, bibl., ill. The Hague: M. Nijhoff.

425. —— *Types of melodic movement in Central Africa.* Ethnomusicology, **6** (2), 1962, bibl., 75–87.

426. **Bruel, Georges.** *Les Pomo et les Boumali.* Rev. ethnog., **1**, London, 1910, 27.

427. —— 1935. *La France Équatoriale Africaine.* Pp. xvi + 558, ill., maps. Paris: Larose.

428. **Chauvet, S.** *Musique et arts nègres en A.E.F.* Le Sud-Ouest economique [Bordeaux] Sept. 1930, 987–97.

429. **Collaer, Paul.** *Notes sur la musique d'Afrique Centrale.* Probl. Afr. Centr., no. 26, 1954, 267–71.

430. **Courlander, Harold.** 1950. *Music of Equatorial Africa.* (Notes by Harold Courlander.) Folkways Records, no. 402.

431. **Cureau, Adolphe.** 1912. *Les sociétés primitives de l'Afrique équatoriale.* Pp. 420. Paris: Colin. [Pp. 91–96.]

432. **Daigre, le R. P.** *Les Bandas de l'Oubangui-Chari.* Anthropos, **26**, 1931, 647–95, ill.; **27**, 1932, 153–81, ill. [P. 655, vol. 26.]

433. **Dekoster, Louis.** *La musique nègre.* Probl. Afr. Centr., **26**, 1954, 265–6. [Editorial preface to La musique nègre.]

434. **Éboué, F.** *The Banda: their music and language.* Revue du monde [Paris], April 1932.

435. **Éboué, Félix.** *Les peuples de l'Oubangui-Chari.* Com. Afr. France, 1933, 75–94, ill. Paris: ....

436. —— *Les peuples de l'Oubangui-Chari.* Rens. col., **42**, 1932, 461–2; **43**, 1933, 14–19, ill.

437. **Encyclopédie Coloniale et Maritime.** (Direction d'Eugène Guernier.) 1950. *Afrique Équatoriale Française.* Pp. x + 590 (vii), bibl., ill., maps. Paris: 3 rue Blaise-Desgoffe.

438. **Feuilloley, R. P.** *Note au sujet de quelques phénomènes psychiques observés chez les primitifs du centre africain.* Bull. & Mém. soc. anthrop. [Paris], 1930, 11–22.

439. **Gaud, Fernand.** 1911. *Les Mandjia.* Pp. xxiv + 574, ill., map. Brussels: Institut Intern. de Bibliographie. [Collection de monographies ethnographiques.]

440. **Gillier, Lt.** *Les Bandas: notes ethnographiques.* Rens. col., **23**, 1913, 392.

441. —— *Parmis les tribus du Haut-Oubangui.* Monde col. ill., 1924, 284–6, ill., map.

442. **Moseley, A. B.** *More about music.* Central Africa, **52**, 1934, 54–55.

443. **Pepper, Herbert.** 1940. *Musique-Centre-Africaine.* Pp. 20, ill. Paris: Gouvernement Général de l'Afrique Equatoriale Francaise.

444. —— *Chant d'adultère.* Le mois de l'Afrique Équatoriale Française, jan. 1945, 22.

445. —— [1946.] *Rythmes et chants de la brousse africaine: Oubangui violon et piano.* Pp. 14. Paris, Bruxelles: H. Lemoine.

446. —— *Musique et pensée africaines.* Presence africaine, **1**, 1947, 149.

447. —— *Musique centre africaine.* Encyclopédie coloniale et maritime (direction d'Eugène Guernier), Afrique Équatoriale Française, 1950, pp. 553–72, ill.

448. —— *L'enregistrement du son et l'art musical ethnique.* Bull. inst. ét. centrafricaines [Brazzaville], n.s. 4, 1952, 143–9, ill.

449. —— *Reflexions sur l'art musical en A.E.F.* Cahiers Charles de Foucauld, L'Afrique Équatoriale Francaise, 1952, pp. 82–85, ill.

450. —— *Considerations sur le langage tambouriné et autres langages musicaux d'Afrique Centrale, sur la pensée musicale africaine.* 40 Conf. Intern. de Africanistas Occidentales, Santa Isabel de Fernando Poo, 1951. Trabajos [Madrid], 2, 1954, 165–76.

451. —— *Essai de définition d'une grammaire musicale noire.* Probl. Afr. Centr., no. 26, 1954, 289–98, ill., map.

452. **Rouget, Gilbert.** *Anthologie de musique centre-africaine.* Présence africaine, no. 7, 1949, 324–5.

453. —— 1948. *Musiques pygmées et nègres d'Afrique Équatoriale Française.* Notice pour BAM (Boite à Musique), Paris.

454. —— 1949. Music of Equatorial Africa. (Notes on the recordings) pour l'album FE 4402. Ethnic Folkways Library, New York.

454a. **Van der Elsken, Eduard.** 1961. *Bagara.* 112 plates + 29 pp. London: ....

455. **Vergiat, A. M.** 1951. *Les rites secrets des primitifs de l'Oubangui.* Pp. 158, ill., map. Paris: Payot. [2nd ed.]

456. **Ziéglè, Henri.** *Notes sur la psychologie des Bantous de l'Afrique Centrale.* Cahiers d'outre-mer [Bordeaux], **4**, 1951, 23–38.

CHAD

457. **Carbou, Henri.** 1912. *La région du Tchad et du Ouadaï. Tome 1, Études ethnographiques.* Pp. 380, bibl., maps. Paris: Leroux. [Publ. de la Faculté des Lettres d'Alger, 47–48.]

458. **Chapelle, Jean.** 1957. *Nomades noirs du Sahara.* Pp. 449, bibl., ill., maps. Paris: Plon.

459. **Chevalier, Auguste.** 1907. *Mission Chari, lac Tchad, 1902–04.* Pp. 776, ill., maps. Paris: Challamel. (Pp. 100–1, 149.]

460. **Cline, Walter.** 1950. *The Teda of Tibesti, Borku and Kawar in the Eastern Sahara.* Pp. 52, bibl., map. Menasha, Wis.: Amer. Anthrop. Assoc. [American Anthrop. Assoc. General Series in Anthropology, no. 12.]

461. **Fuchs, Peter.** 1961. *Die Völker der Südost-Sahara: Tibesti, Borku, Ennedi.* Pp. 254, bibl., ill., map. Vienna: Wilhelm Braumüller. [Veröffentlichungen zum Archiv für Völkerkunde. Museum für Völkerkunde in Wien. [Band 6.]

462. **Gide, André.** *Musiques et danses au Tchad.* Rev. musicale, **9**, 1927, 97.

463. **Heinitz, Wilhelm.** *Eine Melodienprobe von den Sara-Kaba.* Vox [Hamburg], **17**, 1931, 69–71.

464. **Lebeuf, Jean-Paul.** *Beyond Lake Chad.* Geog. mag., Jan. 1953, 434–43, ill.

465. **le Coeur, Charles.** 1950. *Dictionnaire ethnographique Teda.* Pp. 211, ill., maps. Paris: Larose. [Mém. I.F.A.N., no. 9.] [Musical instruments: pp. 123–4, 148, Dance: pp. 55–56, pl. 27.]

466. **Mackenzie, Donald.** 1877. *The flooding of the Sahara.* Pp. xix + (1) 287, ill., map. London: Sampson Low. [Mandingo musical instrument from 'near Chad'.]

467. **Macleod, Olive.** 1912. *Chiefs and cities of Central Africa: across Lake Chad by way of British, French and German territories.* Pp. xiv + 322, ill., maps. Edinburgh: Blackwood. [Music: pp. 20–22, 50, 76, 81–82, 117, 128, 169–71, 174–5, 277.]

468. **Rottier, D. A. A.** *Étude sur le Tibesti (Tchad).* Bull. com. Étud. A.O.F., 1922.

469. **Thomas, Jean.** 1934. *À travers l'Afrique équatoriale sauvage.* Pp. 223, ill., map. Paris: Larose. [Pp. 16, 17, 46, 49, 50, 59, 76–77, 80 (ill.), 86 (ill.), 143.]

CONGO REPUBLIC
(Formerly Middle-Congo, A.E.F.)

470. **Avelot, R.** *La musique chez les Pahouins, les Ba-kalai, les Eshira, les Iveïa, et les Ba-vili (Congo français).* l'Anthropologie, **16**, 1905, 287–93, ill.

471. **Bastian, Adolf.** 1874–5. *Die deutsche Expedition an der Loangoküste* [2 vols.]. Vol. 1, pp. 46, 161–3, ill., map (1874). Vol. 2, pp. xv + 353, ill. (1875). Jena: Hermann Costenoble.

472. **Bemba, Sylvain.** *L'évolution de la musique Congolaise.* Liaison, no. 58, 1957, 37–41.

473. **Darré, E.** *Notes sur la tribu des Bomitaba (Moyen Congo.)* Rev. ethnog. trad. pop., **3**, no. 12, 1922, 304–25.

474. **Guesfeldt, Paul.** *Zur Kenntnis der Loango-Neger.* Z. f. Ethnol., **8**, 1876, 203–16.

475. —— **Julius Falkenstein** and **Eduard Pechuël-Loesche.** 1879–1907. *Die Loango Expedition . . . 1873–1876.* Pt. 1, by Paul Güssfeldt, pp. (6) 232 ill., map. Pt. 2, by Julius Falkenstein, pp. (6), 183, ill. Pt. 3, (1), by E. Pechuël-Loesche, pp. (4), 316, ill., map. Pt. 3 (2) by E. Pechuël-Loesche, pp. vi + 503, ill. Leipzig: Paul Frohberg. Stuttgart: Strecker u. Schröder. [Music: Pt. 1, p 197; Pt. 3 (2), pp. 111–12, 115–32, 260.]

476. **Guiral, Léon.** *Les Batékés (Afrique orientale).* Rev. ethnog. [Paris]., **5**, 1886, 135–66, ill.

477. —— 1889. *Le Congo français du Gabon à Brazzaville.* Pp. xvi + 322, ill., map. Paris: Plon.

478. **Hornbostel, Erich von.** *Die Musik der Pangwe.* Tessmann, Günter, Die Pangwe, vol. 2, 1913, 320–57, ill.

479. **Johnston, Sir Harry Hamilton.** 1884. *The River Congo.* Pp. xviii + 458, ill., maps. London: Sampson Low.

480. **Largeau, V.** 1901. *Encyclopédie Pahouine Congo Francais.* Pp. 697. Paris: E. Leroux. [See under 'Musique' for the principal instruments in use by the Pahouins. See also pp. 163–5.]

481. **Maignan, Capt.** *Études sur le pays Pahouins.* Bull. soc. Rech. Congo, 1930, 90.

482. **Pepper, H.** *Les problèmes généraux de la musique populaire en Afrique noire.* Pp. 3 [duplicated]. Extract from Brazzaville: l'Afrique Equatoriale Française, Service de l'Information, 5–11.11.49.

483. —— *À la recherche des traditions musicales en pays Vili.* Bull. inform. et docum. [Brazzaville], 69, 1950, p. 6.

484. —— *Essai de définition d'une grammaire musicale noire d'après des notations empruntées à un inventaire babembe.* Probl. Afr. Centr., **7**, 26, 1954, 289–98, ill., carte.

485. **Proyart, Liévain Bonaventure.** 1766. *Histoire de Loango, Kakongo et autres royaumes d'Afrique.* Pp. viii + 390. Paris: Berton.

486. **Roche, Jean Baptiste.** 1904. *Au pays des Pahouins.* Pp. 92. Paris: Lauvauzelle.

487. **Rouget, Gilbert.** *Note sur les travaux d'ethnographie musicale de la mission Ogooué-Congo.* Conferência Internacional dos Africanistas Occidentais. 2a Bissau, 1947. Trabalhos, vol. 5.3a Seccão 2A Parte. (Meio Humano), 1952, 193–204. Lisbon: Junta de Investigacões Colóniais.

488. **Soret, Marcel.** 1959. *Les Kongo Nord-Occidentaux.* Pp. viii + 144, bibl., map. Paris: Presses Universitaires de France. [Pp. 108–10.] [Monographies Ethnologiques Africaines Institut International Africain.]

489. **Thonner, Franz.** 1899. *Dans la grande forêt de l'Afrique Centrale.* Pp. x + 115, ill., maps. Brussels: Société Belge de Librairie.

490. —— 1910. *Du Congo à l'Ubangi: mon deuxième voyage dans l'Afrique Centrale.* Pp. xi + 125, ill., maps. Brussels: Misch & Thron.

CONGOLESE REPUBLIC
(Formerly Belgian Congo)

491. **Aequatoria.** *Musique indigène congolaise.* Aequatoria, no. 1, 1956, 37–43.

492. **Anon.** (On Congo music.) Congo illus., **27**, 1892, 216.

493. **Anon.** *La musique (à Congo).* Belg. col., **1**, 1895–6, 565–8.

494. **Anon.** *Ethnographie congolaise: musique, chant et danse.* Belg. col., **7**, 1902, 557–8; **8**, 1903, 5–7, etc.

495. **Baeyens, M.** *Les Lesa.* Rev. Cong., 1914, 327–8.

496. **Bateman, C. S. L.** 1898. *The first ascent of the Kasai.* Pp. xx + 185, ill., maps. London: George Philip & Son. [Note H, pp. 181–2, 'Lhiambo Song' with score.]

497. **Baumann, Oscar.** *Beiträge zur Ethnographie des Congo.* Mitt. anthrop. gesell. Wien, **17**, 1887, 166–79.

498. **Bentley, W. Holman.** 1887. *Dictionary and grammar of the Kongo language.* Pp. xxiv + 718. London: Baptist Missionary Society.

499. **Birnbaum, Martin.** *The long-headed Mangbetus.* Nat. hist., **43**, 1939, 73–83, ill.

500. **Bittremieux, L.** 1911. *De geheime sekte der Bakhimba's.* Pp. 201. Louvain: J. Beekmann-Vanderwaren.

501. —— 1923. *Mayombsch Idioticon, Deel 1 & 2.* Pp. 821. Gent: Erasmus.

502. —— *La société secrète des Bakhimba au Mayombe.* I.R.C.B. (sciences morales), mém. no. 5, 1935–6, 327, ill., map.

503. —— 1937. *Woordkunst der Bayombe. Lied en spel, dans en tooneel in Beneden-Congo.* Pp. 224. Brussels: N. V. Standaard Boekhandel.

504. **Blacking, John.** *Eight flute tunes from Butembo, East Belgian Congo: an analysis in two parts, musical and physical.* Afr. mus. soc., **1**, 2, 1955, 24–52, ill.

504a. **Boelaert, E.,** *Musique et danse.* Aequatoria, **6**, 3, 1943, 77–78.

504b. —— *Muziek en Dans.* Nieuw Vlaanderen, **5**, 1939, 30, 8.

505. —— and **G. Hulstaert.** *La musique et la danse chez les Nkundo.* Brousse, **4**, 1939, 13–14.

506. **Boerens, H.** *La musique indigène au Katanga.* Rev. Cong., **22**, (11), 1950, 25–26, ill.

507. **Brandel, Rose.** *Music of the giants and pigmies of the Belgian Congo.* J. Amer. mus. soc., 5, 1952, 16–28.

508. —— *The music of African circumcision rituals.* J. Amer. mus. soc., **7** (1), 1954, 52–62.

509. —— 1961. *The music of Central Africa: former French Equatorial Africa, the former Belgian Congo, Ruanda-Urundi, Uganda, Tanganyika.* Pp. xii + 272, bibl., ill. The Hague: M. Nijhoff.

509a. **Burrows, Guy.** 1898. *The Land of Pigmies.* Pp. xxx + 299, ill. London: C. A. Pearson. [Pp. 83–84, 183.]

510. **Burssens, H.** 1958. *Les peuplades de l'entre Congo-Ubangi (Ngbandi, Ngbaka, Mbandja, Ngombe et Gens d'Eau).* Pp. xi + 219, bibl., ill., map. London: International African Institute. [Ethnographic Survey of Africa: Central Africa: Belgian Congo, Part IV.]

511. **Butaye, R.** 1910. *Dictionnaire kikongo-francais et francais-kikongo.* Pp. 73. Roulers: Meester. [List of musical instruments: see also Tambours, etc.]

512. **Callewaert, E.** *Les Mousserongos.* Bull. soc. roy. belge géog., **29**, 1905, 200.

513. **Cameron, Verney Lovett.** 1885. *Across Africa.* Pp. 186, 250, 267, 355, ill. London: Philip.

514. **Campbell, Dugald.** 1922. *In the heart of Bantuland.* Pp. 308, ill; map. London: Seeley Service.

515. **Candied, Fr.** *Muziek en zang in Kongo.* Toren, 1951, 23–28, 37–43.

516. **Carrington, J. F.** *La musique chantée dans la région de Stanleyville.* Band, **19**, 2/3, 1960, 85–91.

517. **Chavanne, Josef.** 1887. *Reisen und Forschungen im alten und neuen Kongostaate.* Pp. x + 508, ill., maps. Jena: Costenoble. [Pp. 401–2.]

518. **Claridge, G. Cyril.** 1922. *Wild bush tribes of tropical Africa.* Pp. 314, ill., map. London: Seeley Service. [Pp. 221–46.]

518a. **Closson, E.** *l'Olifant.* La Revue Belge, **4**, 1926, 446–56.

519. **Clymans, Roland.** 1934. *Boula Matari: musique folklorique du Congo belge.* Pp. 14. Brussels: Dogilbert.

520. **Coart, E.,** and **A. de Haulleville.** 1906. *La musique.* Pp. 145–315, ill. Brussels: Musée du Congo Belge, Tervuren. [Annales du Musée du Congo Belge III, tome I, fasc. I.]

521. **Congo.** *Notes sur l'enregistrement de musique indigène au Congo belge.* Congo, mars 1940, 311–13.

522. **Coquilhat, Camille.** 1888. *Sur le haut-Congo.* Pp. 364, ill. Paris: Lebègue.

523. **Daniel, Gaston.** *La musique au Congo.* S.I.M. [Paris], **8**, 1911, 56–64.

524. **Darré, E.** *La tribu Bondjo.* Bull. soc. rech. Congol., **3**, 1923, 53–73.

525. —— and **Le Bourhis.** *Notes sur la tribu Bomitaba.* Bull. soc. rech. Congol., **5**, 1925, 36–37.

526. **de Bouveignes, Olivier.** *La musique indigène au Congo belge,* Maessen, A., and others, Les Arts au Congo belge et au Ruanda-Urundi, 1950, 72–81, ill.

527. —— *La musique indigène au Congo belge.* Afr. mus. soc., Newsletter, I, no. 3, 1950, 19–27.

528. —— *De inheemse muziek in Belgisch-Kongo.* Band, **10**, 1951, 95–102.

529. —— *Musica indigena nel Congo Belga.* Africa [Rome], **6**, 11/12, 1951, pp. 323–3.

530. **de Cleene N.** 1957. *Introduction à l'ethnographie du Congo belge et du Rwanda-Burundi.* Pp. viii+159, bibl., ill., maps. Anvers: Sikkel.

531. **de Hen, F. J.** *Problemen bij de studie van de congolese muziek.* Congo-Tervuren, **2**, 3/4, 1956, 60–64.

532. **Delcourt, L.,** and **A. Dallons.** *Les Mongo du Sankuru.* Bull. jurid. indig., 17e ann. 6 (viii), 186–9.

533. **Deleval, H.** *Les tribus Kabati du Mayombe.* Rev. Cong., **3**, 1912, 261–2, ill.

534. —— 1913. *Les tribus Kabati du Mayombe: notes ethnographiques.* Pp. 53, ill. Brussels: Vromant. [Pp. 50–51.]

535. **Delhaise, Charles Godefroid Félix Francois.** *Chez les Warembas.* Bull. soc. roy. belge géog., **32**, 1908, 263–7, ill.

536. —— *Chez les Warundi et les Wahorohoro.* Bull. soc. roy. belge géog., **32**, 1908, 413–14.

537. —— *Chez les Wasongola du Sud.* Bull. soc. roy. belge géog., **33**, 1909, 182–6, ill.

538. —— 1909. *Les Warega.* Pp. xx + 376, ill., maps. Brussels: Institut Intern. de Bibliographie. [Pp. 269, 271–3.] [Collection de monographies ethnographiques, no. 5.]

539. —— *Les Bapopie.* Bull. soc. roy. belge géog., **36**, 1912, 183–5.

540. **de Middeleer, J.** *La musique indigène et son adaptation au culte religieux.* Brousse, **3**, 1940, 8, 9/13.

541. **Dennett, R. E.** 1898. *Notes on folklore of the Fjort.* Pp. 32 + 169. London: Sampson Low, Marston. [Folklore Society.]

542. **Denys, Pierre.** *Discographie du Congo belge.* Les colloques de Wégimont, I, 1956, 222.

543. —— *Kongo.* A.M.E., 1957, 117–24, ill.

544. **Engels, Lieutenant.** 1912. *Les Wangata (tribu du Congo Belge): étude ethnographique.* Pp. (8) + 101, ill., map. Brussels and Paris: Vromant et Cie. [Pp. 86–91.]

545. **Forrer, R.** *La géographie musicale du Congo belge,* Expansion belge, **9**, 1928, pp. 33–34.

546. **Francois, A.** *Musique indigène (Commémoration du cinquantième anniversaire du comité specialisé du Katanga).* Report of the Congress of Science [Elizabethville], **6**, Aug. 1950, 169.

547. **Francois, Kurt von.** 1888. *Die Erforschung des Tschuapa und Lulongo.* Pp. 101, 138, 173, ill. Leipzig: Brockhaus.

548. **Glave, E. J.** s.d. *Six years of adventure in Congo-land.* Pp. 247, ill. London: Sampson Low. [Numerous drawings of musical instruments and art objects.]

549. **Guattini, Michael Angelo de,** and **Denis Carli de Piacenza.** 1814. *Curious and exact account of a voyage to the Congo . . . 1666–67.* Pp. 148–94. [Pinkerton's Voyages, vol. 16.]

550. **Halkin, Joseph.** 1911. *Les Ababua.* Pp. 620, map. Brussels: Inst. Intern. de Bibliog. [Pp. 249, 427–36.] [Collection de Monographies Ethnographiques, no. 7.]

551. —— *Quelques peuplades du district de l'Uelé.* Mouvements soc. intern., **8**, 1911, 109–15.

552. **Hammar, J.** *Babwende.* Nordenskiöld, Erland, Ethnografiska bidrag af Svenska Missionarer i Afrika, 1907, pp. 151–2. Stockholm: Palmquist.

553. **Harrison, James J.** 1905. *Life among the pygmies.* Pp. 18, ill. London: Hutchinson.

554. **Harroy, F.** *Ethnographie congolaise: les Bakubas.* Bull. soc. roy. belge. géog., **31**, 1907, 237–46, ill.

555. **Hertsens, L.** *De Bahema muziek.* Nieuw Afrika, **56** (7), 1939–40, 275–81.

556. **Hilton-Simpson, Melville William.** 1911. *Land and peoples of the Kasai.* Pp. xx + 356, ill., map. London: Constable. [Pp. 35–36; 254–5.]

557. **Hulstaert, G.** *Musique indigène et musique sacrée.* Aequatoria, **41**, 1949, 86.

558. **Hurt, Ambra H.** *The music of the Congo.* Étude, **53**, 1935, 402, 440.

559. **Jans, Paul.** *Essai de musique religieuse pour indigènes dans le Vicariat Apostolique de Coquilhatville (avec chants indigènes, chants pour indigènes, et bibliographie).* Aéquatoria, **19**, 1, 1956, 1–43.

560. **Jephson, Arthur J. Mounteney.** 1890. *Emin Pasha and the rebellion at the Equator.* Pp. xxiv + 490, ill., map. London: Sampson Low.

561. **Johnston, Sir Harry Hamilton.** 1908. *George Grenfell and the Congo* (2 vols.). Vol. 1, pp. xxiii + 496, ill., maps. Vol. 2, pp. xx + 494 (497–990), ill., map. London: Hutchinson. [Pp. 718–24.]

562. **Joset, Paul E.** 1936. *Les Babira de la Plaine.* Pp. 63, ill., map.

Anvers: L'Association des Étudiants de l'Université Coloniale de Belgique. [P. 58.]

563. **Knosp, G.** *La mélodie nègre.* (Cinquante année d'activité coloniale au Congo, 1885–1935,) l'Avenir Belge, (Bruxelles), 1935, pp. 298–9.

564. **Kunst, J.** *Ein musikologischer Beweis für Kulturzusammenhänge zwischen Indonesien vermutlich Java- und Zentralafrika.* Anthropos, **31**, 1936 (1–2), 134–40, ill.

565. **Labat, Jean Baptiste.** 1776. *Relation historique de l'Éthiopie occidentale contenant la description des royaumes du Congo, Angola et Matamba (traduit de l'italien par le Père Cavazzi de Montecuculo et augmenté de plusiers relations portugaises des meilleurs auteurs).* [5 vols.] Paris: Delespine.

566. **Laman, K. E.** 1922. *The musical accent or intonation in the Congo language.* Pp. xiii (4), 153 (4), maps. Stockholm: Svenska Missionsförbundets Förlag.

567. **Liétard, L.** *Les Warega.* Bull. soc. roy. belge géog., **48**, 1924, 133–45.

568. **Lutten, Eric.** *Les Wasamba et leur usage dans la circoncision.* Minotaure, **2**, 1933, 13–17, ill.

569. **Maes, J.,** and **Olga Boone.** 1935. *Les peuplades du Congo belge.* Pp. iv + 379, maps. Brussels: Musée du Congo belge. [List of names of tribes, places and rivers of the Congo.]

570. **Maesen, A.** *Les Holos du Kwango: notes succintes.* Reflets du monde, no. 9, 1956, 31–44, ill.

571. **Maistre, C.** 1895. *À travers l'Afrique Centrale du Congo au Niger, 1892–1893.* Pp. 300, ill., map. Paris: Hachette.

572. **Maquet, Jean-Noël.** *Musiciens Bapende.* Bull. union femmes colon., **26**, 124, 1954, 28–31, ill.

573. —— *Initiation à la musique congolaise.* Micro magazine, **10**, nos. 462–73, 1954, v.p.

574. —— *La musique chez les Bapende.* Probl. Afr. Centr., **7**, 1954, 299–315, ill., map.

575. —— *Initiation à la musique congolaise.* Afr. mus. soc., **1** (1), 1954, 64–68. [Reprinted from Jeunesses musicales.]

576. —— *La musique chez les Pende et les Tschokwe.* Colloques de Wégimont, **1**, (1954–5), 169–87, ill.

577. —— *Musiques nègres.* Cahiers musicaux, **1**, no. 3, 1955, 25.

578. —— *La tradition du yodel au sud-ouest du Congo belge.* J. int. folk music council, **11**, 1959, 20–22.

579. **Mbiye, B.** *Kasala des Mulumba (ntiite).* Kongo-Overzee, **21**, 1955, 160.

580. **Meeus, F. de.** *Musique africaine.* L'art nègre du Congo belge. Brussels, 1950, 55.

581. **Meeussen, A. E.** *Een en ander over Lega-muziek.* Africa-Tervuren, **7**, 3, 1961, 61–64, ill.

582. **Merriam, Alan P.** *Recording in the Belgian Congo.* Afr. mus. soc., Newsletter, **1**, 5 June 1952, 15–17, ill.

583. —— 1956. *Ekonda: tribal music of the Belgian Congo.* Riverside Records, R.I.P.4006.

584. **Mertens, Joseph.** *Les Ba Dzing de la Kamtsha. Première partie-ethnographie.* I.R.C.B. (sciences morales), mém. no. 4 (1), 381, ill., maps. [Pp. 273–80.]

585. **Milou.** *Instruments et musique nègre.* Illustr. congol., **189**, 1937, 6412–13, ill.

586. **Müller, P., G. T. Pagels** and **E. Gleerup.** 1887. *Tre år i Kongo* [2 vols.]. Vol. 1, pp. 98, 135, 167, 274. Vol. 2, pp. 147, ill. Stockholm: Norstedt.

587. **Nys, F.** 1896. *Chez les Abarambos.* Pp. 216. Anvers: Huybrechts. [Pp. 90–91, 126–8.]

588. —— *Le chant, les danses, la musique.* Belg. col., **3**, 1898, 509–12.

589. **Olbrechts, Frans M.** *De studie van de inheemse muziek van Belgisch-Congo.* Miscellanea Musicologica, dedicated to Floris van der Meueren, 1950, 147–50.

590. **Parke, Thomas Heazle.** 1891. *My personal experiences in Equatorial Africa.* Pp. xxviii + 526, ill., map. London: Sampson Low. [Pp. 219–20 musical instruments of Balegga.]

591. **Pigafetta, Filippo.** 1881. *A report on the kingdom of Congo . . . 1591* [translated by Margarite Hutchinson]. Pp. xx + 174, maps. London: John Murray. [Music: pp. 111–12, 161.]

592. **Pogge, Paul.** 1880. *Im Reiche des Muata Jamvo.* Pp. viii + 246, ill., map. Berlin: Reimer.

593. **Pring, S. W.** *Music on the Congo.* Music student, 1921, 141–2.

595. **Risasi, Pierre M.** *Musique congolaise de demain.* Voix du congolais, **9**, 92, nov. 1953, 725–31, ill.

596. **Rouget, Gilbert.** *Les travaux d'ethnographie musicale de la mission Ogooué-Congo.* Compte-rendus sommaires des séances de l'institut francais d'anthropologie [Paris], **43**, 1947–9, fasc. 3, 4.

597. **Roy, R.** *Le Munyabungu, fumeur et musicien.* Missions Pères blancs, **33**, 1912, 121–5.

598. **Rudyant, F.** *La musique congolaise.* Sélection [Paris], **1**, 1922, 69–72.

599. **Schebesta, Paul.** 1931. *Les pygmées du Congo belge.* Pp. 432, bibl., ill. Brussels: Mém. I.R.C.B. [Pp. 190–6.]

600. —— 1932. *Bambuti, die Zwerge vom Kongo.* Pp. 270, ill., map. Leipzig: Brockhaus. [Pp. 25, 65–66, 96–97, 182–3, 234–7, 244.]

601. —— 1934. *Vollblutneger und Halbzwerge.* Pp. 263, ill. Salzburg: Rustet. [See figs. 58, 94, 23 and 21.]

602. —— 1933. *Among Congo pigmies.* Pp. 288, ill., maps. London: Hutchinson.

603. —— 1936. *My pygmy and negro hosts.* Pp. 288, ill., maps. London: Hutchinson.

604. —— 1937. *Revisiting my pygmy hosts.* Pp. 288, ill., map. London: Hutchinson.

605. —— 1941–50. *Die Bambuti-Pygmäen vom Ituri* [3 vols.]. Band 2, Teil 1. Die Wirtschaft der Ituri-Bambuti, p. 243—Tänze, musikalische und gesangliche Unterhaltungen. Teil 2, Das soziale Leben, p. 481—Die Lärminstrumente im Nkumbi. Brussels: I.R.C.B.

606. —— *Pygmy music and ceremonial.* Man, 57, no. 78, 1957, 62–63.

607. **Scheyven, R.** *Notes sur la musique chez les Bolia et les Ibeke-y-Onkusu.* Arts et métiers indigènes, **1**, 1936, 11–16, ill.

608. **Schmidt, W.** 1910. *Die Stellung der Pygmaenvölker in der Entwicklungsgeschichte des Menschen.* Pp. ix + 315. Stuttgart: Strecker. [Pp. 128–31.]

609. **Schmitz, Robert.** 1912. *Les Baholoholo (Congo belge).* Pp. xxxii + 605, ill., maps. Brussels: Institut Intern. de Bibliographie. [Pp. 407–19, 421–3.] [Collection de Monographies Ethnographiques, 9.]

610. **Schumacher, Le R. P.** *Les pygmées Bagêsêra et Bazigaba aux cascades du Karambo-Bikore.* Congo [Brussels], **1**, 1928, 177–9, ill.

611. **Servatius, Le R. P.** *De besnijdenis bij de Bene Nsamba.* Anthropos, **27**, 1932, 526, 529, 532.

612. **Shaffer, Jacqueline.** *Experiments in indigenous church music among the Batetela.* Afr. mus. soc., **1** (3), 1956, 39–42.

613. **Tanghe, Basiel.** 1928. *De Ngbandi naar het leven geschetst.* Pp. xvii + 245. Bruges: De Gruuthuuse Persen.

614. —— 1929. *De ziel van het Ngbandivolk.* Pp. 144. Bruges: De Gruuthuuse Persen.

615. **Tanghe, Joseph.** *L'étude de la musique nègre.* Beaux-Arts, 7 ann., 1936, 15–17, ill.

616. —— *La musique nègre.* La revue sincère (Bruxelles), **11**, 1933, 274. [Extract: Congo, **15** (1), 3, 1934, 397–401.]

617. **Tilkens, E.** *Les Ababua.* Belg. col., **5**, 1900, 254.

618. **Torday, Emil.** 1895. *On the trail of the Bushongo.* Pp. 286, ill., map. London: Seeley Service.

619. —— *Songs of the Baluba of Lake Moero.* Man, **4**, no. 80, 1904, 117–19.

620. —— 1913. *Camp and tramp in African wilds.* Pp. xvl + 316, ill., map. London: Seeley Service.

621. —— *The Northern Babunda.* Man, **19**, no. 26, 1919, 49–55, ill.

622. —— 1925. *Causeries Congolaises*. Pp. 235, ill. Brussels: Albert Dewit. [Pp. 226–8.]

623. —— and **Thomas Athol Joyce.** *Notes on the ethnography of the Ba-Mbala*. J. anthrop. inst., **35**, 1905, 398–426, ill., map.

624. —— —— *Notes on the ethnography of the Ba-Yaka*. J. anthrop. inst., **36**, 1906, 39–59, ill.

625. —— —— *Notes on the ethnography of the Ba-Huana*. J. anthrop. inst., **36**, 1906, 272–301, ill.

626. —— —— *On the ethnology of the South-West Congo Free State*. J. anthrop. inst., **37**, 1907, 150.

627. —— —— 1910. *Notes ethnographiques sur les peuples . . . appelés Bakuba ainsi que sur les peuplades apparentées les Bushongo*. Pp. 290, ill. Brussels: Annales du Musée du Congo Belge: Ethnographie, Anthropologie Ser 111, tome 2, fasc. 1. [Pp. 98–104, 269.]

628. —— —— 1922. *Notes ethnographiques sur les populations . . . du Kasai et du Kwango oriental*. Pp. 359, ill. Brussels: Annales du Musée du Congo Belge. Ethnographie, Anthropologie, tome 2, fasc. 2. [Pp. 18–25, 55–63, 203–5, 274–8.]

629. **Tracey, Hugh Travers.** *The problem of the future of Bantu music in the Congo*. Probl. Afr. Centr., No. 26, 1954, 272–99.

630. —— *The future of Bantu music in the Congo*. Belgian Congo of today, **4** (2), 1955, 64–68, ill.

631. **Trilles, Henri.** *Les legendes des Bena Kanioka et le folklore Bantou*. Anthropos, **4**, 1909, 950, 954.

632. **Trilles, Le R. P.** 1933. *Les pygmées de la forêt équatoriale*. Pp. xiv + 530, bibl., ill. Paris: Bloud & Gay. [Pp. 331–60.]

633. **Turnbull, Colin M.** *Pygmy music and ceremonial*. Man, **55**, no. 31, 1955, 23–24.

633a. —— *The Molimo, a men's religious association amongst the Ituri Bambuti*. Zaire, **14**, 1960, 307–40, ill.

634. —— 1960. *Music of the Ituri forest people*. Folkways Records, No. F.E.4483.

635. **Van den Bergh, Leonard John.** 1922. *On the trail of the pigmies*. Pp. xiv + 264, ill., map. New York: James A. McCann & Co.

636. **van der Kerken, G.** *L'ethnie Mongo*. I.R.C.B. (sciences morales), Mém. no. 13, 1941. Vol. 1, pp. xii + 504, maps. Vol. 2 and 3, pp. x + 505–1143, ill. [2 vols. in one.] Brussels: I.R.C.B. [Pp. 94, 242, 276, 376–7, 396, 482, 731.]

637. **van Bulck, G.** *Rapport sur une mission d'études effectuées au Congo belge (jan. 1932–aug. 1933). Séjour chez les Bakongo orientaux*. I.R.C.B. (bulletin), sciences morales, **6** (1), 1935, 116–39.

638. **van Loo E.** *Musique et danses des Bakubas et Batshioks*. Sci. et voyage, **29** (24), 1947, 346–8.

639. **van Mol, D.** *La musique de l'Uélé, Vicariat de Niangara*. Grands lacs [Louvain], **56** (4–6), 1939–40, 5.

640. **Van Overbergh, C.** 1908. *Les Basonge*. Pp. xvi + 564, bibl., ill., map. Brussels: Institut intern. de Bibliographie. [Pp. 361–4.] [Collection de Monographies Ethnographiques, 3.]

641. —— and **E. de Jonghe.** 1907. *Les Bangala*. Pp. xv + 458, bibl., map. Brussels: Institut Intern. de Bibliographie. [Pp. 307–14.] [Collection de Monographies Ethnographiques, 1.]

642. —— —— 1907. *Les Mayombe*. Pp. xvi + 470, bibl., map. Brussels: Institut Intern. de Bibliographie. [Pp. 335–7.] [Collection de Monographies Ethnographiques, 2.]

643. —— —— 1909. *Les Mangbetu (Congo belge)*. Pp. xvi + 594, bibl., ill., map. Brussels: Inst. Intern. Bibliog. [Pp. 417–22.] [Collection de Monographies Ethnographiques, 4.]

644. **Védy, Dr.** *Les A-Babuas*. Bull. soc. roy. belge géog., **28**, 1904, 275–6.

645. —— *Ethnographie congolaise: les riverains de l'Uélé*. Bull. soc. roy. belge géog., **30**, 1906, 311–15.

646. **Verbeken, A. L.** *Étude sur la peuplade des Bombesa*. Bull. soc. roy. belge géog., **52**, 1928, 72.

647. **Vereyecken,** [   ]. *La région des cataractes*. Congo illus. (Brussels), **19**, 1895, 148, ill.

648. **Verwilghen, Leo A.** *Wat elk Europeaan weten moet over Kongolese muziek*. Zaire, **4** (5), 1950, 489–99.

649. **Verwilghen, Leo A.** 1952. *Folk music of the Western Congo*. Folkways Records, P.427.

650. **Viaene, Ernest,** and **Bernard.** *Chez les Lessa*. Bull. soc. roy. belge géog., **34**, 1910, 222.

651. **Walschap, Alphonse.** *Réflexions à propos de la musique indigène*. Ann. de N.D. du Sacré Coeur, 1939, 155–8.

652. **Ward, Herbert.** 1910. *A voice from the Congo*. Pp. xvi + 330, ill. New York: Charles Scribner. [Pp. 298–304.]

653. **Weeks, John H.** *Notes on some customs of the Lower Congo people*. Folklore, **20**, 1909, 198, 458–9, 463– .

654. —— *Anthropological notes on the Bangala of the Upper Congo River*. J. anthrop. inst., **40**, 1910, 402–4.

655. **Wollaston, A. F. R.** 1908. *From Ruwenzori to the Congo*. Pp. xxv + 315, ill., map. London: John Murray.

See also, 27, 28.

DAHOMEY

656. **Albéca, Alexandre L. d'.** *Voyage au pays des Eoués*. Tour du monde [Paris], **1**, 1895, 98–99, 104, ill.

657. **Bouche, Pierre.** 1885. *Sept ans en Afrique occidentale*. Pp. viii + 403. Paris: Plon.

658. **Brunet, L.,** and **L. Giethlen.** 1900. *Dahomey et dépendances*. xi + 544, ill. Paris: Challamel.

659. **Cornevin, G.** *Le canton de l'Akébou*. Études. Dah., **7**, 1952, 81–132, bibl., ill., map. [P. 130.]

660. **Dalzel, Archibald.** 1793. *The history of Dahomy*. Pp. xxvi (2) + 230, ill. London: Spilsbury.

660a. **Duvelle, Charles.** *Musiques dahoméennes*. O.C.R. 17, 1964. Office de coopération radiophonique.

661. **Duncan, John.** 1847. *Travels in Western Africa in 1845 and 1846 . . . through the kingdom of Dahomey, etc*. [2 vols.]. Vol. 1, xiv (1) + 304, ill., map. Vol. 2, ix (1) + 314, ill. London: Richard Bentley.

662. **Foa, Édouard.** 1895. *Le Dahomey*. Pp. xv + 429, ill., maps. Paris: A. Hennuyer. [Music: p. 251.]

663. **Forbes, Frederick E.** 1851. *Dahomey and the Dahomans . . . in the years 1849 and 1850* [2 vols.]. Vol. 1, pp. xii + 244, ill. Vol. 2, pp. 248, ill. London: Longman, Brown, Green & Longmans.

664. **Freeman, Richard Austin.** 1898. *Travels and life in Ashanti and Jaman*. Pp. xx + 559, ill., map. London: Archibald Constable. [Pp. 59, 97–99, 104, 152, 257–61, 281, 335.]

665. **Fuchs, P.** *Les figurines en métal d'Ouagadougou*. Notes Afr., I.F.A.N., no. 87, 1960, 76–82, ill. [Fig. 1, Musicians, pp. 78–79, ill.]

666. **Hagen, A.** *La colonie de Porto-Novo et le roi Toffa*. Rev. Ethnog., **6**, 1887, 81–116, ill. [Pp. 110.]

667. **Hajdukiewicz de Pomian, A.** *Dahome, land och folk*. Ymer, **15**, 1895, 113–15.

668. **Herskovits, Melville J.** 1938. *Dahomey* [2 vols.]. Pp. xxi + 402; xiv (2) + 408, bibl., ill. New York: J. J. Augustin.

669. **Humbert-Sauvageot, Mrs. M.** *Quelques aspects de la vie et de la musique dahoméennes*. Zeit. f. vergl. Musikw., **11**, 1934, 76–83.

670. **McLeod, John.** 1820. *A voyage to Africa with some account of the manners and customs of the Dahomian people*. Pp. iv + 162, ill. London: John Murray. [Pp. 96–97.]

670a. **Quénum, Maximilien.** *Au pays des fons: la musique*. Bull. com. d'étud. l'A.O.F., **18**, 1935. 323–35, ill.

671. **Rouget, Gilbert.** 1955. *Music of the princes of Dahomey*. Notes by Gilbert Rouget. E.S.537.

672. —— 1955. *Musiques des princes, fête des tohossou (Dahomey)*.

Jaquette du LD 5/MC 20.093. Musée de l'Homme, Contre-point, Paris.

673. —— 1958. *Musique du roi (Dahomey), musique malinké (Guinée)*. Jaquette du MC 20.146. Paris: Contrepoint.

674. —— 1959. *Rythmes et chants du Dahomey*. Jaquette du LD 376. Paris: Boite à Musique. Radiodiffusion Outre-mer.

675. —— *Un chromatisme africain (de Dahomey)* L'Homme, I, 3, sept.-dec. 1961, 32–46, ill. [Avec disque en annexe—Musée de l'Homme ID 17–3.]

676. —— *Mission d'ethnomusicologie au Dahomey en 1958–1959*. Cah. d'Ét. afr., 2, mai 1960, 198–200.

677. —— *Une chante-fable d'un signe divinatoire (Dahomey)*. J. afr. languages, I (3), 1962, 272–92.

678. —— *Musique vodun (Dahomey)*. Actes du 6th congrès international des sciences anthropologiques et ethnologiques [Paris], 1964.

679. —— *Afrique*. Vols. 1–4. Jaquettes EXTP, 1026, 1092, 1031–2, Vogue, Paris, 1956.

680. —— 1964. *Vocal music and traditional history in the ancient kingdom of Porto-Novo*. Essays on music and history in Africa and Asia. Pt. 2, Africa. [Roy. anthrop. inst.]

681. **Skertchly, J. A.** 1874. *Dahomey as it is*. Pp. xx + 524, ill., map. London: Chapman and Hall. [Pp. 18–20.]

682. **Tiersot, J.** *La musique au Dahomey*. Rev. encycl. [Paris], 15 août 1893.

683. —— *La musique au Dahomey*. Le Ménestrel, 69, 1903, 4–6, 25–26, 33–35, 41–42.

EAST AFRICA
(General)

684. **Baumann, Oscar.** 1894. *Durch Massailand zur Nilquelle*. Pp. xiii + 385, ill., map. Berlin: Reimer.

685. **Iten, Beatus.** *Acerca de la Musica de los negros*. Missions Católicas [Barcelona], 43, 1935, 278–80, 319–21.

686. **Jones, A. M.** 1964. *Indonesia and Africa—an ancient colonial era*. Essays on music and history in Africa and Asia: Pt. 2, Africa. [Roy. anthrop. inst.]

687. **Kolinski, Mieczyslaw.** *La música del Oeste Africano*. Rev. est. musicales, 1949, 191–215.

688. **Kollmann, Paul.** 1898. *Der Nordwesten unserer Ostafrikanischen Kolonie*. Pp. viii + 191, ill. Berlin: Alfred Schall.

689. **Kubik, Gerhard.** *The phenomenon of inherent rhythms in East and Central African instrumental music*. Afr. mus. soc., 3, 1, 1962, 33–42.

690. **Peters, C.** 1891. *New light on dark Africa*. Pp. 18, 597, ill. London: Ward Lock.

692. **Powell-Cotton, P. H. G.** 1904. *In unknown Africa*. Pp. xxiii + 619, ill., maps. London: Hurst & Blackett.

694. **Reinhard, Kurt.** *Tonmessungen an fünf ostafrikanischen Klimpern*. Die Musikforschung, 4, 1951, 366.

695. **Schoeller, Max.** 1901–4. *Mitteilungen über meine Reise nach Äquatorial-Ost-Afrika und Uganda, 1896–97* [3 vols.]. Vol. 1, pp. viii + 237, ill. Vol. 2, pp. 329 (3) + 102 plates + pp. 33. Vol. 3, maps. Berlin: Reimer.

696. **Scott Elliot, G. F.** 1896. *A naturalist in Mid-Africa*. Pp. xvi + 413, ill., maps. London: A. D. Innes. [Note musical instrument of Wawamba is shown on p. 151 and not as in index.]

697. **Stuhlmann, Franz.** 1894. *Mit Emin Pasha ins Herz von Afrika* [2 vols. in one]. Pp. xxi + 901, ill., map. Berlin: Reimer.

698. **Tracey, Hugh.** *Recording tour, May to November 1950, East Africa*. Afr. mus. soc., Newsletter, I (4), 1951, 38–51.

699. —— *Recording in East Africa and northern Congo*. Afr. mus. soc., Newsletter, I, 6, Sept. 1953, 6–15.

700. —— 1954. *Bantu music from British East Africa*. Columbia SL213.

701. **Wachsmann, Klaus P.** *Ostafrika*. F. Blume (*ed.*), Die Musik in Geschichte, u. Gegenwart, 10, 1961, 437–47, ill.

702. **Werth, E.** 1915. *Das Deutsch-Ostafrikanische Küstenland und die vorgelagerten Inseln* [2 vols.]. Band 1, pp. xvi + 334, ill. Band 2, pp. vii + 265, ill., maps. Berlin: Reimer. [Band 1, pp. 270–4.]

703. **Weule, Karl.** 1909. *Native life in East Africa*. Pp. xxiv + 431, ill., map. London: Pitman.

704. —— *Forschungsreise in . . . Deutsch Ostafrikas*. Mitt. Schutz. Ergan, I, 1908, 150, map.

EGYPT

705. **Baikie, James.** *Music (Egyptian)*. Hastings, James (*ed.*), Encyclopaedia of religion and ethics, 9, 1917, 33–36.

706. **Berner, Alfred.** 1937. *Studien zur arabischen Musik auf Grund der gegenwärtigen Theorie und Praxis in Ägypten*. Pp. vi + 124. Leipzig: Schriftenreihe des Stl. Inst. f. deutsche Musikforschung, no. 2.

707. **Blackman, Winifred S.** 1927. *The fellahin of Upper Egypt*. Pp. 331, ill. London: Harrap.

708. **Brandel, Rose.** *La chironomie dans l'Égypte pharaonique*. Ethnomusicology, 5 (3), 1961, 237–40.

709. **Carl Gregor, Duke of Mecklenburg.** 1960. *Ägyptische Rhythmik. Rhythmen und Rhythmusinstrumente im heutigen Ägypten*. Pp. 70. Strassburg: Baden-Baden. Heitz. [In series of dissertations.]

709a. **Cline, Walter.** 1936. *Notes on the people of Siwah and El Garah in the Libyan desert*. Pp. 64, ill. Menasha, Wis.: G. Banta.

710. **Farmer, Henry George.** *Egyptian music*. Grove's dictionary of music and musicians, vol. 2, 1954, 891–7, bibl. [5th ed.]

711. —— *The music of ancient Egypt*. Wellesz, Egon, Ancient and oriental music, 1957, 255–82, ill.

712. **Foucart, E.** *La musique dans l'ancienne Égypte*. Musica, 1933.

713. **Garnot, Jean Sainte-Fare.** 1955. *L'offrande musicale dans l'ancienne Égypte*. Pp. 89. Paris: . . . . [Mélanges d'histoire et d'esthétique musicales, offerts a Paul-Marie Masson.]

714. **Gilbert, Will G.** *Egyptische Muziek*. A.M.E., 1957, 430–2.

715. **Hefny, Mahmoud El.** *Music in Egypt (Egypt in 1945)*. Calcutta, 1946. Pp. 218.

716. —— 1956. *Aegyptische Musik von einst bis heute*. Cairo.

717. **Hickmann, Hans.** *Ueber den Stand der musikwissenschaftlichen Forschung in Aegypten*. Kongress-bericht d. Int. Ges. f. Musikwiss. Basle, 1949, 150.

718. —— 1949. *Music under the Pharaohs*. Pp. 15, ill. Cairo: Egyptian State Tourist Administration.

719. —— *L'état actuel des recherches musicologiques en Égypte*. Comm. au IVième congrès de la soc. intern. de musicologie, 1949. Basle.

720. —— 1956. *Aegyptische Musikgeschichte in Bildern*. Wiesbaden: Breitkopf.

721. —— 1955. *Klingendes Pharaonenland*. Pp. – . Berlin: M. Hesse.

722. —— 195 . *Musique et vie musicale sous les pharaons*. [3 vols.]. Paris: Richard-Masse.

723. —— *Abrégé de l'histoire de la musique en Égypte*. Rev. de musicologie [Paris], 32, 1950, 93–94. Translated into English and published in Cairo, 1950.]

724. —— *Die ältesten Musikernamen*. Musica, 5, 1951, 89.

725. —— *Aegyptische Musik*. Blume, F. (*ed.*), Die Musik in Geschichte u. Gegenwart, I, 1951, col. 92.

726. —— *Le métier de musicien au temps des pharaons*. Cah. hist. égyptienne, 4 (2), 1952; 6 (2), 1954, 5–6.

727. —— *Die Anfänge eines geordneten Musiklebens im Aegypten der Pharaonen*. Comm. Intern. Congress, Vienna, 17–24 May 1952. Vienna (published) 1953.

728. —— *Le problème de la notation musicale dans l'Égypte ancienne*. Bull. de l'inst. d'Égypte, 36, 1955, 489.

728a. —— *Terminologie musicale de l'Égypte ancienne.* Bull. de l'inst. d'Égypte, **36**, 1955, 583.

729. —— *Une scène de musique pharaonique (analyse iconographique).* Rev. de la soc. belge de musicol., **10**, 1956.

730. —— 1956. *Musicologie pharaonique. Études sur l'évolution de l'art musical dans l'Égypte ancienne.* Kehl.

731. ——*L'essor de la musique sous l'ancien empire de l'Égypte pharaonique* (2778–2423 av. J.C.). Ortiz, Gernando, Miscelanea de estudios dedicados a Fernando Ortiz, vol. 2, 1956, 829–36, ill.

732. —— *Les problèmes et l'état des recherches musicologiques en Égypte.* Acta musicol., **28**, 1956, 59.

733. —— 1956. *45 siècles de musique dans l'Égypte ancienne.* Pp. xii+26, ill. Paris: Richard-Masse.

734. —— *Neues Musikleben in Aegypten.* Mitt. d. Inst. f. Auslandsbeziehungen, **2**, 1957.

735. —— *Hufu-anh und andere ägyptische Musiker.* Blume, F., (*ed.*), Die Musik in Geschichte u. Gegenwart, **6**, 1957, 852.

736. —— *Musikerzichung im alten (Aegypten Musikerkenntnis und Musikerziehung).* Festschrift-Mersmann [Kassel Basle], 1957.

737. —— *Rapport préliminaire sur la campagne d'enregistrements de musique folklorique égyptienne.* Bull. de l'inst. d'Égypte, 1958.

738. —— and **Carl Gregor, Duke of Mecklenburg.** 1958. *La musique populaire égyptienne et ses rapports avec l'art musical pharaonique.* Strassburg/Kehl: ....

739. —— *Die Mehrstimmigkeit in der exotischen Musik und ihre Frühesten Belege im Alten Ägypten.* Wissenschaftliche Zeitschrift der Karl-Marx-Universitat [Leipzig], **8**, 1958–9, 519–25.

740. —— 1961. Vol. II. *The music of antiquity.* Pt. I, Egypt. Besseler, Heinrich, and Max Schneider, History of music in pictures. Pp. 168, ill. Leipzig: Deutscher Verlag für Musik.

741. **Kamel, El-Kholay.** *Kitabu 'l'musuqi.* Cairo, 1905.

742. **Lachmann, Robert.** 1932. *Compte rendue d'un voyage après la cloture du congrès pour les récherches musicales.* Pp. 127–30. Cairo: .... [Music of the Delta Oasis, Kharga, Fayoum and El Kantara.]

743. **Lane, E. W.** 1898. *An account of the manners and customs of the modern Egyptians, written in . . . 1833–1835.* Pp. xii + 595, ill. London: Alexander Gardner. [Music, pp. 363–83. Dance, pp. 383–8.]

744. **Lavignac, A. de** and **de la Laurencie.** 1913. *Encyclopédie de la musique.* Pt. I, Égypte. 2485–3401, ill., 1922.

745. **Loret, Victor.** *Quelques documents relatifs à la litterature et à la musique populaire de la Haute-Égypte.* Mémoires de la mission archéologique française au Caire, **I**, 1881–4, 305.

746. **Lyle, Robert.** The music of the ancient Egyptians. Monthly Musical record, **78**, 1948.

747. **Maas, Chr. J.** *Égypte.* Encyclopedie van de muziek, vol. I, 1956, 56.

748. **Machabey, A.** *La musique suméro-chaldéene et égyptienne.* Dufourcq, Norbert, La musique dès origines à nos jours, 1946, 59, ill.

749. **Sachs, Curt.** *Die Tonkunst der alten Aegypter.* Archiv. f. musikw., **II**, 1920.

750. ——*Altägyptische Musik.* Faust, III, fasc. 2/3, 1924–5, 36.

751. ——*Note on Egyptian music.* J. Amer. Mus. soc., **2**, 1949, 204.

753. **Schiffer, Brigitte.** *Die Oase Siwa und ihre Musik.* 1936. 128 S. Bottrop. i. Westfalen.

754. **Schneider, Marius.** *Lieder ägyptischer Bauern (Fellachen).* Festschrift f. Z. Kodály [Budapest], 1943, 154.

755. **Stanley, C. V. B.** *The oasis of Siwa.* J. afr. soc., **II**, 1911–12, 307–8.

756. **Villoteau, Guillaume André.** 1812. *De l'état actuel de l'art musical en Égypte.* Pp. 127–35. Paris: l'Imprimerie Impériale.

757. —— 1821. *Abhandlung über die Musik des alten Aegyptens.* [translated from the French]. Pp. 190. Leipzig: ....

757a. —— 1822–3. *Sur la musique en Égypte.* s.p. – . Paris: ......,

758. **Wellesz, Egon** (*ed.*). 1957. *Ancient and oriental music.* Pp. xxiii + 530, bibl., ill. London: Oxford Univ. Press. [New Oxford History of Music, vol. I.]

ETHIOPIA

759. **Anon.** *Schweizerische Zeitschrift für Instrumentalmusik.* Feuilleton: La Musique ethiopienne. Vol. 24, pp. 294–9, 519, 544–5, 567–8.

760. —— Vol. 25, pp. 41, 51, 63–64, 207–8, 303.

762. **Barblan, G.** 1941. *Musiche e strumenti musicali Africa Orient.* Ital. Pp. 147. Naples.

763. **Basset, R.** *Étude sur l'histoire d'Éthiopie.* Journal asiatique, Aug. 1881.

764. **Bent, J. Theodore.** 1893. *The sacred city of the Ethiopians.* Pp. 309, ill. London: Longmans, Green.

765. **Bianchi, Gustavo.** 1884. *Alla Terra dei Galla: narrazione della Spedizione Bianchi in Africa . . . 1879–80.* Pp. 543, ill. Milan: Fratelli Treves. [Pp. 92–93.]

766. **Bieber, Friedrich.** 1920–3. *Kaffa: ein altkuschitisches Volkstum in Inner-Afrika* [2 vols.]. Vol. I, pp. xxiv + 500, ill. Vol. 2, pp. x+560, ill. Vienna: Verlag Anthropos Administrat ion, St. Gabriel-Mödling. [Vol. 2, pp. 328–34, plates of lute and horn.]

767. **Brotto, Enrico.** 1. *Menestrelli e canzoni del Caffa;* 2. *I Magianghir.* Rass. Studi Etiopici, **6**, 1, 1947, 62–96, ill., map.

768. **Castro, Lincoln de.** 1915. *Nella terra dei Negus.* Vol. I, pp. 309–11 et seq., ill. Milan: Treves. [See also vol. 2, plates 25 and 26.]

769. **Cerulli, Enrico.** 1933. *Etiopia Occidentale* [2 vols.] [Note del viaggio, 1927–8.] Vol. I, pp. 254, ill. Vol. 2, pp. 266, ill., maps. Rome: Sindacto Italiano Arti Grafiche. [Vol. I, pp. 180. Vol. 2, pp. 22.]

770. **Cerulli, Ernesta.** 1956. *Peoples of South-West Ethiopia and its borderland.* Pp. x + 148, bibl., map. [Ethnographic Survey of Africa: North-Eastern Africa, Pt. III.]

771. **Cohen, Marcel.** *Sur la notation musicale éthiopienne.* Studi orientalistici in onore di Guirgio Levi della Vida, vol. I, 1956, 197– . Rome: ....

772. **Courlander, Harold.** *Notes from an Abyssinian diary.* Mus. quart., **30**, (3), 1944, 345–55, ill.

773. —— 1951. *Folk music of Ethiopia.* Pp. 6, ill. New York: Ethnic Folkways Library, P405. Folkways Records & Service Corp.

774. **Doresse, Jean.** 1959. *Ethiopia.* Pp. 239, bibl., ill., maps. London: Elek Books.

775. **Dos Santos, Joao.** 1684. *Histoire de l'Éthiopie orientale.* Pp. (10) 237 (3). Paris: Guillaume de Luyne. [A French translation.]

776. **Dos Santos, Y.** 1891. *Ethiopia oriental.* Pp. 432. Lisbon: .... [Original ed. 1609.]

777. **Duchesne-Fournet, Jean.** 1908–9. *Mission en Éthiopie* (1901–03) [3 vols.] bibl., ill., maps. [Anthropologie et ethnographie, by R. Verneau, vol. 2.] Paris: Masson.

779. **Geyer, F.** *Musica e canto presso i Neri del Sudan.* Nigrizia, 1892, 41–47, 68–74.

780. **Gilbert, Will G.** *Ethiopische Muziek.* A.M.E., 1957, 487–9.

781. **Griaule, Marcel.** 1935. *Jeux et divertissements abyssins.* Pp. 258 (3), ill. Paris: E. Leroux. [Bibliothèque de l'école des hautes études sciences religieuses, XLIX.]

782. **Grottanelli, Vinigi L.** 1940. *Missione Etnografica nel Uollega Occidentale,* Vol. 1, I Mao. Pp. 397, bibl., ill., maps. Rome: Reale Accademia d'Italia. [Pp. 336–41.] [Reale Accademia d'Italia: Centro Studi per l'Africa Orientale Italiana, V.]

783. **Haberland, Eike.** 1963. *Galla Süd-Äthiopiens* [with English summary]. Pp. xix, 815, 82, bibl., ill., maps. Stuttgart: Kohlhammer. [Pp. 721–61, Die Musik der Borana', by Kurt

Reinhard.] [Frobenius-Institut, Frankfurt a/M (Völker Süd-Athiopiens: Ergebnisse d. Frobenius Expeditionen, 1950–2 and 1954–6, Band 2.]

784. **Herscher-Clément, M. J.** *Chants d'Abyssinie.* Z. f. vergleich. Musikwiss., **2**, 1934, 24–38, 51–57.

785. **Herzog, George.** *Notes on music.* Leslau, Wolf, Chansons Harari [notes on music by George Herzog]. Rass. Studi Etiopici, **6**, 1947, 130.

786. **Hickmann, Hans.** *Afrikanische Musik. Äthiopische Musik.* F. Blume (*ed.*), Die Musik in Geschichte und Gegenwart, **1**, 1949–51, 105–11, bibl., ill.

787. **Hough, Walter.** *The Hoffmann abyssinian ethnological collection.* Proc. U.S. national museum, 1911.

788. **Jensen, A. E.** 1936. *Im Lande des Gada: Wanderungen zwischen Volkstrümmern Südabessiniens.* Pp. xv + 608, bibl., ill., maps. Stuttgart: Strecker u. Schröder. [Verlauf und Ergebnisse der 12 Deutschen Inner-Afrikanischen Forschungs-Expedition (DIAFE 1934–5 unter . . . Leo Frobenius.]

789. —— 1959. *Altvölker Süd-Äthiopiens.* Pp. xiv + 455, bibl., ill., maps. Stuttgart: Kohlhammer. [Völker Süd-Äthiopiens: Ergebnisse der Frobenius-Expedition, 1950–2 and 1954–6. With an English summary. Band 1.] [Musikinstrumente, pl. 39. Music and dance, see index.]

790. **Keller, C.** *Ueber Maler und Malerei in Abessinien.* Jahresber. geog.-ethnog. Gesell. in Zürich, 1903–4.

791. **Lefebvre, Theophile.** 1844–5. *Voyage en Abyssinie.* Vol. 1, pp. lxviii–lxx, 300–1. Paris: Bertrand.

792. **Leslau, Wolf.** 1950. *Music of Falashas (Jews of Ethiopia).* Recorded in Ethiopia by Wolf Leslau. Folkways Records. P201.

793. **Lipsky, G. A.,** and **Others.** 1962. *Ethiopia.* Pp. 376, bibl., map. New Haven: Human Relations Area Files.

794. **Lobo, Jerome.** 1789. *A voyage to Abyssinia.* Pp. 500. London: Elliot & Kay.

795. **Lüpke, Theodor von.** 1913. *Profan- und Kultbauten Nord-abessiniens.* Deutsche Aksum Expedition, vol. 3, p. 98, ill. Berlin: Reimer.

796. **Magni-Dufflocq, Enrico.** *Tristezza, lusinghe e furore della musica etiopica.* La Lettura, **35**, 1935, 1112–16.

797. **Mondon-Vidailhet, M.** *La musique éthiopienne.* Lavignac, A., and L. de la Laurencie, Encyclopédie de la musique, Pt. 1, 1922, 3179–96, ill.

798. **Montandon, Georges.** *Au pays Ghimirra.* Bull. soc. Neuchât. géog., **22**, 1913, 194–5, ill.

799. **Pankhurst, Sylvia.** 1955. *Ethiopia: a cultural history.* Pp. xxxviii + 747, ill. London: Lalibela House, Woodford Green. [Music: Pl. 52, pl. 170–1; pl. 65, p. 186; pls. 97–102, p. 442.]

800. **Paulitschke, Philipp.** 1893–6. *Ethnographie Nordost-Afrikas* [2 vols.]. Vol. 1, Die materielle Cultur der Danakil, Galla und Somâl. Pp. xvi + 338, ill., maps. Berlin: D. Reimer. Vol. 2, Die Geistige Cultur der Danakil, Galla und Somâl. Pp. xvii + 312. Berlin: D. Reimer. [Music of Danakil u. Galla, vol. 1, 148 and 250–1; vol. 2, 217–21.]

801. **Petino, Antonio.** *Realtà e leggenda nella musica e poesia d'Etiopia.* La Cultura moderna, **46**, 2, 1937, 74–79.

801a. **Picken, L.** *A note on Ethiopian church music.* Acta musicol., **29**, 1957, 41–42.

802. **Reinhard, Kurt.** *Die Musik der Borana.* Galla Süd-Äthiopiens, by E. Haberland, 1963, 721–61.

803. **Rein, G. K.** 1918–20. *Abessinien* [3 vols.]. Vol. 1, pp. xii + 495, bibl., ill. Vol. 2, pp. xix + 358, ill., map. Vol. 3, pp. xxxii + 395, bibl., ill. Berlin: Reimer.

804. **Rey, Charles Fernard.** 1923. *Unconquered Abyssinia.* Pp. 306, ill., map. London: Seeley Service.

805. **Rohrer, Ernest Friedrich.** 1932. *Beiträge zur Kenntnis der materiellen Kultur der Amhara.* Pp. 174, bibl., ill., map. Schönburg-Bern: Wälchli. [Ex: Jahresber. geog. Gesells. in Bern, **29**, 1929, 30.]

806. **Rosen, Felix.** 1907. *Eine deutsche Gesandtschaft in Abessinien.* Pp. xii + 496, map., ill. Leipzig: Verlag von Veit.

807. **Salt, Henry.** 1814. *A voyage to Abyssinia.* Pp. xiv + 506, ill. maps. London: Rivington. [German ed., Weimar, 1815.]

808. **Simoons, Frederick J.** 1960. *Northwest Ethiopia.* Pp. xvii + 250, bibl., ill., maps. Madison: Univ. of Wisconsin Press.

809. **Straube, Helmut.** 1963. *Westkuschitische Völker Süd-Äthiopiens.* [English summary, pp. 373–87.] Pp. xii + 411, bibl., ill., maps. Stuttgart: Kohlhammer. [Part of the results of the Frobenius Expedition, 1950–2 and 1954–6. Band 3.]

810. **Ullendorf, Edward.** 1960. *The Ethiopians.* Pp. xiv (2) + 232, bibl., ill., map. London: Oxford Univ. Press. [Chap. 8, p. 158. Art and music, pp. 109–73.]

811. **Wellesz, Egon.** *Studien zur äthiopischen Kirchenmusik.* Oriens Christianus, N.S. **9**, 1920, 74– .

FORMER FRENCH WEST AFRICA (A.O.F.)
(General)

812. **Balandier, Georges.** 1957. *Afrique ambiguë.* Pp. 291, bibl., ill., Paris: Plon.

813. **Béart, Charles.** *Contribution à l'étude des langages tambourinés, sifflés, musicaux.* Notes afr., I.F.A.N., no. 57, 1953, 11–14.

814. —— 1955. *Jeux et jouets de l'ouest africain* [2 vols.]. Pp. 438, 443–889, bibl., ill. Dakar: Ifan. [Chap. 29, pp. 653–701.] [Mémoires de l'Institut Français d'Afrique Noire, 42.]

815. **Bernatzik, Hugo Adolph.** 1935. *L'Afrique équatoriale.* Pp. xxvi + 256 plates. Paris: Librairie des Arts Décoratifs.

816. **Brasseur, G.** 1957. *Initiations africaines No. 13 L'A.O.F.* Pp. 69, bibl., ill., map. Dakar: I.F.A.N. [Musical inst., pp. 24–31, ill.]

817. **Chauvet, Stephen.** *Musique et arts nègres en A.E.F.* Sud-ouest economique [Bordeaux], **11**, 1930, 987–91, ill.

818. —— *Musique et arts nègres en A.E.F.* Apollon [Paris], July 1931, 39.

819. **Collaer, P.** *Notes sur la musique d'Afrique centrale.* Probl. Afr. centr., no. 26, 1954, 267–71.

820. **Cureau, Adolphe.** 1912. *Les populations primitives de l'Afrique équatoriale.* Pp. 420, ill., map. Paris: Colin. [Pp. 91–96.]

821. **Dakar: Bulletin Information et Renseignement.** *La musique en A.O.F.* Bull. information et renseignement, **218**, 1939, 243–5.

822. **Gide, André.** 1930. *Travels in the Congo.* Pp. 375, ill., map. New York: Knopf. [Pp. 111–12, 223–6, 232–4.]

823. **Hardy, Georges.** 1937. *L'Afrique occidentale, française.* Pp. 244, bibl., ill., maps. Paris: Laurens. [Music and art, pp. 74–77.]

824. **Perbal, Albert.** *Notes brèves sur la question de la musique indigène.* AFER, **9**, 1937, 161–7.

825. **Problèmes d'Afrique Centrale.** *Numéro consacré à la musique nègre.* Probl. Afr. centr., **26**, 4e trim., 1954.

826. **Rouget, Gilbert.** 1954. *Musique d'Afrique occidentale.* Jaquette du MC 20.145, Contrepoint, Paris.

827. **Rousseau, Madelaine.** *La musique et la danse en Afrique occidentale.* Musée vivant, **12**, 36 37, nov. 1948, 21–22.

GABON

828. **Brandel, Rose.** *The tonal structure of Kele.* Afr. stud., II (4), 1943, 193–209, ill.

829. **Burton, Sir Richard Francis.** *A day among the Fans.* Trans. ethnol. soc., **3**, 1865, 44.

830. **Desvallons, Gilbert.** *La musique et la danse au Gabon.* Rev. musicale, **3**, 1903, 215–18.

830a. **du Chaillu, Paul B.** 1861. *Exploration and adventures in equatorial Africa.* Pp. xviii + 479, ill., map. London: John Murray. [Pp. 87, 294, 467.]

831. **Grébert, F.** 1928. *Au Gabon: Afrique equatoriale française.* Pp. 228, ill. Paris: Sociétés des Missions Évangeliques de Paris. [Chap. 12, L'art musical, pp. 90–98.]

832. —— *L'art musical chez les Fang.* Archiv. suisses anthrop. générale, 5, 1928–9, 75–86, ill.

833. **Hübbe-Schleiden, Wilhelm.** 1879. *Ethiopien: Studien über West-Afrika.* Pp. xvi + 412, map. Hamburg: L. Friedrichsen.

834. **Larsonneur, A.** *Notes sur les Pongoués.* Rev. anthrop., **24**, 1914, 189.

835. **Rouget, Gilbert.** *Les travaux d'ethnographie musicale de la mission Ogooué-Congo.* C.R. sommaires séances inst. franc. anthrop., **3**, janv. 1947–déc. 1949, 4–5.

836. —— *Notes sur les travaux d'ethnographie musicale de la mission Ogooué-Congo.* Bissau, Conferencia International des Africanistas ocidentais. 2a. Conferencia Bissau, 1947, vol. 5, 1952, 193–204.

836a. **Rouget G.,** coll. with **Yvette Grimaud.** *Notes on the music of the Bushmen compared to that of the Babinga pygmies.* Musée de l'Homme and Peabody Museum. Phonodisc LD9.

837. **Tiersot, Julien.** 1889. *Musiques pittoresques.* Pp. 99–108. Paris: Fischbacher.

838. **Trilles, R. P.** 1912. *Chez les Fang.* Pp. 286. Lille: Soc. Saint-Augustin.

839. —— 1912. *Le totémisme chez les Fan.* Pp. 653. Vienna: Aschendorffsche Verlagsbuchhandlung. [Pp. 88–92, 267–9, 333–4, 373–83, 513–14, 533–6, 620.]

GAMBIA

840. **Archer, Francis Bisset.** 1906. *The Gambia colony and protectorate.* Pp. xviii + 364, ill., maps. London: St. Bride's Press.

841. **Béart, Ch.** *Sur les Bassaris de Haute-Gambie.* Notes afr., I.F.A.N., no. 35, 1947, 1–7, ill.; no. 34, 1947, 24–26, ill.

842. **Jobson, R.** 1623 (1904). *The golden trade or a discovery of the river Gambia and the golden trade of the Aethiopians . . .* [ed. by C. G. Kingsley]. [Mary Kingsley Travel Books, no. 1.] Pp. xiii + 210. Teignmouth: Privately printed.

843. **Moore, Francis.** 1738. *Travels into the inland parts of Africa . . . to which is added Capt. Stribb's voyage up the Gambia.* Pp. xiii + 229, 84, 25, ill. London: D. Henry & R. Cave. [2nd ed.] [Music, p. 45. Drums, pp. 84–85. Xylophone described.]

844. **Rancon, André.** 1894. *Dans la haute Gambie, voyage d'exploration, 1891–1892.* Pp. 592, ill., maps. Paris: Soc. d'éditions scientifiques. [Pp. 26–30.]

845. **Reeve, H. F.** 1912. *The Gambia.* Pp. xv + 288, ill., maps. London: Smith Elder.

846. **Southorn, Lady.** 1952. *The Gambia.* Pp. 283, bibl., ill., maps. London: George Allen & Unwin.

GHANA

847. **Acquaye, Saka.** 1950. *Gold Coast Saturday night.* Performed by native musicians. Elektra, E.K.L. 1950.

848. **Asado, F. Onwona.** *An African orchestra in Ghana.* Afr. mus. soc., **I** (4), 1957, 11–12.

849. **Beecham, John.** 1841. *Ashantee and the Gold Coast.* Pp. xix + 376, map. London: John Mason. [Pp. 167–9.]

850. **Bosman, Willem.** 1705. *A new and accurate description of the coast of Guinea.* Pp. (6), 493 (16), ill., map. London: J. Knapton. [Pp. 138–40.]

851. —— 1907. *A new and accurate description of the Coast of Guinea* (1705). Pp. 493, ill. London: Ballantyne Press. [Pp. 138, 353, 453.]

852. **Bowdich, T. Edward.** 1819. *Mission from Cape Coast Castle to Ashantee.* Pp. 10, 512, ill., maps. London: John Murray. [Chap. 10, pp. 361–9, 449–52.]

853. —— 1821. *An essay on the superstitions, customs and art common to the ancient Egyptians, Abyssinians, and Ashantees.* Pp. 72. Paris: J. Smith.

854. —— 1825. *Excursions in Madeira and Porto Santo . . . 1823.* Pp. xii + 278. London: Whittaker. [P. 210.]

855. **Cruickshank, Brodie.** 1853. *Eighteen years on the Gold Coast of Africa* [2 vols.]. Vol. 1, pp. viii + 345. Vol. 2, pp. v + 335. London: Hurst & Blackett. [Vol. 2, pp. 265–9.]

856. **Dupuis, Joseph.** 1824. *Journal of a residence in Ashantee.* Pp. (4) xxx + 264, ill., map. London: Henry Colburn. [Pp. 70–71.]

857. **Ellis, Alfred Burdon.** 1887. *The Tshi-speaking peoples of the Gold Coast of West Africa.* Pp. vii + 343, map. London: Chapman & Hall. [Pp. 325–30.]

858. **Gadzekpo, B. S.** *Making music in Eweland.* W.A.R., **23**, 299, 1952, 817–21, ill.

859. **Gbeho, Philip.** *The indigenous Gold Coast music.* Afr. mus. soc., Newsletter, **I** (5), 1952, 30–33.

859a. **Gbeho, Philip.** *Cross rhythm in African Music.* W.A.R., **23**, 1952, 11.

860. —— *Music of the Gold Coast.* Afr. mus. soc., **I** (1), 1954, 62–64, ill.

861. **Ghana University, Institute of African Studies.** 1961. *Recordings of African music.* Catalogue 1: tape recordings [cyclostyled]. Legon, Accra. [Padmore Res. Library, Afr. Aff., 2, 1962, p. 1.]

862. **Jones, A. M.** 1959. *Studies in African music.* Pp. 8, 295, 238, ill., maps. Oxford: Oxford Univ. Press. [Ewe music.]

862a. **Kyerematen, A. A. Y.** 1964. *Panoply of Ghana.* Pp. viii + 120, ill. London: Longmans.

863. **Labat, Jean-Baptiste.** 1730. *Voyage du Chevalier des Marchais en Guinée, isles voisines et à Cayenne . . . 1725–27.* [4 vols.]. Vol. 1, pp. xxiv + (2) 381, ill., maps. Vol. 2, pp. (4) 364, map. Vol. 3, pp. (4) 350, ill., map. Vol. 4, pp. (4) 337 (345–681), 36, map. Paris: Osmont. [Vol. 1, p. 349. Vol. 2, pp. 62, 194–6, 246–50, 317.]

864. **Macdonald, George.** 1898. *The Gold Coast.* Pp. ix + 352, ill., map. London: Longmans, Green. [Pp. 237–8.]

865. **Mähly, E.** *Zur Geographie und Ethnographie der Goldküste.* Verhand. Naturf. Gesell. in Basel, **7/3**, 1885, 851–2.

866. **Marrée, J. A. de.** 1817–18. *Reizen op en Beschrijving van de Goudkust van Guinea* [2 vols.]. 1817, vol. 1, pp. viii (iv) + 289, ill., maps. 1918, vol. 2, pp. 96, 313, ill. The Hague: van Cleef. [Vol. 2, pp. 185–93.]

867. **Moloney, Sir Cornelius Alfred.** *On the melodies of the Ewe people of West Africa.* J. Manch. geog. soc., **5**, 1889, 277–98, ill.

868. **Nketia, J. H. Kwabena.** *Akanfo Nnwom Bi* [a collection of Akan songs, words only]. London: Oxford Univ. Press. [In Tiv.]

869. —— 1949. *Akanfo Ananses m* [Akan Folktales]. London: Oxford Univ. Press. [In Tiv.]

870. —— 1951. *Ananwoma* [a play]. London: Oxford Univ. Press. [In Tiv.]

871. —— 1953. *Ad.* [The Akwasidae Festival.] London: Macmillan. [In Tiv.]

872. —— *The gramophone and contemporary African music in the Gold Coast.* West African Institute of social and economic research, 4th annual conference [Ibadan], 1956, 191–201.

873. —— *The organization of music in Adangme society.* Universitas [Accra], **3**, 1, Dec. 1957, 9–11.

874. —— *Modern trends in Ghana music.* Afr. mus. soc., **I** (4), 1957, 13–17.

875. —— *Changing traditions of folk music in Ghana.* J. int. folk music council, **9**, 1957, 4–9.

876. —— *The ideal in African folk music: a note on 'Klama'.* Universitas, **3** (2), 1958, 40–42.

877. —— *Traditional music of the Ga people.* Universitas [Accra], **3**, (3), 1958, 76–80.

878. —— *Yoruba musicians in Accra.* Odu, no. 6, 1958, 35–44.

879. —— *Folklore of Ghana.* The Ghanaian, no. 1, 1958.

880. —— *African gods and music.* Universitas, **4** (1), 1959, 3–7.

881. —— 1962. *African music in Ghana: a survey of traditional forms.* Pp. ix + 148, bibl., ill., maps. London: Longmans.

882. —— 1963. *Folk songs of Ghana.* Pp. x + 205. London: Oxford Univ. Press for University of Ghana. 50s. [First of a series designed to provide source material for performers, composers and students of African music.]

883. —— *Historical evidence in Ga religious music.* The historian in tropical Africa [eds. J. Vansina, and others], 1964, 265–80.

884. **Perregaux, Edmond.** *Chez les Achanti.* Bull. soc. Neuchât. géog., **17**, 1906, 182–5, 235–41, 282, 324, ill., maps.

885. **Pfister, G. A.** *Ashanti music at the Empire Exhibition* (1924). Music news, **66**, 1924, 490.

886. —— *La musica ascianti.* Riv. musicale italiana [Turin], **32**, 1925, 213–18.

887. **Reed, E. M. G.** *Music of West Africa.* l, Ashanti. Music and youth, **5**, 1925, 135–9, ill.

888. **Riverson, Isaac D.** 1960. *The teaching of music in primary schools.* Pp. 52. Accra: Methodist Book Depot, 7s 6d.

889. —— 1960. *Atlantis music reader.* Pts. 1 and 2, for primary schools. Pp. 12, 20. Accra: Methodist Book Depot. 2s 3d., 2s. 9d.

890. —— *The growth of music in the Gold Coast.* Trans. Gold Coast and Togoland hist. soc., **1**, 4, 1955, 121–32.

891. **Schneider, Marius.** *Phonetische und metrische Korrelationen bei gesprochenen und gesungenen Ewe-Texten.* Archiv. f. vergl. Phonetik, **7**, 1943–4.

892. —— *Tone and tune.* Ethnomusicology, **5**, (3), 1961. [Ewe.]

893. **Singer, Caroline,** and **Cyrus le Roy Baldridge.** 1942. *White Africans and black.* Pp. 119, ill., map. Cape Coast: Methodist Book Depot. [Pp. 87–88, illustrations of African musical instruments.]

894. **Smith, Edna M.** 1962. *Music education in West Africa* [a plea for bi-musicality]. Pp. 9. Accra: University of Ghana. [First International Congress of Africanists, 11–18 Dec. 1962, Doc. 8.]

895. **Vortisch, H.** *Die Neger der Goldküste.* Globus [Brunswick], **89**, 1906, 294–7, ill.

896. **Ward, William Ernest Frank.** *Music in the Gold Coast.* Gold Coast rev., **3** (2), 1927, 199–223.

897. —— *Spirituals and jazz.* Teachers' Journal (Gold Coast Colony), **2**, 9, 193a, 123–6. [Advice to teachers on music.]

898. —— *Music of the Gold Coast.* Music times, **73**, 1932, 707–10, 797–9, 901–2.

899. —— *Gold Coast music in education.* Oversea education, **5**, 2, 1934, 64–71.

900. **West Africa.** *Ghana's teacher of music* [Mr. Ephraim Amu]. West Afr., 3 Nov., 1956, p. 871, ill.

901. **Wiegrabe, Paul.** *Ewelieder.* Afrika und Übersee, **37** (3), 1953, 99–108; **38** (1), 1953, 17–26; **38** (3), 1954, 113–20; **38** (4), 1954, 155–64.

902. **Witte, Fr.** *Lieder und Gesänge der Ewe-Neger.* Anthropos, **1**, 1906, 65, 194.

903. **Wolfson, Freda.** 1958. *Pageant of Ghana.* Pp. xiii + 266, ill., maps. London: Oxford Univ. Press.

See also 2185, 2266–71, 2281, 2286–9.

GUINEA
(Formerly Guinée Française, A.O.F.)

904. **Arcin, A.** 1907. *La Guinée française.* Pp. 659, ill., maps. Paris: Challamel.

907. **Germain, J.** *Extrait d'une monographie des habitants du Cercle de N'Zérékoré (Guerzé, Kono, Manon). Les artisans, les techniques et les arts.* Études Guin., **13**, 1955, 3–54, ill.

908. **Heim, Arnold.** 1934. *Negro Sahara von der Guineaküste zum Mittelmeer.* Pp. 160, ill., map. Bern: Hans Huber.

909. **Holas, B.** 1954. *Le culte de Zié: elements de la religion Kono (Haute Guinée française).* Pp. 274, bibl., ill., map. [Mém. I.F.A.N., no. 39.]

910. —— 1952. *Les masques Kono (Haute-Guinée française).* Pp. 200, bibl., ill., map. Paris: Paul Geuthner.

911. **Joyeux, Charles.** *Notes sur quelques manifestations musicales observées en Haute Guinée.* Rev. musicale, **10** and **11**, 1910–11, 49, 103.

912. —— *Étude sur quelques manifestations musicales observées en Guinée française.* Rev. ethnog. trad. pop., **5**, no. 18, 1924, 170–212, bibl., ill.

913. **Lestrange, Monique de.** 1955. *Les Coniagui et les Bassari.* [Guinée française.] Pp. vi+86, bibl., ill., map. Paris: Presses Univ. de France. [Monographies ethnologiques africaines de l'Institut International Africain.]

914. **Madrolle, Claudius.** 1895. *Le continent noir en Guinée.* Pp. 407, bibl., ill., maps. Paris: H. Le Soudier. [2nd ed.] [P. 109, pl. 82.]

915. **Mengrelis, Thanos.** *La voix des 'niamou' chez les Guerzé de Guinée française.* Notes afr. I.F.A.N., no. 38, 1948, 8, ill.

917. **Mollien, G.** 1820. *Travels in the interior of Africa to the sources of the Senegal and Gambia in . . . 1818.* Pp. xii + 378, ill., map. London: H. Colburn.

918. **Schaeffner, André.** 1951. *Les Kissi: une société noire et ses instruments de musique.* Pp. 85, ill. Paris: Hermann. [Cahiers d'ethnologie de géographie et de linguistique, 2.]

918a. —— *Musiques rituelles Baga.* 6th congrès international des sciences anthropologiques et ethnologiques, 30 July–6 Aug., 1960, 2, pp. 123–5.

See also 1689, 1693.

IVORY COAST

919. **Chéron, Georges.** *Les Minianka.* Rev. étud. ethnog. sociol., **4**, 1913, 185–6.

920. **Chéruy, P.** *Notes sur les Agnis de l'Indénié.* Rev. étud. ethnog. sociol., 1914, 231–2.

921. **Delafosse, Maurice.** 1908. *Les frontières de la Côte d'Ivoire et du Soudan.* Pp. ix + 256, ill., map. Paris: Masson et Cie.

922. —— 1909. *Le peuple Siéna ou Sénoufo (Ivory Coast) (La musique et la danse).* Pp. 107, ill. Paris: Geuthner. [Reprint from Rev. étud. ethnog. et sociol.]

923. **Eysséric, M. J.** *Rapport sur une mission scientifique à la Côte d'Ivoire.* Nouvelles archives des missions scientifiques, ser. 4, vol. 9, 1899, 248–9.

924. **Holas, B.** 1957. *Les Sénoufo (y compris les Minianka).* Pp. viii + 183, bibl., maps. Paris: Presses Univ. de France. [Monographies ethnologiques africaines de l'Institut International Africain.]

925. —— 1960. *Cultures materielles de la Côte d'Ivoire.* Pp. 96, bibl., ill. Paris: Presses Univ. de France.

925a. **Paulme, D.** *Les Bété.* 1962. Pp. 200, bibl,, ill., maps. Paris: Mouton.

926. **Prouteaux, M.** *Notes sur certains rites magico-religieux de la Haute Côte d'Ivoire.* L'anthropologie, **29**, 1919, 37–52, ill.

927. **Rouget, Gilbert.** 1954. *Africa: Music of the Malinké. Music of the Baoulé.* Esoteric E8529.

928. **Thomann, Georges.** 1905. *Essai de manuel de langue Néoulé parlée dans la partie occidentale de la Côte d'Ivoire.* Pp. viii + 198, bibl., map. Paris: Leroux.

929. **Thurow, Donald.** *The Baoulé of the Ivory Coast.* 1956. Folkways Records, P476.

930. **Verger, Pierre.** 1957. *Notes sur le culte des Orisa et Vodun a Bahia . . . au Brésil et à l'ancienne Côte des Esclaves en Afrique.* Pp. 609, bibl., ill., map. Dakar: I.F.A.N. [Mém. I.F.A.N., no. 51.]

930a. **Zemp, H.** *Musiciens autochtones et Griots Malinké chez les Dan de Côte d'Ivoire.* Cah. étud. afr., **4** (3), 1964, 370–82, ill.

See also 2180, 2245, 2640a.

KENYA

931. **Browne, Granville St. John Orde.** 1925. *The vanishing tribes of Kenya.* Pp. 284, ill., map. London: Seeley Service.

932. **Cagnolo, C.** 1933. *The Akikuyu: their customs, traditions and folklore.* Pp. xv + 324 (2), bibl., ill., map. Nyeri, Kenya Mission Printing School.

933. **Fischer, G. A.** *Das Wapokomo-Land und seine Bewohner.* Mitt. Geog. Gesell. [Hamburg], 1878–9, 30–32.

934. **Heinitz, W.** *Zwei Phonogramme aus Rutenganyo.* Vox, **22**, 4/6, 1937, 50–56. [Commentaires à propos de quelques phonogrammes des Kikuyu, analysés au point de vue musical.]

934a. **Hobley, Charles William.** 1902. *Eastern Uganda.* Pp. 96, ill. London: Anthropological Institute Occ. Paper, No. 1. [The Eastern Province of Uganda was ceded to Kenya in April 1902.]

935. **Hyslop, Graham.** *Kenya's colony music and drama officer.* Afr. mus. soc., **2**, 1, 1958, 37–39.

936. **Kenyatta, Jomo.** 1938. *Facing Mount Kenya: the tribal life of the Gikuyu.* Pp. xxv + 339, ill., map. London: Secker & Warburg. [Pp. 93–97, 101, 104.]

937. **Lindblom, Gerhard.** 1920. *The Akamba in British East Africa.* Pp. xii + 607, bibl., ill. Uppsala: Appelbergs Boktryckeri Aktiebolag. [Archives d'etudes orientales, 17.]

938. **Massam, J. A.** 1927. *The cliff dwellers of Kenya.* Pp. 267, ill., maps. London: Seeley Service.

939. **Merker, M.** 1904. *Die Masai.* Pp. xvl + 421, ill., map. Berlin: Reimer. [Music, Gesang, 122, Wandorobbo, 229. Musical instruments, 122.]

940. **Middleton, John.** 1953. *The central tribes of the north-eastern Bantu (the Kikuyu and Kamba of Kenya).* Pp. viii + 105, bibl., map. London: International African Institute. [Ethnographic survey of Africa: East Central Africa, Pt. 5.]

941. **Oliver, Richard A. C.** *The musical talent of natives of East Africa.* Brit. J. of psychol (gen. sec.), **22**, 1932, 333–43.

942. **Peristiany, J. G.** 1939. *The social institutions of the Kipsigis.* Pp. xxxiv + 288, ill., maps. London: Routledge.

943. **Routledge, W. S.,** and **K.** 1910. *With a prehistoric people: the Akikuyu of British East Africa.* Pp. xxiv + 392, ill., maps. London: E. Arnold.

944. **Werner, Alice.** *Some notes on the Wapokomo of the Tana Valley.* J. Afr. soc., **12**, 1913, 375–6.

945. **Widenmann, A.** *Die Kilimandscharo-Bevölkerung: Anthropologisches und Ethnographisches aus dem Dschaggalande.* Petermanns Mitteilungen: Ergänzungsheft, no. 129, 1899, ix + 104, ill. [Pp. 85–86.]

LIBERIA

946. **Anderson, R. Earle.** 1952. *Liberia: America's African friend.* Pp. (14), 305. Chapel Hill: Univ. of North Carolina Press.

947. **Bouet, F.** *Les Tomas.* Rens. Col., **21**, 1911, 185–200, 220–7, 233–46, ill., maps.

948. **Büttikofer, J.** *Einiges über die Eingeborenen von Liberia.* Intern. archiv. ethnog., **1**, 1888, 87–88, ill.

949. —— 1890. *Reisebilder aus Liberia* [2 vols.]. Vol. 1, pp. xv + 440, ill., maps. Vol. 2, pp. viii + 510, ill. Leiden: Brill. [Vol. 2, music, pp. 334–48.]

950. —— *Few observations on the native tribes of Liberia.* Liberia bull., **10**, 1897, 57–66.

951. **Corry, Joseph.** 1807. *Observations upon the Windward Coast of Africa.* Pp. xvi + 163, ill., map. London: G. & W. Nicol.

953. **Dölter, Cornelius.** 1884. *Über die Capverden nach dem Rio Grande und Futah-Djallon.* Pp. viii+263, ill., map. Leipzig: Frohberg. [Music and dance, pp. 194–6.]

954. **Germann, Paul.** 1933. *Die Völkerstämme im Norden von Liberia.* Pp. 8 + 141, bibl., ill., map. Leipzig: Voigtländer.

[Veröffentlichungen des Staatlich-Sächsischen Forschungsinstitutes für Völkerkunde in Leipzig, Band 1.]

955. **Himmelheber, Hans und Ulrike.** *Die Dan: ein Bauernvolk im Westafrikanischen Urwald.* Pp. 256, bibl., ill., maps. Stuttgart: Kohlhammer. [With L. P. record of songs, harp, sansa, musical bow, drums.] [Music and dance, pp. 232–5.]

956. **Holas, B.** 1952. *Mission dans l'est Libérien (P.-L. Dekeyser-B. Holas, 1948).* Pp. xiii + 566, bibl., ill., maps. Dakar: I.F.A.N. [Mém. de l'institut français d'Afrique noire, no. 14.]

957. **Johnston, Sir Harry Hamilton.** 1906. *Liberia* [2 vols.]. Vol. 1, pp. xxviii + 520, ill., maps. Vol. 2, pp. xvi + 663, ill. London: Hutchinson.

958. **Neel, H.** *Note sur deux peuplades de la frontière Libérienne: les Kisi et les Toma.* L'anthropologie, **24**, 1913, 445–75, ill.

959. **Okie, Packard L.** 1954. *Folk music of Liberia.* Folkways Records, P465.

960. **Schwab, George.** 1947. *Tribes of the Liberian hinterland.* Pp. xix + 526, bibl., ill., maps. Cambridge, Mass: Peabody Museum. [Papers of the Peabody Museum of American Archaeology and Ethnology, Harvard University, vol. 31.]

961. **Strong, Richard Pearson** (ed.). 1930. *The African republic of Liberia and the Belgian Congo* [2 vols.]. Vol. 1, pp. xxvi + 568, ill. Vol. 2, pp. ix + 1064, ill. Cambridge, Mass.: Harvard Univ. Press. [Pp. 55, 64–66, 69, 125, ill.]

962. **Wallis, Braithwaite.** *A tour in the Liberian hinterland.* J. roy. geog. soc., **35**, 1910, 285–95.

963. **Westermann, D.** 1921. *Die Kpelle.* Pp. xvi + 552, bibl., map. Göttingen: Vandenhoeck & Ruprecht.

LIBYA

964. **B.** *Musica e danza nella Tripolitania.* Musica, 1911.

966. **Bates, Oric.** 1914. *The eastern Libyans.* Pp. xviii + 298, bibl., ill., maps. London: Macmillan. [Pp. 153–6.]

967. **Belgrave, C. Dalrymple.** 1923. *Siwah: the oasis of Jupiter Ammon.* Pp. xxix + 275, ill., map. London: John Lane.

968. **Cline, Walter.** 1936. *Notes on the people of Siwah and El Garah in the Libyan Desert.* Pp. 64, ill. Menasha, Wis.: G. Banta Publ. Co.

969. **Cultrera, Gionanni.** 1938. *I canti di Libia.* Pp. – . Studio editoriale moderno.

970. **Falls, J. C. Ewald.** 1908. *Beduinen-Lieder der Libyschen Wüste.* Pp. 240, ill. Cairo: F. Diemer, Finck & Baylaender.

971. **King, W. J. H.** 1925. *Mysteries of the Libyan Desert.* Pp. 348, ill., maps. London: Seeley Service.

972. **Schiffer, Brigitte.** 1936. *Die Oase Siwa und ihre Musik.* Pp. – . Berlin: . . . .

973. **Stumme, H.** 1894. *Tripolitanisch-tunesische Beduinenlieder.* Pp. – . Leipzig: . . . .

MADAGASCAR

974. **Bonnenberger-Rouillon, H.** *De la musique malgache authentique.* Rev. Madagascar, no. 12, déc. 1960, 17–22, ill.

975. **Brot, Fernand.** *L'évolution de la musique à Madagascar.* Rev. Madagascar, 1906, 56–74.

976. **Camboué, R. P.** *Jeux des enfants malgaches.* Anthropos, **6**, 1911, 674– .

977. **Camo, Pierre.** 1931. *La protection de la vie locale à Madagascar, musique, danse et fêtes traditionnelles indigènes.* Pp. 14. Paris: . . . .

978. **Colin, E.** 1899. *Mélodies malgaches, recueillies et harmonisées.* Pp. 68. Antananarivo: Impr. Miss. Catholique.

979. **Decary, Raymond.** 1933. *L'Androy (extréme sud de Madagascar).* Pp. vii + 268, ill. Paris: Société d'Éditions Géographiques, Maritimes et Coloniales. [Music and Games, p. 141.]

980. —— *Poupées Malgaches et Comoriennes.* 1937, 41–52, ill. Rev. Madagascar. 1937, 41–52, ill.

981. **Dubois, Henri M.** 1938. *Monographie des Betsileo (Madagascar).* Pp. xviii+1510, ill., maps. Paris: Institut d'Ethnologie. [Travaux et mémoires de l'institut d'Ethnologie, 34.] [L'art, pp. 1127–48, ill. Musique, pp. 1149–72, ill.]

982. **Ellis, William.** 1858. *History of Madagascar.* Vol. 1, pp. 272–4. London: Fisher.

983. **Gautier, Judith.** 1900. *Les chants de Madagascar. Les musiques bizarres a l'Exposition de 1900.* Pp. 28. Paris: Ollendorff.

984. **Grandidier, Alfred** and **Guillaume.** 1908–14. *Histoire physique, naturelle et politique de Madagascar.* Vol. 4, Ethnographie. Paris: Soc. d'Éditions géog. Marit et Col. [Pp. 66–67.]

985. **Hornbostel, Erich M. von.** 1909. *Phonographierte Melodien aus Madagascar und Indonesien.* Forschungsreise S.M.S. Planet, 1906–07, vol. 5, pp. 139–52 and Append. 1–12. Berlin: Sigismund.

986. **Leblond, Marius-Ary.** *Lettre sur la musique malgache.* J. soc. intern. de musicologie [Paris], **4**, 1908, 877–87.

987. —— 1946. *La grande île de Madagascar.* Pp. vi + 270, bibl., ill. Paris: Editions de Flore. [Pp. 165–76.]

988. **Linton, Ralph.** *The Tanala, a hill tribe of Madagascar.* Field Museum of Natural History: Anthropological series, vol. 22, 1933. [Musical instruments, pp. 264–71, ill. Art, pp. 271–81, ill.]

988a. **Macleod, N.** *The status of musical specialists in Madagascar.* Ethnomusicology, **8**, 1964, 278–89.

989. **Michel, Louis.** 1957. *Moeurs et coutumes des Bara.* Pp. 192, bibl., ill. Tananarive: Imprimerie Officielle. [Méms. de l'académie malgache, fasc. 40.]

990. **Mondain, Gustave.** *Musique malgache.* Le petit messager des missions évangeliques, 1904, 37–46, ill.

991. **Rabearivelo, Jean Joseph.** *Notes sur la musique malgache.* Rev. d'Afrique, no. 8, 1931, 29–31.

992. **Rason, Robert.** *Étude sur la musique malgache (avec notations musicales).* Rev. Madagascar, 1933, 41–91, ill.

993. **Rouget, Gilbert.** *La musique à Madagascar.* Faublée, J. Ethnographie de Madagascar, 1946, 85–92, ill.

994. **Rusillon, H.** 1933. *Un petit continent: Madagascar.* Pp. 201–3. Paris: Soc. des Miss. Évang.

995. **Sibree, James.** 1870. *Madagascar and its people.* Pp. 576. London: Religious Tract Society. [Pp. 234–5.]

996. **Sichel, A.** *Histoire de la musique des malgaches.* Lavignac, A., and L. de la Laurencie, Encyclopédie de la musique, Pt. 1, 1922, 3226–33, ill.

997. **Tiersot, Julien.** *La musique à Madagascar.* Le Ménestrel, **68**, 1902 (35–42), 273–4, 281–2, 289–90, 297–9, 305–7, 313–14, 321–2, 329–30.

MALAWI
(Formerly Nyasaland)

998. **Debenham, Frank.** 1955. *Nyasaland: the land of the lake.* Pp. xi + 239, ill., maps. London: H.M.S.O. [Pp. 144, 157, 160, 176–7, 180, 189, 191.]

999. **Duff, L.** 1906. *Nyasaland under the Foreign Office.* Pp. xxxii + 422, map. London: Geo. Bell [2nd ed.] [Pp. 285–6.]

1000. **Kidney, Ella.** *Native songs from Nyasaland.* J. Afr. soc., **20**, 1921, 116–26. [Musical instruments, p. 118.]

1001. —— *Songs of Nyasaland.* Outward Bound, **1**/7, 1921, 31–37; **1**/12, 1921, 23–29, 74.

1002. **Stannus, Hugh Stannus.** *Notes on some tribes of British Central Africa.* J. roy. anthrop. inst., **40**, 1910, 333–4.

1003. —— *The Wayao of Nyasaland.* Harvard African Studies, vol. 3, Varia Africana III, 229–372, ill. [Pp. 364–72, ill.]

1004. **Stigand, C. H.** *Notes on the natives of Nyasaland, N.E. Rhodesia and Portuguese Zambezia.* J. anthrop. inst., **37**, 1907, 119–32, ill.

1005. **Swann, Alfred J.** 1910. *Fighting the slave-hunters in Central Africa.* Pp. xvi + 359, ill., map. London: Seeley Service.

1006. **Tracey, Hugh.** *Report on the I.L.A.M. Nyasaland recording tour.* Afr. mus. soc., **2** (1), 1958, 65–68.

1007. **Werner, Alice.** 1906. *The natives of British Central Africa.* Pp. xii + 303, bibl., ill., map. London: Constable.

See also 2434.

MALI
(Formerly Soudan Français)

1009. **Anon.** *Art musical indigène au Soudan.* Brousse, nos. 1–2, 1946, 28.

1010. **Bazin, Hippolyte.** 1906. *Les Bambara et leur langue.* Pp. 689. Vienna: Anthropos Verlag.

1011. **Bissuel, H.** 1888. *Les Touareg de l'ouest.* Pp. xix + 210, maps. Alger: A. Jourdan. [Pp. 99–100.]

1012. **Caillie, R.** 1830. *Journal d'un voyage à Temboctou et à Jenné* [3 vols., ill., map]. Vol. 1, pp. xii + 475. Vol. 2, pp. 426. Vol. 3, pp. 404. Paris: Imprimerie Royale. Vol. 1, pp. 360, 428–9; vol. 2, pp. 34, 72–73, 105–6.

1013. —— 1830. *Travels through Central Africa to Timbuctoo . . . 1824–28* [2 vols.]. Vol. 1, pp. viii + 475, ill., map. Vol. 2, pp. xiv + 501, ill., map. London: Colburn. [Music and dance: Vol. 1, pp. 366, 369, 391.]

1014. **Crozals, J. de.** 1883. *Les Peulhs: Étude d'ethnologie africaine.* Pp. 271. Paris: Maisonneuve. (P. 239.)

1015. **Dieterlen, Germaine.** 1951. *Essai sur la religion Bambara.* Pp. xx + 240, bibl., ill. Paris: Presses Univ. de France. [Pp. 152–4, 220–5.]

1016. **Gallieni, Joseph Simon.** 1885. *Mission d'exploration du Haut-Niger: Voyage au Soudan francais (Haut-Niger et pays de Ségou . . . 1879–81).* Pp. 632, ill., maps. Paris: Hachette. [Pp. 76–77.]

1017. **Griaule, Marcel.** 1938. *Jeux Dogons.* Pp. viii + 292, ill., map. Paris: Institut d'Ethnologie. [Pp. 83–99.] [Travaux et mémoires de l'institut d'ethnologie, 32.]

1018. **Henry, Joseph.** 1910. *Les Bambara.* Pp. 238. Münster: Aschendorffschen Buchhandlung.

1019. **Holiday, Finola** and **Geoffrey.** *Tuareg music of the Southern Sahara.* Ethnic Folkways, FE4470.

1020. **Jean, Camille Charles.** 1909. *Les Touaregs du Sud-Est (l'Air).* Pp. iv + 361. Paris: Larose. [Pp. 209–14.]

1020a. **Lanrezac, Lt.** 1905. *L'Art et les croyances chez les Noirs du Soudan francais (Mali), musique et sculpture, etc.* C.R. 26e Congrès nat. soc. franc. Géogr. et soc. assimilées, 453–65. Saint-Étienne.

1021. **Leiris, Michel.** 1948. *La langue secrète des Dogons de Sanga (Soudan francais).* Pp. xxxii + 530, bibl. Paris: Institut d'Ethnologie. [Travaux et mémoires de l'institut d'Ethnologie, 50.]

1022. **Lem, F. H.** *Musique et art nègres.* Lettres du Soudan. Bull. rech. soudanaises, no. 36, 1936, 73–83.

1023. **Lenz, Oskar.** 1884. *Timbuktu: Reise durch Marokko, die Sahara und den Sudan . . . in 1879–80* [2 vols.]. Vol. 1, pp. xvi + 430, ill., map. Vol. 2, pp. x + 408, maps. [Vol. 1, p. 149, 217–18, vol. 2, front.]

1025. **Lyon, G. F.** 1821. *A narrative of travels in northern Africa . . . 1818–20.* Pp. xii + 383, ill., map. London: John Murray. [Pp. 161–234.]

1026. **Monteil, Charles.** 1915. *Les Khassonké: monographie d'une peuplade du Soudan francais.* Pp. 528, ill., map. Paris: Leroux.

1027. **Palau Marti, Montserrat.** 1957. *Les Dogon.* Pp. 122, bibl., maps. Paris: Presses Univ. de France. Monographies ethnologiques africaines de l'Institut International Africain.

1028. **Paques, Viviana.** *Bouffons sacrés du cercle de Bougouni (Soudan francais).* J. soc. africanistes, **24**, 1954, 63.

1029. —— 1954. *Les Bambara.* Pp. viii + 123, bibl., map. Paris:

Presses Universitaires de France. Monographies Ethnologiques Africaines de l'Institut International Africain.

1030. **Park, Mungo.** 1799. *Travels in the interior districts of Africa.* Pp. 278–9. London: Nicol.

1031. —— 1808–14. *Pinkerton's voyages,* 5, 1808–14, 878.

1031a. **Rouch, Jean.** *La religion et la magie songhay.* Pp. 325, ill. Paris: Presses Universit. de France.

1032. —— *Aperçu sur l'animisme Sonrai.* Notes afr. I.F.A.N., no. 20, 1943, 6, ill.

1033. **Rouget, Gilbert.** *Chroniques musicales. Nouvelles des Griots.* Présence africaine, N.S. nos. 1–2, 1955, 153–158.

1034. **Raimond, Georges.** *De la musique chez les Bambaras aux jazz modernes.* Le monde colonial illustré [Paris], no. 145, 1935, 162– .

1035. **Schaeffner, André.** *Musique, danse et danses des masqués dans une société nègre (Dogon).* Deuxième congrès internationale d'esthétique et de science de l'art. 1, 1937, 308–12. [Paris: Alcan.]

1036. **Tellier, Henri Ernest Edmond Gaston.** 1902. *Autour de Kita: étude soudanaise.* Pp. 316. Paris: Lavauzelle. [Pp. 176–85.]

1037. **Zahan, Dominique.** 1960. *Sociétés d'initiation Bambara.* Pp. 438, bibl., ill., map. Paris: Mouton. [Pp. 234–6.]

See also 2155, 2200.

MAURITANIA

1038. **Balandier, G.,** and **P. Mercier.** *Notes sur les théories musicales maures à propos de Chants Enregistrés.* Conferência International dos Africanistas Ocidentais. 2 A Bissau, 1947. Trabalhos, vol. 5. 3 A Secção 2A Partie. (Meio Humano), 1952, 135–91, ill. Lisbon: Junta de Investigações Coloniais.

1039. **du Puigaudeau, Odette.** *Musique du desert.* Table ronde, 64, avr. 1953, 179–84.

1040. **Leriche, Albert.** *Poésie et musique maure.* Bull. I.F.A.N., 12 (3), 1950, 710–43.

1041. **Nikiprowetzky, T.** 1961. *La musique de la Mauritanie.* Communication présentée au 14 congrès du conseil international de la musique populaire. [Quebec.] V. p. (30), ill. Paris: Radio-Diffusion Outre-mer Sorafom.

1042. **Rouget, Gilbert.** 1954. *Musique maure.* Notice pour un album de deux disques microsillon. Institut Français d'Afrique Noire, Saint-Louis du Sénégal.

1043. —— 1960. *Mauritanie, Chants d'homme, Chants de femme.* Jaquette du LD 45–3 & 4. Paris: Musée de l'Homme.

MOROCCO

1044. **Aguila y Tajera, Augustin.** *De musica marroqui.* Revue de la Raza, 1927/28, 24–25.

1045. **Antonio de Vega, Luis.** *Sonaba Tetuán como una inmensa derbuka.* Africa (Madrid), no. 182, 1957, 53–58, ill.

1046. **Bernard, Robert.** *Congrès de musique marocaine à Fès.* Rev. musicale, Dec. 1939, 164–9.

1047. **Bourrily, Joseph.** 1932. *Elements d'ethnographie marocaine.* Pp. viii + 264, ill., map. Paris: Larose.

1048. **Chottin, Alexis.** *Airs populaires receuillis à Fes.* Hespéris, 3, 1923, 275–85; 4, 1924, 225–38. Le Ménestrel, 94 (nos. 35–37), 1932, 351–3, 359–60, 367–8.

1049. —— *La musique marocaine.* Outre-mer, 1 (1), 1929, 32–42.

1050. —— *Les visages de la musique marocaine.* Le Ménestrel, 93, 1931, 217–19, 230–1.

1051. —— *Au congrès de la musique arabe.* Le Caire (Mar.–Apr.), 1932. *Journal d'un congressiste.* Bull. enseign. pub. du Maroc, Jan.–Feb., 1933, 3–21, ill.

1052. —— *La pratique du chant chez les musicians marocains.* Z. f. vergleich. Musikwiss, 1, 1933, 52–55.

1053. ——*Instruments, musique et danse chleuh.* Z. f. vergleich. Musik-wiss, 1, 1933, 11–15, ill.

1054. —— (transl.) 1931. *Corpus de musique marocaine.* Fasc. 1. Nouba de Ochchak (prélude et première phase rythmique: Bsit). Pp. xvi + 67. Paris: Heugel.

1055. —— 1933. *Corpus de musique marocaine.* Fasc. 2. Musique et danses berbères du pays chleuh. Pp. 72, illus. Paris: Heugel.

1056. —— 1949. *Visages de la musique marocaine.* Pp. 429–46, ill. [Encycl.] [Col. et Mar., vol. IV, Maroc: Fasc. 14.] Paris.

1057. —— 1959. *Tableau de la musique marocaine.* Pp. 223, ill. Paris. Paul Geuthner.

1058. **de Hen, F. J.** *Quelques notes ethnographiques sur les Ihansalen.* Jb. S. Mus. Völkerkunde [Leipzig], 20, 1964, 310–12.

1059. **Derwil, G.,** and **Essafi.** *Chansons marocaines.* Rev. Méditerranée, June 1932.

1060. **Dolmetsch, Mabel.** *Music in Morocco.* The consort, 1931.

1061. —— *Musik in Marokko.* Z. f. Instrumentenbau, 52, 1932, 378–80.

1062. **Garcia Barriuso, Patrocinio.** *La Musica marroqui.* Mauritania, 7–10, 1934–7. Vol. 7, pp. 9–11, 49–51, 103–6, 135–7, 169–70, 236–42, 263–6, 364–9. Vol. 8, pp. 16–18, 109–12, 144–7, 269–72, 296–8. Vol. 9, pp. 20–25, 240–3, 277–80, 298–300, 364–8. Vol. 10, pp. 15–18, 60–61, 90–91, 123–8, 251–4, 279–82, 363–7.

1063. —— 1941. *La música hispano-musulmana en Marruecos.* Pp. 318, ill. Larache: Artes Graficas Bosca. [Publ. del inst. General Franco para la investigacion hispanoarabe, ser. VI, no. 4. Inst. de estud. Africanos, Madrid.]

1064. —— *La classica musica de Al-Andalus las Nubas.* Africa [Madrid], no. 26, 1944, 23–26, ill.

1065. —— *Edicion del tradicional repertorio musical y poetico Hispano-Marroqui.* Africa [Madrid], nos. 37–38, 1945, 29–31, ill.

1066. **Garcia Figueras, T.,** and **J. L. Fernandiz-Liebrez.** 1955. *Manuales del Africa Española,* 2 Marruecoes. Pp. 210, ill., map. Madrid: Instituto de Estudios Africanos. [Pp. 97–99.]

1067. **Gilbert, Will G.** *Zuid-zuidoost van Marakesch.* Luister, no. 44, 1956, 219 [Amersfoort.]

1068. —— *Marokkaanse Muziek.* A.M.E., 1957, 469–71.

1069. **Lens, Thérèse de.** 1920. *Ce que nous savons de la musique et des instruments à musique au Maroc.* [Bull. inst. hautes études Marocaines.]

1070. **Lenz, Oskar.** 1886. *Timbouctou: voyage au Maroc, au Sahara et au Soudan* [2 vols.]. Vol. 1, pp. xii + 467, ill. Vol. 2, pp. 438, ill., maps. Paris: Hachette. [Marocaine, vol. 1, p. 169.]

1071. **Mammery, Azouaou.** *La musique et le théâtre populaire à Marrakech.* Atlas, numéro special, 1930, 3, ill.

1072. **Martens, Frederick H.** *The musical observations of a Moroccan ambassador* (1690–91). Mus. quart., 15, Oct. 1929, 574–82.

1073. **Mény de Marangue, Marc.** 1923. *La musique marocaine.* Pp. 16, ill. Nyons: Imp. dauphinoise.

1074. **Oulié, Marthe.** *Musiques et danses berbères au Maroc.* Miroir du monde, 19 Dec. 1931, 690, ill.

1075. **Ricard, Prosper.** *Le conservatoire de musique marocaine de Rabat.* Outre-mer, 1er trim, 1932, 19–29.

1076. —— *Le 8 congrès de l'institut des hautes études marocaines.* 1933, 64–65. Also Actes de 8° congrès de l'institut des hautes études marocaines, Rabat-Fès, 13–20 April 1933 [Paris, 1934], 84–86.

1077. —— *La rénovation des arts musicaux au Maroc.* Rev. d'Afrique July and Oct.–Nov., 1936, 13–20, 3–8.

1078. **Schneider, Marius.** *Nochmals asiatische Parallelen zur Berbermusik.* Ethnologica, 2 (Festband M. Heydrich), 1960, 433–8.

1079. **Thornton, Philip.** 1936. *The voice of Atlas: in search of music in Morocco.* Pp. 12 + 226, ill., maps. London: Alexander Maclehose.

1080. **Tiersot, Julien.** *Musique marocaine.* Le Ménestrel, 3 and 10 Aug. 1934.

MOZAMBIQUE

1081. **Barrett, Otis Warren.** *Impressions and scenes of Mozambique.* Nat. geog. mag., 21, 1910, 807–30, ill.

1082. **Bastos, Maria Henriqueta Calçada,** and **C. Montez.** *Canções Djongas (Magude).* Moçambique [Lourenço Marques], **3**, 1935, 17–29, ill.

1083. —— *Kossi n'quaio . . . A grande festa do Rei Gungunhana.* Moçambique [Lourenço Marques], 4, 1935, 5–24, ill.

1084. **Cabral, Augusto A. P.** 1925. *Raças, usos e costumes dos indigenas da provincia de Mocambique.* Pp. 95, ill. Lourenço Marqués: Imprensa Nacional.

1085. **de Campos, Octavio Rodrigues.** *A arte negra de Mocambique.* Portugal em Afr., **13**, no. 78, 1956, 337–56, ill.

1086. **Curtis, Natalie.** 1920. *Songs and tales from the 'dark continent' recorded from the singing and sayings of C. Kamba Simango and Madikane Cele.* Pp. xxv + 170, ill. New York: G. Schirmer.

1087. **de Matos, Alexandre V.** *Un aspecto do folclore dos Chirimas: os Chirimas e a mūsica.* Bol. mus. Nampula, **1**, 1960, 31–49, ill.

1088. **Dos Santos, J.** 1609. *Ethiopia oriental e varia historia de covsas no travies do oriente.* Lisbon: . . . . [The relevant pp. are reprinted in G. M. Theal, Records of South East Africa, 1901, vol. 7, pp. 1–182, with English translation 183–370.]

1089. **Earthy, E. Dora.** *Some agricultural rites practised by the Valenge and Vachopi (Portuguese East Africa).* Bantu stud., **2** (4), 1926, 265–7.

1090. —— 1933. *Valenge women: the social and economic life of the Valenge women of Portuguese East Africa.* Pp. viii + 251, ill., map. Oxford: Oxford Univ. Press.

1091. **Jorge, Tomás, Jun.** *As aptidões musicais dos indígenas de Moçambique.* Bol. soc. estud. Moc., **17**, 1934, 163–84.

1092. **Junod, Henri Alexandre.** 1897. *Les chants et les contes des Ba-Ronga de la baie de Delagoa.* Pp. 327, ill. Lucerne: Bridel.

1093. —— 1898. *Les Ba-Ronga.* Pp. 500, ill., map. Neuchâtel: Attinger Frères. [Pp. 147–8, 263–5.] [Bull. soc. Neuchât. géog., 10.]

1094. —— 1927. *The life of a South African tribe.* [2 vols.]. Vol. 1, Social life. Vol. 2, Mental life. Pp. 559; 660, ill. London: Macmillan. [2nd ed.] [Vol. 2, pp. 276–300.]

1095. —— 1962. [Latest ed.] *The life of a South African tribe* [2 vols.]. Vol. 1, Social life [Music, p. 431]. Vol. 2, Mental life [Music, pp. 276–300, 294, 423, 484]. Ill., map. New York: University Books Inc.

1096. **Kirby, Percival R.** 1934. *The musical instruments of the native races of South Africa.* Pp. xix + 285, ill., map. Oxford: Oxford Univ. Press. [Pp. 57–65, Chopi instruments and music.]

1097. **Marques, Belo.** 1943. *Musica negra (Estudos de folclore Tonga).* Pp. 121. Lisbon: Agência-Geral das Colónias.

1098. **Monteiro, Rose.** 1891. *Delagoa Bay.* Pp. xi (1) + 274, ill. London: George Philip.

1099. **Müller, Hendrik Pieter Nicolaas,** and **Joh. F. Snelleman.** 1893. *Industrie des Cafres du Sudest de l'Afrique.* Pp. vi + 50, ill. (pls. 21–23). Leiden: Brill. [Pp. 46–47 and app.]

1100. **Rippmann, Ernst.** 1940. *Durch Busch und Sand in Mozambique.* Pp. 164, bibl., ill., maps. Zürich: Wanderer-Verlag.

1101. **Rita-Ferreira, A.** *Timbilas e jazz entre os indígenas de Homoine.* Bol. inst. invest. cient. Moçambique, **1** (1), 1960, 68–79.

1102. **Rocha, Illidio.** *L'art merveilleux du peuple Chope.* [Assoc. hist. int. Océan Indien, 2º Congr. int. Commission int. d'Hist. Maritime, 6º colóquio int.] Lourenço Marques: 1962 Inst. Invest. Cient. Moçambique.

1103. **Salt, Henry.** 1814. *A voyage to Abyssinia and travels, 1809–1810, in which are included an account of the Portuguese settlements on the east coast of Africa, etc.* Pp. xi + 506, lxxv, ill., maps. London: Rivington. [Music: pp. 41–42, 380–1, 447 (illustration of instruments facing p. 408).]

1104. **Theal, George McCall.** 1899–1903. *Records of south-eastern Africa.* Vols. 1–7. Cape Town. [Describes the Sansa of Joa. dos Santos.]

1105. **Tracey, Hugh.** *Três dias com os Bà-Chope.* Moçambique, **24**, 1940, 23–54, ill.

1106. —— *Música poesia e ballados Chopes.* Moçambique, **30**, 1942, 69–112, ill.

1107. —— 1948. *Chopi musicians: their music, poetry, and instruments.* Pp. x + 180, ill., maps. London: Oxford Univ. Press for Int. African Institute.

1108. —— 1946–48), tr. de Barradas, M. H. 1949. *A música Chope: gentes afortunadas (separata do documentàrio trimestral 'Moçambique').* Pp. 273, ill. Lourenço Marques: Imprensa Nacional de Moçambique.

1109. —— *Music is life to the Chopi.* Picture post, 1 Apr. 1950, 14–17.

1110. —— *Recording tour 1949 (Mozambique, Belgian Congo, Rhodesias and Nyasaland).* Afr. mus. soc. newsletter, **1**, 3, July 1950, 33–37.

1111. —— *Musica Africana.* Bol. soc. estud. Moc., **21**, 1951, 61–88.

1112. —— *Wood music of the Chopi: summary.* J. int. folk music council, **16**, 1964, p. 91.

See also 2471.

NATAL

1113. **Aitchison, S. G. Gilkes.** 1917. *Native social life.* Pp. 26–29. Durban: Jones.

1114. **Angas, George French.** 1849. *The Kaffirs illustrated.* London: Hogarth. [Pls. 17, 19 and 25 for Zulu reedpipe, rattles and bow.]

1115. **Caluza, Reuben Tolakele.** *African music.* S. Workman, **60**, 1931, 152–5.

1116. **Campbell, John.** 1815. *Travels in South Africa.* Pp. xv + 400, ill., map. London: Black. [Pp. 433, 518–19.]

1117. **Davis, William J.** 1877. *An English and Kaffir dictionary.* Pp. xiv + 332. London: Wesleyan Missionary Society. [See Index.]

1118. **Dhlomo, H. I. E.** *Nature and variety of tribal drama.* Bantu stud., **13**, 1939, 33–48.

1119. **Fynn, Henry Francis.** 1950. *The diary of Henry Francis Fynn.* Pp. xvi + 341, ill., maps. Pietermaritzburg: Shuter & Shooter.

1120. **Gardiner, Allen Francis.** 1836. *Narrative of a journey to the Zoolu country.* Pp. iv + 412, ill. London: W. Crofts. [Pp. 56–59, 104–5.]

1121. **Grout, Lewis.** 1864. *Zululand.* Pp. 351, ill., map. Philadelphia: Presbyterian Publication Committee. [Pp. 194– .]

1122. **Kirby, P. R.** *Old-time chants of the Mpumuza chiefs.* Bantu stud., **2**, 1923, 23–34.

1123. **Krige, Eileen Jensen.** 1950. *The social system of the Zulus.* Pp. xix + 420, bibl., ill., maps. Pietermaritzburg: Shuter & Shooter. [2nd ed.]

1124. **Mayr, F.** *A short study on Zulu music.* Annals of the Natal museum, **1**, 3, 1908, 257–67, ill.

1125. **Rycroft, David.** *Zulu and Xhosa praise-poetry and song.* Afr. mus. soc., **3**, 1, 1962, 79–85, bibl.

1126. **Samuelson, L. H.** 1928. *Zululand: its traditions, legends customs and folklore.* Pp. 144–6. Mariannhill: Mission Press.

1127. **Samuelson, Robert Charles Azariah.** 1923. *King Cetewayo Zulu dictionary.* Pp. 995. Durban: Commercial Printing Co. [Vernacular names of instruments.]

1128. —— 1929. *Long, long ago.* Pp. 319–21: 386–7. Durban: Knox Printing Co.

1129. **Scully, William Charles,** and **Nora Scully.** *Kaffir music.* Pall Mall magazine, **12**, 1897, 179.

1130. —— *Kaffir music. By veldt and kopje.* 1907. Pp. 285–301. London: Fisher Unwin.

1131. **Shooter, Joseph.** 1857. *The Kaffirs of Natal and the Zulu country.* Pp. iii + 400. London: Stanford. [Pp. 234–8.]

1131a. **Tracey, Hugh.** 1948. *Zulu paradox.* Pp. 110, ill., maps. Johannesburg: Silver Leaf Books.

1132. —— *Zulu find the middle road: a South African sect and its music.* Nat. hist., 1955, 400–6.

See also 2237, 2494.

NIGER

1133. **Abadie, Maurice.** 1927. *La colonie du Niger.* Pp. 466, bibl., ill., map. Paris: Soc. d'Éditions Géog. Maritimes et Coloniales. [Pp. 193–8.]

1134. **Binger, Louis Gustave.** 1892. *Du Niger au Golfe de Guinée par le pays de Kong et le Mossi (1887–89)* [2 vols.]. Vol. 1, pp. (5) 513, ill. Vol. 2, pp. (3) 416, ill., map. Paris: Hachette. [Vol. 1, pp. 76–77.]

1135. **Delafosse, Maurice.** *Le peuple Siéna ou Sénoufo.* Rev. étud ethnog. sociol., 4–5, 1908, 267–9.

1136. **Haywood, A. H. W.** 1912. *Through Timbuctu and across the Great Sahara.* Pp. xvi + 349, ill., map. London: Seeley Service.

1137. **Heinitz, Wilhelm.** *Musikwissenschaftliche Vergleiche an vier afrikanischen (Djarma-Ewe und Yefe-) Gesängen.* Vox, 1935, 23.

1138. **Holas, B.** 1957. *Les Sénoufo (y compris les Minianka).* Pp. viii + 83, bibl., maps. Paris: Presses Universit. de France. [Monographies ethnologiques africaines de l'Institut International Africain.]

1139. **Lutten, Eric.** *Les Wasamba et leur usage dans la circoncision.* Minotaure [Paris], 2, 1933, 13–17, ill.

1139a. **Nikiprowetsky, Tolia.** *Niger: la musique des griots.* Pp. 8, ill., et disque OCR20. Paris: Office de Coopération Radiophonique (OCORA).

1140. —— *L'Ornementation dans la musique des Touareg de l'air.* J.

1141. **Noirot, Ernest.** sd. *À travers le Fouta-Diallon et le Bambouc.* Pp. 326–45. Paris: Dreyfous.

NIGERIA

1142. **Abraham, R. C.** 1940. *The Tiv people.* Pp. x + 177, ill., map. London: Crown Agents. [2nd ed.]

1143. **Alldridge, Thomas Joshua.** 1901. *The Sherbro and its hinterland.* Pp. xvi + 356, ill., maps. London: Macmillan.

1144. **Allen, William,** and **Others.** 1843. *A narrative of the expedition . . . to the River Niger in 1841* [2 vols.]. Vol. 1, pp. xviii + 509, ill., map. Vol. 2, viii + 511, ill. London: Bentley.

1145. **Anon.** *Sur les bords du Niger.* Rev. musicale, 6, 1906, 528–30.

1146. —— *Spielleute und Märchenerzähler Innerafrikas.* Westermanns Monatshefte, Brunswick, 115, 1913, 573–85, ill.

1147. **Basden, George Thomas.** 1921. *Among the Ibos of Nigeria.* Pp. xxxi + 448, ill., map. London: Seeley Service. [Chap. 17, Music.]

1148. —— 1938. *Niger Ibos.* Pp. xxxii + 448, ill., map. London: Seeley Service. [Chap. 17, Music.]

1149. **Baumann, Margaret.** 1933. *Sons of sticks: sketches of everyday life in a Nigerian Bush Village. With music of Yoruba songs and marches.* Appendix 12 pp. London: Sheldon Press.

1150. **Beier, H. Ulli.** *Yoruba folk operas.* Afr. mus. soc., 1, 1954, 32–34, ill.

1151. —— *Yoruba vocal music.* Afr. mus. soc., 1 (3), 1956, 23–28.

1152. —— *Yoruba enclave.* Nigeria magazine, no. 58, 1958, 238–51, ill.

1153. **Boston, John.** *Alosi shrines in Udi division.* Nigeria magazine., no. 61, 1959, 157–65, ill.

1154. **Brackenbury, E. A.** *Notes on the Bororo Fulbe or nomad 'Cattle Fulani'.* J. Afr. soc., 23, 1923–4, 271–2.

1155. **Bradbury, R. E.** *Divine kingship in Benin.* Nigeria magazine, no. 62, 1959, 186–207, ill.

1156. **Campbell, M. J.** *People in trust (Adamawa).* Nigeria magazine, no. 62, 1959, 208–29, ill. [Pp. 216–18.] int. folk music council, 16, 1964, 81–83, ill.

1157. **Claridge, G. Cyril.** 1922. *Wild bush tribes of tropical Africa.* Pp. 314, ill., map. London: Seeley Service. [Chap. 20, Native music. Chap. 21, Musical instruments.]

1158. **D'Avezac, M.** 1845. *Notice sur le pays et le peuple des Yébous.* Pp. 271, map. Paris: Dondey-Dupré. [Pp. 86–94.]

1159. **Davies, J. G.** 1954–6. *The Biu book: a collation and reference book on Biu division (Northern Nigeria).* Pp. 357 (typescript).

1160. **Ellis, A. B.** 1887. *The Tshi-speaking peoples of the Gold Coast of West Africa.* Pp. vii + 343, map. London: Chapman & Hall. [Chap. 22, Music.]

1161. **Euba, Akin.** *Traditional Nigerian music.* Nigeria magazine, special no., Oct. 1960, 193–210, ill.

1162. **Farrow, Stephen S.** 1924. *Faith, fancies and fetich or Yoruba paganism.* Pp. xi + 180, ill. London: S.P.C.K.

1163. **Frobenius, Leo.** 1913. *The voice of Africa* [2 vols.]. Pp. xxii + 349; viii + 363–682, ill., maps. London: Hutchinson. [Vol. 1, p. 118, Court orchestra. Vol. 2, p. 518, Busu on their way to coast.]

1164. **Funke, E.** *Einige Tanz- und Liebeslieder der Haussa.* Z. f. Eingeb. Sprachen., 11, 1921, 259–78.

1165. **Goins, W.** *The music of Nigeria.* Music journal, 19, 1961, 34– , ill.

1166. **Griffith, W. J.** *On the appreciation of African music.* Nigerian field, 16 (2), 1951, 88–93, ill.

1167. **Hall, Leland.** *What price harmony?* Atlantic monthly, 144, 1929, 511–16.

1168. **Harper, F. J.** *Nigerian music.* Nigerian field, 17, 1952, 91–93.

1169. **Hornburg, Friedrich.** *Die Musik der Tiv.* Die Musikforschung, 1, 1948, 47–60.

1170. **Johnson, Samuel.** 1921. *The history of the Yorubas.* Pp. lv + 684, ill., map. London: Routledge.

1171. **King, Anthony.** *Employments of the standard pattern in Yoruba music.* Afr. mus. soc., 2 (3), 1960, 51–54.

1172. —— 1961. *Yoruba sacred music from Ekiti.* Pp. 45 + 1–xlix, ill. Ibadan Univ. Press.

1173. **Kingslake, Brian.** *The art of the Yoruba.* Afr. mus. soc., Newsletter, 1, (4), 1951, 13–18.

1174. —— *Musical memories of Nigeria.* Afr. mus. soc., 1 (4), 1957, 17–20.

1175. **Kirk-Greene, A. H. M.** *A Lala initiation ceremony.* Man, 57, no. 5, 1957, 9–11, ill.

1176. **Köler, Hermann.** 1848. *Einige Notizen über Bonny an der Küste von Guinea.* Pp. iv + 182. Göttingen: Dieterichschen Univ.-Buchdruckerei. [Pp. 35, 72, 130–1.]

1177. **Lander, Richard Lemon.** 1830. *Records of Captain Clapperton's last expedition to Africa* [2 vols.]. Vol. 1, xxii + (1) 310, ill. Vol. 2, pp. vi + 293. London: Colburn. [Vol. 1, 289–98.]

1178. **Lane, Michael G. M.** *The music of Tiv.* Afr. mus. soc., 1, 1, 1954, 12–15, ill.

1179. —— *The origin of present-day musical taste in Nigeria.* Afr. mus. soc., 1, 3, 1956, 18–22.

1181. —— *The Aku-Ahwa and Aku-Maga post-burial rites of the Jukun peoples of northern Nigeria.* Afr. mus. soc., 2 (no. 2), 1959, 29–32, ill.

1182. **Luschan, Felix von.** 1919. *Die Altertümer von Benin.* Pp. 175–95, ill. Berlin: . . . . [Veröff. mus. völk, Bd. 8–10.] [Pls. 36–39; figs. 296–319.]

1183. **Mackay, Mercedes.** *The 'shantu' music of the harims of Nigeria.* Afr. mus. soc., 1, 2, 1955, 56–57, ill.

1184. **Madumere, Adele.** *Ibo village music.* Afr. affairs, 52, 206, Jan. 1953, 63–67.

1185. **Mansfeld, Alfred H.** 1928. *Westafrika aus Urwald und Steppe zwischen Crossfluss und Benue.* Westafrika. Pp. 65 + 143, ill., map. Munich: Muller.

1186. **Meek, C. K.** 1925. *The Northern tribes of Nigeria* [2 vols.]. Vol. 1, pp. xviii + 312, ill., maps. Vol. 2, pp. viii + 277, ill., maps. Oxford: Oxford Univ. Press. [Vol. 2, pp. 155–9.]

1187. **Nadel, S. F.** 1942. *A black Byzantium: the kingdom of Nupe in Nigeria.* Pp. xiv + 420, ill., maps. London: Oxford Univ. Press [for Int. African Institute.]

1188. **Nettl, Bruno.** *Ibo songs from Nigeria, native and hybridized.* Midwest folklore, III, 1954, 237.

1189. **Onyido, Udemezuo.** *The Nigerian institute of music.* Human probl. Brit. central Afr., **19**, 1955, 46–47.

1190. **Parrinder, E. Geoffrey.** 1953. *Religion in an African city.* Pp. (6) 211, ill. London: Oxford Univ. Press. [Pp. 70, 113, 135, 137, 139, 141, 143.]

1191. **Partridge, Charles.** 1905. *Cross River natives.* Pp. 332, ill. London: Hutchinson. [Pp. 226–229.]

1192. **Perron, Michel.** *Chants populaires de la Sénégambie et du Niger.* Bull. ag. génl. col., **23**, 1930, 803– .

1193. **Phillips, Ekundayo.** 1953. *Yoruba music.* Pp. 58, ill. Johannesburg: African Music Society.

1194. **Prietze, Rudolf.** 1916. *Haussa Sänger.* Göttingen: W. Friedrich Kastner.

1195. **Raphael, John R.** 1914. *Through unknown Nigeria.* Pp. xxiii + 361, ill. London: T. Werner Laurie.

1196. **Reed, E. M. G.** *The Nigerian at home.* Music and youth, **5**, 1925, 159–63, ill.

1197. **Reed, L. N.** *Notes on some Fulani tribes and customs.* Africa, **5**, 1932, 436, 438.

1198. **Rhodes, Steve.** *Is Nigerian music losing its national character?* Nigeria magazine, no. 67, 1960, 297–300, ill.

1199. **Roth, Henry Ling.** 1903. *Great Benin: its customs, arts and horrors.* Pp. xliv + 234, ill. Halifax: F. King. [Pp. 77, 153–4, and index. Note figs. 151–3.]

1200. **Rumann, W. B.** *Funeral ceremonies for the late ex-Oba of Benin.* J. Afr. soc., **14**, 1914, 37–38, ill.

1201. **Sowande, Fela.** *African music and Nigerian schools.* Ibadan, **16**, 1963, 13–15.

1202. **Thomas, Northcote Whitridge.** *Notes on Edo burial customs.* J. roy. anthrop. inst., **50**, 1920, 410–11.

1203. **Tremearne, Arthur John Newman.** *Notes on the Kagoro and other Nigerian head-hunters.* J. roy. anthrop. inst., **42**, 1912, 181–2, ill.

1204. —— 1912. *The tailed head-hunters of Nigeria.* Pp. xvi + 341, ill. London: Seeley Service. [Pp. 249–52, 262–9.]

1205. —— 1913. *Some Austral-African notes and anecdotes.* Pp. xii + 215, ill. London: John Bale. [Chap. 13, pp. 158–65.]

1206. **Westcott, Joan A.,** and **Peter Moreton Williams.** *The festival of Iya Mapo.* Nigeria magazine, no. 58, 1958, 212–24, ill.

1207. **Whitehouse, A. A.** *An Ibo festival.* J. afr. soc., **4**, no. 13, 1904, 134–5, ill.

1208. **Whyte, Harcourt.** *Types of Ibo music.* Nigerian field, **18**, 1953, 182–6.

See also 2009, 2045, 2068, 2075–8, 2085–6, 2137, 2139–40, 2147, 2171, 2205–6, 2231, 2246–7, 2316, 2468.

NORTH AFRICA
(General)

1209. **Anon.** *Le congrès de la musique arabe,* Le Ménestrel, **94**, no. 41, 1932, 404.

1210. **Barbès, Léo-Louis.** *Afrique du Nord.* Michel, Francois, –12. 12, Encyclopédie de la musique, **3**, 1961, 940–3, bibl.

1213. **Ben Smail.** *Sur la musique et les musiciens arabes.* France-Maroc, 1919.

1214. **Berner, Alfred.** *Neue Bestrebungen der arabischen Musik in Aegypten.* Allg. Musik, Zeit., 1942.

1215. **Bertholon, L.,** and **E. Chantre.** 1913. *Recherches anthropologiques dans la Berbérie Orientale. Tripolitaine, Tunisie, Algérie* [2 vols.]. Lyon: A. Rey. [Chap. 6, La Musique et la Danse.]

1216. **Caussin de Perceval, A.** *Notices anecdotiques sur les principaux musiciens arabes des trois premiers siècles de l'Islamisme.* Journal asiatique, Dec. 1873.

1217. **Chottin, Alexis.** *La musique arabe en orient et en occident.* Outre-mer, Mar. 1936, 6–19.

1218. —— 1946. *La musique musulmane.* Dufourcq, La musique dès origines à nos jours, 74– . Paris: Larousse.

1219. —— *Nordafrikanische Musik.* Blume, F. (ed.), Die Musik in Geschichte u. Gegenwart, **9**, 1961, 1558–70, bibl., ill.

1220. **Collangettes, Father.** *Étude sur la musique arabe.* Journal asiatique, 1904, 6.

1220a. **Christianowitsch, A.** 1863. *Esquisse historique de la musique arabe aux temps anciens avec dessins d'instruments, etc.* Pp. 32, 42, ill. Cologne: . . . .

1221. **Egypt: Ministère de l'Instruction Publique.** 1934. *Recueil des travaux du congrès de musique arabe . . . tenu au Caire en 1932.* Pp. xii + 711, ill. Cairo: Imprimerie Nationale.

1222. **D'Erlanger, Rodolphe.** 1959. *La musique arabe.* Tome 6. Essai de codification des règles de la musique arabe moderne. Système rhythmique, diverses formes de composition artistique. Pp. lx + 644. Paris: Paul Geuthner. [Chap. 5, pp. 188–98, La musique Maghrebine de tradition Hispano-Arabe. Pièces instrumentales-Morceaux de chant-suites. La Suite Marocaine. La Suite Algérienne. La Suite Tunisienne.]

1223. **Farmer, Henry George.** *The Arab influence on music in the western Sudan.* Musical standard, N.S., 1924, 158– .

1224. —— *Musiki.* Encyclopaedia of Islam, vol. 3, pt. 2, 1936, 751–5, bibl.

1225. —— 1929. *A History of Arabian music to the 13th century,* Pp. xv + 264, ill. London: Luzac.

1226. —— *The influence of Alfarabi's 'Ihsa al-atum' (de scientiis) on the writers on music in western Europe.* J. roy. Asiat. soc., July, 1932, 561–92.

1226a. —— *Early references to music in the Western Sudan.* J. roy. asiat. soc., 1939, 569–80.

1227. —— 1953. *Oriental studies, mainly musical.* A. What is Arabian music? B. Arabian musical instruments on a thirteenth-century bronze bowl. London: . . . .

1228. —— *Articles in Grove,* 5th ed., 1954. Vol. 1, Berber music, p. 632. Vol. 1, Arabian music, p. 179. Vol. 5, Maghribi music, p. 504. Vol. 5, Moorish music, p. 868.

1229. —— *The music of Islam.* Wellesz, Egon, Ancient and oriental music, 1957, 421–77, ill.

1230. —— N.D. *Historical facts for the Arabian musical influence.* Pp. 376. London: William Reeves. [Studies in the music of the Middle Ages.]

1231. **Féline, Pierre.** *Arts maghrébins, musique arabesque.* L'Islam et l'Occident, 1947, 277–84. Marseille: Ed. Cahiers du Sud.

1232. **Fétis, F. J.** 1869. *Histoire générale de la musique depuis les temps les plus anciens jusqu'à nos jours* [5 vols.]. Vol. 2, N. Africa. Paris: Firmin Didot Frères.

1233. **Furness, Clifton Joseph.** *Communal music among Arabians and negroes.* Mus. quart., **16**, 1930, 38.

1233a. **Hartmann, R.** 1863. *Reisen des Freiherrn Adalbert v. Barnim . . . 1859–60.* Pp. xvi + 108, ill., maps. Berlin: Reimer. [Musik Beilagen.]

1234. **Hickmann, Hans.** *Arabische Musik* (with Alexis Chottin). Blume, F. (ed.), Die Musik in Geschichte u. Gegenwart, **1**, 1951, col. 577.

1235. **Hornbostel, Erich von.** *Zum Kongress für arabische Musik, Kairo, 1932.* Z. f. Vergl. Musikwiss., **1**, 1933, 16.

1236. —— and **Robert Lachmann.** *Asiatische Parallelen zur Berbermusik.* Zeit. f. vergleich. Musikwiss., **1**, 1933, 4–11, ill.

1237. **Huart, Cl.** *Étude biographique sur trois musiciens arabes.* Journal asiatique, Ser. 8, no. 3, 1884, 141.

1238. **Idelsohn, A. Z.** *Die Maqamen der arabischen Musik.* Sammelbände der Intern. Mus. Ges., **15**, 1913, 1–63.

1239. **Jean-Darrouy, Lucienne.** *La musique arabe en Afrique du Nord.* Bull. soc. géog. (Alger), 1931, 34–50.

1240. **Kutahialian, Jean Onnik.** 1957. *Ecriture musicale arabe moderne.*

1241. **Lach, Robert.** *Musik im Islam.* Der Auftakt [Prague], **1**, 1920–21, 35.

1242. **Laffage, A.** 1906. *La musique arabe.* Paris: ....

1243. **Land, J. P. N.** *Recherches sur l'histoire de la gamme arabe.* Proc. of the 6th int. congress of orientalists [Leyden], 1883, vol. 11 (1), 1884, 35.

1244. —— 1885. *Essais de notation musicale chez les arabes et les persans.* Études arch. linguistiques et historiques dédièes à M. le Dr. C. Leemans. Pp. 315. Leiden: ....

1245. —— *Remarks on the earliest development of Arabic music.* Proc. of the 9th int. Congress of orientalists [London], 1892, vol. 11, 1893, 155.

1246. **Maitrot de la Motte-Capron, A.** *De l'art dans les objets usuels nord-africains.* Bull. soc. géog. [Alger], 1932, 502–24.

1247. **Martens, Frederick H.** *Mahomet and music.* Mus. quart., **12**, 1926, 376.

1248. **Mu 'Tamar al-Músikā al-'Arabtyah, Cairo,** 1932. *Recueil des travaux du congrès de musique arabe . . . tenue au Caire en 1932.* Pp. xii + 711, ill. At head of title: Royaume d'Égypte. Ministère de l'instruction publique contributions in French or Arabic. Includes music. 1, Music congresses. 2, Folk music Arabic hist. and crit. 3, Folk music Arabic.

1249. **Nachtigal, Gustave.** *Saharâ und Sudân: Ergebnisse sechsjahriger Reisen in Afrika* [3 vols.]. Th. 1, 1879, xxii + 748 (20), ill., maps. Th. 2, 1881, pp. xxiv + 790, ill., maps. Th. 3, 1889, pp. xxii (1) + 548, ill., map. Berlin: Weidmannsche Buchhandlung. Th. 1, Tripolis, Fezzan, Tibesti U. Bornu. Th. 2, Borku, Kanem, Bornu and Bagirmi. Th. 3, Wadai und Dar-For. [Vol. 1, pp. 745–6. Vol. 3, pp. 226, 437.]

1250. **Prince, J. D.** *Muhammadan music.* Hastings, J., Encyclopaedia of religion and ethics, 1917, **9**, 53.

1251. **Rouanet, Jules.** *La musique arabe.* Lavignac, A., and L. de la Laurencie, Encyclopédie de la musique, Pt. 1, 1922, 2676–2812, ill.

1252. —— *La musique arabe dans le Maghreb.* Lavignac, A., and L. de la Laurencie, Encyclopédie de la musique, Pt. 1, 1922, 2813–44. Paris: De la Grave.

1253. —— *Les visages de la musique musulmane.* Rev. musicale, **5**, no. 1, 1923.

1254. —— *La suite dans la musique musulmane.* Rev. musicale, **8**, 1927.

1255. —— and **E. N. Yafil.** 1904. *Répertoire de musique arabe et maure.*

1256. **Rouget, Gilbert.** *Note on some Tuareg songs of historical interest.* J. roy. anthrop. inst.

1257. **S.T.** *Musique et poésie arabe.* La Tribune des Nations, Dec. 1946, 1–6, 20.

1258. **Sachs, Curt.** *Kongress der arabischen Musik zu Kairo.* Z. f. Musikw. [Leipzig], **14**, 1932, 448.

1259. **Servier, Jean H.** *Musique et poésie kabyles.* 4e congr. int. sci. antrop. et ethnol. [Wien, 1952], **3**, 2, 1956.

1260. **Smith, M. L.** *Arab music.* [Translated from the French of M. Jules Rouanet.] J. Afr. soc., **5**, 1905–6, 148–50.

1261. **Stoppani, A.** *La musica degli Arabi.* Nigrizia, 1900, 46–48.

1262. **Tiersot, Julien.** *La musique des arabes.* Le Ménestrel, **68**, 1902 (4–8), 26–27, 35–36, 43–44, 50–51, 60–61; (11), 83, (13–14), 99–100, 106–8; (16) 123–4.

1263. **Zerrouki, Mohammed.** *La musique arabe.* Les Lettres Francaises, **10**, Sep. 1947, 1–5, ill.

1264. —— *La musique arabe et la polyphonie.* J. des instituteurs de l'Afrique du nord, 25 sep. 1948, 4.

1265. —— *Musique occidentale et musique arabe.* IBLA, 3 trim. 1950, 269–78.

1266. **Zöhrer, Ludwig G. A.** *Studien über die Tuareg (Imohag) der Sahara.* Z. f. Ethnol. **72**, 1940, 138–52.

See also 2360.

NORTH AFRICAN MUSIC IN RELATION TO THAT OF THE IBERIAN PENINSULA

1267. **Garcia Barriusi, P. Patrocinio.** 1941. *La musica hispano-musulmana en Marruecos.* Pp. 318, ill. Larache: Artes Graficas Bosca.

1268. —— *Edicion del tradicional repertorio musical y poetico Hispano-Marroqui.* Africa [Madrid], nos. 37–38, 1945, 29–31, ill.

1269. **Hasan Husni 'Abd Al-Wahhab.** 1918. *Le développement de la musique arabe en orient, Espagne et Tunisie.* Tunis: ....

1270. **Larrea Palacin, Arcadio de.** *La musica hispano-arabe.* 'Crece o Muere [Madrid]., no. 11, 1957.

1270a. —— *Recherches sur la musique hispano-arabe.* VIe Congrès Int. des Sciences anthrop. et ethnol. Tome 2, 107–8. Pubd. Paris, 1964, at Musée de l'Homme.

1271. **Mohammed el Fasi.** *La musique marocaine dite 'Musique Andalouse'.* Hespéris Tamuda, **3** (1), 1962, 79–106.

1272. **Ribera, Julian.** 1929. *Music in ancient Arabia and Spain.*

1273. **Sachs, Curt.** *Die Marokkaner.* Zeit. f. vergleich. Musikwiss., i, 1933, 17–18. [Contributed to an article 'Zum Kongress für Arabische Musik-Kairo', 1932. Detects Andalusian ancestry in the music of the Moroccans.]

1274. **Schneider, Marius.** *A propósito del influenjo árabe (Ensayo de ethnografía musical de la Espana medieval).* Anuario musical, **1**, 1946 (60 Notenbeispiele). Barcelona: ....

1275. —— *Le verset 94 de la sourate VI du Coran étudiée en une version populaire et en trois nagamât de tradition hispano-musulmane.* Anuario músical, **9**, 1954 (8 Seiten Notenbeispiele).

1276. —— *Studi e proposto per une corpus delle musiche populari mediterranee.* Atti del congresso di Palermo.

1277. —— *Le style vocal dans les pays méditerranéens.* Colloque d'Hammamet, Tunis. 1963. Bull. 1 (edition du centre culturel).

1278. ——*Das Maqamsystem in der italienischen Ars nova.* Colloques de Wégimont, Ars Nova, vol. 2, 1964. [In preparation.]

1278a. **Ursprung, Otto.** *Um die Frage arabischen bzw. maurischen Einfluss auf die abendländische Musik des Mittelalters.* Z. f. Musikw., **16**, 1934, 129–41.

1279. **Yafil, E.,** and **J. Rouanet.** 1904. *Répertoire de musique arabe et maure: collection de mélodies.* Algiers: ....

PORTUGUESE GUINEA

1280. **Bernatzik, Hugo Adolf.** *Meine Expedition nach Portugiesisch Guinea.* Atlantis [Leipzig], **1**, 1932, 197–208, ill.

1281. —— 1933. *Äthiopen des Westens* [2 vols.]. Vienna: Seidel.

1282. —— *Afrikanische Musikinstrumente.* Atlantis [Leipzig], **6**, 1934, 645–51, ill.

1283. **Carreira, Antonio.** 1947. *Mandingas da Guiné Portuguesa.* Pp. (12), 326 (3), ill., map. Bissau: (Printed in Lisbon). [Centro de Estudos da Guiné Portuguesa, no. 4.]

1284. **Gomes, Abílio.** *Notas sobre a música indigena da Guiné.* Bol. cultural da Guiné Portuguesa, vol. 5, no. 19 (1950), 412–24, ill.

1285. **Lux, A. E.** 1880. *Von Loando nach Kimbundu . . . Forschungsreise im Äquatorialen West-Afrike,* 1875–76. Pp. viii + 219, ill. Vienna: [Musical instruments, 120–2, ill.]

1285a. **Méo, Dr.** *Études sur le Rio Nunez.* Bull. com. étud. A.O.F., nos. 3 and 4, 1919, 281–317; 341–69.

RWANDA
(Formerly part of Rwanda Urundi)

1286. **Arnoux, Alex.** *Le culte de la société secrète des Imándwa au Ruanda.* Anthropos, **7**, 1912, 546–51, 852–74; **8**, 1913, 111–12.

1287. **Coupez, A.,** and **M. Rutaremara.** *Trois chansons Rwanda.* Africa-Tervuren, 10 (1), 1964, 19–25.

1288. **Dufays, Félix.** *Lied und Gesang bei Brautwerbung und Hochzeit in Mulera-Ruanda.* Anthropos, **4**, 1909, 847–78.

1289. **Guenther, Robert.** *Eine Studie zur Musik in Ruanda* (1). Les Colloques de Wégimont, III, 1960, 163–86. [Ethnomusicologie II.] Paris: Société d'Édition 'Les Belles Lettres'.

1289a. —— 1964. *Musik in Rwanda.* Pp. vii + 128, bibl., ill. Tervuren. Mus. roy. Afr. Centr.

1290. **Hornbostel, Erich von.** 1917. *Gesänge aus Ruanda.* Czekanowski, Jan, Wissenschaftliche Ergebnisse der Deutschen Zentral-Afrika-Expedition, 1907–8, vol. 6, pt. 1, pp. 379–412 and append. Leipzig: Klinkhardt.

1291. **Pauwels, Marcel le R. P.** *Jeux et divertissements au Rwanda.* Annali. Lat. **24**, 1960, 219–363, ill.

1292. **Schumacher, P.** 1910. *Die Ehe in Ruanda.* Anthropos, **5**, 1910, 897–906.

See also 2226.

SÃO TOMÉ

1293. **Barros, M.** *Folclore musical da ilha de Sao Tomé (velhas danças, suas músicas e cantares).* Conf. int. Africanistas ocid., 6ª sessão (S. Tomé, 1956), **5**, 101–12.

SENEGAL

1294. **Ames, David.** 1955. *Wolof music of Senegal and the Gambia.* Ethnic Folkways Library Album, P462. Pp. 7, ill. New York: Folkways Records & Service Corp.

1295. **Bailly, Edmond.** *Le pittoresque musical à l'exposition.* L'Humanité nouvelle 1900, 177–92.

1296. **Balandier, Georges.** *Femmes 'Possédées' et leurs chants.* Présence africaine, no. 5, 1948, 749–54.

1297. **Bérenger-Féraud, L. J. B.** 1879. *Les peuplades de la Sénégambie.* Pp. xvi + 420. Paris: E. Leroux.

1298. —— *Étude sur les griots des peuplades de la Sénégambie.* Rev. ethnog. [Paris], **5**, 1882, 266–79.

1299. **Boilat, P. D.** 1853. *Esquisses sénégalaises.* Pp. – , ill., maps. Paris: Bertrand.

1300. **Ca Da Mosto, Alvise de.** 1895. *Relation des voyages à la côte occidentale d'Afrique . . . 1455–57.* Pp. xix + 206. Paris: Leroux.

1301. **Chauvet, Stephen.** *La musique nègre en Afrique occidentale française.* Encyclopédie coloniale et maritime, France, vol. 2, 1949, 371–6, ill.

1302. **Forwerg, Rudolph.** *Die Bewohner der Guineaküste.* Jahresber. Verh. Erdk. Dres., **27**, 1901, 139–40.

1303. **Froger, Francois.** 1699. *Relations d'un voyage fait en 1695–1697 aux côtes d'Afrique.* Paris: Nic Le Gros.

1304. **Gamble, David P.** 1957. *The Wolof of Senegambia.* Pp. x + 110, bibl., map. London: International African Institute. [Ethnographic Survey of Africa: Western Africa, Pt. 14.]

1305. **Gray, William,** and **S. S. Dochard.** 1825. *Travels in Western Africa, 1818–21.* Pp. xvi + 413, ill., map. London: Murray.

1306. **Hecquart, Hyacinthe.** 1853. *Voyage sur la côte et dans l'interieur de l'Afrique occidentale.* Pp. 123. Paris: Benart et Cie.

1307. **Hovelacque, Abel.** 1889. *Les nègres de l'Afrique sus-equatoriale (Sénégambie-Guinée, Soudan, Haut-Nil.)* Pp. xiv + 468. Paris: Lecrosnier et Babe.

1308. **Jobson, Richard.** 1932. *The golden trade: or a discovery of the river Gambra (1620–1621).* Penguin Press.

1309. —— Ed. by C. G. Kingsley. 1904. Teignmouth: Speight & Walpole.

1310. **Labarthe, Pierre.** 1802. *Voyage au Sénégal,, 1784–85.* Pp. xii + 262, map. Paris: The Author.

1311. **Labat, Jean Baptiste.** 1728. *Nouvelle relation de l'Afrique occidentale* [4 vols. in 2, ill., maps.] Paris: Cavelier.

1312. **Lasnet, Dr.,** and **Others.** 1900. *Une mission au Sénégal.* Pp. 348, ill. Paris: A. Challamel.

1313. **Laveda, L.** *Les Mandingues dans le cercle de Tambacounda.* Sénégal, **11**, nos. 50 and 51, 1943, 109– , 143– .

1314. **Lemaire, Jacques Joseph.** 1695. *Les voyages du Sieur Lemaire aux isles Canaries . . . Sénégal et Gambie.* Pp. 205, ill., map. Paris: Collombat.

1315. **Mage, M. E.** 1867. *Du Sénégal au Niger: relation du voyage d'exploration de M. M. Mage et Quintin au Soudan occidentale de 1863–1866.* Pp. 496, map. Paris: Paul Dupont. [Pp. 57, 104.]

1316. **Raffenel, Anne.** 1856. *Nouveau voyage dans le pays des nègres suivi d'études sur la colonie du Sénégal.* [Vol. 1 only.] Pp. xv, xxii + 512, ill. Paris: Imprimerie et Librairie Centrales des Chemins de Fer.

1317. **Tautain, L.** *Sur l'ethnologie et l'ethnographie des peuples du bassin du Sénégal.* Rev. ethnog. [Paris], **4**, 1885, 61–80, 137–47, 254–68, ill.

1318. **Tauxier, Louis.** 1917. *Le noir du Yatenga.* Pp. 315, 522. Paris: Larose.

1319. **Verneuil, V.** 1848. *L'Art musical au Sénégal et dans l'Afrique centrale.* Paris: . . . .

SIERRA LEONE

1320. **Banbury, G. A. Lethbridge.** 1888. *Sierra Leone or the white man's grave.* Pp. (6) 296, ill. London: Swan Sonnenschein. [P. 160, Mandingo musicians.]

1321. **Clarke, Robert.** 1843. *Sierra Leone.* Pp. – . London: Ridgway.

1322. **Godel.** *Ethnographie des Soussous.* Bull. soc. anthrop. [Paris], **4**, 1892, 166–7.

1323. **Great Britain: Admiralty: Naval Staff Intelligence Reports.** 1919. *Sierra Leone.* Pp. 19. London: Admiralty. [Music and games, pp. 17–18.]

1324. **John, J. T.** *Village music of Sierra Leone.* W.A.R., **23**, 301, Oct. 1952, 1043–4, 1071.

1325. **Laing, Alexander Gordon.** 1825. *Travels in the Timannee, Kooranko and Sooliman countries in western Africa.* Pp. x (2) + 465, ill., map. London: Murray.

1326. **Little, K. L.** *A Mende musician sings of his adventures.* Man, 48, no. , 1948, 27–28.

1327. **Margai, M. A. S.** *Music in the protectorate of Sierra Leone.* Wasu, **2**, 1926, 38–40.

1328. **Matthews, John.** 1791. *A voyage to the river Sierra Leone on the coast of Africa . . . in 1785–87.* Pp. 183, ill., maps. London: B. White & Son. [Pp. 104–6.]

1329. **Migeod, Frederick William Hugh.** 1926. *A view of Sierra Leone.* Pp. x + 345, bibl., ill., map. London: Kegan Paul.

1330. **Newland, Harry Osman.** 1916. *Sierra Leone.* Pp. xv + 251, ill. London: J. Bale.

1331. **Taylor, N. Ballanta.** *Ein Klavier für afrikanische Musik.* Der Kolonialdeutsche, 4, 1924, 197.

1332. **Winterbottom, Thomas Masterman.** 1803. *Account of the native Africans in the neighbourhood of Sierra Leone* [2 vols.]. Vol. 1, pp. xi (3) + 362 (22), ill., map. Vol. 2, pp. (2), 283 (10), map. London: J. Hatchard. [Pp. 108–14.]

SOMALIA
(Including former British Somaliland)

1332a. **Balilla-Pratella, F.** 1927. *La musica nelle nostre colonie d'Africa.* Musica d'oggi [Milan], Nov. 1927, 313–16; Dec. 1927, 351–5.

1333. **Barblan, Guglielmo.** 1941. *Musiche e strumenti musicali dell' Africa orientale Italiana.* Pp. 147, bibl., ill., map. Naples: Edizioni della Triennale d'Oltremare.

1334. **Caravaglios, Cesare.** *Per lo studio della musica indigena delle nostre colonie.* Roy. ist. superiore di scienze sociali e politiche 'Cesare Alfieri', Centro di studi col., **4** (3), Ott. 1934, 113–28. Atti del 2 congresso di studi col. riv. col. Ital., **8**, 1934, 937–46. [Rome.]

1335. **Dainelli, G.,** and **O. Marinelli.** 1912. *Risultati scientifici di un viaggio della colonia Eritrea.* Pp. – . Florence: . . . .

1336. **Elliott, J. A. G.** *A visit to the Bajun islands.* J. Afr. soc., **25**, no. 97, 1925, 10–22; **25**, no. 98, 1926, 147–63; **25**, no. 99, 1926, 245–63 (music); **25**, no. 100, 1926, 338–58.

1337. **Grottanelli, Vinigi L.** *Asiatic influences on Somali culture.* Ethnos, **4**, 1947, 148–80.

1338. —— 1955. *Pescatori dell' Oceano Indiano.* Pp. xxi + 409, ill., map. Rome: Cremonese.

1339. **Heinitz, W.** *Über die Musik der Somali.* Z. f. Musikw., **11**, 1920, 257–63.

1340. **Paulitschke, Philipp.** 1893–96. *Ethnographie Nordost-Afrikas* [2 vols.]. Vol. 1, Die materielle Cultur der Danâkil, Galla und Somâl. Pp. xvi + 338, ill., maps. Berlin: D. Reimer, Vol. 2, Die Geistige Cultur der Danâkil, Galla und Somâl. Pp. xvii + 312. Berlin: D. Reimer. [Somali music, vol. 1, pp. 143, 148, 232, 250–1. Vol. 2, pp. 164, 217–21.]

1341. **Pesenti, Gustavo.** *Canti e ritmi arabici, somalici e swahili.* B. R. soc. geog. Ital., **47**, 1910, 1409–1432.

1342. —— *Di alcuni canti arabici e somalici.* B. R. soc. geog. Ital., **49**, 1912, 58–63.

1342a. —— *Canti Sacri e profani danze degli Arabi, dei Somali e dei Suaheli.* 1929.. Mailand:..........

1343. **Vianney, John J.** *La musica somala,* Somalia d'oggi, **2**, 3, Ott. 1957, 37–39.

1344. **Vignato, A.** *Musica.* Nigrizia, 1911, 168–73.

1345. **Vivladi, Le R. P.** 1901. *Tre anni in Eritrea.* Milan:.........

1346. **Wachsmann, K. P.** *Somali.* Blume, F. (*ed.*), Die Musik in Geschichte und Gegenwart, vol. 11, 1964. 856–861.

1347. **Williams, Chet.** *The Freedom Songs of the Somali Republic.* [With Abdullah Ke/shi and Ahmed Sherif. Collected by Chet Williams with Hussan Hussein (wireless) and by Mussa Gallal, with voices, and lute, drums and tambourine.] 12 in. L.P. Folkways FD5443. Descriptive pamphlet with 4 pp., ill.

SOUTH AFRICA

1348. **A., T.** *Bantu music.* S. Afr. outlook, **64**, 1931, 116–17.

1349. **Anon.** *Bantu music on the gramophone.* S. Afr. outlook, **61**, 1931, 78.

1350. **Anderson, Andrew Arthur.** 1887. *Twenty-five years in a waggon in the gold regions of Africa* [2 vols.]. Vol. 1, pp. vi + 253, ill. Vol. 2, pp. x + 307, ill. London: Chapman & Hall. [Vol. 1. pp. 106, 140–1.]

1351. **Balfour, Alice Blanche.** 1895. *Twelve hundred miles in a waggon.* Pp. xix + 265, ill., map. London: Arnold. [Pp. 64, 150–3, 247.]

1352. **Barrington, George.** 1803. *Account of a voyage to New South Wales.* Pp. 467, ill. London: Jones. [Pp. 189–90, 218, 250–1.]

1353. **Basile, Frère.** *Le dilemme de la musique réligieuse indigène en Afrique du Sud.* La musique sacrée au 30 congrès int. de musique sacrée, 1957, 255–9.

1355. **Blacking, John.** *Problems of pitch, pattern and harmony in the ocarina music of the Venda.* Afr. mus. soc., **2** (2), 1959, 15–23.

1356. —— *The identification of different musical styles and their historical and sociological foundations, with special reference to the music of the Venda.* Essays on music and history in Asia and Africa, Pt. 2, Africa. [Roy. anthrop. inst.]

1357. **Bleek, E.,** and **Dorothea, F.** *Note on songs and instruments.* Tongue, H. M., Bushman paintings, 1909, 36–37.

1358. **Bomos, J.** 1946. *Musik in Südafrika.* Bruges: Voorland.

1359. **Bouws, Jan.** 1946. *Musiek in Suid-Afrika.* Pp. 143. Uitgeverij Voorland Brugge.

1360. **Breuil, H.** *Rock paintings of S. Africa.* Anthrop. Q. 27, 1954, 31–42.

1361. **Bruwer, J.** 1956. *Die Bantoe van Suid-Afrika.* Pp. (xii) + 240, bibl., ill., map. Johannesburg: Afrikaanse Pers-Boekhandel. [Pp. 173–7.]

1362. **Burchell, William J.** 1953. *Travels in the interior of Southern Africa* [2 vols.]. Vol. 1, pp. xxix + 381, ill., map. Vol. 2, pp. xvi + 473, ill., map. [Original ed. 1822–4.] London: Batchworth Press. [Music and musical instruments, see index, vol. 2, p. 460.]

1363. **Campbell, D.** *Music of Africa.* S. Afr. panorama, **4** (2), 1959, 37–39, ill.

1364. **Cape, S.** *La musique bantoue. Les chanteurs à la croix de cuivre.* Artisan et arts liturgiques, **18**, 4, 1949, 382.

1365. **Collaer, P.** *Bantoe.* A.M.E., 1957, 328–33, ill.

1366. **Courlander, Harold.** 1957. [*Music of*] *Africa south of the Sahara.* Folkways Records, FE4503.

1367. **Dart, R. A.** *South Africa and the prehistory of music.* S. Afr. J. of science, **53**, no. 7, 1957, 192– .

1368. **Duggan-Cronin, A. M.** 1928–36. *The Bantu tribes of South Africa.* Vols. 1 (1); 2 (1–3); 3 (1–5); 4 (1–2). [11 vols. containing in all 9 plates of musical instruments of high technical standard.] Cambridge: Deighton, Bell.

1369. —— and **D. F. Bleek.** 1942. *The bushman tribes of southern Africa.* Pp. 14 + 40 plates and a map. Kimberley: Alexander McGregor Memorial Museum.

1370. **Dunn, E. J.** 1931. *The bushman.* Pp. xii + 130, ill. London: Charles Griffin.

1371. **Du Plessis, I. D.** 1944. *The Cape Malays.* Pp. ix + 95, ill. Cape Town: Maskew Miller. [Folk songs with scores, pp. 58–67.]

1372. —— and **C. A. Luckhoff.** 1953. *The Malay quarter and its people.* Pp. 91, bibl., ill. Cape Town: A. A. Balkema. [Chap. 3, Song and music, pp. 43–52.]

1373. **Fleming, F.** 1853. *Kaffraria.* Pp. (8), 144, ill., map. London: Smith Elder.

1374. **Fritsch, Gustav.** 1872. *Die Eingeborenen Südafrikas.* Pp. xxiv + 528, ill. Breslau: F. Hirt. [Music of Zulus, Bushmen and Bechuana.]

1375. **Gane, Margaret.** *Bushmen music.* Music in schools, **2**, 171–2.

1376. **Gottschling, E.** *Bawenda.* J. anthrop. Inst. **35**, 1905, 365–85, ill.

1378. **Hellwald, Friedrich von.** 1882. *Naturgeschichte des Menschen* [2 vols.]. Vol. 2, 20. Stuttgart: Spemann.

1379. **Holden, William Clifford.** 1866. *The past and future of the Kaffir races.* Pp. xii + 516, ill., map. London: The author.

1380. **Holub, Emil.** 1881. *Sieben Jahre in Süd-Afrika* [2 vols.]. Vol. 1, pp. xvi + 528, ill. Vol. 2, pp. xi + 532, maps. Vienna: Holder. [Vol. 2, pp. 148–9, 162, 198–200, 294–5.]

1381. —— 1881. *Seven years in South Africa* [2 vols.]. Vol. 1, pp. xi + 426, ill., map. Vol. 2, pp. xi + 479, ill. London: Sampson Low. [Vol. 2, pp. 136, 168–72, 223, 228–9, 259, 264.]

1384. **Kirby, Percival R.** *Some problems of primitive harmony and polyphony with special reference to Bantu practice.* S. Afr. J. of science, **23**, 1926, 951–70.

1385. —— 1928. *Primitive and exotic music.* S. Afr. J. of science, **25**, 507–14. [Remarks on South African native music and musical instruments, pp. 513–14.]

1386. —— *The study of South African native music.* S. Afr. Rlwys. & Harbours Mag., Dec. 1928, 2001–2006, ill.

1387. —— *Musical origins in the light of the musical practices of the Bushmen, Hottentot and Bantu.* Proc. mus. assoc., Leeds, 1933.

1388. —— 1934. *The effect of western civilisation on Bantu music.* [Pp. 131–40.] Schapera, I., Western civilisation and the natives of South Africa. Pp. xiv + 312, bibl., ill., maps. London: George Routledge.

1389. —— *The principle of stratification as applied to South African native music.* S. Afr. J. of science, **32**, 1935, 72–90.

1390. —— *A Study of Bushman music.* Bantu stud., **10**, 2, 1936, 205–52. [With transcriptions.]

1391. —— *The musical practices of the auni and khomani bushmen.* Bantu stud., **10**, 4, Dec. 1936, 373–431, ill.

1392. —— *The musical practices of the native races of South Africa.* Schapera, I. Bantu-speaking tribes, etc., 1937, 271–89.

1393. —— *Bantu*. F. Blume (*ed.*), Die Musik in Geschichte und Gegenwart, **1**, 1951, 1219.

1394. —— *Buschmann- und Hottentottenmusik.* Blume, F. (*ed.*), Die Musik in Geschichte und Gegenwart, **2**, 1952, 501.

1395. —— *African music.* Hellmann, E. and L. Abrahams, Handbook on race relations in South Africa, chap. 29, 1949, 619–27.

1396. —— 1934. *The musical instruments of the native races of South Africa.* Pp. xix + 285, ill., map. London: Oxford Univ. Press. [Reprinted 1953.]

1397. —— *The use of European musical techniques by the non-European peoples of southern Africa.* J. int. folk music council [Cambridge], **11**, 1959, 37–40.

1398. —— *Physical phenomena which appear to have determined the bases and development of harmonic sense among Bushman, Hottentot and Bantu.* Afr. mus. soc., II, 1961, 6–9.

1399. —— 1964. *The changing face of African music south of the Equator, with particular reference to that south of the 22nd parallel.* Essays on music and history in Africa and Asia, pt. 2, Africa. [Roy. anthrop. inst.]

1400. **Lieberman, Helena.** *The music of the South African natives.* Afr. world, **132**, 1935, 162.

1401. **Long, R.** *African folk song: some notes on music of Bantu tribes of southern Africa.* Hinrichsens musical year book, **7**, 1952, 57–93.

1402. **Longmore, L.** *Music and song among the Bantu people in urban areas on the Witwatersrand.* Afr. mus. soc., Newsletter, **1**, 6, Sept. 1953, 15–27.

1403. **Mackenzie, John.** 1871. *Ten years north of the Orange River.* Pp. xix + 523, ill., map. Edinburgh: Edmonston & Douglas. [Picture of Goura, p. 328; Sansa, p. 354.]

1404. **Magyar, Ladislaus.** 1859. *Reisen in Südafrika in . . . 1849–57.* Vol. I (all published), pp. xii + 450, ill., map. Pest and Leipzig: Lauffer & Stolp. [Pp. 311–14.]

1405. **Marais, Joseph.** *Music of the African bushveld.* Étude, **60**, May 1942, 316.

1406. **Molema, S. M.** 1920. *The Bantu past and present.* Pp. xix + 398. Edinburgh: Green. [Pp. 162–3.]

1407. **Raemsdonck, M. van.** *Jazz et musique Bantoue.* Jeune Afr., **6**, 1952, 7.

1409. **Rycroft, David R.** *Tribal style and free expression (Ila and Tonga).* Afr. mus. soc., **1** (1), 1954, 16–27.

1410. —— *Melodic imports and exports: a byproduct of recording in southern Africa.* Bull. Brit. Inst. of Recorded Sound, no. , 1956, pp. 19– .

1411. —— *African music in Johannesburg: African and non-African features.* J. int. folk music council, **11**, 1959, 25–30.

1412. —— 1964. *Stylistic evidence in Ngunisong.* Essays on music and history in Asia and Africa, pt. 2, Africa. [Roy. anthrop. inst.]

1413. **Schapera, I.** 1930. *The Khoisan peoples of South Africa: Bushmen and Hottentots.* Pp. xi + 450, bibl., ill., maps. London: George Routledge.

1414. —— 1937. *The Bantu-speaking tribes of South Africa.* Pp. xv + 453, bibl., illus., map. London: Routledge & Kegan Paul. [The musical practices of the native races of South Africa, by P. R. Kirby, pt. XII, pp. 271–89.]

1415. **Schumann, C.** *Volksmusik der Eingeborenen.* Die Brücke, **7**, 1, 1929, 2–8.

1416. **Serpa Pinto, Alexandre de.** 1881. *Comment J'ai traversé l'Afrique* [2 vols.]. Vol. 1, pp. xxx + 456, ill., maps. Vol. 2, pp. 485, ill., maps. Paris: Hachette. [Vol. 1, pp. 55–56, 224–5, 235–6, 289, 396. Vol. 2, pp. 21, 31–33.]

1417. **Smith, Andrew.** 1939–40. *The diary of Dr. Andrew Smith, director of the 'Expedition for exploring Central Africa, 1834–36.'* Edited by Percival R. Kirby [2 vols.]. Vol. 1, 1939, pp. 413, ill. Vol. 2, 1940, pp. 342, ill., map. Cape Town: Van Riebeeck Society.

1418. **Speight, W. L.** *The evolution of native music.* The Sackbut, **14**, 1933, 18–20.

1419. —— *Notes on South African music.* Mus. quart., **20**, 1934, 344–53, ill.

1420. **Stow, G. W.** 1905. *The native races of South Africa.* Pp. xii + 618, ill. London: Macmillan.

1420a. **Theal, George McCall.** 1910. *The yellow and dark-skinned people of Africa south of the Zambesi.* Pp. xvi + 397. London: Swan Sonnenschein.

1421. **Tongue, Helen M.** 1909. *Bushman paintings.* Pp. 39, ill. Oxford: University Press. [Pls. 14, 15, 36.]

1422. **Torrend, J.** 1891. *A comparative grammar of the South African Bantu language.* Pp. xlviii + 340. London: Kegan Paul. [Pp. 296–320.]

1423. **Tracey, Hugh Travers.** 1948. *Ngoma: an introduction to music for southern Africans.* Pp. 91 + xxi, illus. Cape Town: Longmans.

1424. —— *Short survey of southern African folk music for the international catalogue of folk music records.* Afr. mus. soc., Newsletter, **1**, 6, Sept. 1953, 41–46.

1425. —— *The state of folk music in Bantu Africa.* [International folk music council, Biarritz, July 1953.] Afr. mus. soc., **1** (1), 1954, 8–11.

1426. —— *Bantu music.* Grove, Dictionary of music, vol. 1, 1954, 416–17. [5th ed.]

1427. —— *Music of South Africa.* Music journal, **19**, 1961, 76–77.

1428. **Wachsmann, K. P.** *The sociology of recording in Africa south of the Sahara.* Afr. mus. soc., **2** (2), 1959, 77 79. [Reprint from Bull. British Institute of Recorded Sound. No. 14, 1959, 24–26.]

1429. **Webb, Maurice.** *Music in South Africa.* Voorslag [Durban], **1**, 1926, 23–26.

See also 2079–80, 2296, 2339, 2341, 2346–52, 2395–8, 2401, 2424, 2427–8, 2433, 2471–2, 2479, 2490, 2492–4.

SOUTH-WEST AFRICA

1430. **Fischer, Hans.** *Musik und Tanz bei den Eingeborenen in Südwestafrika.* Musik. Wochenbl., **40**, 1909, 354–6, 371–3. Allg. Musik. Zeit., **37**, 1910, 418–21.

1431. **Galton, Francis.** 1853. *Narrative of an explorer in tropical South Africa.* Pp. xx + 320, ill., map.

1432. **Gentz, P.** *Beiträge zur Kenntnis der südwestafrikanischen Völkerschaften.* Globus (Brunswick), **83**, 1903, 301; **84**, 1903, 156–7; **85**, 1904, 82, ill.

1433. **Grimaud, Yvette.** *Note sur la musique vocale des Bochiman! Kung et des pygmées Babinga.* Colloques de Wégimont, **3**, 1956, 105–26.

1433a. **Grimaud, Yvette,** and **Gilbert Rouget.** *Notes on the music of the Bushmen compared to that of the Babinga pigmies.* [Issued as L.P. record L.D.9 by the Peabody Mseum (Harvard) and by the Musée de l'Homme, Department of Ethnomusicology.]

1433b. **Günter, Robert.** 1961. *Die Gutussu der Mbarakwengo Buschmänner.* Pp. 193–99, ill. Cologne: . . . . [Fellerer-Festschrift.]

1434. **Hahn, C. H. L.,** and **Others.** 1928. *The native tribes of South West Africa.* (1) The Ovambo, by C. H. L. Hahn. (2) The Berg Damara, by H. Vedder. (3) The bushmen of South West Africa, by L. Fourie. (4) The Nama, by H. Vedder. (5) The Herero, by H. Vedder. Pp. 209, bibl., ill. Cape Town: Cape Times Ltd. [Pp. 95–98, 141–2, Music and dance.]

1435. **Hahn, Theophilus.** *Die Nama Hottentotten,* Globus (Brunswick), **12**, 1867, 278, 335.

1436. —— *Die Buschmänner.* Globus (Brunswick), **18**, 1870, 121–2.

1437. —— 1881. *Tsuni- Goam: the supreme being of the Khoi-Khoi.* Pp. xi + 154. London: Trubner & Co. [Pp. 27–29.]

1438. **Heilborn, Adolf.** *Die Musik der Naturvölker unserer Kolonien.* Deut. Kol. Zeitg., **21**, 1904, 347–8.

1439. **Irle, I.** 1906. *Die Herero.* Pp. viii + 352, ill., map. Gütersloh: C. Bertelsmann. [Pp. 124–5.]

1440. **Loeb, Edwin M.** 1962. *In feudal Africa.* Pp. xxii + 383, bibl., ill., maps. Bloomington (Indiana): Pubn. 23 Indiana University Research Center in Anthropology, Folklore and Linguistics.

1441. **Rycroft, D.** 1964. *Comments on Dr. Westphal's Bushman and Hottentot recordings.* Essays on music and history in Africa and Asia, pt. 2, Africa. [Roy. anthrop. inst.]

1442. **Schinz, Hans.** 1891. *Deutsch-Südwest-Afrika: Forschungsreisen . . . 1884–1887.* Pp. xvi + 568, ill., map. Oldenburg and Leipzig: Schulzesche Hof-Buchhandlung. [Pp. 31–32, 95–96.]

1443. **Schultze, Leonhard.** 1907. *Aus Namaland und Kalahari . . . Forschungs reise . . . in 1903 05.* Pp. xi + 752, ill., map. Jena: Gustav Vischer. [Pp. 374–83, 644–5.]

1444. **Shaw, Barnabas.** 1840. *Memorials of South Africa.* Pp. 371, ill. London: J. Mason.

1445. **Stopa, Roman.** 1938. *Studies on the population and culture of South West Africa.* Pp. 134, ill. Warsaw: . . . . [Travaux du centre d'études de la ligue maritime et coloniale polonaise, vol. 1, fasc. 1.]

1446. **Tönjes, Hermann.** 1911. *Ovamboland.* Pp. viii + 316, ill. Berlin: Warneck. [Pp. 81–83.]

1447. **Vedder, H.** 1923. *Die Bergdama* [2 vols.]. Teil 1, pp. (4) + 199, ill. Teil 2, pp. (6) + 131. [Hamburg Universität; Abhandlungen aus dem Gebiet der Auslandskunde, Band 11.]

1448. **von Francois, H.** 1894. *Nama und Damara: Deutsch-Süd-West-Afrika.* Pp. 6, 334 (1–xxviii), ill., map. Madgeburg: E. Baensch. [Pp. 188, 228, 253.]

1450. **Werner, H.** *Anthropologische, ethnologische und ethnographische Beobachtungen über die Heikum- und Kungbuschleute.* Z. f. Ethnol., **38**, 1906, 251–2.

1451. **Westphal, E. O. J.** 1964. *Observations on current bushman and Hottentot musical practices.* Essays on music and history in Africa and Asia, pt. 2, Africa. [Roy. anthrop. inst.]

See also 2029, 2117, 2431.

SOUTHERN RHODESIA

1452. **Bent, J. Theodore.** 1891. *The ruined cities of Mashonaland.* Pp. xi + 376, ill., map. London: Longmans, Green.

1453. **Gelfand, Michael.** 1959. *Shona ritual.* Pp. (10) + 217, ill. Cape Town: Juta & Co.

1454. **Gibbons, A. St. H.** 1898. *Exploration and hunting in Central Africa.* Pp. xi + 408, ill., map. London: Methuen. [P. 264.]

1455. **Kuper, Hilda,** and **Others.** 1954. *The Shona and Ndebele of Southern Rhodesia.* The Shona, by Hilda Kuper. The Ndebele, by A. J. B. Hughes and J. van Velsen. Pp. vii + 129, bibl., map. International African Institute. [Ethnographic Survey of Africa: Southern Africa, pt. 4.]

1455a. **Lenherr, Joseph.** *Einheimische Kirkenmusik.* Neue Zeitschrift f. Missionswissenschaft, **20**, 1964, 133–43.

1456. **Mauch, Carl.** *Reisen im Inneren von Südafrika,* 1865–72. Petermanns Mag. Ergänz., **37**, 1874, 43.

1458. **Richartz, F. J.** *Habits and customs of the Mashonas.* Zambezi mission rec., **2** (27), 508–13, 1905; **2** (28), 551–3, 1905; **2** (29), 589–92, 1905.

1459. **Taylor, Guy A.** *Some Mashona songs and dances.* Nada [Bulawayo], **4**, 1926, 38–42.

1460. **Tracey, Hugh Travers.** *Some observations on native music of Southern Rhodesia.* Nada [Bulawayo], no. 7, 1929, 96–103.

1461. —— *African folk music.* Man, **32**, 1932, 118–19.

1462. —— *Recording journey from the Union into the Rhodesias.* Afr. mus. soc., Newsletter, **1**, 1948, 12–14.

1463. —— *A study of native music in Rhodesia.* Nada [Bulawayo], **26**, 1949, 27–29.

1464. —— *Recording in the lost valley.* Afr. mus. soc., **1** (4), 1957, 45–47.

See also 2491.

SPANISH GUINEA

1465. **De Aranzadi, Iñigo.** 1962. *La Adivinanza en la Zona de los Ntumu: Tradiciones orales del Bosque Fang.* [Historiografia y musicografia de la Adivinanza Fang.] Pp. 310 + (18). Madrid: Instituto de Estudios Africanos.

1466. **de Unzueta y Yuste, Abelardo.** 1944. *Guinea continental Española.* Pp. 394, bibl., ill., maps. Madrid: Instituto des Estudios Politicos. [Pp. 337–40 Manifestaciones artisticas.]

1467. **Dicenta Segui, Jose.** *El Curanderismo en los pueblos primitivos del Golfo de Guinea.* Africa [Madrid], no. 48, 1945, 24–26, ill.

1469. **Gonzalez-Echegaray, Carlos.** *La musica indígena en la Guinea Española.* Arch. inst. est. Afr., **9** (38), 1956, 19–30, ill.

1470. **Ibarrola, Ricardo.** *La musica y el baile en los territorios del Golfo de Guinea.* Africa [Madrid], **10**, 142, 1953, 15–17, ill., map.

1471. **Panyella, Augusto.** 1959. *Esquema de etnologia de los Fang Ntumu de la Guinea Española.* Pp. 77 + (14), bibl., ill. Madrid: Instituto de Estudios Africanos. [Musical bow, p. 58.]

SPANISH WEST AFRICA

1472. **Baumann, Oscar.** 1888. *Eine afrikanische Tropen-Insel Fernando Poo und die Bube.* Pp. ix + 150, ill., map. Vienna: Holzel. [Pp. 98–100, ill.]

1473. **Cano, Domingo Manfredi.** *Fiesta en un poblado Bubi.* Africa [Madrid], no. 114, 1951, 287–9, ill.

1474. **Crespo Gil-Delgado, Carlos.** 1949. *Notas para un estudio antropologico y etnologico del Bubi de Fernando Poo.* Pp. xi + 290, bibl., ill. Madrid: Institutos de Estudios Africanos y Bernardino de Sahagún, de Antropologia y Etnologia.

1475. **Garcia Barriuso, P. G.** 1950. *La musica hispano-musulmana en Marruecos.* Pp. 56, ill. Madrid: Instituto de Estudios Africanos.

1476. **Guinea, Emilio.** 1947. *En el Pais de los Pamues.* Pp. 156, ill. Madrid: Instituto de Estudios Africanos. [Pp. 49–50.]

1477. **Iradier, Manuel.** 1887. *Africa, viajes y trabajos de la associacion Euskara* [2 vols.]. vol. 2, pp. 269–81. Vitoria: La Exploradora. [Rio Muni.]

1478. **Johnston, Sir Harry Hamilton.** 1908. *George Grenfell and the Congo* [2 vols.]. Vol. 2, p. 959, ill. London: Hutchinson.

1479. **Kingsley, Mary.** 1897. *Travels in West Africa.* Pp. xvi + 743, ill. London: Macmillan.

1480. —— 1901. *West African studies.* Pp. xxxii + 507, ill., map. London: Macmillan. [2nd ed.]

1481. **Mulero Clemente, Manuel.** 1945. *Los territorios españoles del Sahara y sus Grupos Nómadas.* Pp. x + 442, bibl., ill., maps. Gran Canaria: 'El Siglo'. [P. 119.]

1482. **Robles, Fernando.** *Mimos y juglares de la Puerta de Tánger.* Africa [Madrid], no. 186, 1957, 246–8, ill.

1483. **Tessmann, Günter.** 1923. *Die Bubi auf Fernando Po.* Pp. 218, ill. Hagen: Folkwang.

SUDAN
(Formerly Anglo-Egyptian Sudan)

1484. **Adolf Friedrich, Duke of Mecklenburg.** 1913. *From the Congo to the Niger and the Nile* [2 vols.]. Vol. 1, pp. xvi + 241, ill., map. Vol. 2, pp. xii + 285, ill. London: Duckworth. [Vol. 1, plates, music, nos. 44, 49, 181; dancing, no. 86. Vol. 2, plates, music, nos. 71, 79, 110; dancing, nos. 75, 107, 201.]

1485. **Anon.** *La musique chez les nègres.* Congo illus. [Brussels], no. 6, 48; no. 9, 1893, 66–67, ill.

1486. **Baker, Sir Samuel White.** *The Albert Nyanza* [2 vols.].

Vol. 1, xxx + 395, ill., maps. Vol. 2, pp. xi + 384, ill. London: Macmillan. [6. 243–44.]

1487. —— *Ismailia* [2 vols.]. Vol. 1, pp. viii + 448, ill., map. Vol. 2, pp. viii + 588, ill., map. [Vol. 1, pp. 241–2, 276.] London: Macmillan.

1488. **Basil, Rev. Brother.** *Towards a solution of African music problems: an assessment of the work of Father Giorgetti.* Afr. mus. soc., **2** (2), 1959, 90–92.

1489. **Baumann, Hermann.** *Die materielle Kultur der Azande und Mangbetu.* Baessler archiv., **11**, 1927, 1–131, ill., maps.

1490. **Baxter, P. T. W.** and **Audrey Butt.** 1953. *The Azande and related peoples of the Anglo-Egyptian Sudan and Belgian Congo.* Pp. x + 150, bibl., map. [International African Institute. Ethnographic Survey of Africa: East Central Africa, pt. IX.]

1491. **Bernatzik, Hugo Adolf.** 1948. *Gari-gari: Leben und Abenteuer bei den Negern am Oberen Nil.* Pp. 198, ill., map. Bern: Aare.

1492. **Bianchi, Gustavo.** 1884. *Alla Terra dei Galla: narrazione della Spedizione Bianchi in Africa . . . 1879–80.* Pp. 543, ill. Milan: Fratelli Treves. [Pp. 92–93.]

1493. **Burrows, Guy.** 1898. *The land of pygmies.* Pp. xxx + 299, ill. London: C. Arthur Pearson. [Pp. 83–84, 183.]

1494. **Casati, Gaetano.** 1891. *Zehn Jahre in Aequatoria und die Rückkehr mit Emin Pascha* [2 vols.]. Vol. 1, pp. x + 334, ill. Vol. 2, pp. (4), 364, ill. Bamberg: C. C. Buchner. [Vol. 1, pp. 48, 195.]

1495. **Cummins, S. L.** *Sub-tribes of the Bahr-el-Ghazal Dinkas.* J. anthrop. inst., **34**, 1904, 149–66, ill.

1496. **Czekanowski, Jan.** 1924. *Forschungen im Nil-Kongo-Zwischengebiet. Wissenschaftliche Ergebnisse der deutschen Zentralafrika-Expedition, 1907–1908, unter Führung Adolf Friedrichs, Herzog zu Mecklenburg.* Vol. 6, pt. 2, Ethnographie-Anthropologie. Pp. xvi + 714, ill., map. Leipzig: Klinkhardt & Biermann. [Pp. 38–40, 146–8.]

1497. **Dixon, D. M.** 1964. *A note on Kushite contact with the south.* Essays on music and history in Africa and Asia, pt. 2, Africa. [Roy. anthrop. inst.]

1498. **Domville Fife, C. W.** 1927. *Savage life in the black Sudan.* Pp. 284, ill., maps. London: Seeley Service.

1499. **Duchesne-Fournet, J.** 1909. *Mission en Ethiopie. 1901–3.* Paris.

1500. **Elisofon, E.** *The Nile.* Life. 1950. Pp. 56–57, ill.

1501. **Frobenius, Herman.** 1893. *Die Heiden-Neger des Ägyptischen Sudan.* Pp. (6) + 483, map. Berlin: Reimer.

1502. **Giorgetti, Filiberto.** *Musica d'Africa.* Strenna, Missioni Africane, 1940, 67–69.

1503. —— 1951. *Note de musica Zande: Con trascrizioni musicali di uccelli, tainburi, xilofoni e canti Zande.* Pp. 36. Verona: Missioni Africane (Mus. combonianum, n. 5).

1504. —— *Musica e tamburi fra gli Azandè.* Nigrizia [Verona], **70**, 1, Jan. 1951, 15–18.

1505. —— *Musica e tamburi fra gli Azande. Hanno la musica nel sangue.* Africana, **11**, 1955, 12–15, ill.

1506. —— *African music (with special reference to the Zande tribe).* Sudan notes and records, **33**, (2), 1952, 216–23.

1507. **Hartmann, R.** 1884. *Die Nilländer.* Pp.   - . Leipzig: Freytag. [Pp. 50, 89, 158.]

1509. **Heinitz, Wilhelm.** *Transkription zweier Lieder aus Nil-Nubien.* Z. f. Musikw., **2**, 1920, 733.

1510. **Herzog, Rolf.** 1957. *Die Nubier.* Pp. 218, bibl., ill., map. Berlin: Akademie-Verlag. [Deutsche Akad, Wiss, Berlin: Völkerkundliche Forschungen, Band 2.]

1511. **Hilke, H.** *Die Ingessana im Dar-Fung.* Z. f. Ethnol., **84**, 1959, 220–37.

1512. **Hofmayr, Wilhelm.** 1925. *Die Schilluk.* Pp. xvi + 524, ill., maps. Saint-Gabriel, Mödling, Vienna. Verlag: Anthropos Administration. [Pp. 403–82, 483–513.]

1513. **Junker, Wilhelm.** 1889–91. *Reisen in Afrika, 1875–86* [3 vols.]. Vol. 1 (1875–8), pp. xvi + 585, ill., maps. Vol. 2 (1879–82), pp. xvi + 560, ill., maps. Vol. 3 (1882–6), pp. xvi + 741, ill., maps. Vienna and Olmutz: Eduard Holzel. [Vol. 1, pp. 175, 301, 425, 434. Vol. 3, pp. 15.]

1514. —— 1890. *Travels in Africa* [3 vols.]. Vol. 1 (1875–8), pp. viii + 582, ill., map. Vol. 2 (1879–82), pp. viii + 477, ill., map. Vol. 3 (1882–6), pp. viii + 573, ill., map. London: Chapman and Hall. [Musical instruments, etc. Vol. 1, pp. 246, 364, 418–19. Vol. 2, Drum, 140, 217, 314, 366. Vol. 3, 14–15, 16, 21.]

1515. **Karsten, Paula.** *Tambura der Krieger des Mahdi (Sudanneger).* Chorgesang [Stuttgart], no. 24, 1889.

1516. —— *Tambura der Krieger des Mahdi (Sudanneger).* Neue Musik. Rundschau, no. 1, 1908.

1517. **Larken, P. M.** *Impressions of the Azande.* Sudan notes and records, **10**, 1927, 103–8.

1518. —— *Zande Notes.* Sudan notes and records, **6**, 1923, 235–47.

1519. —— *Account of the Zande.* Sudan notes and records, 1926, 1–55.

1520. **Mann, Anthony.** 1954. *Where God laughed: the Sudan to-day.* Pp. xviii + 221, ill., maps. London: Museum Press. [Pp. 72–73, 131.]

1521. **Mischlich, A.** 1942. *Über die Kulturen im mittel-Sudan.* Pp. xi + 198, ill. Berlin: Dietrich Reimer. [Pp. 103–12.]

1522. **Morlang, Franz.** *Reisen östlich und westlich von Gondokoro, 1859.* Petermanns Mitteilungen, Ergänz., **2**, 1862, 119.

1523. **Paulitschke, Philipp.** 1885. *Die Sudanländer.* Pp. xi + 511, bibl., ill., map. Freiburg im Breisgau: Herdersche Verlagshandlung.

1524. **Pritchard, E. E. Evans.** *The Zande corporation of witch-doctors.* J. roy. anthrop. inst., **62**, 1932, 302, 315, 317–20.

1525. **Robertson, J. W. R.** *Further notes on the Ingessana tribe.* Sudan notes and records, **17**, 1934, pt. 1, 121–3.

1526. **Schweinfurth, Georg August.** 1875. *Artes Africanae.* Leipzig: Brockhaus. [Plates of musical instruments, etc., with descriptive text.]

1527. —— 1878. *The heart of Africa* [2 vols.]. Vol. 1, pp. xvi + 559, ill., map. Vol. 2, pp. x + 521, ill., map. London: Sampson Low. [Vol. 1, pp. 130–3, 197–8, 293–5. Vol. 2, pp. 29, 58, 61, 248.]

1528. —— 1918. *Im Herzen von Afrika.* Pp. xviii + 578, bibl., ill., map. Leipzig: Brockhaus. [3rd ed.]

1530. **Tucker, Archibald Norman.** *Music in south Sudan.* Man, **32**, 1932, 18–19.

1531. —— *Children's games and songs in the southern Sudan.* J. roy. anthrop. inst., **63**, 1933, 165–87, ill.

1532. —— 1933. *Tribal music and dancing in south Sudan at social and ceremonial gatherings.* Pp. 57, ill. London: W. Reeves.

1533. **Vanden Plas, Joseph.** 1910. *Les Kuku.* Pp. xlii + 407, bibl., ill., map. Brussels: Institut Intern. de Bibliographie. [Collection de monographies ethnographiques, VI.]

1534. **Zöllner, Heinrich.** *Einiges über sudanesische Musik.* Musik. Wochenbl., **16**, 1885, 446.

See also 2150, 2236.

SWAZILAND

1535. **African Music Society.** *The music of the Swazis* (contributed). Afr. mus. soc., Newsletter, **1** (5), 1952, p. 14.

1536. **Kuper, Hilda.** 1952. *The Swazi.* Pp. vi + 89, bibl., map. [International African Institute: Ethnographic survey of Africa: Southern Africa, pt. I.]

1537. **Marwick, B. A.** 1940. *The Swazi.* Pp.   - . Cambridge: . . . .

1538. **Myburgh, A. C.** 1949. *The tribes of Barberton district.* Pp. 146, ill., map. Pretoria: Government Printer. [Union of S. Africa: Dept. of Native Affairs, Ethnological publications, no. 25.]

TANGANYIKA

1539. **Baumann, Oscar.** 1891. *Usambara und seine Nachbargebiete.*

Pp. xi + 375, ill., maps. Berlin: Reimer. [Pp. 50–55, 136–8, 350–3.]

1540. —— 1894. *Durch Massailand zur Nilquelle . . . in 1891–93.* Pp. xvi + 385, ill., map. Berlin: Reimer.

1541. **Blohm, Wilhelm.** 1933. *Die Nyamwezi: Gesellschaft und Weltbild.* Pp. xiii + 208, ill. Hamburg: Friedrichsen.

1542. **Brandel, Rose.** 1961. *The music of Central Africa. Former French Equatorial Africa: the former Belgian Congo, Ruanda-Urundi, Uganda, Tanganyika.* Pp. xli + 272, bibl., ill. The Hague: M. Nijhoff.

1543. **Burton, Sir Richard F.** *The lake regions of Central Africa* [2 vols.]. Vol. 1, pp. xvi + 412, ill., map. Vol. 2, pp. vi + 468, ill. London: Longmans. [Vol. 2, pp. 98, 291–5.]

1544. **Césard, Le R. P. Edmond.** *Le Muhaya (l'Afrique orientale).* Anthropos, **31**, 1936, 489–90 (music); 490–2 (dance); 492–3 games).

1545. **Claus, Heinrich.** *Die Wagogo.* Baessler Archiv [Leipzig], **2**, 1911, 36– . [Beiheft, 2.]

1546. **Culwick, A. T., and G. M.** 1935. *Ubena of the rivers.* Pp. 444, ill., map. London: George Allen & Unwin.

1547. **Dempwolff, Otto.** *Die Sandawe.* Abh. Hamburger Kol. Inst., **34**, 1916, 102–3.

1548. **Fabry, Hermann.** *Aus dem Leben der Wapogoro.* Globus, **91**, 1907, 218–19.

1549. **Fülleborn, Friedrich.** 1906. *Das deutsche Njassa- und Ruwumagebiet.* Pp. xx + 636, ill., maps. Berlin: D. Reimer. [Pp. 165, 234–42, 338, 458, 554–5, Deutsch Ost-Afrika, vol. 9 + bildatlas.]

1550. **Grant, James Augustus.** 1864. *A walk across Africa.* Pp. xviii + 453. Edinburgh: Blackwood. [Pp. 182–5.]

1551. **Hagemann, Carl.** 1919. *Spiele der Völker.* Pp. – . Berlin: Schuster.

1552. **Heinitz, Wilhelm.** *Lied aus Dar es Salaam.* Festschrift Heinrich Wilhelm Augustin, Glückstadt, 1932.

1553. **Herrmann, G.** *Die Wasiba und ihr Land.* Mitt. Schutz., **7**, 1894, 51.

1554. **Hornbostel, Erich von.** *Wanyamwezi-Gesänge.* Anthropos, **4**, 1909, 684–701, 919–30. [Phonograph recordings.]

1554a. —— *Gesang der Wasukuma.* Bul. Acad. Sci. Cracovie: Sciences Naturelles, 1910, 711–13. [Phonograph recordings.]

1555. **Hossfeld, Carl.** *Ein Beitrag zur ostafrikanischen Lyrik.* Globus [Brunswick], **88**, 1905, 82–83.

1556. **Jacques, Victor, and Émile Storms.** *Notes sur l'ethnographie de la partie orientale de l'Afrique équatoriale.* Bull. soc. anthrop. Brux., **5**, 1886, 127–35, ill.

1557. **Jaeger, Fritz.** *Das Hochland der Riesenkrater und die umliegenden Hochländer Deutsch-Ostafrikas.* Mitt. Schutz. Ergänz. **4**, 1911, 100–1.

1558. **Karásek, A., and August Eichhorn.** *Beiträge zur Kenntnis der Waschambaa.* Baessler Archiv. [Leipzig], **1**, 1911, 184–5,; **7**, 1918, 61–68, ill.

1559. **Kohn.** *West and East African songs.* Cunard, Nancy (ed,), Negro Anthology, 1934, 416–18.

1560. **Kollmann, Karl Paul.** 1899. *Der Nordwesten unserer ostafrikanischen Kolonie, etc.* Pp. viii + 191, ill., map. Berlin: A. Schall.

1561. —— 1899. *The Victoria Nyanza.* Pp. x + 254, ill., map. London: Swan Sonnenschein.

1562. **Kootz-Kretschmer, Elise.** 1926. *Die Safwa* [3 vols.]. Vol. 1, pp. xi + 316, ill. Vol. 2, pp. xi + 337, ill., map. Vol. 3, pp. – . Berlin: Reimer. [Vol. 1, 124–38.]

1563. **Krauss, H.** *Spielzug der Suahelikinder.* Globus [Brunswick], **92**, 1907, 357–9, ill.

1564. **Lechaptois, Mgr.** 1913. *Aux rives du Tanganyika.* Pp. xii + 282, ill., map. Alger: Maison-Carée. [Pp. 223–32.]

1565. **Luschan, F. von.** 1898. *Beiträge zur Ethnographie des Abflusslosen Gebiets von Deutsch-Ost-Afrika.* W. C. Waldemar, Die mittleren Hochländer des nördlichen Deutsch-Ostafrika. Wiss.

Ergebnisse der Irangi-Expedition, 1896–7, ill., maps. Pp. 340, 361, 374.

1566. **Lussy, K.** *Some aspects of work and recreation among the Wapogoro of southern Tanganyika.* Anthrop. quart., **26**, 1953, 109.

1567. **Mackenzie, D. R.** 1925. *The spirit-ridden Konde.* Pp. 318, ill., map. London: Seeley Service.

1568. **Maytain, Philémon de Neudaz.** *Le chant et la musique des nègres.* Rev. romande [Dar-es-Salaam], **9**, 1930, 103–7, 126–8.

1569. **Molitor, H.** *La musique chez les nègres du Tanganyika.* Anthropos, **8**, 1913, 714–35.

1570. **Ngubane, Simon S.** *Music north of the Limpopo.* Afr. mus. soc., Newsletter, **1**, 1948, 21–25.

1571. **Pfeil, Joachim.** *Beobachtungen während meiner letzten Reise in Ostafrika.* Petermanns Mitteilungen, **34**, 1888, 7–8.

1572. **Reche, Otto.** *Zur Ethnographie des abflusslosen Gebietes Deutsch-Ostafrikas.* Abh. Hamburger Kol. Inst., **17**, 1914, 19, 65, 89–91, 100, ill.

1573. **Rehse, Hermann.** 1910. *Kiziba: Land und Leute.* Pp. 394, ill. Stuttgart: Strecker.

1574. **Roscoe, John.** 1921. *Twenty-five years in East Africa.* Pp. xvi + 288, ill., map. Cambridge: Cambridge Univ. Press.

1575. **Schneider, Marius.** *Die musikalischen Beziehungen zwischen Urkulturen, Altpflanzern und Hirtenvölkern.* Z. f. Ethnol., **70**, 1938, 287–306. [P. 295, reference to Ngoni music.]

1576. —— *Kriterien zur Melodiegestalt (Nyamwezi).* Festschrift für H. Engel, 1963.

1577. **Schuman, C.** *Der musikalische Ton in der Benasprache.* Afr. u. Übersee, **8** (3), 1918, 164–9.

1578. **Sick, Eberhard von.** *Die Waniaturu.* Baessler Archiv [Leipzig], **5**, 1915, 22–62, ill.

1579. **Spellig, Fritz.** *Die Wanyamwezi.* Z. f. Ethnol, **59**, 1927, 250–1.

1580. **Stern, Rudolf.** *Lieder und Sageweisen und Geschichten der Wanyamwezi.* Mitt. Sem. Orient. Sprach. Afr. Stud., **4**, 1901, 45–62.

1581. **Stuhlmann, Franz.** 1894. *Mit Emin Pascha ins Herz von Afrika.* Pp. xxiv + 901, ill., maps. Berlin: Reimer.

1582. **Thurnwald, Richard C.** 1935. *Black and white in East Africa.* Pp. xxii + 419, ill. London: Routledge.

1583. **Tracey, Hugh.** *Recording tour in Tanganyika by a team of the African music society.* Tanganyika notes and records, **32**, 1952, 43–49, ill. [Reprinted from the African music society's Newsletter, June 1951, but with the addition of plates.]

1584. **Weber, Wolfgang.** *Negermusik: eine Urform der Unsrigen.* Die Musik [Berlin], **19**, 1927, 697–702, ill.

1585. **Weiss, Max.** 1910. *Die Völkerstämme im Norden Deutsch-Ostafrikas.* Pp. xx + 443, ill., map. Berlin: Marschner.

1586. **Werth, Emil.** 1915. *Das Deutsch-Ostafrikanische Küstenland und die Vorgelagerten Inseln,* [2 vols.]. Vol. 1, pp. xvi + 334, ill., maps. Vol. 2, pp. vii + 265, ill., maps. Berlin: Reimer. [Vol. 1, pp. 271–4.]

1587. **Weule, Karl.** 1908. *Wissenschaftliche Ergebnisse meiner ethnographischen Forschungsreise in den Südosten Deutsch-Ostafrikas.* Pp. x + 150, ill, maps. Berlin: Ernst Siegfried Mittler & Sohn. [Pp. 95–96.] [Mitt. Schutz. Erganz., no. 1.]

1588. —— 1909. *Native life in East Africa.* Pp. xxiv + 431, ill., map. London: Pitman.

1588a. **Widenmann, A.** *Die Kilimanscharo-Bevölkerung. Anthropologisches u. Ethnographisches aus dem Dschaggalande.* Petermanns Mitt. Ergänzungsheft, no. 129, 1890, ix + 104, ill. [Pp. 85–86.]

TOGO

1589. **Anon.** *Les arts à Togo.* Togo/Cameroun, **6**, 1931, 154–5.

1590. **Anon.** [R. Cornevin]. *Les arts, la musique et la toponymie (Togo).* Encyclopédie de l'Afrique francaise, 'Cameroun-Togo', 1951, 564–6.

1591. **Froelich, J. C.** 1954. *La tribu Konkomba du Nord Togo.* Pp. 253, bibl., ill., maps. Dakar: I.F.A.N. Mém. no. 37.

1592. **Heilborn, Adolf.** *Die Musik der Naturvölker unserer Kolonien.* Deut. Kol. Zeitg., **21**, 1904, 347–8.

1593. **Henrici, Ernest.** 1888. *Das deutsche Togogebiet und meine Afrikareise, 1887.* Pp. 152, map. Leipzig: Reissner.

1594. **Hornbostel, Erich von.** 1920. *Musik der Eingeborenen.* Deutsches-Kolonial-Lexicon, ed. H. Schnee, Vol. 2, pp. 602–5, ill.

1595. **Kling, Hermann.** *Bericht über seine letzte, von Lome über Kpandu, Salaga und Naparri nach Bismarckburg ausgeführte Reise.* Mitt. Schutz., **3**, 1890, 162.

1596. **Klöse, Heinrich.** 1899. *Togo unter deutscher Flagge.* Pp. xxii + 561, ill. Berlin: Reimer.

1597. —— *Musik, Tanz und Spiel in Togo.* Globus, **89**, 1906, 9–13, 69–75, ill.

1598. **Luschan, Felix von.** 1897. *Beiträge zur Völkerkunde der deutschen Schutzgebiete.* Pp. 87, ill. Berlin: Reimer.

1599. **Schönhärl, Josef.** 1909. *Volkskundliches aus Togo.* Pp. x + 204, ill. Dresden: Kochs.

1600. **Smend, J. von, Oberleut.** *Negermusik und Musikinstrumente der Togo.* Globus, **93**, 1908, 71–75, 89–94, ill.

1601. **Spieth, Jakob.** 1906. *Die Ewe-Stämme.* Pp. 80 + 962, ill., maps. Berlin: Reimer.

1602. **Witte, P. A.,** and **Wilhelm Schmidt.** *Lieder und Gesänge der Ewe-Neger (Gedialekt).* Anthropos, **1**, 1906, 65–81, 194–209.

See also 2212, 2325, 2326, 2509.

TRANSVAAL

1603. **Blacking, J. A. R.** 1956–7. *The role of music amongst the Venda of the Northern Transvaal, Union of South Africa.* Pp. 51. Johannesburg: Typescript.

1604. **Duggan-Cronin, A. M.** 1928–36. *The Bantu tribes of South Africa.* Vols. 1 (1); 2 (1–3); 3 (1–5); 4 (1–2). Cambridge: Deighton, Bell. [11 vols. containing in all 9 plates of musical instruments of high technical standard.]

1604a. **Krige, Eileen Jensen** and **J. D. Krige.** 1943. *The Realm of the Rain-queen.* Pp. xv + 335, maps. London: Oxford Univ. Press. [Published for the International African Institute.]

1605. **Lestrade, G. P.** 1928. *The Bavenda.* Pp. 21, pls. 16 and 17. Cambridge: Cambridge Univ. Press.

1606. **Stayt, Hugh A.** 1931. *The Bavenda.* Pp. xviii + 392, ill., map. London: H. Milford. [Published for the International African Institute by the Oxford Univ. Press.] [Pp. 316–29.]

1607. **van Warmelo, N. J.** 1932. *Contributions towards Venda history, religion and tribal ritual.* Pp. 207, xxviii, ill., maps. Pretoria: Government Printer. [Union of S. Africa: Dept. of Native Affairs, Ethnological Publications, no. 3.] [Pp. 101, 192–6, etc.]

TUNISIA

1608. **Erlanger, Rodolphe D'.** 1937. *Mélodies tunésiennes (Hispanoarabes, arabes-berbères, juive, nègre).* Paris: ....

1609. **Gironcourt, Georges.** *Recherche de géographie musicale dans le sud tunisien.* La géog., **71** (2), 1939, 65–74.

1610. **Hornbostel, Erich von.** *Phonographierte Tunesische Melodien.* Sammelb. der Intern. Mus. Ges., VIII, 1907. Reprinted in ...... Sammel. f. vergl. Musikw., **1**, 1922, 311.

1611. **Lachmann, Robert.** *Die Musik in den tunesischen Städten.* Archiv. f. Musikw., **5**, 1923.

1612. —— *Musikwissenschaftliche Forschungen in Tunesien.* Forsch. u. Fortschritte, **6**, 31, 1930, pp. 402–3.

1613. —— 1940. *Jewish cantillation and song in the island of Djerba.* Pp. 115. Jerusalem: Hebrew University. [Archives of oriental music.]

1614. **Mahdi, S.** 1963. *Patrimoine musical tunisien.* 2nd Fascicule, Ensemble des Tawchihs et Zajals tunisiens. [s.p.] Tunis: ....

1615. **Messadi, M.** 1960. *Patrimoine musical tunisien.* 1st Fascicule, Ensemble des Bachrafs tunisiens. Tunis: ....

1616. **Stumme, H.** 1894. *Tripolitanisch-tunesische Beduinenlieder.* Leipzig: ....

UGANDA

1617. **Ansorge, W. J.** 1899. *Under the African sun.* Pp. xiv + 355, ill. London: Heinemann.

1618. **Bansisa, Y.** *Music in Africa.* Uganda J., **4**, 1936, 108–14.

1620. **Brandel, Rose.** 1961. *The music of Central Africa, Former French Equatorial Africa, the former Belgian Congo, Ruanda-Urundi, Uganda and Tanganyika.* Pp. xii + 272, bibl., ill. The Hague: M. Nijhoff.

1621. **Castellani, Aldo,** and **Aldobrandino, Mochi.** *Contributo all'antropologia dell'Uganda.* B.R. Soc. geog. Ital., **41**, 1904, 1087–1089.

1622. **Cunningham, J. Francis.** 1905. *Uganda and its peoples.* Pp. 92, 289–90, ill., map. London: Hutchinson.

1623. **Driberg, John Herbert.** *A preliminary account of the Didinga.* Sudan notes and records, **5**, 1922, 222.

1624. —— 1923. *The Lango.* Pp. 468, bibl., ill., map. London: T. Fisher Unwin. [Pp. 123–37.]

1625. **Duncan, J. M.** *Native music.* By X.Y.Z. Uganda J., **1** (1), 1934, 63.

1626. —— *Music in Uganda, old and new.* Uganda J., **3** (4), 1936, 314–17.

1627. **Girling, F. K.** 1964. *The Acholi of Uganda.* Pp. x + 236, bibl., map. London: H.M.S.O. [Pp. 35, 38, 43, 56, 58, 64, 86–87, 98, 102–3, ill, 113, 115, 121, 229.]

1628. **Grant, James Augustus.** 1864. *A walk across Africa.* Pp. xviii + 453. Edinburgh: William Blackwood. [Pp. 103–4, 182–5.]

1630. **Ingrams, William Harold.** 1960. *Uganda.* Pp. xvi + 365, bibl., ill., maps. London: H.M.S.O.

1631. **Johnson, T. Broadwood.** 1908. *Tramps round the mountains of the Moon.* Pp. xxiii + 316, ill. London: T. Fisher Unwin. [Busoga harp, p. 243. Royal Band.]

1632. **Johnston, Sir Harry Hamilton.** 1904. *The Uganda Protectorate* [2 vols.]. Pp. xxvi + 470; xiii + 471–1018, ill., maps. London: Hutchinson. [2nd ed.] [Vol. 1, p. 210. Vol. 2, pp. 558, 664–6, 697, 778, 834, 851.]

1633. **Kagwa, Sir Apolo.** 1934. *The customs of the Baganda.* Pp. 199. New York: Columbia Univ. Press. [Columbia University contributions to anthropology, vol. 22.] [Chap. 28, p. 140, musical instr. and music.]

1634. **Kintu. Y. Q.** *Kisoga music.* Uganda teachers' journal, **2**, (2), 1940. [With notes by K. P. Wachsmann.]

1635. **Kitching, A. L.** 1912. *On the backwaters of the Nile.* Pp. xxiv + 295, ill., map. London: T. Fisher Unwin. [Pp. 228, 234–5, 255.]

1636. **Kmunke, Rudolf.** 1913. *Quer durch Uganda . . . in 1911–1912.* Pp. xiii + 186, ill., maps. Berlin: Reimer.

1637. **Kollmann, Paul.** 1898. *Der Nordwesten unserer Ostafrikanischen Kolonie.* Pp. — , ill. Berlin: Schall.

1638. ——1899. *The Victoria Nyanza.* Pp. x + 254, ill., map. London: Swan Sonnenschein.

1639. **Kyagambiddwa, Joseph.** 1956. *African music from the source of the Nile.* Pp. xii + 255, ill., map. London: Atlantic Press. [But really from Uganda.]

1640. —— 1963. *Ten African religious hymns.* Pp. 24. Munich: Uni-Druck.

1641. **La Fontaine, J. S.** 1959. *The Gisu of Uganda.* Pp. 68, bibl., map. International African Institute. [Ethnographic Survey of Africa: East Central Africa, pt. 10.]

1642. **Lawrence, J. C. D.** 1957. *The Iteso: fifty years of change in* *a Nilo-Hamitic tribe of Uganda.* Pp. xx + 280, ill., bibl., map. London: Oxford Univ. Press.

1643. **Meldon, James Austin.** *Notes on the Sudanese in Uganda.* J. Afr. soc., **7**, 1907, 142–3, ill.

1644. —— *Notes on the Bahima of Ankole.* J. Afr. soc., **6**, 1907, 235–9, ill.

1645. **Molinaro, Luigi.** *I Didinga, tribù dell' Africa Orientale.* Anthropos, **30**, 1935, 421–31.

1646. **Ness, Mrs. Patrick.** 1929. *Ten thousand miles in two continents.* Pp. xii + 278, ill., maps as end-papers. London: Methuen.

1647. **Powell-Cotton, Percy Horace Gordon.** 1904. *In unknown Africa.* Pp. xxiii + 619, ill. London: Hurst & Blackett.

1648. **Rodger, George.** *Ceremony in Bunyoro.* Nat. Hist., **64**, no. 4, 1955, 184, ill.

1649. **Roscoe, John.** *The Bahima.* J. anthrop. inst., **37**, 1907, 93–118, ill.

1650. —— 1911. *The Baganda.* Pp. xix + 547, ill., map. London: Macmillan. [Pp. 25–37.]

1651. —— 1915. *The northern Bantu.* Pp. xii + 305, ill., map. Cambridge Univ. Press. [Drums: pp. 87–88, 140, 189.]

1652. —— 1922. *The soul of Central Africa.* Pp. xv + 327, ill., map. London: Cassell. [Drums: p. 94.]

1653. —— 1923. *The Bakitara or Banyoro.* Pp. xvi + 370, ill., map. Cambridge Univ. Press.

1654. —— 1923. *The Banyankole.* Pp. xii + 176, ill., map. Cambridge Univ. Press.

1655. —— 1924. *The Bagesu.* Pp. xiii + 205, ill., map. Cambridge Univ. Press.

1656. **Schneider, Marius.** *Gesänge aus Uganda (Acholi only).* Archiv. f. Musikfors., **11**, 1937, 185–224.

1657. **Schoeller, Max.** 1901. *Mitteilungen ueber meine Reise nach Äquatorial Ostafrika und Uganda, 1896–97* [2 vols.]. Vol. 2, p. 306, ill. Berlin: Reimer. [See index to illus. in vol. 2.]

1658. **Scott, R. R.** *Kenya exhibition of musical instruments from Uganda and demonstrations of Uganda music.* Afr. mus. soc., Newsletter, **1**, no. 2, 1949, 22–27.

1659. **Sempebwa, E. K. K.** *Baganda folk-songs.* Uganda J., **12**, 1948, 16.

1660. **Shay, Felix.** *Fife and drum corps of a Uganda chief.* Nat. geog. mag., **47**, 1925, 174, 181, 189, 191.

1661. **Speke, John Hanning.** 1863. *Journal of the discovery of the source of the Nile.* Pp. xxxii + 658, ill., map. London: Blackwood. [2nd ed.]

1663. **Wachsmann, K. P.** *An approach to African music.* Uganda J., **6**, 3, Jan. 1939, 138–63.

1664. —— *The teaching of African music.* I and II. Uganda church Rev., pp. 71–95.

1665. —— *Kisoga music.* Kintu, Y. Q., Kisoga music (with notes by K. P. Wachsmann), Uganda teachers' J., **2**, 1940, 86–93.

1667. —— *Musicology in Uganda.* J. roy. anthrop. inst., **83**, 1, Jan.-June 1953, 50–57.

1668. —— *Harp songs from Uganda.* J. int. folk music council, **8**, 1956, 23–25.

1669. —— 1956. *Folk musicians in Uganda.* Pp. 10. Kampala: Uganda Museum (Occ. Pap. 2).

1670. —— *A study of norms in the tribal music of Uganda.* Ethnomusicology [Middletown, Conn.], **1**, 11, Sept. 1957, 9–15.

1671. —— *A century of change in the folk music of an African tribe.* J. int. folk music council [Cambridge], **10**, 1958, 52–56.

1672. —— *Ostafrika.* Die Musik in Geschichte und Gegenwart, ed. F. Blume, **10**, 92/93, 1961, 437–8, ill.

1673. —— (Joint author.) 1953. *Tribal crafts of Uganda*, by Margaret Trowell and K. P. Wachsmann. Pt. 2, The sound instruments, pp. 311–422, ill., map. London: Oxford Univ. Press.

1674. —— 1964. *Musical instruments in Kiganda historical tradition and their place in the East African scene.* Essays on music and history in Africa and Asia, pt. 2, Africa. [Roy. anthrop. inst.]

1674a. —— *The earliest sources of folk music from Africa.* J. int. folk music council, 1965.

1675. **Wayland, E. J.** *Preliminary studies of the tribes of Karamoja.* J. roy. anthrop. inst., **61**, 1931, 196, ill.

1676. **Weiss, Max.** 1910. *Die Völkerstämme im Norden Deutsch-Ostafrikas.* Pp. xx + 455, ill., maps. Berlin: Marschner. [Pp. 54, 112, 145–7, 237–40, 298–9, 308, 314–16.]

1677. **Wilson, C. T.,** and **R. W. Felkin.** 1882. *Uganda and the Egyptian Sudan* [2 vols.]. Vol. 1, x + 372, ill., map. Vol. 2, vii + 379, ill., maps. London: Sampson Low.

See also 2082, 2252, 2429, 2451.

VOLTAIC REPUBLIC

1678. **Cansdale, G. S.** *Kusasi musicians.* Geog. mag., **18** (4), 1945–6, 176–8, ill.

1679. **Chéron, Georges.** *Les Minianka.* Rev. Étud. Ethnog. Sociol, **4**, 1913, 185–6.

1680. **Labouret, Henri.** 1931. *Les tribus du rameau Lobi.* Pp. vii + 510, ill., maps. Paris: Institut d'Éthnologie. [Travaux et mémoires de l'instit. d'Éthnologie, XV.]

1681. —— 1958. *Nouvelles notes sur les tribus du rameau Lobi.* Pp. 295, bibl., map. Dakar: I.F.A.N. [Mémoires de l'I.F.A.N., no. 54.]

1682. **Marc, Lucien.** 1909. *Les pays Mossi.* Pp. 127, ill. Paris: Larose.

1683. **Ruelle, E.** *Notes anthropologiques, ethnographiques, et sociologiques sur quelques populations noires . . . de l'Afrique occidentale française.* L'Anthropologie, **15**, 1904, 519–61, 657–703.

See also 2097, 2300.

WEST AFRICA
(General)

1684. **Alberts, Arthur S.,** and **Others.** 1954. *The field recordings of new songs of the African coast.* [Modern café music of Liberia and the Gold Coast.] Riverside Records, RLP4003.

1685. —— —— 1954. *The field recordings of African coast rhythms.* [Tribal and folk music of West Africa.] Riverside Records, R.L.P.4001.

1686. **Ballanta, Nicholas George Julius.** *An African scale.* Music courier, **84/26**, 1922, 6.

1687. —— *Gathering folk-tunes in the African country.* Musical America, **44/23**, 1926, 3 and 11.

1688. —— *Music of the African races.* West Afr., **14**, 1930, 752–3. [Note also extracts in Work, M. N., Negro year-book [Tuskegee], 1931-2, 441–4.]

1689. **Barbot, John.** 1732. *A description of the coasts of North and South Guinea.* Churchill's Voyages. Vol. 5:3, 52, 55, 261, 264–5, 275, 308, 372, ill.

1690. **Boulton, Mrs. L. C.** *West African music.* Man, **37**, no. 160, August 1937, 130.

1691. **Butt-Thompson, Frederick William.** 1929. *West African secret societies.* Pp. xi + 320, bibl., ill., map. London: Witherby.

1691a. —— *Land of Poetry.* W.A.R., 1957, 360, 870–3.

1692. **Ca da Mosto, Alvise.** 1895. *Relation des voyages à la côte occidentale d'Afrique . . . 1455–1457.* Pp. xi + 206. Paris: E. Leroux.

1693. **Daniell, W. F.** 1849. *Sketches of the medical topography and native diseases of the Gulf of Guinea, etc.* Pp. viii + 200. London: S. Highley. [Consult p. 60 for use of rattles.]

1694. **Gilbert, Will G.** *Soedanese Negermuziek.* A.M.E., 1957, 361–71, bibl., map.

1695. **Hovelacque, Abel.** 1889. *Les nègres de l'Afrique sus-équatoriale (Sénégambie, Guinée, Soudan, Haut-Nil).* Pp. xiv + 468, bibl., ill. Paris: Lecrosnier et Babe. [Pp. 374–85.]

1696. **Isert, Paul Erdmann.** 1790. *Neue Reise nach Guinea.* Pp. 31, 141, 191–2. Berlin: . . . .

1697. **Kingsley, Mary.** 1901. *West African studies.* Pp. xxxii + 507, ill, map. London: Macmillan. [2nd ed.]

1698. **Kolinski, Mieczyslaw.** *Die Musik Westafrikas.* [MS. deposited in the Department of Anthropology, North-Western University, Chicago.]

1699. **Lemaire, Charles, Lt.** 1897. *Africaines: contribution à l'histoire de la femme en Afrique.* Pp. 11, 256, ill. Brussels: Ch. Bulens. [P. 109, Griots playing musical instruments.]

1700. **Mensah, Atta A.** *Music of Africa (adapting itself to the 20th century).* W.A.R., 33, 412, Apr. 1962, 29–33, ill.

1701. **Moloney, Sir Cornelius Alfred.** *On the melodies of the Volof, Mandingo, Ewe, Yoruba and Houssa people of West Africa.* J. Manchester geog. soc., 5, 1889, 277–98, ill.

1702. **Nketia, J. H. Kwabena.** *The problem of meaning in West African music.* Ethnomusicology, 6, no. 1, 1962, 1–7.

1703. —— 1964. *History and organisation of music in West Africa.* Essays on Music and History in Africa and Asia, pt. 2, Africa. [Roy. anthrop. inst.]

1704. **Rouget, Gilbert.** 1954. *Music of occidental Africa* [Africa: Music of the Malinké; music of the Baoulé.] Unesco, Esoteric ES 529.

1705. —— *Chroniques musicales: nouvelles des Griots.* Présence Afr., 1–11, 1955, 153–8.

1706. —— 1958. *Pondo Kakou, musique de société secrète.* Jaquette du LD 17/MC 20.141. Paris: Musée de l'Homme Contrepoint.

1707. —— *La musique de société secrète en Afrique occidentale.* Revue de musicologie [Paris], 46, 1960, 265–7.

1708. **Schneider, Marius.** *Tone and tune in West African music.* Ethnomusicology, 5, 1961, 204–15.

1709. **Smith, Edna M.** *Musical training in tribal West Africa.* Afr. mus. soc., 3, 1, 1962, 6–10.

1710. —— *Popular music in West Africa.* Afr. mus. soc., 3, 1, 1962, 11–14.

1711. **Sowande, Fela.** *A West African school of music.* W.A.R., 15, 196, Jan. 1944, 22–23.

1712. —— *African music (report of a talk).* Africa, 14, 6, April 1944, 340–2.

1713. —— *African music.* U. Empire, 39 (4), 1948, 165–7.

1714. **Villault, Le Sieur.** 1669. *Relation des costes d'Afrique appellées Guinée.* Pp. 310–18. Paris: Thierry.

1715. —— 1670. *Relation of the coasts of Africa called Guinée.* Pp. 216–23. London: John Starkey.

See also 207, 814.

ZAMBIA
(Formerly Northern Rhodesia)

1716. **Béguin, Eugène.** 1903. *Les Ma-Rotse.* Pp. 144–5. Lucerne: Benda.

1717. **Bertrand, Alfred.** 1898. *Au pays des Ba-rotse.* Pp. 148–9, ill. Paris: Hachette. [See ill., pp. 151, 161.]

1717a. —— 1899. *The kingdom of the Barotsi, Upper Zambezia.* Pp. xx + 304, ill., maps. London: T. Fisher Unwin. [P. 157, picture of royal musical instrument.]

1718. **Burnier, Théophile.** 1927. *Chants zambéziens.* Pp. 31, ill. Paris: Soc. des Miss. Evan.

1719. —— *Notes d'ethnographie Zambézienne.* Archives suisses anthrop. générale, 12, 1946, 92–107, ill.

1721. **Doke, Clement M.** 1931. *The Lambas of Northern Rhodesia.* Pp. 407, bibi., ill., map. London: Harrap.

1722. **Gamitto, A. C. P.** 1960. *King Kazembe and the Marave, Cheva, Bisa, Bemba, Lunda and other peoples of Southern Africa.* Vol. 1, pp. 208, ill., map. Vol. 2, pp. 228, ill., map. Lisbon: Junta de Investigações do Ultramar: Estudós de Ciências Politicas e Sociais. Nos. 42 and 43. [Musical instruments: Vol. 1, 70, 109, 146, 206. Vol. 2, 20, 57, 95 (ill.). Glossary, 213–16.]

1723. **Gouldsbury, Cullen,** and **Hubert Sheane.** 1911. *The great plateau of Northern Rhodesia.* Pp. xxiii + 360, ill., map. London: Arnold. [Pp. 263–9.]

1723a. **Jalla, Louis.** 1928. *Sur les rives du Zambèze: notes ethnographiques.* Pp. 160, ill. Paris: Société des Missions Evangéliques.

1724. **Johnston, Sir Harry Hamilton.** 1906. *British Central Africa.* Pp. xx + 646, ill., maps. London: Methuen. [3rd ed.]

1725. **Jones, A. M.** 1949. *African music in Northern Rhodesia and some other places.* Pp. 78. Livingstone: Rhodes-Livingstone Museum. [Occasional Papers of the Rhodes-Livingstone Museum, no. 4.]

1726. —— 1943. *African music* [Chap. 8, Lala Tribe.] Pp. 33. Livingstone: Rhodes-Livingstone Museum. [Occasional Papers, 2.]

1727. **Lungsonga, C.** *Bemba music.* Afr. mus. soc., 3 (2), 1963, 27–35.

1728. **McHarg, James.** *African music in Rhodesian native eduction.* Afr. mus. soc., 2, 1, 1958, 46–50.

1729. **Melland, Frank H.** *Some ethnographic notes on the Awemba . . . of North Eastern Rhodesia.* J. Afr. soc., 4, 1904–5, 337–45. [Musical instruments: pp. 342–3.]

1730. **Njungu, Agrippa M.** *The music of my people.* Afr. mus. soc., 2 (3), 1960, 48–50.

1731. **Rhodes-Livingstone Institute.** *Fieldwork co-operation in the study of Nsenga music and ritual.* Human probl. Brit. Cen. Afr., 31, June 1962, 51–52.

1733. **Richter, Martin.** 1908. *Kultur und Reich der Marotse.* Pp. 165–76. Leipzig: Voigtländer.

1734. **Sibson, A. R.** *African and European musical culture in the Federation of Rhodesia and Nyasaland.* Afr. mus. soc., 2 (2), 1959, 58–61.

1735. **Smith, Edwin W.,** and **Andrew Murray Dale.** 1920. *The Ila-speaking peoples of Northern Rhodesia* [2 vols.]. Vol. 1, pp. xxiv + 423, ill., map. Vol. 2, pp. xiv + 433, ill. London: Macmillan. [Vol. 2, chap. 25, p. 262.]

1736. **Spillmann, Joseph.** 1882. *Vom Cap zum Sambesi.* Pp. 221. Freiburg i.B.: Herder.

1737. **Stirke, D. W.** 1922. *Barotseland.* Pp. xii + 136, ill., map. London: John Bale.

1738. **Torrend, J.** 1921. *Specimens of Bantu folk-lore from Northern Rhodesia.* [With musical illustrations.] Pp. iv + 187. London: Kegan Paul.

1739. **Tracey, Hugh.** *Recording in the lost valley* [Zambesi]. Afr. mus. soc., 1 (4), 1957, 45–47.

1740. **Turner, V. W.** 1952. *The Lozi peoples of North-Western Rhodesia.* Pp. vii + 62, bibl., map. [London: International African Institute. Ethnographic survey of Africa: West Central Africa, pt. III.]

1740a. **White, C. M. N.** 1948. *The Material culture of the Lunda-Lovale peoples.* Pp. 3–15, ill. Livingstone: Rhodes-Livingstone Museum. [Occ. papers of the Museum, no. 3.]

See also 2033, 2094, 2096.

ZANZIBAR

1741. **Burton, Sir Richard Francis.** 1872. *Zanzibar.* Vol. 1, pp. 430–1. Vol. 2, pp. 91–92, 137. London: Tinsley.

1742. **Ingrams, William Harold.** In *Zanzibar: an account of its people, industries and history* (British Empire Exhibition, Wembley, 1924), pp. 12–14.

1743. —— 1931. *Zanzibar: its history and its people.* Pp. 527, ill., map. London: Witherby.

1744. **Prins, A. H. J.** 1961. *The Swahili peoples of Zanzibar.* Pp. 143, map. London: Int. African Inst. Ethnographic survey of Africa, East Central Africa, 12.

1745. **Pruen, S. Tristram.** 1891. *The Arab and the African.* Pp. – . London: Seeley Service.

1746. **Sacleux, Charles.** 1891. *Dictionnaire français-swahili.* P. 645, List of instruments. Zanzibar: Miss. des Pères du St. Ésprit.

1747. **Schmidt, Karl Wilhelm.** 1888. *Sansibar.* Pp. – . Leipzig: Brockhaus.

See also 1795.

MUSICAL INSTRUMENTS

GENERAL

1748. **Alexander, Boyd.** 1907. *From the Niger to the Nile* [2 vols.]. Vol. 1, pp. xv + 358, ill., maps. Vol. 2, pp. xi + 420, ill., maps. London: E. Arnold.

1749. **Andree, R.** *Signale bei Naturvölkern.* Z. f. Ethnol., **20**, 1888, 410–11.

1750. **Ankermann, Bernard.** *Kulturkreise in Afrika.* Z. f. Ethnol., **37**, 1905, 68–69, map.

1751. —— *Über den gegenwärtigen Stand der Ethnographie der Südhälfte Afrikas.* Archiv. f. Anthrop., **32**, 1905, 274–5.

1752. —— *L'Ethnographie actuel de l'Afrique meridionale,* Pt. 7, La musique. Anthropos [Vienna], **1**, 1906, 926–8, map.

1754. —— *Die afrikanischen Musikinstrumente.* Ethnol. Notizbl., **III**, 1901, 1–134, ill.

1755. **Baglioni, S.** *Contributo alla conoscenza della musica naturale.* Atti della soc. Roma d'anthrop., tome 5, 1910. Also in Globus, **98**, 1910, 232, 249, 264, under the title Ein Beitrag zur Kenntnis, der natürlichen Musik.

1756. **Béart, Ch.** *Contribution à l'étude des langages tambourinés, sifflés, musicaux.* Notes afr., I.F.A.N., no. 57, 1953, ii–14, ill.

1757. **Belker, J.** *Afrikanische Musikinstrumente,* Deut. Kol. Zeitg., **6**, 1941, 137–9.

1758. **Bernatzik, Hugo Adolf.** *Afrikanische Musikinstrumente.* Atlantis [Leipzig], **11**, 1934, 645–51, ill.

1758a. **Bonanni, F.** 1964. *The Gabinetto Armonico (of 1723),* renamed and reissued as *The Show Case of Musical Instruments,* pp. 170, ill. London: Constable.

1759. **Boulton, Laura C.** *Bronze artists of West Africa.* Nat. hist., **36**, 1925, 17–22, ill.

1760. **Büchner, Alexander.** 1960. *Musical instruments through the ages.* Pp. xv, 38, ill. London: Spring Books.

1761. **Cameron, V. L.** 1877. *Across Africa* [2 vols.]. Vol. 1, xvi + 389, ill., maps. Vol. 2, xii + 366, ill., maps. London: Daldy Isbister.

1762. **Chauvet, Stephen.** 1929. *Musique nègre.* Pp. 242, bibl., ill. Paris: Soc. d'Éditions géographiques, Maritimes et Coloniales.

1763. **Cuney-Hare, Maud.** 1936. *Negro musicians and their music.* Pp. xii + 439, bibl., ill. Washington: Associated Publishers Inc. [Appendix: African musical instruments, pp. 386–412.)

1764. **Éboué, Félix.** *La clef musicale des langages tambourinés et sifflés* [*Mossi, Gourounsi, Bobo*]. Bull. com. étud. A.O.F., **18**, 2/3, avr.-sept. 1935, 353–60, ill., *and* Bull. soc. rech. congol., **28**, 1941, 89–98.

1765. **Francolini, Bruno.** 1944. *Bianchi e Neri in Africa.* Pp. 375, bibl., ill., maps. Florence: Casa Editrice del Dott. Carlo Cya.

1766. **Grame, Theodore C.** *Bamboo and music: a new approach to Organology.* Ethnomusicology, **6**, 1, Jan. 1962, 8–14.

1767. **Granner, Erwin.** *Ein Afrikanisches Musikinstrument.* Kosmos [Stuttgart], **10**, 1913, 269–70.

1768. **Griaule, Marcel,** and **Jean-Paul Lebeuf.** *Fouilles dans la région du Tchad.* Pt. 2, Midigué. J. soc. Africanistes, 20, 1950, 1–152, ill.

1769. **Gröger, Helene.** 1946. *Die Musikinstrumente im Kult der Afrikaner.* Pp. 289 [typescript]. Wien: Institut f. Völkerkunde.

1770. **Heinitz, Wilhelm.** 1928. *Instrumentenkunde.* Pp. 152, ill. Wild Park. Potsdam: [Ernst Bücken. Handbuch der Musikwissenschaft, 4.]

1771. **Heins, E. L.** *Musikale exotica.* Kultuurpatronen, **1**, 1959, 115–19, ill.

1772. **Hickmann, Hans.** 1956. Articles on music, musicians, musical instruments, in W. Helck and E. Otto *Kleines Wörterbuch der Aegyptologie.* Wiesbaden: ....

1773. —— *Afrikanische Musik.* Blume, F. ed. Die Musik in geschichte u. gegenwart. I, 1951, 123.

1774. —— *Orchester: Aussereuropäische und antike Instrumentalgruppen.* Blume, F. (*ed.*), Die Musik in Geschichte und Gegenwart, vol. 10, 1962, 167–71, ill.

1775. **Hornbostel, Erich von.** *The ethnology of African sound instruments.* Africa, **6**, 1933, 129–54, 277–311.

1776. —— and **Curt Sachs.** *Systematik der Musikinstrumente.* Z. f. Ethnol., **46**, 1914, 553.

1777. **Jones, A. M.** *Instruments de musique africaine.* Présence Africaine, **34–35**, 1961, 132–50.

1777a. —— *Africa and Indonesia: the evidence of the xylophone and other musical instruments and cultural factors.* Pp. viii + 248, ill. Leiden: E. J. Brill.

1778. **Lane, Sara.** *Some musical instruments of the primitive African.* Southern workman [Hampton Institute], **56**, 1927, 552–6, ill.

1779. **Lavauden, Thérèse.** *African orchestics.* Chesterian, **10**, 1929, 127–33.

1780. —— *Orchestique africaine.* Guide musical [Paris], **3**, 1930, 230–3.

1781. **Leach, Maria** (*ed.*). 1949–50. *Standard dictionary of folklore and legend* [2 vols.]. Vol. 1, pp. x + 531. Vol. 2, pp. 532–1196. New York: Funk & Wagnall. [Contains brief articles on cymbals, dance, drums, harp, horns, lute, lyre, masks, musical bow, primitive song (G. Herzog), sistrum, trumpets, xylophones.]

1782. **Lehmann, J.** *Beiträge zur Musikinstrumentenforschung.* Abh. zur Anthr. Ethn. Urgesch., **2**, 1925, 113–25.

1783. **Macculloch, J. A.** *Horns.* Hastings, J., Encyclopaedia of religion and ethics, VI, 1909, 791–6.

1785. **Marcuse, S.** 1964. *Musical instruments: a comprehensive dictionary.* Pp. 608. New York: Loveday.

1786. **Montandon, Georges.** *La généalogie des instruments de musique et les cycles de civilisation.* Archiv. suisses anthrop. générale, **3** (I), 1919, 1–71, ill.

1787. **Nketia, J. H. Kwabena.** *Musical instruments.* Daily graphic, 9 May 1961, 5.

1788. **Norlind, Tobias.** 1941. *Musikinstrumentens Historia i Ord och Bild.* Pp. – , ill. Stockholm: ....

1789. *Notes and queries on anthropology.* 1951. Pp. xii + 403, bibl., ill. London: Routledge. [6th ed.] [Music, 315–31; dance, 331–2; art, 308–15.]

1790. **Pauli, F. W.** 1956. *Ausserdeutsche Volksmusik. Erster Katalog mit volkskundlichen Erläuterungen.* Frankfurt a/M: Lautarchiv des deutschen Rundfunks.

1791. **Pepper, Herbert.** *L'Enregistrement du son et l'art musical ethnique.* Bull. inst. ét. centrafricaines, no. 4, 1952, 143–8, ill.

1792. **Plant, R. W.** *Notes on native musical instruments.* Blythswood rev., **8** (1931), supplement, p. 97.

1793. **Rey Pailhade, Emile.** 1911. *Essai sur la musique et l'expression musicale. Les instruments de musique.* Paris: ....

1794. **Ris, Paquot.** 1889. *La céramique musical et instrumentale.* Paris: ....

1795. **Rose, Algernon S.** *African primitive instruments.* Proc. mus. assoc., **30**, 1903–4, 91–108.

1796. —— *A private collection of African instruments and South African clickers.* Zeit. Intern. Musikgesell., **6**, 1904–5, 60–66, 283–6, ill.

1797. **Rouget, Gilbert.** *Les éléments de formation des échelles extérieurs à la résonance facture instrumentale et résonance.* Colloques internationaux du centre national de la recherches scientifique: sciences humaines, 1960, 223–34. [1963.]

1798. **Sachs, Curt.** 1913. *Reallexikon der Musikinstrumente.* Pp. xvii + 442, ill. Berlin: J. Bard. [Reproduced under the date 1962.]

1799. —— 1920. *Handbuch der Musikinstrumentenkunde.* Pp. 412. Leipzig: Breitkopf and Händel.

1800. —— 1923. *Die Musikinstrumente.* Pp. – . Breslau: Jeder-mann's Bücherei.

1801. —— The following articles in Ebert, Max (*ed.*), Reallexikon der Vorgeschichte. Vols. 1–15, 1924–32, ill., maps. Berlin: De Gruyter. Vol. 1, *Becken,* p. 376. Vol. 3, *Flöte,* p. 390. Vol. 5, *Harfe,* p. 125. Vol. 7, *Leier,* p. 281. Vol. 11, *Rassel,* p. 23. Vol. 11, *Sackpfeife,* p. 178. Vol. 13, *Trommel,* p. 448; *Trompete,* p. 450.

1802. —— 1940. *The history of musical instruments.* Pp. 505, ill. New York: Norton.

1803. **Santandrea, S.** 1938. *Strumenti musicali indigeni in Africano fotografato.* Pp. 222–3. Verona:............

1804. **Schaeffner, André.** *Projet d'une nouvelle classification méthodique des instruments de musique.* Rev. musicale, **13**, 1932, 215.

1805. —— *Note sur la filiation des instruments à cordes.* Mélanges de musicologie offerts à M. Lionel de la Laurencie [Paris], 1933.

1806. —— 1936. *Origines des instruments de musique.* Pp. 405, bibl., ill. Paris: Payot.

1807. —— 1939. *Contribution à l'étude des instruments de musique d'Afrique et d'Océanie.* Compte rendu de la 2ième session du Congrès intern. des sciences Anthropologiques et Ethno-logiques. Pp. 268–70. Copenhagen: Einar Munksgaard.

1808. 1946. *Les instruments de musique.* Dufourq, La musique dès origines à nos jours. Pp. 13– . Paris: Larousse.

1809. —— 1951. *Musique et instruments primitifs.* Guide de la musique. Paris:............

1810. **Stern, Theodore.** *Drum and whistle languages.* Amer. anthrop. **59**, 1957, 487.

1811. **Tracey, H.** *The tuning of (African) musical instruments.* Nada [Bulawayo], **13**, 1935, 35–44, ill.

1812. **Vilheno, Julio de.** *Folklore activities of the Museo do Dundo.* Afr. mus. soc., II (2), 1959, 42–43, ill.

1813. **Vincent, Frank.** 1895. *Actual Africa or the coming continent.* Pp. xix + 451, ill., map. London: William Heinemann.

1814. **Weber, Wolfgang.** *Afrikanische Musikinstrumente.* Reclams Universum, **7**, 1926–7, 189–91, ill.

See also 117.

MUSICAL INSTRUMENTS (GEOGRAPHICALLY ARRANGED)

ALGERIA (INSTRUMENTS)

See 1210, 1215, 1219, 1222, 1231.

ANGOLA (INSTRUMENTS)

1815. **Bastin, Marie-Louise.** 1961. *Art décoratif tshokwe* [2 vols.] Pp. 395; 277, ill. Lisbon: Companhia de Diamantes de Angola. [Pp. 202–4, 205–30.]

1816. **Sacadura, Fernando de.** *Usos e costumes de Quiteve.* Bol. soc. geog. [Lisbon], **46**, 1928, 369–72.

See also 296, 312, 313, 2011, 2029, 2038a.

ARAB (INSTRUMENTS)

1817. **Chottin, Alexis.** *Instruments, musique et danse Chleus.* Z. f. vergleich. Musikwiss., **1**, 1933, 11–15, ill.

1817a. —— *Le luth et les harmonies de la nature. L'ésoterisme dans la musique arabe.* Rev. musicale, 1940, 197–203.

1818. **Farmer, Henry George.** *A Maghribi work on musical instru-ments.* J. roy. Asiat. soc., **11**, 339, 1935, 1–15.

1819. ——*A Maghribi work on musical instruments.* Studies in oriental musical instruments. 2nd series B, 1939. Glasgow:..........

1820. **Salvador-Daniel, Francesco.** 1863. *La musique arabe.* Alger, 1863.

1821. ——1915. *The music and musical instruments of the Arab . . .* [edited with notes, memoir, bibliography and musical examples by Henry George Farmer]. London/New York:............

See also 2360–2.

BASUTOLAND (INSTRUMENTS)

1821a. **Mabille, H. E.** *The Basuto of Basutoland.* J. Afr. soc., **5**, 1905–6, 241–2.

1821b. **Widdicombe, John.** 1891. *Fourteen years in Basutoland.* Pp. 58–59. London: Church Printing Co. [Drum, goura and guitar.]

See also 323.

BECHUANALAND (INSTRUMENTS)

See 336–7.

BURUNDI (INSTRUMENTS)

1821c. **Burundi.** *Instruments de musique du Burundi.* Nos. 6, 7, 8, and 15, Feb.–Apr. 1962.

See also 343, 345.

CAMEROONS (INSTRUMENTS)

1822. **Lembezat, Bertrand.** 1952. *Mukulehe: un clan montagnard du Nord-Cameroun.* Pp. x + 228, bibl., ill., map. Paris: Éditions Berger-Levrault. [P. 119.]

1823. **Lyée de Belleau, M. de.** 1945. *Du Cameroun au Hoggar.* Pp. 175, ill. Paris: Editions Alsatia. [Illustrations of musical instruments and of art objects.]

1824. **Meyer, Hans.** 1909–10. *Das Deutsche Kolonialreich* [2 vols.]. Vol. 1, Ostrafrika und Kamerun. [Pl. 26.] P. 490, map showing the distribution of the following musical instruments: marimba, drum, harp, sansa.]

1825. **Schaeffner, André.** *Sur deux instruments de musique des Bata (Nord-Cameroun).* J. soc. africanistes, **13**, 1943, 123–51, ill.

1826. **Sieber, J.** 1925. *Die Wute.* Pp. xi + 114, ill. Berlin: Reimer. [Pp. 96–99, ill.]

See also 376, 390, 2038, 2207.

CANARY ISLANDS (INSTRUMENTS)

1827. **Nuez Caballero, Sebastian de la.** *Instrumentos musicales populares en las Islas Canarias.* Ortiz, Fernando, Miscelanea de Estudios dedicados a Fernando Ortiz. Vol. 2, 1956, 1143–62, bibl., ill.

CAPE PROVINCE (INSTRUMENTS)

See 412, 1357, 1368, 1955–7.

CAPE VERDE ISLANDS (INSTRUMENTS)

See 421a.

CENTRAL AFRICAN REPUBLIC (INSTRUMENTS)

1828. **Empain, A.** *Les Bakela de la Loto.* Bull. soc. roy. belge. géog., **46**, 1922, 257–60, ill.

1829. **Jameson, S. J.** 1890. *Story of the rear column of the Emin Pasha relief expedition.* Pp. xxxii + 455, ill., maps. London: R. H. Porter.

1830. **Jephson, A. J. M.** 1980. *Emin Pasha and the rebellion at the*

Equator. Pp. xxiv + 490, ill., map. London: Sampson Low. [Pp. 39, 106.]

1831. **Savage-Landor, A. Henry.** 1907. *Across widest Africa* [2 vols.]. Vol. 1, pp. xv + 396, ill., map. Vol. 2, pp. xii + 511, ill., map. London: Hurst & Blackett.

1832. **Thomas, Thomas Morgan.** 1872. *Eleven years in Central Africa.* Pp.   –   . London: Snow.

1833. **Torday, Emil.** *Der Tofoke.* Mitt. Anthrop. Gesell. [Wien], **41**, 1911, 192–3.

1834. **Wintersgill, H. G.** *Orchestras of Central Africa.* S. Workman, **34**, 1905, 657–62, ill.

1835. **Wissmann, Hermann,** and **Ludwig Wolf.** 1888. *Im innern Afrikas.* Pp. 253–4. Leipzig: Brockhaus.

See also 2071.

CHAD (INSTRUMENTS)

1835a. **Dyboski, Jean.** 1893. *La route du Tchad du Loango au Chari.* Pp. 381, ill., maps. Paris: Firmin-Didot. [Pp. 85–86, 150, 197–9, 303, 347.]

1835b. **Regelsperger, Gustave.** *Les instruments de musique dans le pays du Chari-Tchad.* La Nature, 37, 1908, 19–22, ill.

See also 465, 467, 2042, 2408.

CONGO AND CONGOLESE REPUBLICS (INSTRUMENTS)

1836. **Costermans, B.** *Muziekinstrumenten van Watsa-Gombari.* Zaïre, 1947, 516–42, 129–63, ill.

1837. **De Hen, Ferdinand J.** 1960. *Beitrag zur Kenntnis der Musikinstrumente aus Belgisch-Kongo und Ruanda-Urundi.* Pp. 259, ill., maps. Tervuren: Musée Royale de l'Afrique Centrale.

1838. **Forrer, Raymond.** *La géographie musicale du Congo belge.* L'Expansion belge [Brussels], 1928, 33–34. [Distribution of instruments in the Congo.]

1839. **Hulstaert, G.** *Note sur les instruments de musique à l'Equateur.* Congo, **2**, 1935, 185–200, 354–75, ill.

1840. **Maes, J.** *Musique et sculpture congolaises.* Illustr. congol., **192**, 1937, 6533–4, 6539–42, ill.

1841. —— *Les instruments de musique.* Pp. 144, ill. Tervuren: Annales du Musée du Congo: Ethnographie and Anthropologie [série 3, tome 1, fasc. 1.]

1842. —— 1937. *Sculpture décorative ou symbolique des instruments de musique du Congo belge.* (Artes Africanae.) Pp. 19. Bruxelles: Commission pour la Protection des Arts et Métiers Indigènes.

1843. **Manoly, J.** *Les arts traditionnels de quelques chefferies katangaises.* Beaux-arts, **7**, 1937, 13–16.

1845. **Maquet, J.-N.** 1956. *Note sur les instruments de musique congolais.* Pp. 71. ill. A.R.S.C. (sciences morales), Mém. 6 (4). Brussels: . . . .

1846. **Masson, P.** *Armes, outils et instruments de musique employés par les Shi.* Kongo-Overzee, **24**, 4/5, 1958, 239–55, ill.

1847. **Mertens, Joseph.** 1935. *Les Ba Dzing de la Kamtsha. Première partie-ethnographie.* Pp. 381, ill. maps. Brussels: G. van Campenhout. I.R.C.B. (sciences morales), Mém. no. 4.

1848. **Milou.** *Instruments et musique nègre.* Illustr. congol., **189**, 1937, 6412–13, ill.

1849. **Pigafetta, Filippo.** 1881. *A report on the kingdom of Congo . . . (1591),* [translated by Margarite Hutchinson]. Pp. xxi + 174, maps. London: John Murray. [Pp. 111–12, 161.] s

1850. **Schmeltz, Johannes Diedrich Eduard.** 1904–16. *Ethnographisch Album van het Stroomgebied van den Congo.* Pl. 183–98. The Hague: Rijks Ethnografisch Museum, ser. 2, no. 2.

1851. **Söderberg, Bertil.** *Musical instruments used by the Babembe.* Ethnos [Sweden], **17**, 1952, 51–63, ill. [Reprinted in African music society, Newsletter, vol. 1, no. 6, 1953, 46–56, ill.]

1852. —— 1956. *Les instruments de musique au Bas-Congo et dans les régions avoisinantes: étude ethnographique.* Pp. 285 + XXVI pl.,

carte. Stockholm: Ethnographical Museum of Sweden [monograph ser. no. 3].

1853. **Starr, Frederick.** 1912. *Congo natives: an ethnographic album.* Pp. 38, ill. Chicago: Lakeside Press. [Pl. 1, 18, 19, 43, 46, 48, 49, 61, 123.]

1854. **Torday, Emil.** *The new Congo collection.* Mus. J. phil., **4**, 1913, 21–24, ill.

1855. **Ward, Herbert.** 1890. *Five years with the Congo cannibals.* Pp. xv + 308, ill. London: Chatto & Windus. [2nd ed.]. [Bakongo musical instruments, p. 68.]

1856. —— 1910. *A voice from the Congo.* Pp. xv + 299, ill. London: W. Heinemann. [Pp. 267–71.]

1856a. **Wauters, A. J.** *La musique chez les nègres. Congo.* Illus. 2, 6, 1893, 48, ill.; 2, 9, 1893, 66–67, ill. [Guitars and rattles of the Niam-Niam.]

1857. **Weeks, John H.** 1914. *Among the primitive Bakongo.* Pp. xvi + 318, ill., map. London: Seeley Service. [Pp. 122, 126, 128; 132, 160, 178, 188, 250.]

See also 511, 520, 548, 590, 605, 2005, 2007, 2036, 2040–1, 2062, 2064, 2102, 2106, 2130, 2141, 2148, 2156, 2159, 2173–4, 2196, 2253, 2254, 2306, 2318, 2349, 2355, 2392, 2399, 2402–3, 2405–6, 2418, 2477–8, 2608.

DAHOMEY (INSTRUMENTS)

1858. **Bertho, J.** *Personnification d'instruments de musique à percussion au Dahomey.* Notes afr., I.F.A.N., no. 25, 1945, 1, ill.

1859. —— *Instruments de musique des rois de Nikki au Dahomey.* Notes afr., I.F.A.N., no. 52, 1951, 99–101, ill.

1860. **da Cruz, Clément.** *Les instruments de musique dans le Bas-Dahomey (populations Fon, Adja, Kotafon, Péda, Aïzo).* Études Dah. [Porto-Novo], **12**, 1954, pp. 79 + xx, ill.

1861. **Lombard, J.** *Aperçu sur la technologie et l'artisanat Bariba.* [Section 6, Musical instruments.] Études Dah., **18**, 1957, 5–59, ill.

See also 659, 662, 665, 2126, 2194, 2449.

EAST AFRICA (INSTRUMENTS)

1862. **Wachsmann, K. P.** *Ostafrika.* F. Blume [ed.] Die Musik in Geschichte und Gegenwart, **10**, 1961, 437–47, ill.

See also 696, 2391, 2497.

EGYPT (INSTRUMENTS)

1863. **Carl Gregor, Duke of Mecklenburg.** 1960. *Ägyptische Rhythmic. Rhythmen und Rhythmusinstrumente im heutigen Ägypten.* Pp. 70. Strassburg: Baden-Baden. Heitz. [In series of dissertations.]

1864. **Farmer, Henry George.** *Ancient Egyptian instruments of music.* Trans. Glasgow univ. oriental soc., 6, 1934.

1865. **Hickmann, Hans.** 1949. *Catalogue générale des antiquités égyptiennes du musée du Caire-instruments de musique.* Pp. iv + 213, ill. Cairo: Imprimerie de l'Institut Français d'Archéologie Orientale.

1866. —— *miscellanea musicologica.* (12) *La scène musicale d'une tombe de la 6e dynastie à Guîzah (Idou).* Ann. Service antiq. Égypte, **54**, 1957, 213–37, ill.

1867. —— (13) *Note sur un objet en forme d'instrument de percussion.* Ann. service antiq. Égypte.

1868. —— (14) *Une nouvelle cymbalette à manche.* Ann. service antiq. Égypte.

1869. —— *Miscellanea égyptologica.* Journ. of the Galpin Soc., **1**, 1951, 25.

1870. —— *Aegyptische Volksinstrumente.* Musica [Kassel], **8**, 1954.

1871. —— *Dieux et déesses de la musique.* Cah. hist. égyptienne, **6**, 1954, 31.

1872. —— 1956. *Musik, Musiker-namen und -instrumente.* Handwörterbuch der Aegyptologie. Wiesbaden: ....

1873. **Loret, Victor.** *Notes sur les instruments de musique de l'Égypte ancienne.* Lavignac, A. and L. de la Laurencie, Encyclopédie de la musique, pt. 1, 1913, 1–34, ill.

1874. **Sachs, Curt.** *Die namen der altägyptischen Musikinstrumente.* Z. f. Musikw., **1**, 1917–18, 265.

1875. —— *Altägyptische Musikinstrumente.* Der Alte Orient, **21**, 1920.

1876. —— 1921. *Die Musikinstrumente des alten Aegyptens.* Pp.   – . Berlin: ....

1877. **Whyte, E. T.** *Egyptian musical instruments.* Proc. soc. biblical arch., **21**, 1899.

See also 709, 2018–28, 2030, 2215–16, 2218, 2370–89, 2420–1, 2439, 2442–3, 2446, 2453–5, 2459, 2463–5, 2469–70, 2475, 2498, 2515.

ETHIOPIA (INSTRUMENTS)

1877a. **Harris, W. C.** *The highlands of Aethiopia.* 1844. 3 vols. Vol. 3, 283–6.

1878. **Sandford, Christine.** *The church in Ethiopian life.* Geog. mag., **23**, 1950–1, 565–8, ill.

See also 783, 787, 789.

FORMER FRENCH WEST AFRICA (INSTRUMENTS)

See 813, 816–18.

GABON (INSTRUMENTS)

See 831, 832.

GAMBIA (INSTRUMENTS)

See 841, 843.

GHANA (INSTRUMENTS)

1879. **Nketia, J. H. Kwabena.** *The development of instrumental music in Ghana.* Music in Ghana, **1**, no. 1, 1958, 5–27.

1880. **Onwona Osapo, F.** *An African orchestra in Ghana.* Afr. mus. soc., **1** (4), 1957, 11–12.

See also 893, 2266–72, 2274, 2295.

GUINEA (INSTRUMENTS)
(Formerly Guinée Française, A.O.F.)

1881. **Barret, Paul.** *Sénégambie et Guinée—la région Gabonaise.* 1888. L'Afrique occidentale [2 vols.]. Vol. 1, pp. xiii + 402, map. Vol. 2, pp. 438, map. Paris: Challamel. [Pp. 227–8.]

1882. **Germain, J.** *Extrait d'une monographie des habitants du cercle de N'zérékore (Guerzé, Kono, manon). Les artisans, les techniques et les arts.* Études Guin., **13**, 1955, 47–53, ill.

1883. **Köler, Hermann.** 1848. *Einige Notizen über Bonny an der Küste von Guinea.* Pp. iv + 82. Göttingen: Dieterichschen Univ. Buchdrukerei. [Pp. 35, 72, 130–1.]

1884. **Schaeffner, André.** 1951. *Les Kissi: Une société noire et ses instruments de musique.* Pp. 86, ill. Paris: Hermann (L'Homme: Cah. ethnol., géog., et ling., no. 2).

See also 2070, 2336, 2359.

IVORY COAST (INSTRUMENTS)

1885. **Brisley, Thomas.** *Some notes on the Baoulé tribe.* J. Afr. soc., **8**, 1908–9, 299–300.

1886. **Ménard, P. René.** *Contribution à l'étude de quelques instruments de musique baoulé.* Jb. f. musikalische Volks- u. Völkerkunde., **1**, 1963, 48–99. Berlin: de Gruyter.

See also 2180–1, 2245.

KENYA (INSTRUMENTS)

1887. **Hobley, Charles William.** 1910. *Ethnology of A-Kamba and other East African tribes.* Pp. xvi + 172, ill., map. Cambridge: Cambridge Univ. Press.

1888. **Hollis, Sir Alfred Claude.** 1909. *The Nandi.* Pp. xl + 328, ill., map. Oxford: Clarendon Press.

1889. **Hyslop, Graham.** *African musical instruments in Kenya.* Afr. mus. soc. [Roodespoort], **2**, 1, 1958, 31–36, ill.

1890. ——*More Kenya musical instruments.* Afr. mus. soc., **2**, 2, 1959, 24–28, ill.

See also 939, 2402.

LIBERIA (INSTRUMENTS)

1891. **Johnston, Sir Harry Hamilton.** 1906. *Liberia* [2 vols.]. Vol. 1, pp. xxviii + 520, ill., maps. Vol. 2, pp. xvi + 663, ill. London: Hutchinson.

See also 955.

LIBYA (INSTRUMENTS)

See 1215.

MADAGASCAR (INSTRUMENTS)

1892. **Kaudern, Walter.** 1913. *Pa Madagascar.* Pp. 124–8, ill. Stockholm: Albert Bonniers Forlag.

1893. **Petit, Georges.** *Collection ethnographique provenant de Madagascar.* L'Anthropologie, **33**, 1923, 364. [Instrument called 'farai' described.]

1894. **Sachs, Curt.** 1938. *Les instruments de musique de Madagascar.* Pp. viii + 96, ill. Paris: Université de Paris. [Travaux et mémoires de l'institut d'ethnologie, 28.]

1895. **Sichel, A.** *La musique des Malgaches.* Rev. Musicale, **6**, 1906, 389–91, 448–52, ill.

MALAWI (INSTRUMENTS)
(Formerly Nyasaland)

See 1000, 1003, 2434.

MALI (INSTRUMENTS)
(Formerly Soudan Français)

1896. **Ibn Batoutah.** 1922. *Voyages* [trad. par C. Defremery et le Dr. B. R. Sanguinetti]. Pp. 479. Paris: Impr. Nat. [4th ed.] [Pp. 105 and 411, Balafons et Ares à Mali.']

1897. **Ibn Fadl Allah Al-Omari.** 1927. *L'Afrique moins l'Égypte* [trad. par Gaudefroy-Demombynes]. Pp. 284, maps. Paris: Geuthner. [Musical instruments, p. 69. Tambours et guitares à Mali.]

See also 2155, 2200, 2358, 2368–9, 2435, 2504.

MAURITANIA (INSTRUMENTS)

1898. **Leriche, Albert.** *Instruments de musique Maure et griots.* Bull. I.F.A.N., **12** (3), 1950, 744–50, ill.

MOROCCO (INSTRUMENTS)

1899. **Dupuis, J.** *Les instruments de musique au Maroc.* Terra Mairala, sept. 1947, 7.

1900. **Jean-Léon L'Africain.** 1956. *Description de l'Afrique* [2 vols.]. Pp. xvi + 630, ill., maps. Paris: Maisonneuve. [Orchestra of negroes at Fez, p. 217.]

1901. **Thornton, Philip.** 1936. *The voice of Atlas: in search of music in Morocco.* Pp. xii + 226, ill., map. London: Alexander Maclehose & Co.

See also 1053, 1069.

MOZAMBIQUE (INSTRUMENTS)

1902. **Marques, Belo.** *Musica negra: estudo do folclore tonga.* Pp. 121, ill. Lisbon: Agencia Geral das Colónias.

1903. **Maugham, R. C. F.** 1906. *Portuguese East Africa.* Pp. xii + 340, ill., maps. London: John Murray. [Pp. 287-8.]

1904. **Quay, Georges Stucky de.** *Vieux souvenirs de chasse au Zambèze, suivi d'une étude sur les cafres de la région de Quelimane, 1897-1915.* Pp. 224, ill. Avinhão: Aubanal Freres.

1904a. **Santos Junior, Norberto.** *A chitata: Contribuiçao para o estudo dos instrumentos musicais dos indigenas de Moçambique.* Garcia de Orta [Lisboa], **6**, 1958, 347-64; 3, 527-34, ill.

See also 1081, 1096, 1103, 1107, 2057, 2061a.

NATAL (INSTRUMENTS)

See 1114, 1127.

NIGER (INSTRUMENTS)

1904b. **Nikiprowetzky, Tolia.** *Les instruments de musique au Niger.* 1963. s.p. ill. Paris: O.C.O.R.A.

See also 1139a.

NIGERIA (INSTRUMENTS)

1905. **Bouquiaux, L.** *Les instruments de musique birom (Nigeria septentrional).* Africa-Tervuren, **8** (4), 1962, 105-11, ill.

1906. **Day, C. R.** *Native musical instruments.* 1892. Mockler-Ferryman, A. F. Up the Niger . . . to which is added a chapter on native musical instruments. Pp. xx + 326, ill., map. London: G. Philip. [Pp. 264-81.]

1907. **Echezona, W. Wilberforce.** *Ibo musical instruments.* Music educators journal, 1964, 23-27, 130-1, ill.

1908. **Erokwu, Edward.** *The musical instruments of my district.* Nigerian field, **5**, 1932, 18-20, ill.

1909. **Gunn, Harold D.** 1956. *Pagan peoples of the central area of northern Nigeria.* Pp. x + 144, bibl., map. London: Intern. African Inst. [Ethnographic survey of Africa: Western Africa, pt. xii.]

1910. —— 1953. *Peoples of the plateau area of northern Nigeria.* Pp. 110, map. London: Intern. African Inst. [Ethnographic survey of Africa: Western Africa, pt. VII.]

1911. —— and **F. P. Conant.** 1960. *Peoples of the middle Niger region northern Nigeria.* Pp. viii + 138, bibl., map. London: Intern. African Inst. [Ethnographic survey of Africa: Western Africa, pt. XV.] [Pp. 51-52.]

1912. **Hambly, Wilfrid D.** 1935. *Culture areas of Nigeria.* Pp. 365-502, bibl., ill., maps. Chicago: Field Museum. [Field Museum of Natural History: Anthropological series, vol. 21, no. 3.] [Musical instruments: 430, 462, 477. Drums: 430-1, 458, 475. Bull-roarers: 397, 457, 477. Rattles: 430-1.]

1913. **Harris, Percy Graham.** *Notes on drums and musical instruments seen in Sokoto province, Nigeria.* J. roy. anthrop. inst., **62**, 1932, 105-25, ill.

1914. **Johnson, Samuel.** 1921. *The history of the Yorubas.* Pp. lv + 684, ill., map. London: Routledge. [Pp. 120-1.]

1915. **Lannert, E.** *Ekwechi-Anokehi festival.* Nigeria magazine, **80**, 1964, 44-56, ill.

1916. **Mackay, Mercedes.** *Nigerian folk musical instruments.* Nigeria, **30**, 1949, 337-9, ill.

1917. —— *The traditional instruments of Nigeria.* Nigerian field, **15**, 3, July 1950, 112-33, ill.

1918. **Meek, Charles Kingsley.** 1925. *The northern tribes of Nigeria* [2 vols.]. London: Milford. [Vol. 2, pp. 155-9.]

1919. —— *The Katab and their neighbours.* J. Afr. soc., **27**, 1927-8, 375; **28**, 1928-9, 388.

1920. —— 1931. *Tribal studies in northern Nigeria* [2 vols.]. London: Kegan Paul.

1921. —— 1931. *A Sudanese kingdom.* Pp. xxxiii + 548, ill. London: Kegan Paul.

1922. **Migeod, F. W. H.** 1924. *Through Nigeria to Lake Chad.* Pp. 330, ill., maps. London: Heath Cranton. [Pp. 58, 95.]

1923. **Nicholson, W. E.** *Notes on some of the customs of the Busa and Kyenga tribes at Illo.* J. Afr. soc., **26**, 1926-7, 93-100. [P. 100.]

1925. **Okosa, A. N. G.** *Ibo musical instruments.* Nigeria magazine, 1962, 4-14, ill.

1926. **Omoneukanrin, C. O.** 1942. *Itsekiri law and custom.* Pp. 115. Lagos: Ife-Olu Printing Works.

1927. **Partridge, C.** 1905. *Cross River natives.* Pp. xvi + 332, ill., maps. London: Hutchinson. [Pp. 226-9.]

1929. **Talbot, Percy Amaury.** 1932. *Tribes of the Niger Delta.* Pp. xi + 350, ill., map. London: Sheldon Press. [Pp. 318-19, Plates: p. 31, a Buan sacred drum; p. 140, Ibo ceremonial xylophone; pp. 318, pottery drum, drums and gong.]

1930. —— 1926. *The peoples of southern Nigeria.* Ethnology . . . Vol. 3, pp. x + 425-976, ill., maps. London: Oxford Univ. Press. [Pp. 807-16, 819.]

1931. —— 1912. *In the shadow of the bush.* Pp. xiv + 500, ill., map. London: Heinemann. [Pp. 297-303.]

1932. **Vischer, Hanns.** *Journeys in northern Nigeria.* J. Roy. Geog. Soc., **28**, 1906, 373.

1933. **Yeatman, W. B.** *Ibo musical instruments.* Nigerian teacher, **1** (3), 1934, 17-20, ill.

See also 1147-8, 1163, 2009, 2045, 2068, 2077-8, 2085-6, 2131, 2137, 2139-40, 2147, 2204-6, 2240, 2246-7, 2316, 2468, 2488, 2501.

NORTH AFRICA (INSTRUMENTS)

1934. **Barbès, L. L.** *Afrique du Nord in Michel.* F. Encycl. de la musique. Vol. 3, 1961, 940-3, bibl.

See also 1215, 1219, 1228.

PORTUGUESE GUINEA (INSTRUMENTS)

See 1282, 1284-5.

RHODESIA (SOUTHERN) (INSTRUMENTS)

1937. **Livingstone, David,** and **Charles.** 1865. *Narrative of an expedition to the Zambesi . . . 1858-64.* Pp. xv + 608, ill., map. London: John Murray. [Pp. 254-5, ill. Pp. 98, 105, 255.]

1938. **Schebesta, Paul.** *Zur ethnographie der Asena am unteren Sambesi.* Bibl. Afr., **2**, 1926, 207-8.

1939. **Snowden, A. E.** *Some common musical instruments found among the native tribes of Southern Rhodesia.* Nada [Bulawayo], **15**, 1938, 99-103, ill.; **16**, 1939, 72-75, ill.

1940. **Taylor, M.** *Did Pharaoh Necho's minstrels visit S. Africa?* I.L.N., **171**, 1927, 1058-9, ill. [Rock paintings of musical instruments in Southern Rhodesia.]

1941. **Von Rosen, Eric.** 1916. *Trasfolket Svenska Rhodesia-Kongo-Expeditionens etnografiska Forsknigsresultat.* Pp. 468, ill. Stockholm: Bonniers Forlag. [Map showing distribution of musical instruments.]

See also 1722, 1729, 2036, 2041a, 2084, 2094, 2094a, 2096, 2118-19, 2418, 2491.

RWANDA (INSTRUMENTS)

1941a. **Merriam, Alan P.** *Musical instruments and techniques of performance among the Bashi.* Zaïre, **9**, 1955, 121-32, ill.

1941b. **Pauwels, Le P. Marcel.** *Les metièrs et les objets en usage au Rwanda: (4) Instruments de musique* Annali Lat., **19**, 1955, 217-21, ill.

See also 2226, 2276, 2399.

SÃO TOMÉ (INSTRUMENTS)

See 1293.

SENEGAL (INSTRUMENTS)

1942. **Ca da Mosto, Alvise de.** 1895. *Relation des voyages à la côte occidentale d'Afrique* . . . 1455–57. Pp. xix + 206. Paris: Leroux. [P. 121, Tambours et guitares à deux cordes au Sénégal.]

1943. **Nikiprowetzky, Tolia.** *Les griots du Sénégal et leurs instruments The griots of Senegal and their instruments Die Zauberer* . . . Communication présentée au 15ᵉ congr. du conseil int. musique populaire (Gottwaldov, 1962). Pp. 30, ill. Paris: Office de Coopération Radiophonique OCORA.

1944. **Tautain, L.** *Sur l'ethnologie et l'ethnographie des peuples du Sénégal.* Rev. ethnog. **4**, 1885, 61–80, 137–47, 254–68, ill.

SIERRA LEONE (INSTRUMENTS)

See 1320, 1329, 1331.

SOMALIA (INSTRUMENTS)
(Including Former British Somaliland)

See 1333, 1338, 1340, 1347.

SOUTH AND SOUTH-WEST AFRICA (INSTRUMENTS)

1946. **Balfour, Henry.** *Musical instruments of South Africa.* Rep. Brit. ass. (S. Africa), 1905, 528–9. London: . . . .

1947. **Breuil, Henri.** *The white lady of Brandberg, South West Africa: her companions and her guards.* S. Afr. archaeol. bull., **3**, no. 9, 1948, 2–11, ill. [P. 9.]

1948. **Dunn, Edward John.** 1908. *Ethnological collections made in South Africa.* Pp. 44. Kew, Victoria.

1949. —— 1931. *The Bushman.* Pp. xii + 130, ill. London: Griffin.

1950. **Holub, Emil.** 1879. *Eine Culturskizze des Marutse-Mambunda-Reiches, in Süd-Central Afrika.* Pp. 210, ill. Vienna: K. K. geog. Gesell. [Pp. 135–44.]

1951. —— 1881. *Seven years in South Africa* [2 vols.]. Vol. I, pp. xi + 426, ill., maps. Vol. 2, pp. xi + 479, ill. London: Sampson Low.

1952. **Jeanneret, Philippe.** *Les Ma-Khoca.* Bull. soc. Neuchât. géog., **8**, 1895, 126–55, ill.

1953. **Kaufmann, Hans.** *Die Auin.* Mitt. Schutz., **23**, 1910, 150–1.

1954. **Kidd, Dudley.** 1904. *The essential Kafir.* Pp. xv + 435, bibl., ill., map. London: Adam and Charles Black. [Pp. 332–5.]

1955. **Kirby, Percival R.** *The music and musical instruments of the Korana.* Bantu Stud., **6**, 2, 1932, 183–204, ill.

1956. —— *Musical instruments of the native races of South Africa.* Pp. xix + 285, ill., map. Oxford University Press. l1953 (reprint). Johannesburg: Witwatersrand University Press.]

1957. —— *Musical instruments of the Cape Malays.* S. Afr. J. of science, **36**, 1939, 477–88. [Description of a kind of drum and guitar used by the Cape Malays and which has been adopted by other indigenous peoples, notably the Hottentots.]

1958. —— *My museum of musical instruments.* S.A.M.B., **4**, 1947, 7– .

1959. **Lebzelter, Viktor.** 1934. *Eingeborenen in Südwest-und Südafrika.* Pp. – . Leipzig: Hiersemann. [Pp. 41, 119, 207–8, 284.]

1960. **Lestrade, G. P.** 1928. *The Bavenda.* Pp. 21, pl. 16 and 17. Cambridge: Cambridge Univ. Press.

1961. **Lloyd, Lucy C.** *A short account of further bushman material collected by L.C.L.* Pp. 17–18. London: Nutt.

1963. **Metchnikoff, Léon.** *Bushmen et Hottentots.* Bull. Soc. Neuchât. géog., **5**, 1889–90, 76.

1964. **Müller, Hendrik P. N.,** and **Joh. F. Snellman.** 1893. *Industrie des caffres du Sud-Est de l'Afrique: collection . . . et notice ethnographique,* par H. P. N. Müller. *Description des objets,* par Jon. F. Snelleman. Pp. 55. Leiden: E. J. Brill. [Note pl. xii.]

1965. **Natal Province.** 1911. *Descriptive guide and official handbook.* Pp. xi + 574, ill., maps. Durban: S. A. Railways. [Musical instruments illustrated pp. 462–3.]

1966. **Passarge, Siegfried.** 1908. *Südafrika.* Pp. xii + 355, ill. Leipzig: Quelle & Meyer.

1967. **Ridsdale, Benjamin.** 1883. *Scenes and adventures in Great Namaqualand.* Pp. 94–95. Woolmer.

1968. **Vedder, H.** 1938. *South West Africa in early times.* Pp. xv + 525, bibl., maps. London: Oxford Univ. Press. [Musical instruments of the Bergdama, p. 62.]

1969. **Walton, James.** 1956. *African village.* Pp. xii + 170, bibl., ill. Pretoria: J. L. van Schaik. [Pp. 29–30.]

1970. **Wangemann, Hermann Theodor.** 1886. *Ein zweites Reisejahr in Süd-Afrika.* Pp. 140, 158, 161–2, 167. Berlin: Verlag des Missionshauses.

1971. **Widdicombe, John.** 1891. *Fourteen years in Basutoland.* Pp. 58–59. London: Church Printing Co. Ltd. [Drum, goura and guitar.]

See also 1357, 1362, 1368, 1385, 1396, 1418, 2006, 2237, 2239, 2242, 2301, 2339–41, 2344, 2347–8, 2350, 2351–2, 2393, 2395–8, 2413–16, 2424, 2427–8, 2431, 2448, 2471–2.

SPANISH GUINEA (INSTRUMENTS)

1972. **De Larrea Palacin, Arcadio.** *Organografia de Ifni.* Africa [Madrid], no. 187, 1957, 295–7, ill.

1973. **Perramon, Ramón.** *Al habla con los Buetis.* Guinea espan., **59**, 1554, Mar. 1962, 72–73; 1555, Apr., 109–10.

SUDAN (INSTRUMENTS)

1974. **Bernatzik, H. A.** 1948. *Gari-gari.* Pp. 198, ill., map. Bern: Aare.

1975. **Giorgetti, Filiberto.** *Musica a tamburi fra gli Azande. Hanno la musica nel sangue.* Africana, **11**, 1955, 12, 12–15, ill.

See also 1504–5, 1514–16, 1526, 2150, 2198, 2236, 2292, 2294, 2342, 2487, 2495.

SWAZILAND (INSTRUMENTS)

See 1956.

TANGANYIKA (INSTRUMENTS)

1976. **Eichhorn, A.** *Musikinstrumente nebst zugehörigen Liedern.* Baessler-Archiv, N.F.7, 1918–22, 61–68, ill. [In Beiträge zur Kenntnis der Waschambaa.]

1977. **Kubik, G.** *Musikinstrumente und Tänze bei den Wapangwa in Tanganyika.* Mitt. anthrop. Gesell., [Wien], **91**, 1961, 144–7, ill.

1978. **Tenraa, W. F. E. R.** *Sandawe musical and other sound-producing instruments.* Tanganyika notes and records, **60**, Mar. 1963, 23–48, bibl., ill.

1980. **Wachsmann, K. P.** *Ostrafika.* Blume, F. ed. Die Musik in Geschichte u. Gegenwart, **10**, 1961, 437–47, ill.

See also 2179, 2224, 2303, 2338, 2445.

TOGO (INSTRUMENTS)

1981. **Westermann, Diedrich.** 1935. *Die Glidyi-Ewe in Togo.* Mitt. Sem. Orient. Sprach. Afr. Stud., **38** (Beiband), p. 207.

See also 1600, 2212.

TRANSVAAL (INSTRUMENTS)

See 1604, 1956.

TUNISIA (INSTRUMENTS)

1982. **Balout, L.** 1959. *Collections ethnographiques.* Album no. I, Touareg Ahaggar. s.p. 76 plates with descriptive text. Tunis: Musée d'Ethnographie et de Préhistoire du Bardo (Tunis).

1982a. **Revault, Jacques.** *Notes sur les instruments traditionnels de musique populaire dans le sud tunisien.* 6th congrès international des sciences anthropologiques et ethnologiques, 30 July–6 Aug. 1960, tome 2, pp. 113–20.

UGANDA (INSTRUMENTS)

1983. **Coutts, P. G.** *Some musical instruments of Usuku.* Uganda J., **14**, 1950, 160–2, ill.

1984. **Fallers, Margaret Chave.** 1960. *The eastern Lacustrine Bantu (Ganda, Soga).* Pp. ix + 86, bibl., map. International African Institute. [Ethnographic survey of Africa: East Central Africa, pt. 11.]

1985. **Kearton, Cherry, and James Barnes.** 1915. *Through Central Africa from East to West.* Pp. xviii + 283, ill., map.

1986. **Peters, Carl.** 1891. *New light on dark Africa . . . the narrative of the German Emin Pasha expedition.* Pp. xviii + 597, ill., map. London: Ward Lock. [Musical instruments of Waganda, p. 410.]

1987. **Scott, R. R.** *Kenya exhibition of musical instruments from Uganda and demonstration of Uganda music.* Afr. mus. soc., Newsletter [Johannesburg], **1**, 2, Mar. 1949, 22–27.

1989. **Stam, Father N.** *Music in Uganda.* St. Joseph's Advocate, 1906, 588–9, ill.

1990. **Stigler, Robart.** *Ethnographische und Anthropologische Mitteilungen über einige wenig bekannte Volkstämme Ugandas.* Mitt. anthrop. Gesell. [Wien], 52 and 53, 1923, 113–261, ill., map.

1991. **Trowell, Margaret, and K. P. Wachsmann.** 1953. *Tribal crafts of Uganda.* Pt. 1, Domestic and cultural. Pt. 2, The sound instruments, by K. P. Wachsmann. Pp. xxi + 423, ill., map. London: Oxford Univ. Press.

See also 1674, 2060–1, 2082, 2227, 2252, 2429.

VOLTAIC REPUBLIC (INSTRUMENTS)

1992. **Nicolas, Francois J.** (3) *Le langage sifflé;* (4) *Usages; Bibliographie des langages tambourinés et sifflés.* Nicolas, F. J., Les surnoms-devises des l'éla de la haute Volta (A.O.F.), Anthropos, **45** (1–3), 1950, 81–118.

See also 1678, 2097, 2300.

WEST AFRICA (INSTRUMENTS)

1992a. **Ellis, G. W.** 1914. *Negro Culture in West Africa.* Pp. 290, ill. New York: Neale Publ. Co. [List of musical instruments.]

1993. **Valdez, Francisco Travassos.** 1861. *Six years of a traveller's life in western Africa* [2 vols.]. Vol. 1, pp. xv (1) + 354, ill. Vol. 2, pp. viii + 363, ill. London. Hurst & Blackett. [Pp. 221–5, vol. 2.]

See also 1690, 1695, 2050, 2508.

ZAMBIA (INSTRUMENTS)
(Formerly Northern Rhodesia)

See 1722, 1728, 1735, 2033, 2096.

ZANZIBAR (INSTRUMENTS)

1994. **Anon.** *Les instruments de musique en usage à Zanzibar.* Rev. musicale, **6**, 1906, 165–8, ill.

See also 1746.

AFRO-CUBAN (INSTRUMENTS)
See Introduction, p. vii.

1995. **Ortiz, Fernando.** *El estudio de la musica afrocubana.* Musicalia Habana, **4**, 1928, 115–19.

1996. —— *La musica sagrada de los negros Yoruba en Cuba.* Estudios Afrocubanos, **2**, 1938, 89.

1997. —— *Las musicas Africanas en Cuba.* Rev. de Arqueo- y Etnologia, **11**, 1947, 235.

1998. —— 1950. *La Africania de la musica folorica de Cuba.* Pp. 16 + 477, bibl., ill. Havana: Ediciones Gardens.

1999–2001. —— 1952. *Los instrumentos de la musica afrocubana* [3 vols.]. Vol. 1, Los instrumentos anatómicos y los palos percusivos. Pp. 306. Vol. 2, Los instrumentos sacudivitos, los frotativos y los hierros. Pp. 344. Vol. 3, Los tambores xilofónicos y los membranófonos abiertos A a N. Pp. 472, bibl., ill. Habana: Dirección de Cultura del Ministerió de Educación.

2002. —— *Los instrumentos de la música afrocubana.* Vol. 4, Los membranófonos abiertos, Ñ a Z. Los bimembranófonos y otros tambores especiales. Pp. 452, ill. Habana: Gardenas.

2003. —— *Los instrumentos de la música afrocubana.* Vol. 5. Los pulsativos, los fricativos, los insuflativos y los aeritivos. Indices generales. Pp. 529, ill. Habana: Cardenas.

2004. **Törnberg, G.** *Musical instruments of the Afro-Cubans.* Ethnos, **19**, 1954, 105–26.

INSTRUMENTS
(Types)

IDIOPHONES
(Including certain Pot Drums; excluding Xylophones, Lithophones, Sansas and Slit-drums)

2005. **Bennet-Clark, M. A.** *Iron gongs from the Congo.* Man, **55**, no. 196, 1955, 176.

2006. **Bleek, D. F.** *Beliefs and customs of the XAM Bushmen.* Bantu stud., **7** no. 4, 1933, 391–2. [Bushman rattles.]

2006a. **Boston, J. S.** *Ceremonial iron gongs among the Ibo and the Igala.* Man, **64**, 1964, 52.

2007. **Carrington, J. F.** *Notes on an idiophone used in Kabile initiation rites by the Mbae.* Afr. mus. soc., **1** (1), 1954, 27–31 ill.

2008. **Cunnison, I.** *Central African chronology.* Man, **55**, no. 157, 1955, 143–4.

2009. **Daniel, F.** *Note on a gong of bronze from Katsina, Nigeria.* Man, **29**, no. 113, 1929, 157–8, ill.

2010. **de Chastonay, Ph.** *Pour une systématique des instruments de musique. 1. Les idiophones.* Musées de Génève, 16e ann., 1959, 10, 3, ill.

2011. **Delachaux, Th.** *Omakola (ekola), instrument de musique du sud-ouest de l'Angola.* Anthropos, **35–36** (1–3), 1940–1, 341–5, ill.

2012. **Dworakowska, Maria.** *The origin of bell and drum.* Prace etnologiczne, 1938, 26 pp.

2013. **Focquet-Vanderkerken, G.** *Les populations indigènes des territoires de Kutu et de Nseontin.* Congo [Brussels], **2**, 1924, 170–1, ill.

2014. **Günther, Robert.** *Schlaginstrumente (c. Aussereuropa und Europäische Folklore).* Die Musik in Geschichte und Gegenwart, ed. F. Blume, vol. 11, 1964, 1755–78, ill.

2015. **Hambly, Wilfrid D.** 1937. *Dancing and singing and percussive instruments (music).* Hambly, Source book for African anthropology, vol. 2, pp. 446–56, bibl., ill. [Field Museum of Natural History: Anthropological series, vol. 26.]

2016. **Hawley, E. H.** *Distribution of the notched rattle.* Amer. anthrop., **11**, 1898, 344–6.

2017. **Hirschland, Heinz.** *A Bantu suite for piano, xylophone, whistles and voices.* Afr. mus. soc., **1**, 1957, 40–44.

2018. **Hickmann, Hans.** *The rattle-drum and Marawe-sistrum.* J. Roy, Asiat. soc., 1950.

2019. —— *La castagnette égyptienne.* Ann. service antiq. Egypte, **51**, 1951.

2020. —— *Cymbales et crotales dans l'Egypte ancienne.* Ann. service antiq. Egypte, **49**, 1950, 451–545, ill.

2021. —— *Die Altaegyptische Rassel.* Z. f. Aegypt. Sprache u. Altertumskunde, **79**, 2, 1954, 116.

2021a. —— *Le Menat Kêmi revue,* **13**, 1954, 99–102.

2022. —— *Miscellanea musicologica.* (15) *Le grelot dans l'Égypte ancienne.* Ann. service antiq. Egypte, **57**, 1958.

2023. —— *Rassel.* Blume, F. (*ed.*), Die Musik in Geschichte u. Gegenwart, **11**, 1962, 1–11, bibl., ill.

2024. —— *La cliquette instrument de percussion de l'époque copte.* Bull. soc. d'archéol. copte [Cairo], 13, 1960.

2025. —— *Du battement des mains aux planchettes entrechoquées.* Bull. de l'inst. d'Egypte, **37**, 1954–5, 67– .

2025a. —— *Glocken.* Altertum und aussereuropaische Glocken. Blume, F. (*ed.*), Die Musik in Geschichte u. Gegenwart, **5**, 1956, 267.

2026. —— *Die altaegyptischen Becken (cymbals).* Z. f. Instrumentenbau, **12**, 1957, 2.

2027. —— *La castagnette dans l'Égypte ancienne.* Bull. soc. amis de l'art Copte, 1958.

2028. —— *Klappern.* Blume, F. (*ed.*), Die Musik in Geschichte u. Gegenwart, **7**, 1958, 980–6, ill.

2028a. **Jeffreys, M. W. D.** *A musical pot from Southern Nigeria.* Man, **40**, no. 215, 1940, 186–7, ill.

2028b. **Lindblom, G.** *A noose-trap appliance for the capture of the fruit-eating bats of the Lower Congo Region.* Man, **28**, no. 69, 1928, 93–95, ill. [Alarm bells.]

2029. **Kirby, Percival R.** *A secret musical instrument: the ekola of the Ovakuanyama of Ovamboland.* S. Afr. J. of science, **37**, 1942, 345–51, ill.

2029a. **Laforest, F.** *Une boîte à musique unique au Monde.* Courier, **9**, 1956, 12.

2030. **Loret, Victor.** *Les cymbales égyptiennes.* Sphynx, **5**, 1902.

2031. **Lutten, Eric.** *Les Wasamba et leur usage dans la circoncision.* Minotaure [Paris], **2**, 1933, 13–17, ill. [Calabash-rattle.]

2032. **Ménard, P. René.** *Contribution à l'étude de quelques instruments de musique Baoulé-région de Béoumi.* Bose, Fritz (*ed.*), Jahrbuch für Musikalische Volks u. Völkerkunde, vol. 1, 1963, 48–99. Berlin: Walter de Gruyter.

2033. **Reynolds, Barrie.** *Iron gongs from Northern Rhodesia.* Man, **58**, 255, 1958, 194–5, ill., map.

2034. **Schweeger-Hefel, A.** *Les insignes royaux des Kouroumba (Haute-Volta).* J. soc. africanistes, **32**, 1962, 275–323, bibl., ill. [Bells, pp. 315–20.]

2034a. **Simmonds, Donald C.** *Efik iron gongs and gong signals.* Man, **55**, no. 117, 1955, 107–8, ill.

2035. **Törnberg, Gerda.** *Afro-Cuban rattles.* Miscelanea de Estudios dedicados a Fernando Ortiz, vol. 3, 1957, 1417–25, ill.

2036. **Walton, James.** *Iron gongs from the Congo and Southern Rhodesia.* Man, **55**, no. 30, 1955, 20–23, ill.; **56**, no. 20, 1956, 16.

2037. **Wheeler, A. J.** *Gongs and bells.* Hastings, James (*ed.*), Encyclopaedia of religion and ethics, **6**, 1913, 316.

XYLOPHONES

2038. **Ankermann, Bernhard.** *Ethnographische Forschungsreise im Grasland von Kamerun.* Z. f. Ethnol., **17**, 1910, 309, ill.

2038a. **Anon.** *An African dulcitone: the Marimba played in the Ambaca region of Angola.* The Field, 24 June, 1922, 878.

2039. **Bellile.** *Notes sur la musique orientale: lettres et photographies du Haut-Sénégal et de Batavia.* Rev. musicale, **5**, 1905, 564–5, ill.

2040. **Boone, Olga.** 1936. *Les xylophones du Congo belge.* Pp. 73–144, ill., maps. Tervuren: Musée Royal de l'Afrique Centrale.

2041. **Burrows, Guy.** 1898. *The land of pigmies.* Pp. xxx + 299, ill. London: C. Arthur Pearson. [P. 58, plate of xylophone.]

2041a. **Davidson, M.** *A Lunda Kalendi.* Afr. mus. soc., **3** (2), 1963, 15–16, ill.

2042. **De Ganay, Solange.** *Le xylophone chez les Sara du Moyen Chari.* J. soc. africanistes, **12**, 1942, 203–39, ill.

2043. **Demanet, L Abbé.** 1767. *Nouvelle histoire de l'Afrique française* [2 vols.]. Vol. 1, pp. xxxi + 266, maps. Vol. 2, pp. 352. Paris: Duchesne. [Vol. 2, pp. 69–70, description of a xylophone.]

2044. **Evrard, W.** *Sur les xylophones africains.* Brousse, **2**, 1940, 15–21, ill.

2045. **Fagg, William.** *A Yoruba xylophone of unusual type.* Man, **50**, 234, 1950, p. 145, ill.

2047. **Froger, Francois.** 1698. *Relation of a voyage made in . . . 1695.* Pp. – . Gillyflower. [Description of a xylophone seen near Gorea.]

2048. **Gilbert, Will G.** *De cultuurhistorische beteekenis van de Marimba.* De Wereld der Muziek, **9**, 1943, 344.

2049. —— *Marimba.* A.M.E., 1957, 465–6, ill.

2050. **Herzog, George.** *Canon in West African xylophone melodies.* J. Amer. mus. soc., **2** (3), 1949, 196–7.

2051. **Heins, E. L.** *Exotics in Music, 2 Marimba (African Xylophone).* Kultuurpatronen, **1**, 1959, 125–6.

2052. **Husmann, H.** *Marimba u. Sansa der Sambesikultur.* Z.f. Ethnol. **68**, 1938, 1–3, 197–210.

2054. **Johnson, Amandus.** 1929. *In the land of the marimba.* Pp. – . Stockholm: . . . .

2056. —— *Indonesia and Africa; the xylophone as a culture-indicator.* J. roy. anthrop. inst., **89**, 2, 1959, 156–68, map.

2057. **Junod, Henri-Philippe.** 1936. *The Vachopi of Portuguese East Africa.* Pp. 39–58, bibl., ill. Cambridge: Deighton, Bell. [Xylophones, pl. 70, and orchestra, pl. 71.] [Bantu tribes of South Africa, vol. 4, sec. 2.]

2058. **Kamitin, F. R.** *The Rongo.* Sudan notes and records, **28**, 1947, 179–80, ill.

2059. **Kammerer, R.** *Marimba.* Musical America, **81**, 1961, 11– .

2060. **Kubik, Gerhard.** *The structure of Kiganda xylophone music.* Afr. mus. soc., **2** (3), 1960, 6–30, ill.

2061. —— *The endara xylophone of Bukonjo.* Afr. mus. soc., **3**, 1, 1962, 43–48.

2061a. —— *Discovery of a troughxylophone in Northern Mozambique,* Afr. mus. soc., **3** (2), 1963, 11–14.

2062. **Laurenty, J. S.** *Note sur un xylophone Pende.* Congo-Tervuren, **5**, 1, 1959, 16–18, ill.

2063. **Maes, J.** *Xylophone des Bakuba.* Man, **12**, no. 46, 1912, 90–93, ill.

2064. —— *Xylophones du Congo belge.* Rev. Cong., 1912, 116–23, ill.

2065. **Nadel, Siegfried F.** *Zur Ethnographie des afrikanischen Xylophons.* Forsch. u. Fortschritte [Leipzig], **35–36**, 1932, 444–5, map.

2066. —— 1931. *Marimba-Musik.* Pp. 65, ill. [Aus den Sitz.-Ber. philos.-hist. Kl. Akad. Wissensch. Wien, Bd. 212, 3. Abh. separat abgedruckt.] Wien and Leipzig: Holder-Pichler-Tempsky [62. Mitt. der Phonogrammarchivs Kommission].

2067. **Nicolas, Francois-J.** *Origine et valeur du vocabulaire désignant les xylophones africains.* Zaire, **11** (1), 1957, 69–89.

2068. **Pepper, H.** *Sur un xylophone Ibo.* Afr. mus. soc., Newsletter, **1**, 5 June 1952, 35–38.

2069. **Santos Rufino, José dos.** 1929. *Albuns fotogràficos e descritivos . . . da . . . colónia de Moçambique.* Vol. 10, p. 30, ill. Hamburg: Broschek.

2070. **Smith, William.** 1745. *A new voyage to Guinea* (1744). Pp. 21, ill. London: Nowell. [P. 21, xylophone. The volume of drawings (thirty different drafts of Guinea) is an exact contemporary representation of the British forts of the African Company.]

2071. **Stannus, Hugh Stannus.** *A rare type of musical instrument from Central Africa.* Man, **20**, no. 20, 1920, 37–39, ill.

2072. **Tracey, Hugh T.** *Marimbas: Os xilofones dos Changanes.* Moçambique, **31**, Outubro 1942, 49–61, ill.

2073. **Trilles, Henri.** *La marimba et l'anzang.* Rev. musicale, **5**, 1905, 473.

2074. **Vela, David.** *Noticia sobre la marimba, instrumento representativo de Guatemala.* La marimba en el Africa. El Imparcial [Guatemala], 23 Sept. 1953.

LITHOPHONES

2075. **Fagg, Bernard E. B.** *The cave paintings and rock gongs of Birnin Kudu.* Proc. 3rd Pan-African congress of prehistory held at Livingstone, 1955, 306–12, ill., map.

2076. —— *The rock gong complex today and in prehistoric times.* J. hist. soc. Nigeria, **I**, 1, Dec. 1956, 27–42, ill.

2077. —— *The discovery of multiple rock gongs in Nigeria.* Man, **56**, no. 23, 1956, 17–18, ill., map. [Reprint in African music, **I** (3), 1956.]

2078. —— *Rock gongs and rock slides.* Man, **57**, nos. 32 and 142, 1957, 30–32, 112, ill.

2079. **Goodwin, A. J. H.** *Rock-gongs, chutes, paintings and fertility.* S. Afr. archaeol. Bull., **12**, 1957, 37–40, ill.

2080. **Jeffreys, M. D. W.** *Rock gongs or sounding stones,* S. Afr. archaeol. bull., **14**, 55, Sept. 1959, 111–12.

2081. **King, Anthony.** *A report on the use of stone clappers for the accompaniment of sacred songs.* Afr. mus. soc., **2**, 4, 1961, 64–71.

2082. **Lanning, E. C.** *A ringing rock associated with rainmaking, Uganda (Mawogola county).* S. Afr. archaeol. bull., **13**, 51, Sept. 1958, 83–84, ill.

2083. **Mauny, Raymond.** *Nouvelles pierres sonnantes d'Afrique occidentale.* Notes afr. IFAN, 79. juil. 1958, 65–66, ill.

2084. **Robinson, K. R.** *Venerated rock gongs and the presence of rock slides in Southern Rhodesia.* S. Afr. archaeol. bull., **13**, 50, June 1958, 75–77.

2085. **Morton-Williams, P.** *A cave painting, rock gong and rock slide in Yorubaland.* Man, **57**, no. 213, 1957, 170–1, ill.

2086. **Vaughan, James.** *Rock paintings and rock gongs among the Marghi of Nigeria.* Man, **62**, no. 83, 1962, 49–52, ill.

2087. **Walton, James.** *Villages of the paramount chiefs of Basutoland,* (I) *Butha Buthe.* Le Sotho, **I**, 1959, 15–21, ill.

SANSAS

2088. **Blacking, John.** *Patterns of Nsenga kalimba music.* Afr. mus. soc., **2** (4), 1961, 26–43.

2089. —— and **Raymond Apthorpe.** *Fieldwork co-operation in the study of Nsenga music and ritual.* Africa, **32** (1), 1962, 72–73.

2090. **Brisley, Thomas.** *Some notes on the Baoulé tribe.* J. Afr. soc., **8**, 1909, 300.

2091. **Cabrita, Carlos L. Antunes.** 1954. *Em Terras de Luenas.* Pp. 195, ill. Lisbon: Agência Geral do Ultramar. [P. 165.]

2092. **Fraser, Douglas.** 1927. *Through the Congo Basin.* Pp. xii + 283, ill., maps. London: H. Jenkins.

2093. **Gilbert, Will G.** *Sansa.* A.M.E., 1957, 219.

2094. **Husmann, Heinrich.** *Marimba und Sansa der Sambesikultur.* Z. f. Ethnol., **68** (1–3), 1936, 197–210.

2094a. —— *Zur Kurt Reinhards 'Tonmessungen an fünf ostafrikanischen Klimpern'.* Die Musikforschung, **5**, 1952, 218.

2095. —— *Nochmals die Mwere-Sansen.* Die Musikforschung, **6**, 1953, 49– .

2096. **Jones, A. M.** *The kalimba of the Lala tribe, Northern Rhodesia.* Africa, **20**, 4, Oct. 1950, 324–33, ill.

2097. **Jourdain, M.** *Un instrument du pays Bobo (Haute Volta).* L'Anthropologie, **42**, 1932, 676.

2098. **Junod, Henri Philippe.** *The mbila or native piano of the Tsopi tribe.* Bantu stud., **3** (3), 1929, 275–85, ill.

2099. **Kerr, Walter Montagu.** 1886. *The far interior* (2 vols.). Vol. 1, pp. 316, ill. Vol. 2, pp. 318, ill., map. London: Sampson Low.

2100. **Kirby, Percival R.** *Note on Hornbostel 'The ethnology of African sound instruments.,* Africa, **7**, 1934, 107–9. [Origin of Sansa.]

2101. **La Caille, Nichlas Louis de.** 1763. *Journal historique du voyage fait au Cap de Bonne Esperance.* Pp. 192–3. Paris: Guillyn.

2102. **Laurenty, J. S.** 1962. *Les Sanza du Congo* [2 vols.]. Pp. xiii + 249, bibl., ill., maps. Tervuren: Musée Royal del'Afrique Centrale. [Annales ser. in 4, Sciences humaines, 3.]

2103. **Macdonald, Duff.** 1882. *Africana or the heart of heathen Africa* [2 vols.]. Vol. 1, Native customs and beliefs, pp. xvi + 301, ill. Vol. 2, Mission life, pp. ix + 371, ill. London: Simpkin Marshall. [Sansa, vol. 1, p. 272.]

2104. **Mackenzie, John.** 1871. *Ten years north of the Orange River.* Pp. xix + 523, ill., maps. Edinburgh: Edmonston & Douglas. [Sansa, p. 355.]

2105. **Maes, Joseph.** *Notes sur quelques objets des Pygmées-Wambuti.* Anthropos, **6**, 1911, 135.

2106. —— *La sanza au Congo belge.* Congo [Brussels], **I**, 1921, 542–72, ill., map. [Distribution map of the four types.]

2107. **Mathers, E. P.** 1891. *Zambesia.* Pp. vii + 480, ill., maps. London: King, Sell & Railton. [Sansa, p. 386]

2108. **Monard, A.** *Voyage de la mission suisse en Angola, 1928–29.* Bull. Soc. Neuchât. géog., **39**, 1930, 43–44, ill.

2109. **Montandon, Georges.** *La généalogie des instruments de musique et les cycles de civilisation.* Archiv. suisses anthrop. générale, **3** (1), 1919, 1–71, ill. [Describes a sanza d'Amérique, pp. 40–41.]

2110. **New York: Metropolitan Museum of Art.** 1914. *Catalogue of the musical instruments of Oceania and America by Frances Morris.* New York: The Museum. [P. 243, Ewbank., Life in Brazil, pp. 92, 111 and 112, 117, illustrates and describes the sansa, an instrument in common use among the slaves, who play African airs upon it.]

2111. **Pepper, Herbert.** *Le sanzi compagnon dans la solitude.* Tropiques, no. 316, 1949.

2112. —— *Notes sur une sanza d'Afrique equatoriale.* Ortiz, Fernando, Miscelanea de Estudios dedicados a *Fernando Ortiz,* vol. 2, 1956, 1191–1201, ill.

2113. **Redinha, José.** 1953–55. *Campanha Etnografica au Tchiboco (Alto Tchicapa).* Pp. 99, ill., maps. Lisbon: Museu do Dundo.

2114. **Roumeguère-Eberhardt, Jacqueline.** 1963. *Pensée et société Africaines.* Chap. 55, pp. 63–76, ill. Paris: Mounton & Co. The Hague: Cahiers de L'homme, N.S. 3. [Morphologie, symbolisme et usage d'un instrument de musique Lemba: leurs rapports avec la mythologie et la structure sociale.]

2115. **Santos, Junior, Norberto.** *Contribuicão para o estudo dos instrumentos (musicais) dos indígenas de Mocambique—A chitata.* Garcia de Orta, **6** (2), 1958, 347–64, ill. [English summary.]

2116. —— *Contribuicão para o estudo dos instrumentos musicais dos indigenas de Mocambique—O Pango, ou panco.* Garcia de Orta, **6** (3), 1958, 527–34, ill. [English summary.]

2117. **Tönjes, Hermann.** 1911. *Ovamboland.* Pp. viii + 316. Berlin: Martin Warneck. [Sansa and drum, pp. 81–84.]

2118. **Tracey, Andrew.** *Mbira music of Jege A. Tapera.* Afr. mus. soc., **II** (4), 1961, 44–63, ill.

2119. —— *Three tunes for Mbira dza Vadzimu,* Afr. mus. soc. **3** (2), 1963, 23–26, ill.

2120. **Tracey, Hugh T.** *The tuning of musical instruments.* Nada, Bulawayo, **13**, 1935, 35–44, ill. [Mashona methods of tuning a sansa.]

2121. —— *A case for the name Mbira.* Afr. mus. soc., **2**, 4, 1961, 17–25.

2122. **Werner, Alice.** 1933. *Myths and legends of the Bantu.* Pp. 335, bibl., ill. London: Harrap. [Pp. 240, 284.]

2123. **Wessmann, R.** *The Bawenda of the Spelonken, Transvaal.* African World [London], 1908, 154, ill., map.

SLIT-DRUMS AND MEMBRANE DRUMS

2124. **Adandé, A.,** and **P. Verger.** *Tam-tam avohu.* Notes Afr. I.F.A.N., no. 59, 1953, 72–76, ill.

2125. **Adolf Friedrich, Duke of Mecklenburg.** 1912. *Vom Kongo zum Niger und Nil.* Vol. 1, pp. 57. Leipzig: Brockhaus.

2126. **Alapini, Julien.** *Note sur les tam-tams dahoméennes.* L'Education Afrique, **27**, 1938, 50–56.

2127. **Albert, A.** *Chez les Banjouns.* Missions catholiques, **71**, 3315, 1939, 301–3. [Sortes de tronçons d'arbres creux, servant de gong et sur quelques moyens de correspondre.]

2128. **Allan, George.** 1885. *Notes of life in the Cameroons.* Pp. 52–53, ill. Newcastle upon Tyne: Reid.

2129. **Anon.** *Le langage tambouriné en Fang.* Courier (UNESCO), nos. 112–13, 1950, 4.

2130. **Anon.** *Les tambours.* Congo illus., **19**, 1893, 152, ill.

2131. **Armstrong, Robert G.** *Talking drums in the Benue-Cross River region of Nigeria.* Phylon [Atlanta, Georgia], **15**, 4, 1954, 355–62.

2132. —— *Talking instruments in West Africa.* Exploration, **4**, 1955, 140–53.

2133. **Avermaet, E. van.** *Les tons en kiluba samba et le tambour-téléphone.* Aequatoria, 8, 1945, 1–12.

2134. **Baker, Richard St. Barbe.** 1949. *Tambours africains.* Pp. 239, ill. Paris: Stock. [2nd ed.]

2135. —— *Africa drums.* Pp. 159, ill. London: Lindsay Drummond. [1951 (rev. ed.) London: G. Ronald.]

2137. **Bascom, Wm.** 1953. *Drums of the Yoruba of Nigeria: introduction and notes on the recordings.* Ethnic Folkways Library Album P441. Pp. 6, ill. New York: Folkways Records & Service Corp.

2138. **Basile, Frère.** 1949. *Aux rythmes des tambours: la musique chez les Noirs d'Afrique.* Pp. 172, ill. Montréal: Frères du Sacré-Coeur.

2139. **Beier, H. Ulli.** *The talking drums of the Yoruba.* Afr. mus. soc., **I**, 1954, 29–31, ill.

2140. —— *Three igbin drums from Igbomina.* Nigeria magazine, no. 78, 1963, 154–63, ill.

2141. *The language of the tom-toms.* Belgian Congo of to-day, **2** (3), 1953, 88–91, ill.

2143. **Bernatzik, Hugo Adolf.** *Meine Expedition nach Portugiesisch Guinea.* Atlantis [Leipzig], **1**, 1932, 197–208, ill.

2144. **Betz, R.** *Die Trommelsprache der Duala.* Mitt. Schutz., **11**, 1898, 1–86, ill.

2145. **Bland-Sutton, J.** 1911. *Man and beast in eastern Ethiopia.* Pp. xii + 419, ill. London: Macmillan. [Chap. vii, pp. 83–91, drums, ill.]

2146. **Boelaert, E.** *De Zwarte telefoon.* Congo, **I** (3), 1933, 356–64.

2147. **Bohannan, Laura and Paul.** 1953. *The Tiv of Central Nigeria.* Pp. viii + 100, bibl., map. London Ethnographic Survey of Africa, Western Africa, part 8. International African Institute [Pp. 35–37, drums.]

2148. **Boone, Olga.** 1951. *Les tambours du Congo belge et du Ruanda-Urundi.* Pp. 122, ill., maps. Tervuren: Musée royale du Congo Belge. [Ann. mus. Congo, N.S. in 4, no. 1.]

2149. **Brandel, Rose.** *The African hemiola style.* Ethnomusicology, **III** (3), 1959, 106–17.

2150. **Braunholtz, H. J.** *War drum from Khartoum.* B.M.Q., **12**, 1937–8, 7–9.

2151. **Bryant, Alfred T.** 1905. *Zulu-English dictionary.* Pp. 778. Pinetown, Natal: Mariannhill Mission Press.

2152. **Buchholz, R.** 1876. *Land und Leute in Westafrika* [Samm. Gemein. Wiss. Vorträge Virchow und Wattenbach, ser. 11, heft 257]. Pp. 46–47. Hamburg:............

2153. **Buchner, Max.** 1887. *Kamerun.* Pp. 37–38. Leipzig: Dunker.

2154. **Burssens, A.** *Le luba, langue à intonation, et le tambour-signal.* Proc. 3rd int. Congress of phonetic science [Ghent], 1938, 503–7, ill.]

2155. **Calame-Griaule, Geneviève.** *Note complémentaire sur le symbolisme du tambour kunyu (Soudan français).* Notes Afr., I.F.A.N., no. 72, 1956, 121–3.

2156. **Carrington, John F.** *The drum language of the Lokele tribe.* Afr. studies, **3**, 2, June 1944, 75–88.

2157. —— *The initiation language: Lokele tribe.* Afr. studies, **6**, 4, Dec. 1947, 196–207.

2158. —— 1949. *Talking drums of Africa.* Pp. 96, illus. London: Carey Kingsgate Press.

2159. —— *A comparative study of some Central African gong-languages.* I.R.C.B. (sciences morales), **18** (3), 1949, 119, bibl., ill., maps.

2160. —— *Individual names given to talking-gongs in the Yalemba area of Belgian Congo.* Afr. mus. soc., **I** (3), 1956, 10–17, map.

2161. —— *La transmission de messages par 'tam-tam'.* Probl. Afr. centr., **9**, 32, 1956, 86–94, ill.

2162. —— *Four-toned announcements on Mbole talking gongs.* Afr. mus. soc. [Roodeport], **I**, 4, 1957, 23–26.

2163. **Chapin, J. P.** *The travels of a talking drum.* Nat. hist., **50**, 1942, 63–68.

2164. **Cleather, Gabriel G.** *The musical aspects of drums.* J. roy. soc. arts, **57**, 1909.

2165. **Courlander, Harold.** 1954. *African and Afro-American drums.* Folkways Records, P502.

2166. **Crawley, Alfred Ernest.** *Drums and cymbals.* Hastings, James (ed.)., Encyclopaedia of religion and ethics, vol. 5, 1912, 89–94.

2167. —— 1931. *Dress, drinks and drums* . . . [Ed. by T. Besterman.] Pp. x + 274. London: Methuen.

2168. **Cudjoe, S. D.** *The techniques of Ewe drumming and the social importance of music in Africa.* Phylon [Atlanta, Georgia], **14**, 3, 1953, 280–91.

2169. **Cuney-Hare, Maud.** *The drum in Africa.* The Metronome [New York], **34**, 1918.

2170. **D.M.M.** *La signalisation chez les Baribas de Kandi, Dahomey* [par M.M.D.]. Notes afr., I.F.A.N., no. 23, 1944, 7.

2171. **Daniel, F. de F.** *The regalia of Katsina.* J. Afr. Soc., **31**, 1932, 80–83, ill. [P. 82, The batchelor drum of Katsina and other drums.]

2172. **da Offeio, Francesco.** *Proverbi Abissini in Lingua Tigray.* Anthropos, **1**, 1906, 296–301, ill. [Fig. 3, Tamburini per il canto sacro.]

2173. **DeHen, F. J.** 1955. *Tam-tams in Belgisch Kongo.* Pp. 147, ill., map. Antwerp: Licentiaatsverhandeling: Universitair Inst. voor Overzeese Gebieden, Akademiejaar 1954–5.

2174. —— *Les tambours à fente Congolais.* Kultuur Patronen [Patterns of culture, Delft], 3–4, 1961, 141–221, bibl., ill., maps.

2175. **Dennett, R. E.** 1906. *At the back of the black man's mind.* Pp. xv + 288, ill. London: Macmillan. [Pp. 72–73, 76–78, 191.]

2176. **Dieterlen, Germaine.** *La morphologie et la symbolique de deux instruments de musique Bambara: la guitare du Sema et le tambour royal.* C. R. Sommaires Séances Inst. franc, Anthrop. [Paris], 3 Jan. 1947, Dec. 1949, 13–14.

2177. **Djan [O.S. edited by M. S. Cockin].** *Drums and victory: Africa's call to the empire.* J. roy. Asiat. soc., **41** (162), 1942, 29–41.

2178. **Drost, Dietrich.** *Tönerne Trommeln in Afrika.* Jb. S. Mus. Völkerkunde [Leipzig], **14**, 1955 (1956), 31–61, ill.

2179. **Fabry, Hermann.** *Aus dem Leben der Wapogoro.* Globus [Brunswick], **91**, 1907, 218–19.

2180. **Fagg, William B.** *A drum probably from the Ivory Coast.* B.M.Q., **15**, 1941–50, 109.

2181. —— *Further note on a West African drum.* B.M.Q., **21**, 1957–9, 107.

2182. **Ffoulkes, Arthur.** *The company system in Cape Coast Castle.* J. Afr. soc., **7**, 1908, 267, 272.

2183. **Fisch, Rudolf.** *Die Dagbamba.* Baessler Archiv., **3**, 1913, 132–64.

2184. **Fischer, Heinrich.** *Die Trommeln von Wuwulo.* Stuttgart: Jahr. Ver. Handelsgeogr, **24–25** (1905–6), 1907, 79–86.

2185. **Fortes, M.** *Ritual festivals and social cohesion in the hinterlands of the Gold Coast.* Amer. Anthrop., **38**, 1936, 595– .

2186. **Fourneau, Jacques.** *Des transmissions acoustiques chez les indigènes du Sud-Cameroun.* Togo-Cameroun, 1930, 387–8.

2187. **Francois, Curt von.** 1888. *Die Erforschung der Tschuapa und Lulongo.* Pp. 101. Leipzig: Brockhaus.

2188. **Frobenius, Leo.** *Über Trommeln.* Mutter Erde, **3** (1899).

2189. **Gamory-Dubourdeau, P. M.** *Notice sur les coutumes des Toma.* Bull. com. étud. A.O.F., 1926, 288–350. [La signalisation sonore, pp. 345–50.]

2190. **Gani, O.** *Notes sur les coutumes funéraires des Pila.* Études Dah., **4**, 1950, 13–21.

2191. **Gbeho, Phillip.** *Africa's drums are more than tom-toms.* W.A.R., **22**, 1951, 1150.

2192. —— *Beat of the master drum.* W.A.R., **22**, 1951, 1263.

2193. —— *African music deserves generous recognition.* W.A.R., **22**, 1951, 910.

2194. **Germann, Paul.** *Zwei Trommeln aus Dahomey im Leipziger Museum für Völkerkunde.* Jb. S. mus. Völkerkunde [Leipzig], **11**, 1952 (1953), 101–5, ill.

2195. **Gide, André.** *Afrikanische Flussfahrt.* Atlantis [Leipzig], **1**, 1929, 204–5, ill. [Ill. of tom-tom.]

2196. **Gilbert, Dorothy R.** *The lukumbi: a six-toned slit drum of the Batelela.* Afr. mus. soc., **1**, 2, 1955, 21–23.

2197. **Gilbert, Will G.** *Trommel: Buiten-Europa Trommeltypen.* A.M.E., 1957, 569–74, ill.

2198. **Giorgetti, Filiberto.** *Musica e tamburi fra gli Azande.* Nigrizia, **70**, 1951, 15–18, ill.

2199. **Good, A. I.** *Drum talk.* Nat. hist., **50**, 1942, 69–74, ill.

2200. **Griaule, Marcel.** *Symbolisme des tambours soudanais.* Mélanges d'histoire et d'esthétique musicales offerts à Paul-Marie Masson, tome 1, 1955, 79–86.

2201. **Grootaert, J. E. A.** *Pensées autour d'un tam-tam lokombe (Mutetela).* Brousse, **3/4**, 1946, 20–22.

2202. **Guillemin, Le R. P.** *Le tambour d'appel des Ewondo.* Études Cam., nos. 21–22, 1948, 69–84.

2203. **Hall, Henry Usher.** *Notes on some Congo and West African woodcarvings.* Mus. J. phil., **14**, 1923, 101–34, ill.

2204. —— *A drum from Benin.* Mus. J. phil., **19**, 1928, 130–43, ill.

2205. **Harris, P. G.** *Notes on drums and musical instruments seen in Sokoto province, Nigeria.* J. roy. anthrop. inst., **62**, 1932, 105–25.

2206. **Heath, D. F.** *Bussa regalia (drums and kettle drums, etc.).* Man, **37**, no. 91, 1937, 77–80, ill.

2207. **Heepe, M.** *Die Trommelsprache der Jaunde in Kamerun.* Z. f. Eingeb.-Sprachen, 1919–20, 43–60.

2208. **Heinitz, Wilhelm.** *Die Trommelsprache in Afrika und in der Südsee* [in collab. with Prof. Thilenius and Prof. Meinhof]. Vox, **4**, 1916, 179.

2208a. —— *Musikinstrumente und Phonogramme des Ost-Mbam-Landes.* F. M. Thorbecke, Im Hochland von Mittelkamerun, vol. 3.

2209. —— *Zum Problem der afrikanischen Trommelsprache.* Afr.-Rdsch., **6** (10), 1941, 142–3.

2210. —— *Probleme der Afrikanischen Trommelsprache.* Beitr. Kol.-Forschung, **4**, 1943, 69–100, ill.

2211. **Henry, B.** *De telefoon van de Congolese wildernis.* Ontwakend Afrika, **22**, no. 71, 1957, 7– .

2212. **Herold, Captain.** [Letter concerning a Togo drum.] Ethnol. Notizbl., **1**, 1895, 39–40, ill.

2213. **Herzog, George.** *Remarks on Ovimbundu singing and drumming.* Hambly, W. D., The Ovimbundu of Angola [Field Museum of Natural History, Anthrop. series 21, 1934, pp. 217, 219, 223; pls. 25, 26, 27].

2214. —— *Drum-signalling in a West African tribe.* Word, 1945, 317–38.

2215. **Hickmann, Hans.** *Miscellanea musicologica.* 10. *Le tambourin rectangulaire du nouvel empire.* Ann. service, antiq. Égypte, **51**, 1951, 317–33, ill.

2216. —— *La Daraboukah.* Bull. de l'inst. d'Égypte, **33**, 1952, 229.

2217. —— *La musique polyphonique dans l'Égypte ancienne.* Bull. de l'inst. d'Égypte, **34**, 1953, 229.

2218. —— *Die Gefässtrommeln der Aegypter.* Mitt. Deutschen Archaeol. Inst. Abt. Kairo, **14**, 1956. Wiesbaden: Festschrift H. Kees.

2219. **Hives, Frank.** 1930. *Ju-ju and justice in Nigeria.* Pp. xi + 254, ill., map. London: J. Lane.

2220. —— 1932. *Justice in the jungle.* Pp. ix + 239. London: J. Lane.

2221. **Holub, Emil.** 1890. *Von der Capstadt ins Land der Maschukulumbe* [2 vols.]. Vol. 2, p. 83. Vienna: Holder.

2222. **Hornbostel, Erich von.** *Trommeln und Trommelsprache.* Schnee, H. (*ed.*), Deutsches Koloniallexikon, vol. 3, 1920, 536–7.

2223. **Hulstaert, G.** *De telefoon der Nkundo.* Anthropos, **30**, 5–6, 1935, 655–68.

2224. **Hunter, G.** *Hidden drums in Singida district.* Tanganyika notes and records, **34**, Jan. 1953, 28–32, ill., map.

2225. **Ilunga, Camille L.** *Téléphone-tambour en Afrique centrale.* Voix du congolais [Léopoldville], **134**, 1957, 339–40.

2226. **Inforcongo.** *The royal drums of Ruanda.* Belgian Congo today, no. 3, 1953, 103–5.

2227. **Ingrams, William Harold.** 1960. *Uganda.* Pp. xvi + 365, ill., maps. London: H.M.S.O. [Drums.]

2228. **Jacobs, J.** *Signaaltrommeltaal bij de Tetela.* Kongo-Overzee, **20**, 4/5, 1954, 409–22.

2229. —— *Le message tambouriné, genre de littérature orale bantoue (Tetela, Sankuru, Congo belge).* Kongo-Overzee, **25**, 2/3, 1959, 90–91.

2230. —— and **B. Omeonga.** *Le bois qui parle.* Jeune Afr., **32**, 1960, 25–33, ill.

2231. **Jahn, Janheinz.** *World congress of black writers.* P. 40, E. L. Lasebikan demonstrates the Yoruba talking drum. Black Orpheus, no. 1, 1957, 39–46, ill.

2232. **Jones, A. M.** 1934. *African drumming.* Bantu stud., **8**, 1–16.

2233. —— *Drums down the centuries.* Afr. mus. soc., **1** (4), 1957, 4–10.

2234. **Kamal, Prince Youssouf.** 1926–51. *Monumenta cartographica Africae et Aegypti* [16 vols.]. Pp. 1684. Cairo and Leiden: Brill. [P. 953, Tambours énormes pour le commerce muet de l'or.]

2235. **Kappe, G.** *Tanz und Trommel der Neger.* Festschrift zum 70. Geburtstage von H. H. Schauinsland [Bremen], 1927, 64–67.

2236. **Karsten, Paula.** *Musikinstrumente fremder Völker.* 8, *Die Tambura der Sudan-Neger.* D. Instrbau Ztg. [Berlin], **10**, 1909, 95–96.

2237. **Kirby, P. R.** *The drums of the Zulu.* S. Afr. J. of Science, **29**, 1932, 655–9, ill.

2238. —— *The kettle-drum.* London: Oxford Univ. Press.

2239. —— *South African native drums.* S.A.M.B., **3**, 1943, 42.

2240. **Kirk-Greene, Anthony.** *Makidi—the Hausa drummer.* Nigeria Magazine, **71**, Dec. 1961, 338–55, ill.

2241. **Krause, Edouard.** *Die ältesten Pauken.* Globus [Brunswick], **78**, 1900, 193–6, ill.

2242. **Krige, E. Jensen,** and **J. D. Krige.** 1943. *The realm of a rain-queen.* Pp. xv + 335, ill., map. London: Oxford Univ. Press for the International African Institute. [Drums, p. 126.]

2243. **Labouret, H.** *Langage tambouriné et sifflé.* Bull. com. étud. A.O.F., 1923, 120–58, ill.

2244. —— *La langage tambouriné en Afrique centrale.* Congo, **2**, 4, nov. 1923, 587–92.

2245. —— and **A. Schaeffner.** *Un grand tambour de bois Ebrié (Côte d'Ivoire).* Bull. mus. ethnog. troc., **2**, 1931, 48–55.

2246. **Laoyel, Timi of Ede.** *Yoruba drums.* Nigeria, no. 45, 1954, 4–13, ill.

2247. —— *Yoruba drums.* Odu, no. 7, 1959, 5–14, ill.

2248. **Laszlo, Andras E.** 1956. *Doctors, drums and dances.* Pp. 286, ill., map. London: R. Hale.

2248a. **Lewis, Roy.** 1954. *Sierra Leone.* Pp. ix + 263, ill., maps. London: H.M.S.O.

2249. **Lhermitte, L.** *Les langages tambourinés de l'Afrique centrale.* Avenir col. Belge, 1950, 1.

2250. **Lindblom, G.** *Die Stosstrommel, insbesondere in Afrika* [a stamping tube]. Ethnos, **10**, 1, Jan.–Mar. 1945, 17–38, ill.

2251. **Lo Cascio, A.** 1940. *The tom-toms speak.* Pp. 163. Boston: Meador.

2252. **Lush, Allan J.** *Kiganda drums.* Uganda J., **3**, 1, July 1935, 7–25, ill.

2253. **Maes, J.** *Les tam-tam du Congo belge.* Rev. quest. scientif. [Bruxelles], 1912. [See 'Africa', 1934, p. 182.]

2254. —— *Un tamtam d'initiation du Haut-Kwilu.* Man, **29**, no. 128, 1929, 167–9, ill.

2255. **Mähly, E.** *Zur Geographie und Ethnographie der Goldküste.* Verhand. Naturf. Gesell. in Basel, **7/3**, 1885, 851–2.

2255a. **Marc, Lucien.** 1909. *Les Pays Mossi.* Pp. 127, ill. Paris: Larose.

2255b. **Matagne, A.** *Vraies nouvelles et fausses nouvelles.* Rev. Cong, **31** (12), 1960, 16–20, ill.

2256. **Meinhof, Carl.** *Die Geheimsprachen Afrikas.* Globus, **66**, 1894, 117–19. [Drum signalling in the Cameroons and Congo.]

2258. **Mentzel, O. F.** 1787. *Beschreibung des Vorgebirges der Guten Hoffnung* [2 vols.]. Vol. 1, Vol. 2, pp. 519. Glogau:........

2259. **Migeod, F. W. H.** *Mendi drum signals.* Man, **20**, no. 22, 1920, 40–41.

2260. **Milheiros, Mario.** *O tom nas palavras gentilicas.* Mensario admin., **18**, Fev. 1949, 15–16.

2261. **Monod, Th.** *Un résonateur inusité.* Notes Afr., I.F.A.N., **20**, 1943, 3, ill.

2262. **Moreno Moreno, José A.** *El 'Yangüe' Fernandino.* Africa [Madrid], 83/84, Nobr.–Dic. 1948, 411–12, ill.

2263. **N'Doye, M. C.** *Le son du tabala dans le Rip.* Notes Afr., I.F.A.N., no. 38, 1948, 9–10. [Drums with magical properties.]

2265. **Nekes, P. Hermann.** *Trommelsprache und Fernruf bei den Jaunde und Duala in Südkamerun.* Mitt. Sem. Orient. Sprach. Afr. Stud., **15**, 1912, 69–83.

2266. **Nketia, J. H. Kwabena.** *The role of the drummer in Akan society.* Afr. mus. soc., **1** (1), 1954, 34–43.

2267. —— *The poetry of drums.* Voices of Ghana [Accra], Ministry of information, 1958, 17–23; New world writing, no. 15 (June 1959), 190–7.

2268. —— *Drum proverbs.* Voices of Ghana, 1958, 49–53.

2269. —— *Drums, dance and song.* Atlantic monthly, **203**, no. 4, 1959, 67–72.

2270. —— *Drums and language:* (1) Daily Graphic, 16/5/61, 5; (2) Daily Graphic, 23/5/61, 5; (3) Daily Graphic, 2/6/61, 5; (4) Daily Graphic, 9/6/61, 5; (5) Daily Graphic, 13/6/61, 5.

2271. —— 1963. *Drumming in Akan communities of Ghana.* Pp. x + 212, bibl., ill., map. London: Nelson for Ghana Univ.

2272. **Ngoma Lungundu.** *Eine afrikanische Bundeslade.* Studia Ethnographica Upsaliensia, **5**, pp. 192.

2273. **Obama, Jean Baptiste.** *Du 'folklore' grégorien au tam-tam africain.* Africa [Rome], **18**, May–June 1963, 138–44.

2274. **Onwona-Osapo, F.** *Talking drums in the Gold Coast.* Gold Coast Teachers' J., **2**, Apr. 1957, 9–12.

2275. **Passarge, Siegfried.** *Die Mambukuschu.* Globus [Brunswick], **87**, 1905, 296, ill.

2276. **Pauwels, Marcel.** *Le kalinga, tambour enseigne du royaume et de la dynastie des rois Banyiginya (Abasindi) du Rwanda.* Ann. lateranensi, **26**, 1962, 221–56, bibl., ill., carte.

2277. **Pechuel-Loesche, Edouard.** 1882. *Die Loango-Expedition* [2 vols.]. Vol. 2, 117–19. Leipzig: Frohberg.

2278. **Peeraer, S.** *Over Seintrommels.* Bull. amis. art. indig. Kat., 1938, 1.

2279. **Pepper, H.** *Histoire contée sur un vieux tambour de Bois.* Jeune Afr., **6**, 1949, 13–16.

2280. **Perron, Michel.** *Instruments à percussion du son en Europe et en A.O.F. (Nacaires ou timbales, tambours, tam-tams).* Bull. com. étud. A.O.F., **7** (4), 1924, 692–715. ill.

2281. **Pfister, G. A.** *Les chansons historiques et le 'timpam' des Achantis.* Rev. musicale, **4**, 1923, 230–5.

2282. **Prouteaux, Maurice.** *Le culte de Séké.* Rev. Ethnog. Trad. Pop., **7**, 1931, 173–99.

2283. **Puleston, Fred.** 1930. *African drums.* Pp. 352, ill. London: V. Gollancz.

2284. **Quix, J. P.** *Au pays de Mahagi.* Congo, **1**, 1939, 387–411.

2286. **Rattray, Robert Sutherland.** 1955. *Ashanti.* Pp. 348, ill. London: Oxford Univ. Press. [2nd ed.]

2287. —— 1927. *Religion and Art in Ashanti.* Pp. xviii + 414, ill. Oxford Univ. Press.

2288. —— *The drum language of West Africa.* J. Afr. soc., **22**, 1923, 226–36, 302–16, ill.

2289. —— *What the African believes as revealed by the talking drums.* W.A.R., **6**, 1935, 12.

2291. **Reininghaus, Fr. W.** *Die Trommel- und Pfeifsprache.* Arch. Völkerkunde [Wien], **5**, 1950, 187–90.

2292. **Reynolds, F. G. B.** *The 'drum of succession' of the Emirs of Fika.* Man, **30**, no. 9, 1930, 155–6.

2293. **Roberts, Noel.** *Bantu methods of divination.* S. Afr. J. of science, **13**, 1916, 406–8. [Ritual drums.]

2294. **Robinson, A. E.** *Some notes on the regalia of the Fung Sultans of Sennar.* J. Afr. soc., **30**, 1931, 361–76, ill. [P. 369, copper nahas or kettle-drum.]

2294a. —— *Note on the sketches and notes of Bazumi Effendi.* Man, **32**, no. 300, 259–61, ill.

2295. **Rohrer, Ernst Friedrich.** *Eine Tanztrommel der Goldküste.* Jb. Bern. hist. mus., **25**, 1945, 17–24, ill.

2296. **Rose, Cowper.** 1829. *Four years in southern Africa.* Pp. 141, 146. London: Colburn. ['Kaffir' oxhide and shield-drums.]

2297. **Rose, Fr.** *De seintamtam de Baloeba's.* Africa-Christo, **6** (5), 1951, 7–9, ill.

2298. **Ryckmans, A.** *Étude sur les signaux de mondo (tambour-téléphone) chez les Bayaka et Bankanu du territoire de Popokabaka.* Zaïre, **10**, 1956, 493–515.

2299. **Schneider, Marius.** *Zur Trommelsprache der Duala.* Anthropos, **47**, 1952, 235–43.

2300. **Schweeger-Hefel, A.** *Les insignes royaux des Kouroumba (Haute-Volta).* J. soc. africanistes, **32**, 1962, 275–323, bibl., ill. [Les tambours, pp. 279–85.]

2301. **Seligmann, C. G.** *An Avungura drum.* Man, **11**, no. 7, 1911, 17.

2302. **Sicard, Harald von.** *The ancient East African Bantu drum.* Ethnos [Stockholm], **7**, 1942, 49–54.

2303. **Slevin, B.** *Le tam-tam chez les Wa-Luguru.* Ann. Pères Saint-Esprit, **55**, 1939, 23–26.

2304. **Smith, M. F.** 1954. *Baba of Karo: a woman of the Muslim Hausa.* Pp. 299, ill., map. London: Faber.

2305. **Sobchenko, A.** 1952. *Poredacha soobschenii na barabanakh u narodov zapadnoi Afriki* [The drum signals of the people of West Africa]. Moscow: Academy of Sciences of the U.S.S.R. (Inst. of Ethnog.).

2306. **Stairs, Capt.** *Les tambours (du Kassai).* Congo illus., **2**, no. 19, 1893, 150–1, ill.

2307. **Stannus, Hugh S.** *A rare type of musical instrument from Central Africa.* Man, **20**, no. 20, 1920, 37–39, ill.

2308. **Stefahiszyn, B.**, and **Others.** *Mutivi* [a drum]. Nada [Bulawayo], **27**, 1950, 56–59, ill.

2309. **Stern, Theodore.** *Drum and whistle 'languages': an analysis of speech surrogates.* Amer. anthrop., **59** (3), 1957, 487–506, bibl.

2310. **Thoonen, J. P.** 1941. *Black martyrs.* Pp. xviii + 302. London: Sheed & Ward. [P. 88 describes the Kigowa drums.]

2311. **Tracey, Hugh.** *Music of the tribes.* African drum, **1**, 1, Mar. 1951, 12–13, 48, ill. [in continuation].

2312. **Tripe, W. B.** *The death and replacement of a divine king in Uha.* Man, **39**, no. 21, 1939, 22–25, ill.

2313. **Tsala, Th.** *'Nkui' ou le tam-tam.* Presses missionaires, no. 22, 1955, 3.

2314. **Tucker, A. N.** *African alphabets and the telegraph system.* Bantu stud., **10**, 1936, 67–73.

2315. **Tucker, J. T.** 1927. *Drums in the darkness.* Toronto: Doran.

2316. **Underwood, Leon.** 1949. *Bronzes of West Africa.* Pp. 32 + 64 pls. London: Tiranti. [Plaque du Bénin représentant un joueur de tam-tam, pl. 56.]

2317. **Vancoillie, G.** *Recueil de signaux claniques ou kumbu des tribus Mbagani et du Kasai (Congo belge).* Afr. studies, **8** (1), 1949, 35–45, ill.; **8** (2), 1949, 80–99.

2318. **Van Goethem, L.** *Lokole of Tam-Tam bij de Nkundo-negers.* Congo, 1927, 711–16; Jan. 1928, 33–38; Fev. 1928, 181–7.

2319. **Vanden Plas, Joseph.** 1910. *Les Kuku.* Pp. xlii + 407, bibl., ill., map. Brussels: Institut Intern. de Bibliographie. [Collection de monographies ethnographiques, VI.] [Drum, pp. 311–12.]

2320. **Van Hoepen, A. E.** *Op soek na 'n Bawenda-Trommel.* Die Huisgenoot, **33**, 1931, 77, ill.

2321. **Van Saefthingen, W.** *Trommeltaal.* Nieuw Afrika, **71**, 3, 1955, 135–6.

2322. **van Valen, Leigh.** *Talking drums and similar African tonal communications.* Southern folklore quart., **19**, 1955, 252.

2322a. **Verbeken, A.** *La communication à distance chez les noirs* (Elizabethville, 1920).

2322b. —— *Le tambour-téléphone chez les indigènes de l'Afrique Central.* Congo, **1**, 1924, 721–8.

2323. —— *Le langage tambouriné des congolais.* Afr. mus. soc., Newsletter, **1**, 6, 1953, 28–41.

2324. —— *Le langage tembouriné des congolais.* Rev. congol., ill. **31** (9), 1960, 15–16, ill.

2325. **Westerman, Diedrich.** *La langue du tambour à Togo.* Anthropos, **1**, 1906, 665–8.

2326. —— *Zeichensprache des Ewevolkes in Deutsch-Togo.* Mitt. Sem. orient. sprach. Afr. Stud., **10** (3), 1907, 1–14.

2327. **Weule, Karl.** *Schädeltrommeln aus dem Otschigebiet.* Ethnol. Notizbl., **1**, 1896, 35–37.

2328. —— 1924. *Trommelsprache und Trommelsignale bei den Negern.* Illus. Zeitung [Berlin], **163**, 4156, S. 664. [Bezieht sich namentlich in den Abb. auf den Kongo.]

2329. **Wieschhoff, Heinz.** 1933. *Die Ausserafrikanischen Trommeln und ihre Beziehungen. Studien zur Afrikanischen Kulturkunde* Städt. Völkermuseums, Frankfurt a/M. Bd. 2, p. 148, + bibl., ill., maps. Strecker & Schröder. [Bd. 11 der Studien zur Kulturkunde.]

2330. **Wilson, W. A. A.** *Talking drums in Portuguese Guinea.* Est. Etnol. ultramar portug., **3**, 1963, 199–220, bibl., ill.

2331. **Witte, A.** *Zur Trommelsprache bei den Ewe-Leuten.* Anthropos, **5**, 1910, 50–53, ill.

2332. **Zeller, Rudolf.** *Die Goldgewichte von Asante.* Baessler-Archiv, Beiheft, **III**, 1912, 1–72, ill. [Mention of drums and other instruments on pp. 60, 62–63.]

FRICTION DRUMS AND KAZOOS

2333. **Balfour, Henry.** *The friction-drum.* J. anthrop. inst., **37**, 1907, 67–92, ill.

2334. —— *Ritual and secular uses of vibrating membranes as voice-disguisers.* J. roy. anthrop. inst., **78**, 1951, 45–69, bibl., ill.

2335. **Collaer, Paul.** *Le tambour à friction.* (11) *et Idiophones frottés.* Colloques de Wégimont, **III**, 1956, 91–104.

2336. **Maclaud, D.** *Note sur un instrument de musique employé au Fouta-Djallon, l'Anthropologie,* **19**, 1908, 271–3.

2338. **Werner, Alice.** *Some notes on the Wapokomo of the Tana Valley.* J. afr. soc., **12**, 1912–13, 375–6. ['Ngadzi- sacred friction drum.']

CHORDOPHONES

2339. **Alberti, Lodewyk.** 1810. *De Kaffers aan de Zuidkust van Afrika.* Pp. 165–6. Amsterdam: Maaskamp.

2340. **Alberti, Louis.** 1811. *Description physique et historique des Caffres sur la côte méridionale de l'Afrique.* Pp. xii + 255. Amsterdam: Maaskamp. [Pp. 165–6, Gonaquois bow instrument.]

2341. **Anon.** 1851. *Sketches of . . . various classes and tribes . . . of the Cape of Good Hope and . . . interior of South Africa with a brief account descriptive of the manners and customs of each.* S.P. 42 pls. with descriptive text. London: W. R. & Lowes Dickinson. [Pl. 35, 'A Hottentot musician' (with text). Shows musical bow, plectrum (feather) and gourd resonator: leather rings at ankles.]

2342. **Anon.** *Spielleute und Märchenerzähler Innerafrikas.* Westermanns Monatshefte [Brunswick], **115**, 1913, 573–85, ill. [Sudan harps.]

2343. **Anon.** 1922. *Un instrument soudanais—la Kora.* Encyclopédie de la musique et dictionnaire du conservatoire, ed. Lavignac, La Laurencie: vol. 5, pt. 1, pp. 3224–5. Paris.

2344. **Backhouse, James.** 1844. *A narrative of a visit to the Mauritius and South Africa.* Pp. xvi + 648, lvi, ill., maps. London: Hamilton Adams.

2345. **Balfour, Henry.** 1899. *The natural history of the musical bow.* Oxford: Oxford Univ. Press.

2346. —— *The goura: a stringed wind musical instrument of the Bushmen and Hottentots.* J. Anthrop. inst., **32**, 1902, 156.

2347. **Barnard, Lady Anne.** 1910. *South Africa a century ago (1797–1801).* Pp. x + 316. London: Smith Elder. [Pp. 259–60.]

2348. **Barrow, Sir John.** 1804. *An account of travels into the interior of southern Africa* [2 vols.]. Vol. 1, pp. viii + 419, ill., map. Vol. 2, pp. xii + 452, ill., map. London: T. Cadell & W. Davis. [Vol. 1, pp. 148–9, Goura.]

2349. **Belgian Congo of To-day.** Illustration of girl playing a 'Longoma' (musical bow), Bofete Village, Tshuapa District. Belgian Congo of to-day, **6** (1), 1957, facing p. 36.

2350. **Burchell, William J.** 1822. *Travels in the interior of southern Africa* [2 vols.]. Vol. 1, viii (iii) + 582, ill., map. Vol. 2, vi + 648, ill. London: Longman, Hurst, Rees, etc. [Goura, Vol. 1, 458, 499–500; vol. 2, 24, 45, 63–67, 287–88.]

2351. **Camp, Charles,** and **Bruno Nettl.** *The musical bow in southern Africa.* Anthropos, **50**, 1955, 65–80, ill.

2352. **Chapman, James.** 1868. *Travels in the interior of South Africa* [2 vols.]. Vol. 1, pp. xvi + 454, ill. Vol. 2, pp. xii + 480, ill., map. London: Bell & Daldy. [Vol. 1, pp. 271–2.]

2353. **de Bary, Maxime.** 1910. *Grand gibier et terres inconnues.* Pp. viii + 341, ill., map. Paris: Plon. [3rd ed.]

2354. **de Chastonay, Ph.** *Pour une systématique des instruments de musique—les chordophones.* Musées de Genève, **2**, 1960, 8–11, ill.

2355. **de Macar, Ghislain.** *Chez les Bakubas.* Congo illus., **4**, no. 21, 1895, 172–4, ill., [Pl. p. 173, 'Musicien Zappo-Zap'. Kassai.]

2356. **Demba, Coly.** *Chant mandingue de Casamance.* Notes Afr., I.F.A.N., no. 38, 1948, 22–24, ill. [P. 23, sketch of 'Corra', a kind of guitar.]

2357. **Dieterlen, Germaine.** *La morphologie et la symbolique de deux instruments de musique Bambara: la guitare du Sema et le tambour royal.* C.R. sommaires séances inst. franc. anthrop. [Paris], 3 Jan. 1947: dec. 1949, 13–14.

2358. —— 1951. *Essai sur la religion Bambara.* Pp. xx + 240, bibl., ill. Paris: Presses Univ. de France. [La harpe divinatoire du Soma, p. 222.]

2359. **Duchemin, G-J.** *Autour d'un arc musical du Saloum oriental.* 1ᵉ conf. int. africanistes de l'ouest, C.R., **2**, 1951, 248–58, ill.

2359a. **Duvelle, Charles.** *Valiha Madagascar, disques Okora,* **18**, 1964.

2360. **Farmer, Henry George.** *A North African folk instrument (Guenbri).* J. roy. Asiat. soc., 1928, 25–34, ill.

2361. —— *The origin of the Arabian lute and rebec.* J. roy. Asiat. soc., Oct. 1930, 767–83. [Studies in oriental musical instruments, 1st ser. H.]

2362. —— *An old Moorish lute tutor.* J. roy. Asiat. soc., 1931, 349–66. [Studies in oriental musical instruments, 2nd ser. C.]

2364. **Flood, Grattan.** 1905. *The story of the harp.* Pp. 228, ill. London: Scott.

2365. **Frobenius, Leo.** *Die Saiteninstrumente der Naturvölker.* Prometheus, **12**, 1901, 625–8, 648–52, ill.

2366. —— 1922. *Atlas africanus. Heft* 3, *Blatt No.* 8. [Map showing the distribution of the harp and lyre.] Munich: Beck.

2367. **Granner, Erwin.** *Ein afrikanisches Musikinstrument.* Kosmos, [Stuttgart], **10**, 1913, 269–70, ill.

2368. **Griaule, Marcel,** and **Germaine Dieterlen.** *La harpe-luth des Dogon.* J. soc. africanistes, **20**, (2), 1950, 209–27, ill.

2369. —— *Nouvelles remarques sur la harpe-luth des Dogon.* J. soc. africanistes, **24** (2), 1954, 119–22, ill.

2370. **Heinitz, Wilhelm.** *Analayse eines abessinischen Harfenliedes.* Festschrift Meinhof, 1927, 263–74.

2371. **Hickmann, Hans.** *Un instrument à cordes inconnu de l'époque copte.* Bull. soc. d'archéol. copte., **12**, 1946–7, 63.

2372. —— *Miscellanea musicologica (2) sur l'accordage des instruments à cordes (lyres, harpes, luths).* Ann. service antiq. Égypte, **48**, 1948, 649–56, ill.

2373. —— *Un luth inconnu de l'époque Copte.* Bull. soc. d'archéol. copte, **12**, 1949.

2374. —— *Quelques précurseurs égyptiens du luth court et du luth échancré.* Ann. service antiq. Égypte, **49**, 1949, 417. [Miscellanea musicologica, 6.]

2376. —— *Les harpes de la tombe de Ramsès III.* Ann. service antiq. Égypte, **50**, 1950, 523–36, ill. [Miscellanea musicologica, 7.]

2377. —— *Ein unbekanntes ägyptisches Saiteninstrument aus Koptischer Zeit.* Die Musikforschung, **3**, 1950.

2378. —— *Fragment d'un instrument à cordes.* Ann. service antiq. Égypte, **50**, 1950, 540–5, ill.

2379. —— *Das Harfenspiel im alten Aegypten.* Die Musikforschung, **5**, 1952, 21.

2380. —— *Le jeu de la harpe dans l'Égypte ancienne.* Arch. Orientální [Prague], **20** (3–4), 1952, 449.

2381. —— *Quelques documents concernant le jeu de la harpe et l'emploi de la chironomie dans l'Égypte pharaonique.* Konggressber. Intern. Ges., 1952, 263. [Amsterdam, 1953.]

2382. —— *Note sur une petite Harpe en forme de bèche ou de Pelle.* [Miscellanea musicologica, 5. 1949.]

2383. —— *Miscellanea musicologica (11) Les Luths aux frettes du nouvel Empire.* Ann. service antiq. Égypte, **52**, 1952, 161–83, ill.

2384. —— *Usage et signification des frettes dans l'Égypte pharaonique.* Kemi [Paris], **13**, 1954.

2385. —— *Miscellanea musicologica (1) Note sur une harpe au musée du Caire.*

2386. —— *Les harpes de l'Égypte pharaonique (essai d'une nouvelle classification).* Bull. de l'Inst. d'Égypte, **35**, 1954, 309.

2387. —— *A new type of Egyptian harp.* Acta musicol., 1954, 127.

2388. — *Harfe.* Blume, F. (*ed.*), Die Musik in Geschichte und Gegenwart, **5**, 1956, 1507.

2389. —— *Gitarre, Vorgeschichte und aussereuropäische Formen.* Blume, F. (*ed.*), Die Musik in Geschichte und Gegenwart, **5**, 1956, 17.

2390. **Hilberth, J.** 1962. *Les Gaya.* Pp. viii + 143, ill. Lund: Studia Ethnographica Upsaliensia 19.

2391. **Johnson, T. Broadwood.** 1912. *Tramps round the mountains of the moon.* Pp. xxiv + 316, ill., map. London: T. Fisher Unwin. [P. 242, illus. of Busoga harp.]

2392. **Johnston, Sir Harry Hamilton.** 1908. *George Grenfell and the Congo* [2 vols.]. Vol. 1, pp. xxiii + 496, ill., map. Vol. 2, pp. xx + 494 (497–990), ill., map. London: Hutchinson. [Musical bow, vol. 2, 716.]

2393. **Junod, Henri-Philippe.** 1935. *The Vathonga (the Thonga-Shangaan people).* Pp. 28, bibl., ill. Cambridge: Deighton, Bell. [Music: pl. 39, musical bow.] [Bantu tribes of South Africa, vol. 4, sec. 1.]

2393a. **Karsten, Paula.** *Musikinstrumente fremder Völker.* 8 Die Tambura der Sudan-Neger. D. instrbau. Ztg. [Berlin], **10**, 1909, 95–96.

2394. **Kirby, Percival R.** *The study of the music of the native people.* Blythswood Rev., **8** (1931), 81–82.

2395. —— *The gora and its Bantu successors: a study in South African native music.* Bantu stud., **5** (1931), 89–109, ill.

2396. —— *The mystery of the grand gom gom.* S. Afr. J. of science, **28**, 1931, 521–5, ill.

2397. —— *A further note on the gora and its successors.* Bantu stud., **9** (1), 1935, 53–62, ill.

2398. —— *The recognition and practical use of the harmonics of stretched strings by the Bantu of South Africa.* Bantu Stud., **6** (1932), 31–46, ill.

2399. **Laurenty, J. S.** 1960. *Les cordophones du Congo belge et du Ruanda-Urundi.* Pp. 230 [+ 37 planches et 5 cartes, bound separately], bibl. Tervuren: Ann. Mus. Roy. Congo Belge (sér. in-4°, sci. de l'homme, 2.)

2400. **Lehmann, Johannes.** 1925. *Beiträge zur Musikinstrumental-Forschung. Saiteninstr. Flöten. Festschrift zur Feier. 25. Jähr. Best. d. Frankfurter Ges f. Anthrop. Ethnol. u. Urgesch.* Pp. 113–25, ill. Frankfurt a/M.: Bechhold.

2401. **Lichtenstein, Henry.** 1928. *Travels in Southern Africa* [2 vols.]. Vol. 1, xxiv + 470 + x, ill. Vol. 2, xxiii + 498 + xv, map. Cape Town: Van Riebeeck Society. [Pp. 292–3, vol. 2.]

2402. **Lindblom, G.** *Notes ethnographiques sur le Kavirondo septentrional et le Colonie du Kenya.* Revista del Instituto de Ethnologia, **2**, 1932, 395–440, ill. Univ. Nacional de Tucumán.

2403. **Mackenzie, John.** 1871. *Ten years north of the Orange River.* Pp. xix + 523, ill. Edinburgh: Edmonston & Douglas.

2404. **Maes, J.** *Les Warumbi Anthropos,* **4**, 1909, 627.

2405. —— *Snaarspeeltuigen in Belgisch Congo.* Onze Kongo, **3**, 1912–13, 359–89, ill. [Stringed instruments of the Congo.]

2406. —— *Les lukombe ou instruments de musique à cordes des populations Du Kasai—lac Léopold II-Lukenie.* Z.f. ethnol, **70**, 1938, 240–54, ill.

2407. —— *Sculpture décorative ou symbolique.* Artes Africanae, 1–9.

2408. **Mahillon, V.** *Catalogue descriptif . . . du Musée au Conservatoire royal de musique.* 1893–1922, 5 vols. [Brussels, etc.]

2409. **Manoly, J.** *Les arts traditionels.* Beaux-Arts, **7**, 1937, 13–16.

2410. —— *Notules sur les manifestations artistiques des Baluba.* Bull. Amis. Arts. indig. Katanga, 1–3, 1937.

2411. **Mason, Otis Tufton.** *Geographical distribution of the musical bow.* Amer. Anthrop., **10**, 1897, 377–80.

2412. **Meinhof, Carl.** 1916. *Eine Studienfahrt nach Kordofan.* Pp. xii + 134, bibl., ill., map. [Abh. Hamburger Kol.-Inst. Band 35, p. 91.]

2413. **Moffat, Robert.** 1842. *Missionary labours and scenes in southern Africa.* Pp. xv + 624, ill., map. London: John Snow. [P. 58.]

2414. **Montandon, Georges.** *Nouveaux exemplaires africains de la cithare en radeau.* L'Anthropologie, **42**, 1932, 676–8, ill.

2415. **Oates, Frank.** 1889. *Matabeleland and the Victoria Falls.* Pp. xlix + 433, ill., maps. London: Kegan Paul. [Pp. 115, 143.] [2nd. ed.]

2416. **Percival, Robert.** 1804. *An account of the Cape of Good Hope.* Pp. xii + 339. London: C. & R. Baldwin.

2417. **Rensch, R.** 1950. *The harp.* Pp. – . New York: . . . .

2418. **Rycroft, David.** *The guitar improvisations of Mwenda Jean Bosco.* Afr. mus. soc., **2** (4), 1961, 81–98, ill.; **3**, 1, 1962, 86–101, ill.

2419. **Sachs, Curt.** *Der Ursprung der Saiteninstrumente.* Festschrift P. W. Schmidt, 1928, 629–34. Vienna: Mechitharisten-Congregations-Buchdruckerei.

2420. —— *Die altägyptische Namen der Harfe.* Festschrift-Hermann Kretschmar [Leipzig], 1918.

2421. —— *Eine aegyptische Winkelharfe.* Z. f. ägypt. Sprache u. Altertumskunde, **69**, 1933, 68.

2422. **Saint-Saëns, Camille.** *Lyres et cithares.* A. Lavignac and La Laurencie, L., Encyclopédie de la musique. Iᵉ Partie, vol. 1, 1913, 538– .

2423. **Schaeffner, André.** 1933. *Note sur la filiation des instruments à cordes.* Mélanges de musicologie offerts à M. Lionel de la Laurencie. Paris: . . . .

2424. **Stow, George W.** In Bleek, D. F., Rock paintings in South Africa, 1930; pl. 72, 'Illustration of a bushman bow'.

2425. **Ten, Kate H.** *Geographical distribution of the musical bow.* Amer. anthrop. O. S., **11**, 1898, 93.

2426. **Thomas, J.** *The harp.* Pp. 19, ill. London: Hutchings.

2427. **Thurlé, M.** *Sur les Bochimans.* Bull. soc. anthrop. [Paris], **4**, 1881, 404.

2428. **Valentyn, Francois.** 1726. *Oud en Nieuw Oost Indien.* Vol. 5, pt. 2, p. 105b. Dordrecht: van Braam. [Hottentot goura.]

2429. **Wachsmann, Klaus P.** *An equal-stepped tuning in a Ganda harp.* Nature [London], **165**, Jan. 1950, p. 4.

2430. —— *Human migration and African harps.* J. int. folk music council, **16**, 1964, 84–88, map.

2431. **Wängler, Hans-Heinrich.** *Über Südwestafrikanische Bogenlieder.* Afr. u. Übersee, **39**, 1955, 49–63; **40**, 1956, 163–74, ill.

2432. **Wallaschek, Richard.** *Urgeschichte der Saiteninstrumente.* Mitt. anthrop. Gesell. [Wien], **28** (1)–(5), 1898.

2433. **Webster, William Henry Bailey.** 1834. *Narrative of a voyage to the South Atlantic Ocean . . . 1828–30 [2 vols.].* Vol. 1, 274–5. London: Bentley.

2434. **Werner, Alice.** *On a stringed instrument obtained at Ntumbi, Nyasaland.* Bantu stud., **5**, 1931, 257.

2434a. **Wissmann, Hermann von.** *My second journey through equatorial Africa from the Congo to the Zambesi in . . . 1886 and 1887.* Pp. xiv + 326, ill., map. London: Chatto & Windus. [P. 102, aeolian harps—description and plate.]

2435. **Zahan, D.** *Notes sur un luth dogon.* J. soc. africanistes, **20**, 2, 1950, 193–207, ill., map.

AEROPHONES
(Excluding Whirling Aerophones)

2436. **Abou Hamid.** *Tufat al-albab (vers 1162). Extraits traduis en Anglais* Palmer, H. R. Sudanese memoirs, vol. 2, 1928, 119, map. Lagos: Government Printer. [P. 91.]

2437. **B., A. M.** *The ordeal of manhood.* J. Afr. soc., **15**, 1916, 250– .

2438. **Bernatzik, H. A.** 1930. *The dark continent.* Pp. xvi + 256, ill. London: The Studio. [Illus. of Niambara flute-player.]

2439. **Bodley, Nicholas B.** *A study of the Greek-Egyptian auloi found at Meroë, Egypt.* Amer. J. of arch., 2nd ser., vol. 50, 1946, 217–40, ill.

2440. **Closson, Ernest.** 1902. *L'instrument de musique comme document ethnographique.* Brussels.

2441. ——*Les conques sonores dans la préhistoire.* Guide musical, 1912. Brussels.

2442. —— 1930. *Une nouvelle série de hautbois égyptiens antiques.* Festschrift-Guido Adler, p. 17. Berlin.

2443. —— *La flûte égyptienne antique de Fétis.* Acta musicol., **4**, 1932, 145.

2444. **Culwick, G. M.** *Degeneration of a wind instrument.* Man, **34**, no. 138, 1934, 112.

2445. —— *A pogoro flute.* Man, **35**, no. 39, 1935, 40–42, ill.

2446. **Dixon, D. M.,** and **K. P. Wachsmann.** *A sandstone statue of an Auletes from Meroë.* Kush, **12**, 1964, s.p., ill.

2447. **Douillez, J.** *Aulos.* A.M.E., 1957, 237–8, ill.

2448. **Gibson, Gordon D.** *The Himba trumpet.* Man, **62**, no. 258, 1962, 161–3, ill.

2449. **Gigliolo, Enrico H.** *La kpwen, tromba de guerra delle Amazzoni del Dahomii.* Archivio antrop. etnol., **26**, 1896, 106–10.

2450. **Haddon, Ernest B.** *Whistled signals.* Uganda J., **17** (2), Sept. 1953, 189–91.

2451. **Haddow, A. J.** *Whistled signals among the Bakonjo.* Uganda J., **16**, 2, Sept. 1952, 164–7.

2452. **Hickmann, Hans.** *The Egyptian Uffatah.* J. roy. Asiat. soc., 1952.

2453. —— 1945. *La trompette dans l'Égypte ancienne.* Cairo.

2454. —— 1950. *Die Kultische Verwendung der altägyptischen Trompete.* Stuttgart. [Die Welt des Orients, 5.]

2455. —— *Fabrikationsmarken an altägyptischen Blasinstrumenten.* Die Musikforschung, **3**, 1950, 241.

2456. —— *Horninstrumente. B. Frühgeschichte, Orient und Altertum.* Blume, F. (ed.), Die Musik in Geschichte und Gegenwart, **6**, 1957, 733– .

2457. —— *Die aussereuropäischen und antiken Klarinetteninstrumente Vor-und Frühgeschichte.* Blume, F. (ed.), Die Musik in Geschichte und Gegenwart, **7**, 1958, 993–1005, ill.

2458. —— *The antique cross-flute.* Acta musicol., **24**, 1952, 108.

2459. —— *Unbekannte ägyptische Klangwerkzeuge. (2) Muschelpfeifen und Gefässflöten, (3–4) Knochenpfeifen, Blockflöten, Sackpfeife, Querflöte.* Die Musikforschung, **8**, 1955, 314, 398.

2460. ——*La flûte de Pan.* Chronique d'Égypte [Brussels], **30**, 1955, 217.

2461. ——*Flöteninstrumente. Flötencharacter und Form.* Blume, F. (ed.), Die Musik in Geschichte und Gegenwart, **4**, 1956, 319.

2462. —— *Flöteninstrumente: Altertum: Orient und Antike.* Blume, F. (ed.), Die Musik in Geschichte und Gegenwart, **4**, 1956, 323.

2463. —— *Deux vases siffleurs de l'Égypte ancienne.* Ann. service antiq. Égypte, tom. 50, 1950, 537–9, ill. [Miscellanea musicologica (8).]

2464. —— *Note on an Egyptian wind instrument.* J. int. folk music council, **III**, 1951, 108.

2465. —— *Classement et classification des flûtes, clarinettes et hautbois de l'Égypte ancienne.* Chronique d'Égypte, **26**, no. 51, 1951, 17.

2466. —— *Un sifflet de l'époque préhistorique.* Miscellanea musicologica (4).

2467. **Jackson, Wilfrid.** *Shell-trumpets and their distribution in the Old and New World.* Mem. Manchester lit. soc., **60**, fasc. 8, 1916.

2469. **Kirby, Percival R.** *The trumpets of Tut-Ankh-Amen and their successors.* J. roy. anthrop. inst., **77**, 1947, 33–45, ill.

2470. —— *The trumpets of Tut-ankh-amen and their successors.* Man, **49**, 13, 1949, 19.

2471. ——*A note on the Shipalapala of the Tonga.* S. Afr. J. of science, **35**, 1938, 361–3.

2472. —— *The reed-flute ensembles of South Africa. A study in South African native music.* J. roy. anthrop. inst., **63**, July–Dec. 1933, 313–89.

2473. **Lagercrantz, Sture.** 1950. *Bagpipes.* S. Lagercrantz, Contribution to the Ethnography of Africa. Pp. 286–90, ill., map. Lund: Hakan Ohlssons Boktryckeri. [Studia ethnographica Upsaliensia, 1.]

2474. **Le Roy, Alexandre.** 1928. *Les pygmées: negrilles d'Afrique et négritos d'Asie.* Pp. 129–30, ill. Paris: Beauchesne.

2475. **Loret, Victor.** *Les flûtes égyptiennes antiques.* Journal Asiatique. **64**, 1889, 133.

2476. **Maquet, J. N.** *Les instruments à vent du Congo belge.* Journal mensuel de la féderation nationale des jeunesses musicales de Belgique, 1956.

2477. **Merriam, Alan P.** *The Bashi Mulizi and its music: an end-blown flute from the Belgian Congo.* J. Amer. Folklore, **70**, 276, 1957, 143–56.

2478. —— *The Epudi: a Basongye ocarina.* Ethnomusicology, **6** (3), 1962, 175–80, bibl., ill.

2479. **Morelet, Arthur.** 1864. *Journal du voyage de Vasco da Gama en 1497.* Pp. 9. Lyons: Perrin. [Includes Hottentot flute-greeting at the Cape.]

2480. **Niemeyer, Wilhelm.** *Flöteninstrumente Vor-und Frühgeschichte.* Blume, F. (ed.), Die Musik in Geschichte und Gegenwart, **4**, 1956, 330.

2481. **Pages, P.** *Des joueurs de flûte et de cithare.* Brousse, **3**, 1940, 6–8. [Description de la flûte de roseau et de l'instrument à corde *inanga*.]

2482. **Schaeffner, André.** *Timbales et longues trompettes.* Bull. I.F.A.N, **14**, 4, oct. 1952, 1466–89.

2483. —— *Sur deux instruments de musique des Bata (Nord-Cameroun).* J. soc. Africanistes, **13**, 1943, 123–51, ill.

2484. **Schlesinger, K.** 1939. *The Greek Aulos.* London: Methuen.

2485. **Schmitz, Hans Peter.** *Flöteninstrumente.* Blume, F. (*ed.*), Die Musik in Geschichte und Gegenwart, **4**, 1955, 311.

2486. **Schofield, J. F.** *Four debatable points.* S. Afr. archaeol. Bull., **4** (no. 15), 1949, 98–106. [See p. 104, iv, The Greek Aulos.]

2487. **Schultze, Arnold.** 1910. *Das Sultanat Bornu.* Pp. (4), 128, maps. Langensalza: Julius Beltz. [P. 95.]

2488. **Schweeger-Exeli, Annemarie.** *Ein Elfenbeinblashorn aus Benin.* Arch. f. Völkerkunde [Wien], **13**, 1958, 227–35, ill.

2489. **Shaffer, Jacqueline M.** *Bamboo pipes of the Batetela children.* Afr. mus. soc., **1**, 1954, 74–75.

2490. *South African archaeological society bulletin,* vol. 12, no. 47 (1957), 77. [Cover design maroon kilted figure playing on a reed or (more probably) a bark pipe.] [Instrument mentioned by Meerhoff in 1661 among the Nama (bull. 25, vol. 7, 1952, 48. Modern illus., p. 3.]

2491. *South African archaeological society bulletin,* 15, no. 60. 1960. *Rock-paintings in Africa.* Cape Town: The Society. [Cover design: 'Solitary piper from Southern Rhodesia'.]

2491a. **Struck, Bernhard.** *Afrikanische Kugelflöten.* Kol. Rund. Heft 2–6, 1922, 56–251, ill., map.

2492. **Tachard, G.** 1686. *Voyage de Siam des Pères Jésuites, envoyez par le Roy aux Indes et a la Chine.* Pp. 102–3, 106. Paris: Seneuze. [Namaqua flute ensembles and dances.]

2493. **Van Riet Lowe, Clarence.** *Rock paintings near Cathedral Peak.* S. Afr. archaeol. bull., **4** (no. 13), 1949, 28–33, ill.

2494. **Veenstra, A. J. F.** *The Begu Zulu vertical flute.* Afr. mus. soc., **2**, 1, 1958, 40–45, ill.

2495. **Wachsmann, K. P.** *A rare Nuba trumpet collected by the Seligmans.* Man, **63**, no. 110, 1963, 85–86, ill.

2496. **Werner, Alice.** *Note on 'fufuriye' flutes.* J. Afr. soc., **13**, 1913, 102–3.

2497. **Widenmann, August.** 1899. *Die Kilimandscharo-Bevölkerung.* Pp. ix + 104, ill. Gotha: J. Perthes. [Dschagga trumpet.]

WHIRLING AEROPHONES

2498. **Hickmann, Hans.** *Unbekannte ägyptische Klangwerkzeuge.* (1) *Schwirrholz und Schwirrscheibe.* Die Musikforschung, **8**, 1955, 151.

2499. **Hirschberg, Walter.** *Der Ahnencharakter des afrikanischen Schwirrholzes.* Ethnos, **5**, 1940, 112.

2501. **Jeffreys, M. D. W.** *The bull-roarer among the Ibo.* Afr. stud., **8**, 1949, 23–34, ill.

2502. **Labouret, Henri.** *Rhombes sacrés provenant de l'Afrique occidentale.* L'Anthropologie, **35**, 1925, 345.

2503. **Lang, A.** *Bull Roarer.* Hastings, James, Encyclopaedia of religion and ethics, vol. 2, 1909, 889–91.

2504. **Leiris, Michel.** *Rhombes dogon et dogon pignari.* Bull. mus. ethnog. troc., no. 7, 1934, 3–15.

2505. **Marett, R. R.** *Savage supreme beings and the bull-roarer.* The threshold of religion, 1914.

2506. **Ménard, René.** 1961. *Le Rhombe dans quelques traditions africaines.* Pp. – . Abidjan: . . . .

2508. **Murdoch, John.** *The whizzing-stick or bull-roarer on the West Coast of Africa.* Amer. Anthrop., **3**, 1890, 258 (note). [cf. Moloney, Sir C. A., On the melodies of the Ewe people of West Africa.]

2509. **Plehn, R.** 1898. *Beiträge zur Völkerkunde des Togogebietes.* Pp. – . Halle: . . . .

2510. **Schmeltz, J. D. E.** *Das Schwirrholz.* Verhandl. des Vereins f. Naturwiss. Unterhaltung zu Hamburg, **9**, 1896.

2511. **Sinclair, Gordon.** S.D. *Loose among devils.* Pp. 287, ill. London: Hurst & Blackett. [Chap. 18, pp. 257–78, 'Bull Roarers'.]

2513. **Weeks, John H.** 1914. *Among the primitive Bakongo.* Pp. xvi + 318, ill., map. London: Seeley Service. [Bull-roarer, p. 126.]

2514. **Wissmann, Hermann von.** 1891. *My second journey through equatorial Africa from the Congo to the Zambesi in . . . 1886 & 1887.* Pp. xiv + 326, ill., map. London: Chatto & Windus. [P. 102, aeolian harps (description and plate).]

2515. **Zába, Zbynèk.** *Die 'Sackpfeifen-Syrinx' der Berliner Terrakotta no. 8798 und ihre Stellung in der Geschichte der Musikinstrumente.* Aegyptol. Stud., 1955, 411.

2516. **Zerries, Otto.** 1942. *Das Schwirrholz.* Stuttgart: . . . .

DANCE

GENERAL

2517. **Boas, Franziska.** *Percussion music and its relation to the modern dance.* Dance observer, **7**, 1940, 6–7.

2518. **Breuil, J. H.** *Rythmes africains.* Tropiques, **441**, 1961, 33–41.

2519. **Chilkovsky, Nadia.** *African dance* (bibliography). Afr. stud. bull., **5**, no. 2, 1962, 45–47.

2520. **de Bouveignes, Olivier.** *Les danses nègres.* Afr. mus. soc., Newsletter, **1**, no. 5, 1952, 21–30. [With English Summary.]

2521. **Delavignette, Robert.** 1946. *Les paysans noirs: le quatrieme mois 'L'Afrique Danse'.* Pp. 261. Paris: Editions Stock.

2522. **Eberle, Oscar.** 1954. *Cenalora: Leben, Glaube, Tanz und Theater der Urvölker.* Pp. 575, ill. Freiburg i. Breisgau: Walter Verlag.

2523. **Fodeba, Keita.** *The true meaning of African dances.* Courier [UNESCO], Jan. 1959, 18–23, ill.

2524. **Gaspar, D.,** *Quand l'Afrique chante et danse.* Rev. col. belge, **7**, 1952, 170.

2525. **Gorer, G.** 1938. *Africa dances: a book about West African negroes.* Pp. 254, ill., map. London: Lehmann. [Revised edition, 1949.]

2526. **Hambly, W. D.** 1926. *Tribal dancing.* Pp. 296, bibl., ill. London: Witherby.

2527. **Hambly, W. D.** 1937. *Dancing and singing and percussive instruments (music).* Hambly, Source book for African anthropology, vol. 2, pp. 446–56, bibl., ill. [Field Museum of Natural History: Anthropological series, vol. 26.]

2528. **Holas, B.** *Organisations socio-religieuses en Afrique noire.* Bull. I.F.A.N., **26**, 1964, 40–70, ill.

2529. **Huet, Michel and Keita Fodeba.** 1954. *Les hommes de la danse.* Pp. 135, ill. Lausanne: Editions Clairefontaine.

2530. **Italiaander, R.** 1960. *Tänzer, Tiere und Dämonen. Afrikanische Graphiken.* Pp. 86, ill. Vienna/Stuttgart: Eduard Wancura Verlag.

2531. **Jahn, Janheinz.** 1961. *Muntu.* Pp. 267, bibl., ill., maps. London: Faber & Faber. [Dance: pp. 78–90.]

2532. **Jeffreys, M. D. W.** *African tarantula or dancing mania.* Eastern anthropologist [Lucknow], **6**, (2), 1952–3, 98–105.

2533. **Junk, Viktor.** 1930. *Handbuch des Tanzes.* Pp. 264. Stuttgart: Klett.

2534. **Kappe, Gustave.** *Tanz und Trommel der Neger.* Festschrift-Prof. Schauinsland [Bremen], 1927.

2535. **Kersaint-Gilly, F. de.** *Notes sur la danse en pays noir.* Études historiques et scientifiques, 1922, 77–80.

2536. **Lanternari, Vittorio.** *Choreography.* Encyclopaedia of world art, vol. 3, 1960, 578–80.

2537. **Lenoir, Raymond.** *La danse comme institution sociale.* L'Anthropologie, **40** (4), 1930, 411–29.

2538. **Magriel, P. D.** *A bibliography of dancing 1936 and Supplements 1936–40, etc.* Pp. 229. New York: H. W. Wilson.

2539. **Menjaud, Henri.** *Danse sacrée.* Le monde colonial illustré, 138, janv. 1935.

2540. **Nketia, J. H.** *Possession dances in African societies.* J. int. folk music council [Cambridge], **9**, 1957, 4–9.

2541. 1951. *Notes and queries on anthropology.* Pp. xii + 403, bibl., ill. [London: Routledge. 6th ed.]

2542. **Nys, F.** *Le chant, les danses, la musique.* Belg. col. **3**, 1898, 509–12.

2543. **Oldenburg, R.** *Musik und Tanz der Neger.* Erdball, 1930, **4**, S. 413–14, ill.

2544. **Ortiz, Fernando.** 1951. *Los bailes y el teatro de los negros en el folklore de Cuba.* Pp. 466, ill. Havana: Ed. Gardenas.

2545. **Primus, Pearl E.** *African dance.* Davis, John A. Africa from the point of view of American negro scholars, 1958, 163–73.

2546. **Questerley, W. O. E.** 1923. *The sacred dance.* Pp. 234. Cambridge: Cambridge Univ. Press.

2547. **Sachs, Curt.** 1933. *Eine Weltgeschichte des Tanzes.* Pp. 325, bibl., ill. Berlin: Reimer.

2548. —— 1937. *World history of the dance.* Pp. 469, ill. New York: Norton.

2549. **Schäppi, Franz S.** *Moraltheologische Beleuchtung der (afrikanischen) Eingeborenen-Tänze, I.* Neue Z. Missionswiss. (Switzerland), **1**, 1945, 204–16.

2549a. **Segy, L.** *The mask in African dance.* Negro hist. bull., **14**, 1953, 6, ill.

2550. **Sources Orientales.** 1963. *Les danses sacrées.* Pp. – . Paris: Seuil. [Symposium by members of C.N.R.S. and École des hautes études.]

2551. **Thibangu, Th.** *Comment assumer dans l'église le chant et l'art chorégraphique africains.* Band, 1960, 19e jg., 2–3, 94–105. [Échange de vue sur la place et le rôle de la musique religieuse africaine dans le culte: la question du tam-tam à l'église; le cantique d'enseignement; la danse religieuse.]

2552. **Verger, Pierre.** 1954. *Dieux d'Afrique: culte des Orishas et Vodouns à l'ancienne Côte des Esclaves en Afrique et à Bahia, la Baie de tous les Saints au Brésil.* Pp. 193, ill., map. Paris: P. Hartmann.

2553. **Wattenberg, Ben,** and **Ralph Lee Smith.** 1963. *The new nations of Africa.* Pp. 479, ill., maps. New York: Hart Publish. Co. [See under 'Dance' in index.]

See also 27, 116, 159, 256, 2886a.

DANCE GEOGRAPHICALLY ARRANGED

ALGERIA (DANCE)

See North Africa (Dance).

ANGOLA (DANCE)

2554. **Nicod, Henri.** 1955. *La danseuse du roi.* Pp. 160, ill. Neuchâtel: Delachaux & Niestle, S.A. Paris: [2nd ed.]

2555. **Osório de Oliveira, José.** 1958. *Flagrantes da Vida na Luanda.* Pp. 192, ill. Lisbon: Companhia de Diamantes de Angola.

See also 295.

BASUTOLAND (DANCE)

2556. **Ashton, Hugh.** 1952. *The Basuto.* Pp. xi + 355, bibl., ill., map. London: Published for the International African Institute by the Oxford Univ. Press.

BECHUANALAND (DANCE)

2557. **Zerwick, W.** *Note on a Bechuana reed dance.* Berliner Missions Berichte 2, 1855, 180–1.

See also 336, 337.

BURUNDI (DANCE)

2558. **Bourgeois, R.** *Banyarwanda et Barundi.* Tome 3 (Magie et religion). Mém. A.R.S.C. (sciences morales), **4** (2), 1954, bibl., ill. [Pp. 131–2.]

2558a. —— *Banyarwanda et Barundi.* Tome 1. Mém A.R.S.C. (sciences morales), **15**, 1957, 792, bibl., ill., map. [Pp. 628–35.]

2559. **Kna, H.** *Die Watussi als Springkünstler.* Erdball, **2**, 12, 1928, 459–62.

2560. **Saillez, P. J.** *Où les pages du Roi Mutara Rudahigwa dansent au son d'une melodie sur dix notes.* Congo-Namur, no. 5, 1948, 10–11.

2561. **Sandrart, Georges,** and **Others.** 1953. *Ruanda-Urundi (now Burundi Rwanda).* Pp. 16 + 119 pl., map. Brussels: Charles Dessart. [Images du Congo.]

2562. **Sassoon, J. M.** *Two African dances.* Geog. mag., **25**, 1952–3, 242–7, ill.

2563. **Theza.** *Danse Batutsi.* Echo du tourisme au Congo belge, no. 7, 1956, 1–4.

See also 360.

CAMEROONS (DANCE)

2564. **Ardener, Edwin.** 1956. *Coastal Bantu of the Cameroons.* Pp. 116, map, bibl. London: International African Institute. [Ethnographic survey of Africa: Western Africa, pt. XI.]

2564a. **Egerton, F. C. C.** 1938. *African majesty.* Pp. xx + 348, ill., maps. London: Routledge.

2564b. **McCulloch, Merran,** and **Others.** 1954. *Peoples of the Central Cameroons. Tikar,* by Merran McCulloch. *Bamum and Bamileke,* by Margaret Littlewood. *Banen, Bafia and Balom,* by I. Dugast. Pp. vii + 174, bibl., map. London: International African Institute. [Ethnographic survey of Africa: Western Africa, pt. IX.]

2565. **Pepper, H.,** and **E. Barat Pepper.** *Trois danses chantées avec accompagnemement de linga.* Études Cam., **21–22**, 1948, 85–89, ill.

2566. **Schmidt, A.** 1955. *Die Rote Lendenschnur als Frau im Grasland Kameruns.* Pp. 197, ill. Berlin: Dietrich Reimer.

2566a. **Tessmann, Günther.** 1934. *Die Baja: Ein Negerstamm im mittleren Sudan. Teil 1 Materielle und seelische Kultur.* Pp. xi + 243, bibl., ill., map. Stuttgart: Strecker u. Schröder. [Abschnitt, 7 Bildende Kunst, 187–96: 9 Musikinstrumente, 212–19 (Anhang- 'Tanz').]

See also 369, 393.

CANARY ISLANDS (DANCE)

See 407.

CAPE PROVINCE (DANCE)

See 1396.

CAPE VERDE ISLANDS (DANCE)

2566b. **Ribas, Tomaz.** *Notas para uma introdução ao estudo das danças da Africa Portuguese.* Est. Ultramarinos, **3**, 1959, 187–93.

2566c. —— *Introdução ao estudo das danças de Cabo Verde.* Garcia de Orta, **9** (1), 1961, 115–21, bibl.

CENTRAL AFRICAN REPUBLIC (DANCE)

See 424.

CHAD (DANCE)

See 462, 465, 467.

CONGO REPUBLIC (DANCE)
(Formerly Middle-Congo, part of A.E.F.)

2567. **Ballif, Noël.** 1954. *Les danseurs de Dieu, chez les pygmées de la Sangha.* Pp. 272, ill., carte. Paris: Hachette.

2568. —— tr. by **Cameron, James.** 1955. *Dancers of God* [an account of the Ogowe-Congo Mission to French Equatorial Africa]. Pp. 213, ill. London: Sidgwick & Jackson.

2570. **Scohy, A.** *Jour de fête à Medje.* L'Eventail-album, **7** (n° spécial), 1954, 7, ill. [Description d'une danse traditionnelle des Meje, le *nebobo*.]

2571. **Tidjani, A. Serpos.** *La danse des Égoungoun.* Tropiques [Paris], **368**, déc. 1954, 29.

2572. **Tsamas, Sylvère.** *Le Kyebe-Kyebe.* Liaison, **59**, 1957, 61–65, ill.

CONGOLESE REPUBLIC (DANCE)

2572a. **Antonius, Rév. P.** *Heidensch dansfeest op het dorp Bamania Bokale.* Het Missiewerk, **2**, 8, 1905, 150–4.

2573. *Danses Basala Mpasu.* Belgique d'outremer, **280**, July 1958, 443–8, ill.

2574. *The Congo's thousand tribes.* Belgian Congo of to-day, **8** (3), 1959, 34–36, ill.

2575. **Bentley, W. Holman.** 1887. *Dictionary and grammar of the Kongo language.* Pp. xxiv + 718. London: Baptist Missionary Soc.

2576. **Biebuyck, D.** *Kongolese dansen.* Band 17e jg., **5**, 1958, 171–81, ill.

2577. **Bittremieux, Leo.** 1911. *De geheime Sekte der Bakhimba's.* Pp. 94–100, 171–2. Louvain: Reekmans.

2578. **Brusseaux.** *Note sur les Moundans.* Bull. soc. rech. Congol., **2**, 1922, 35–37, 47. [Dance, pp. 67–69.]

2579. **Cable, G. W.** *The dance in Place Congo.* Century mag., **31**, 1886, 517–32.

2580. **Campbell, Dugald.** 1922. *In the heart of Bantuland.* Pp. 313, ill., map. London: Seeley Service.

2581. **Comhaire-Sylvain, Jean (Mde).** *Les danses Nkundu du territoire d'Oshwe au Congo belge.* Afr. Stud., **6** (3), 1947, 124–30, ill.

2581a. **Cormerais, R. P. C.** *Rejouissances indigènes.* Missions d'Afr. Pères Blancs, 1930, 105–10.

2582. **Cuvelier, J.** *Les missions catholiques en face des danses des Bakongo.* A.F.E.R., **17**, 1939, 143–70.

2583. **de Beaucorps R.** *Les Basongo de la Luniungu et de la Gobari.* I.R.C.B. (sciences morales), Mém. 10 (3), 1941, 172, ill., maps. [Pp. 48–49.]

2584. **de Capmaker, I.** *Danses des Bakongo.* Sem. missiologie Louvain, **16**, 1938 (1939), 40–62.

2585. **Delhaise, Charles Godefroid Félix Francois.** 1909. *Les Warega.* Pp. xx + 376, ill., maps. Brussels: Institut Intern. de Bibliographie. [Collection de monographies ethnographiques, no. 5. [Dance pp. 265–6.]

2586. **D'Hont, M.** *Cérémonial de danse des indigènes à la région de Mwanza.* Bull. amis art indig. Katanga, avril 1938, 18.

2587. **de Sousberghe, L.** *Les danses rituelles Mungonge et Kela des Ba Pende (Congo belge).* A.R.S.C. (sciences morales), Mém. 9, 1956–9, 62, ill.

2589. **Hulstaert, G.** *Mission et divertissements populaires.* Aequatoria, 1940, I, 16/21. [Mus. Congo, p. 873.]

2590. **Iyandze-Lopoloko, Joseph.** 1961. *Bobongó: danse renommée des Ekonda du Lac Léopold II, une institution parascolaire.* Pp. ix + 169, ill., map. Tervuren: Musée Roy. Afrique Centrale. [Archives d'ethnographie, 4.]

2590a. **Lecoq, R.** *Danse à Bandjoon.* Jeune Afr., **4**, 1950, 13–20, ill.

2591. **Louillet, P.** *Quelques couplets de la danse ngwava.* Ann. Pères Saint Esprit, **55**, 1939, 121–3. [Danse des indigènes de Kongolo texte en langue indigène et explication.]

2592. **Louvain: Semaine de Missiologie.** 1938. *La mission et les joies populaires: compte rendu de la 16e semaine de missiologie de Louvain, 1938.* Pp. 448, Bruxelles: Ed. Universelle.

2593. **Mupende.** *Bapende-dansen.* Band, **6**, 1, Jan. 1947. 9–12.

2594. **Peeraer, Servais.** *La danse chez les Baluba Shandaki.* Bull. Amis Art indig. Katanga [Élisabethville], **2**, oct. 1937, 4–6.

2595. **Plancquaert, M. Le R. P.** 1930. *Les sociétés secrètes chez les Bayaka.* Pp. 131, ill., map. Brussels: J. Kuyl-Otto.

2596. **Regnault, M.** *Les Babenga.* L'Anthropologie, **22**, 1911, 261–88, ill., map. [Dance + music: pp. 280–1, ill.]

2597. **Rosmant, M.** *Au pays des pages danseurs.* Bull. tour. club, Congo belge, no. 1, 1950, 13–23.

2598. **Sulzmann, Erika.** *Les danseurs ekonda à 'Changwe Yetu' [spectacle à l'Exposition Universelle de Bruxelles].* Zaïre, **13**, 1, 1959, 57–71, ill.

2599. **Tiarko Fourche, J. A.** *La danse de Tshishimbi chez les Lulus du Kasai.* I.R.C.B. (Bull. des séances), **8**, 1937, 395–448.

2600. **Tonnoir, René.** *Bobongo ou l'art chorégraphique chez les Ekonda, Yembe et Tumba du Lac Léopold II.* Probl. Afr. Centr. [Bruxelles], **6**, 20, 1953, 87–109, ill.

2601. **Torday, Emil.** *Land and peoples of Kasai basin.* J. roy. geog. soc., **36**, 1910, 30–31.

2602. **Tshibangu.** *An experiment in Congolese dancing: Choreography by Tshibangu.* Belgian Congo of to-day, **2** (3), 1953, 106–9.

2603. **Vandewalle, I.** *De dans bij de Pamitu.* Nieuw Afrika, **67**, 6, 1951, 261–5.

2604. **Van Loo, E.** *Musique et danses des Bakubas et Batshioks.* Sci. et voyage, **29** (24), 1947, 346–8.

2606. **Van Mol, O. P.** *Pubertertsviering en besnijdenis bij Mambutu's.* Congo [Brussels], **1**, 1924, 362–74.

2607. —— *Het huwelijk bij de Mambutu's.* Congo [Brussels], **2**, 1932, 207–11.

2608. **Vansina, J.** 1954. *Les tribus Ba-Kuba et les peuplades apparentées.* Pp. xiii + 64, bibl., map. Tervuren: Musée Royale du Congo Belge. [Sciences de l'homme: Monog. ethnog., vol. 1.] Also in International African Institute [Ethnographic Survey of Africa, Central Africa, Belgian Congo, Part 1.]

2609. **Van Wing, J.** *Les danses Bakongo.* Congo, **2**, 2, 1937, 121–31.

2610. —— 1959. *Études Bakongo: sociologie: religion et magie.* Pp. 512, bibl., map. Léopoldville: Desclée de Brouwer. [2nd ed.] [Pp. 480–9.]

2611. **Weeks, John H.** 1914. *Among the primitive Bakongo.* Pp. xvi + 318, ill., map. London: Seeley Service. [Dance: pp. 127–33.]

2612. **Wilverth, Lieut.** *Chez les Mongwandies.* Congo illus., **22**, 1894, 175.

See also 27, 28, 494, 503, 504a, 504b, 505, 584, 588, 605, 638.

DAHOMEY (DANCE)

2612a. **Bernolles, J.** *Première étude sur les rites et danses funéraires des pila-pila de bele foungou (Djougou Dahomey).* Ét. Dah., **1**, 1963, 125–34, ill.

2613. **Kehron, P.** *La danse au Dahomey: Africain (Alm. des missions africains, Lyon).* 1925, 46–48, ill.

See also 668.

EAST AFRICA (DANCE)

2614. **Culwick, A. T.,** and **G. M.** 1935. *Ubena of the rivers.* Pp. 444, ill., map. London: Allen & Unwin.

2615. **Doull, Alex.** *Native dances of eastern Africa.* Dancing Times, 1936, 131–2, ill.

2616. **Hagemann, Carl.** 1919. *Spiele der Völker.* Pp. 495. Berlin: Schuster & Loeffler. [Pp. 13–24, Negertänze in Deutsch Ost-Afrika.]

2617. **Hichens, W.** *Demon dances in East Africa.* Discovery, **17**, 198, 1936, 185–8, illus.

2617a. **Hill, Peter.** *Tribal dances in Kenya's Nyanza Province.* E. Afr. ann. [Nairobi], 1949–50, 57–59, ill.

2618. **Hobley, Charles William.** 1922. *Bantu beliefs and magic.* Pp. 312, ill. London: Witherby. [Chap. 7, pt. 3, pp. 266–73.]

EGYPT (DANCE)

2619. **Brunner-Traut, E.** *Der Tanz im alten Ägypten.* Pp. 63. Glückstadt.

2620. **Curtis, G. W.** 1852. *Nile notes of a 'Howadji'.* Pp. viii + 227, ill. London: Vizetelly. [Pp. 89–91.]

2621. **Hickmann, Hans.** *Quelques considérations sur la danse et la musique de danse dans l'Égypte pharaonique.* Cah. hist. égyptiennes, **5**, 1953, 161.

2622. —— *La danse au miroirs. Essai de reconstruction d'une danse pharaonique de l'ancien empire.* Bull. de l'inst. d'Égypte [Cairo], **37**, 1956, 151.

2623. —— *Un zikr dans le mastaba de Debhen Guîzah (4th Dynasty).* J. Int. folk music council, **9**, 1957, 59.

2624. **Lexová, Irená.** 1935. *Ancient Egyptian dances.* Pp. 84, ill. Prague. [Orientalni Ustav.]

2625. **Seligman, Brenda Z.** *On the origin of the Egyptian zar.* Folk-lore, **25**, 1914, 300–3.

See also 743.

ETHIOPIA (DANCE)

2626. **Bieber, Friedrich J.** 1920–23. *Kaffa: ein altkuschitisches Volkstum in Inner-Afrika* [2 vols.]. Pp. xxiv + 500; x + 560, bibl., ill. Vienna: Verlag: Anthropos Administration. [Dance: vol. 2, pp. 334–7.]

2627. **Courlander, Harold.** *The Ethiopian dance of Gobeta.* Negro history bull., **5**, Oct. 1943, 21–23.

2628. **Grühl, Max.** *Der Tanz der Priester (Abessinien).* Der Erdball, **4**, 3, 1930, 83–90, ill.

See also 770, 783, 788, 789, 809.

GABON (DANCE)

2629. **Alexandre, Pierre,** and **Jacques Binet.** *Le groupe dit Pahouin Fang, Boulou-Beti.* Pp. vi + 152, bibl., map. Paris: Presses Univ. de France. [Monographies ethnologiques africaines de l'Institut International Africain.]

2630. **Briault, Maurice.** *Ivanga: danse des Mpongwe.* Ann. Pères St. Esprit., 1938, 251–6.

See also 830.

GAMBIA (DANCE)

2631. **Palmer, Sir Richmond.** *The Gambia.* Geog. mag., **16** (7), 1943, 335, ill.

See also 841, 846, 917.

GHANA (DANCE)

2632. **Banton, Michael.** *The dancing compin [Freetown association].* W.A.R., 1915, 7 Nov. 1953, 1041–2, ill.

2632a. **Bertonoff, Deborah.** 1963. *Dance towards the earth.* Pp. 233, ill. Tel-Aviv: Alityros Books.

2633. **Price, J. H.** *A bori dance in Accra.* W.A.R., **28**, 352, Jan. 1957, 20–23, ill.

2634. **Wolfson, Freda.** 1958. *Pageant of Ghana.* Pp. xiii + 266, ill., maps. London: Oxford Univ. Press.

See also 852.

GUINEA (DANCE)
(Formerly Guinée Française, A.O.F.)

2635. **Balandier, Georges.** *Danses de sortie d'excision à Boffa (Guinée française) [Soussou].* Notes afr., IFAN, **38**, avr. 1948, 11–12, ill.

2636. **Holas, Bohumil.** *Danses masquées de la Basse-Côte.* Études Guin., **1**, 1947, 61–67.

2637. —— 1954. *Le culte de Zié: elements de la religion Kono (Haute-Guinée française).* Pp. 274, bibl., ill., map. Dakar: I.F.A.N. [Mémoires de l'inst. française d'Afrique noire, 39.]

2638. —— *Echantillons du folklore Kono (Haute-Guinée française).* Études Guin., **9**, 1953, 3–90, ill.

2639. **Lassort, R. P.,** and **R. P. Lelong.** *Chez les Kpele et les Guerze.* Études Guin., **2**, 1948, 9–20, ill.

2639a. *Notes afr. I.F.A.N.,* 1949, no. 43. Légende dela couverture. 'Danseur Masqué Guerzé-Conon N'Zérékoré(Guinée).'

2639b. **Rouch, J.** *La danse.* Présence Africaine, **8–9**, 1950, 219–26, ill.

2640. **Traoré, Mamadou.** *Une danse curieuse: le Moribayasa.* Notes. afr., I.F.A.N., **15**, 1942, 5–6.

IVORY COAST (DANCE)

2640a. **Olbrechts, F. M.** *Maskers en dansers in de Ivoorkust.* Pp. 183, ill. 1940. Davidsfonds Volksboek, no. 290.

2641. **Olbrechts, Frans M.** *Een spectaculaire dans bij de Dan van de Boven-Cavally: Het jongleeren met kleine meisjes.* Alumni, **10**, juin 1939, 279–88, ill.

2642. **Petit, André.** *Une danse fétiche à la Côte d'Ivoire.* Rev. ethnog. trad. pop., **3**, 1920, 174–6.

2643. **Proteaux, M.** *Divertissements de Kong (Diula).* Bull. com. étud., A.O.F. [Paris], **8** (4), 1925, 606–50, ill.

See also 922.

KENYA (DANCE)

2643a **Adamson, Joy.** *Headdresses of Kenya witch-doctors and dancers.* E. Afr. Ann., 1951/2, **54–55**, ill.

2644. **Dundas, K. R.** *Notes on the tribes inhabiting the Baringo district, East African Protectorate.* J. roy. anthrop. inst., **40**, 1910, 49–72, ill.

2645. **Emsheimer, Ernst.** *Drei Tanzgesänge der Akamba.* Ethnos, **2**, 1937, 137–43, ill.

2646. **Hillaby, John.** 1964. *Journey to the Jade Sea.* Pp. vii + 234, ill. London: Constable. [Dance of the Elmolo, pp. 112–14.]

2647. **Joyce, T. A.** *Note on a series of Kikuyu 'ndomi' in the British Museum.* Man, **6**, no. 33, 1906, 49–51, ill. [Description of dancing shields.]

See also 931–2, 936–8, 940, 942.

LIBERIA (DANCE)

2648. **Donner, Etta.** 1939. *Hinterland Liberia.* Pp. xiv + 302, ill., maps as end-papers. Glasgow: Blackie.

2649. **Leroy, Marcel.** 1954. *Land of the Niamoo: travels in the forests of Equatorial Africa.* Pp. 175, ill. London: Arthur Barker.

2650. **West African Review.** *Africa dances [picture-essay of West Africa's traditional dancing].* W.A.R., **33**, 413, May 1962, 4–13.

See also 955–6.

MADAGASCAR (DANCE)

2651. **Coze, Mlle. M.-L.** *Curieuses danses malgaches.* Rev. Madagascar (Tananarive), 3° trim, no. 12, 1952, 21–25, ill.

2652. **Deschamps, H. J.** *Les danses Antaiska.* Bull. acad. malg., **17**, 1934, 31–47.

2653. —— and **Suzanne Vianès.** 1959. *Les malgaches du sud-est.* Pp. xii + 118, ill., maps. Paris: Presses Universitaires de France. [Monographies ethnologiques. Africaines de l'Institut International Africain.]

2654. **Faublée, Marcelle et Jacques.** *À Madagascar, toute danse est sacrée.* Marco Polo [Paris], no. 14, 36–40, ill.

2655. **Mondain, Gustave.** *Danses malgaches.* Bull. acad. malgache, **7**, 1909, 123–8.

2656. **Silberman, Leo.** *Mysterious Madagascar.* Geog. mag., **31** (11), 1959, 549–60, ill., map. Dance and accordion player, pp. 550–1.

See also 979, 981.

MALAWI (DANCE)
(Formerly Nyasaland)

2657. **Cartmel-Robinson, S.** 1962. *Lupanda dance.* Nyasaland journal, vol. 15 (2), 20–23.

2658. **Elmslie, W. A.** 1901. *Among the wild Ngoni.* Pp. 319, ill., map. Edinburgh: Oliphant Anderson.

2658a. **Gelfand, M.** 1959. *Shona ritual.* Pp. (5) + 217, ill. Cape Town: Juta & Co.

2659. **Gulliver, Pamela.** *Dancing clubs of the Nyasa.* Tanganyika notes and records, **41**, Dec. 1955, 58–59.

2659a. **Moloney, Joseph.** *With Captain Stairs to Katanga.* Pp. xii + 280, ill., map. London: Sampson, Low. [Pp. 77–78, dance of Wangoni.]

MALI (DANCE)
(Formerly Soudan Français)

2659b. **Anon.** *Art musicale indigène undigene au Soudan.* Brousse, 1–2, 1946.

2660. **Anon.** *Casques et masques de danse au Soudan français.* Minotaure [Paris], no. 2, 1933, 20–21, ill.

2661. *Bambara dancers.* Travel, **68**, 1937, 42–43, ill.

2662. **Chéron, Georges.** *Les Tyèblenké.* J. soc. africanistes, **1**, 2, 1931, 281–3. [Masked dancers.]

2663. **Lestrange, Monique.** *À propos des Koré du Fouta-Djalon.* Notes afr., I.F.A.N., **46**, avr. 1950, 42–43, ill.

2664. **Dermenghem, E.** *Les masques et les danses rituelles des Bambaras.* Sci. et voyages [Paris], août 1939, 50–53.

2665. **Leiris, Michel.** *Danses funéraires dogon.* Minotaure [Paris], **1**, 1933, 73–76, ill.

2666. —— 1948. *La langue secrète des Dogons de Sanga (Soudan français).* Pp. xxxii + 530, bibl. Paris: Institut d'Ethnologie. [Travaux et mémoires de l'inst. d'ethnologie, 50.]

2667. **Michaut, Pierre.** *Les danses des Dogons, d'après un film de Griaule.* Opinion, **31**, 15 sep. 1938, 14–16.

2667a. **Rouch, J.** *Culte des génies chez les Sonray.* J. soc. africanistes, **15**, 1945, 15–32.

See also 1031a, 1035–6.

MOZAMBIQUE (DANCE)

2667b. **Albert, M. S.** *O mapico, danca dos Macondes,* Império, 1951, 51.

2668. **dos Santos Junior, Joaquim N.** *O marombo ou malombo (Tete., Moçambique).* Garcia de Orta, **5**, 4, 1957, 773–88.

2669. **Fernando, Francisco Alfredo.** *Mapico: danca dos Macondes.* Bol. Museu Nampula, **1**, 1960, 67–72.

2670. **Melo, G. J.** *Etnografia indigena: A dança do Nhau.* Imperio [Lourenço Marques], **7/8**, Nôv.-Dic. 1951, p. 33.

See also 1095.

NIGER (DANCE)

2671. **Dupire, Marguerite.** 1962. *Peuls nomades.* Pp. viii + 336, bibl., ill., maps. Paris: Institut d'Ethnologie. [Travaux et mémoires de l'inst. d'ethnologie, 64.]

2672. **Estreicher, Z.** *Chants et rythmes de la danse d'hommes Bororo.* Bull. soc. Neuchât. géog., **51** (10), 1954-5, 57–93.

NIGERIA (DANCE)

2673. **Ardener, Edwin.** *Bakweri elephant dance.* Nigeria magazine, no. 60, 1959, 31–38, ill.

2674. **Beier, H. U.** *Obatala festival.* Nigeria, no. 52, 1956, 10–28, ill.

2675. **Beier, Ulli.** *The dancers of Agbor.* Odù, no. 7, 1959, 41, ill.

2676. —— *Osezi festival in Agbor.* Nigeria magazine, no. 78, 1963, 184–95, ill.

2676a. —— *The Agbegijo Masqueraders.* Nigeria magazine, **82**, 1964. 188–99, ill.

2677. **Bradbury, R. E.** *Divine kingship in Benin.* Nigeria magazine, no. 62, 1959, 186–207, ill.

2678. —— and **P. C. Lloyd.** 1957. *The Benin kingdom and the Edo-speaking peoples of south-western Nigeria . . . together with a section on the Itsekiri* (by P. C. Lloyd). Pp. xii + 210, bibl., map. International African Institute. [Ethnographic survey of Africa: Western Africa, pt. XIII.]

2679. **Campbell, M. J.** *People in trust.* Nigeria magazine, no. 62, 1959, 208–29, ill.

2680. **Clifford, G. M.** *The spring festivals at Farei—a picturesque Nigerian dance.* Nigeria, no. 16, 1938, 270–1, ill.

2681. **Horton, R.** *The Kalebari Ekine society.* Africa, **33**, 1963, 94–114, ill.

2682. **Kennett, B. L. A.** *The Afoshi dancers of Kabba division, Northern Nigeria.* J. roy. anthrop. inst., **61**, 1931, 435–42.

2683. **Kennet, F. K.** *Dances of the Bassas at Abaji.* **88**, 1936, J. roy. geog. soc., 457–8, ill.

2684. **King, A. V.** *Nigerian traditional dances and music* [Ibadan University, 18 Nov. 1963]. African notes [Ibadan], **1**, 2, Jan. 1964, 15–19.

2685. **Kirk-Greene, A. H. M.** *Festival at Farei.* Nigeria, no. 45, 1954, 60–74, ill.

2686. —— 1958. *Adamawa past and present.* Pp. ix + 230, maps. Oxford: Oxford Univ. Press. [Published for the Int. African Inst.] [Pp. 208–13.]

2687. **MacKay, Mercedes,** and **Augustine Ene.** *The atilogwu dance.* Afr. mus. soc., **1**, 4, 1957, 20–22, ill.

2688. **Mellor, Capt.** *The Fulani dance of Northern Nigeria.* Saturday review, **162**, 1936, 571.

2689. **Murray, K. C.** *Dances and plays.* Nigeria, no. 19, 1939, 214–18, ill.

2690. —— *Ayologbe* [Ibo dance]. Nigerian field, **12**, 2, Oct. 1948, 73–75.

2691. **Nadel, S. F.** 1942. *A black Byzantium: the kingdom of Nupe in Nigeria.* Pp. xiv + 420, ill., maps. London: Oxford Univ. Press for the International African Institute.

2692. —— 1954. *Nupe religion.* Pp. x + 288, ill. London: Routledge.

2693. **Nigeria Magazine.** *Efik dances.* Nigeria magazine, no. 53, 1957, 150–69, ill.

2694. —— *Egbukere dance* (*Ahoada district, Nigeria*). Nigeria magazine, no. 56, 1958, 52–64, ill.

2695. —— *Igogo festival.* Nigeria magazine, no. 77, 1963, 91–104, ill.

2696. **Nzekwu, Onuora.** *Masquerade* (*S. Nigeria*). Nigeria magazine special no., Oct. 1960, 134–92, ill.

2697. —— *Ibo dancing.* Nigeria magazine, no. 73, June 1962, 35–43, ill.

2698. —— *The Edda.* Nigeria magazine, no. 76, 1963, 16–28, ill.

2698a. **Obe, Peter O.** *Igogo festival at Owo. Dance of the Olowo.* W.A.R., **29** (375), 1958, 1007–13, ill.

2699. **Okeke, L. E.** *The Ogwulugwu dance of Awka.* Nigerian teacher, **2** (6), 1936, 39–41, ill.

2700. **Seton, R. Sydney.** *Notes on the Igala tribe of northern Nigeria.* J. Afr. soc., **29**, 1929–30, 42–52, 149–63. [Pp. 158–9.]

2701. **Ukeje, L. O.** *Urhore.* Nigeria magazine, no. 76, 1963, 29–44, ill.

2702. **Wilson-Haffenden, J. R.** *Notes on the Kwottos of Toto district.* J. Afr. soc., **27**, 1927–8, 44.

See also 1164, 2672.

NORTH AFRICA (DANCE)

2703. **Andrews, J.-B.** 1903. *Les fontaines des génies* (*Seba Aioun*), *croyances soudanaises à Alger.* Pp. 36, ill. Alger: A. Jourdan. [Danses de possession, textes rituels songhay.]

2704. **Blanco Izaga, Emilio.** *Las danzas rifeñas.* Africa [Madrid], **55**, 1946, 315–16, ill.; **56/57**, 1946, 414–19, ill.; 59/60, 1946, 547–51, ill.

2705. **Brulard, M.** *La sebbiba d'Achoura à Ghat.* Bull. liaison sahariennes, **8**, 26, juin 1957, 89–93.

2706. **Chapelle, Jean.** 1957. *Nomades noirs du Sahara.* Pp. 449, bibl., ill., maps. Paris: Plon.

2707. **Chottin, A.** *Chants et danses berbères au Maroc.* Le Ménestrel, 1933.

2708. **Deloncle, Pierre.** 1937. *La vie et les moeurs en Algérie.* Pp. – . Orleans. [Pp. 58–64.]

2709. **Deyrolle, E.** *Les danseurs Tunisians.* Bull. & mém. soc. anthrop. [Paris], ser. 6, vol. 3, 1911, 262–6.

2710. **Dunoéli.** *Tänze der Aissaouas.* Der Tanz [Berlin], **4** (11), 1931, 7, ill. [Islamsekte in Nordafrika.]

2711. **du Puigaudeau, Odette.** 1937. *Barefoot through Mauritania.* Pp. xiv + 286, ill., maps. London: Routledge.

2712. **Fisher, T.** *Spring dance in North Africa.* Folk-lore, **45**, 1934, 157–8.

2713. **Gay, Capt.** *Sur la sébiba.* J. soc. africanistes, **5**, 1, 1935, 61–66, ill.

2714. **Hector, Paul.** *Poési et danse dans une tribu Berbère du Moyen Atlas.* Le maroc. cath., **13**, 1933, 15–17, 41–43.

2715. —— *Notes et observations sur l'étude de la danse Berbère.* Le maroc. cath., **14**, 1934, 348–51; **15**, 1935, 20–23, 98–102.

2716. **Johnson, F. E.** *Dancing in northern Africa.* Nat. geog. mag., **25**, 1914, 13–31, ill.

2717. **Lafuente, Domenech.** *El Mulud.* Africa [Madrid], nos. 37–38, 1945, 32–39, ill.

2718. **Laubat, F. de C.** *Le sens du Haut-Mertoutek.* J. soc. Africanistes, **12**, 1942, 139–47, ill.

2719. **Menjaud, Henri.** [s.d.] *Suite de danses berbères: un film du centre cinématographique marocain* [Album de planches]. Pp. 14 f. dont 7 p. de texte. Rabat: Éd. Studios du Souissi.

2720. **Nicolaisen, Johannes.** *Essai sur la religion et la magie Touarègues.* Folk, **3**, 1961, 113–62, bibl., ill.

2721. **Wassing, R. S.** 1957. *Afrika danst.* Meded. Afrika inst., 11 jg. 12, 1957, 399–403, ill.

2722. **Work, T. H.** *Bedouin in wedding-feast.* Geog. mag., **30**, 1957-8, 219–33, ill.

2723. **Young, Clemson.** *Arab music and dancing in North Africa.* Dancing Times, 1931, 220–1, ill.

RWANDA (DANCE)

2724. **Moeller, A.** *Danses* (*Hutu*). Beaux arts, **227**, 1937, 18–19.

2725. **Molitor, H.,** and **Others.** *Danseurs du Ruanda* [in English, French, and Flemish]. Pp. 20 + 10 pl. Bruxelles: Éd. des Artistes (Coll. 'Europe-Afrique').

2726. **Poelmans, René.** *En regardant danser les Banya-ruanda.* Pages congolaises [Léopoldville], Éd. B. 9, 1951, 3.

2727. **Schumacher, le R. P.** *Tanz und Spiel in Ruanda.* 16e semaine missiologie [Louvani], 1938, 381–407.

SENEGAL (DANCE)

2728. **Adam, Paul.** *La musique et le ballet au Sénégal.* S.I.M. [Paris], **10**, 1914, 6–9.

2729. **Ossendowski, F.** 1928. *Slaves of the sun.* Pp. 378, ill., maps. London: Geo. Allen.

2730. **Paulay, Guy.** *Historique de la danse des chasseurs de Touba.* Notes afr., I.F.A.N., **55**, juil. 1952, 83.

2731. **Raffenel, Anne.** 1846. *Voyage dans l'Afrique occidentale . . . en 1843 & 1844.* Pp. vii + 512. Paris: Bertrand. [Pp. 295–6.]

See also 917.

SIERRA LEONE (DANCE)

2732. **Banton, Michael.** *Ambas geda.* West Afr., **31**, Oct. 1953, 995.

2733. **de Hart, J.** *The dance of the Wundu society.* Sierra Leone stud., no. 3, 1919, 5-7.

2734. **Donner, Etta.** *Stelzentänzer.* Atlantis, 1938, 78-81, ill.

2735. **Lewis, Roy.** 1954. *Sierra Leone.* Pp. ix + 263, ill., maps. London: H.M.S.O.

2736. **Little, K. L.** *The Mende of Sierra Leone.* Pp. 307, bibl., maps. London: Routledge.

2737. **Migeod, F. W. H.** *A Mende dance.* Man, **17**, no. 102, 1917, 153-6. [Description in Mende with translation.]

2738. **Tremearne, Arthur John Newman.** *The hammock dance in Sierra Leone.* Man. **12**, no. 53, 1912, 105, ill.

2739. —— 1914. *The ban of the Bori.* Pp. 504, ill. London: Heath, Cranton. [Pp. 251-2, 281-5.]

SOMALIA (DANCE)

2740. **Clark, J. Desmond.** *Dancing masks from Somaliland (Eile tribe).* Man, **53**, 72, Apr. 1953, 49-51, ill.

2740a. **Massari, C.** *Maschere di danza degli Uaboni.* Arch. antrop. e etnol. (Firenze), **80-81**, 1950-1, 143-6, ill.

2741. **Pesenti, G.** 1929. *Canti sacri e profani, danze e ritmi degli Arabi, dei Somali e dei Suahili.* Pp. – . Milan: Eroica.

See also 1340.

SOUTH AND SOUTH-WEST AFRICA (DANCE)

2742. **Alexander, Sir James Edward.** *Report of an expedition of discovery, through the country of the Great Namáquas, Boschmans and the Hill Dámaras in South Africa.* J. roy. geog. soc., **8**, 1838, 19-20.

2743. —— 1838. *Expedition of discovery into the interior of Africa* [2 vols.]. Vol. 1, xxiv + 302, ill., map. Vol. 2, pp. viii + 306, ill. London: Henry Colburn.

2745. **Arbousset, J. Thomas,** and **F. Daumas.** 1842. *Relation d'un voyage d'exploration au nord-est de la Colonie du Cap de Bonne-Espérance.* Pp. 54, 487-91. Paris: Bertrand.

2746. —— 1852. *Narrative of an exploratory tour to the north-east of the Cape of Good Hope.* [Translated from the French.] Pp. xvi + 453, map. London: John C. Bishop. [Pp. 353-4, 417-18.]

2747. **Baines, Thomas.** 1864. *Explorations in South West Africa.* Pp. xiv + 535, ill., maps. London: Longmans, Green.

2748. **Blacking, John.** *Musical expeditions of the Venda.* Afr. mus. soc., **3**, 1, 1962, 54-78, ill.

2749. **Campbell, John.** 1822. *Travels in South Africa.* Vol. 1, pp. 84-85. London: Westley.

2751. **Chapman, James.** 1868. *Travels in the interior of South Africa* [2 vols.]. Vol. 1, pp. xiii + 454, ill., map. Vol. 2, pp. viii + 480, ill., map. London: Bell & Daldy.

2752. **Cook, P. A. W.** *Social organisation and ceremonial institutions of the Bomvana.* Pp. xi + 171, ill. Cape Town: Juta & Co.

2753. **Demery, Felix.** *Native dances of Johannesburg.* Dancing Times, 1935, 582-3, ill.

2754. **Doke, C. M.** *Games, plays and dances of the khomani bushmen.* Bantu Stud., **10**, 1936, 461-71.

2755. **Dornan, S. S.** *Tati bushmen.* Hastings, James, Encyclopedia of Religion and Ethics, vol. 12, 1921, 206. [Dance, music and musical instruments.]

2756. **Drury, J.** *Preliminary report on the anthropological researches carried out by . . . the S. African Museum in S. W. Africa.* Ann. S. African Museum, **24/2**, 1935, 101-3, ill. [Pp. 101-3.]

2757. **Duggan-Cronin, A. M.** 1942. *The bushman tribes of southern Africa.* Pp. 14, pl. 40, map. Kimberley: Cape Times Ltd.

2758. **Fischer, Eugen.** 1961. *Die Rehobother bastards.* Pp. xi + 323, bibl., ill. Graz: Akademische Druck. [Pp. 276-8.]

2759. **Fourie, L.** *The bushmen of South West Africa.* Native tribes of South West Africa, 1928, 211, bibl., ill. [Pp. 95-98.]

2761. **Holden, William C.** 1866. *The past and future of the Kaffir races.* Pp. xii + 516, ill., map. London: Published for the author.

2763. **Krige, E. J.,** and **J. D.** 1950. *The social system of the Zulus.* Pp. xix + 420, bibl., ill., maps. Pietermaritzburg: Shuter & Shooter. [2nd ed.]

2764. **Kuper, Hilda.** 1961. *An African aristocracy.* Pp. xii + 251, bibl., ill., map. Oxford: Oxford Univ. Press. [Published for the International African Institute.]

2765. **Lerner, Rose.** *Tribal dancing among the Bantu.* Dancing Times, 1935, 253-4, ill.

2766. **Livingstone, David.** 1857. *Missionary travels and researches in South Africa.* Pp. x + 687, ill., maps. London: John Murray. [P. 225, ill. of Bechuana reed dance.]

2767. **Lloyd, Theodosia.** *Sunday morning at Randfontein.* New Statesman, **16**, 1938, 218-19.

2768. **Makin, William J.** *The Zulus dance at Eshowe.* Travel, **58**, 1931, 30-31, ill.

2769. **Mentzel, O. F.** 1787. *Beschreibung des Vorgebirges der Guten Hoffnung* [2 vols.]. Vol. 2, pp. 513-14, 516-19. Glogau: Gunther.

2771. **Moritz, Eduard.** *Die ältesten Reiseberichte über Deutsch-Südwestafrika: H. J. Wikar, 1778.* Mitt. Schutz., **31**, 1918, 73, 87.

2773. **Paterson, William.** 1789. *A narrative of four journeys into the country of the Hottentots of Caffraria, 1777-79.* Pp. vi + 171, ill., map. London: J. Johnson.

2774. **Schwarz, Ernest Hubert Lewis.** 1928. *The Kalahari and its native races.* Pp. 244, bibl., ill., maps. London: Witherby. [Pp. 161-2.]

2775. **Schweiger, Albert.** *Der Ritus der Beschneidung unter den ama Xosa und ama Fingo in der Kaffraria, Südafrika.* Anthropos, **9**, 1914, 53-65, ill. [Masked dancers.]

2776. **Sutherland, John.** 1845. *Memoir respecting the Kaffers, Hottentots and Bosjemans of South Africa* [2 vols.]. Cape Town: Pike & Philip. [Vol. 2, pp. 245, 647-8.]

2777. **Torrend, J.** 1892. *A comparative grammar of the South African Bantu languages, etc.* Pp. xlviii + 336. London: Kegan Paul. [Pp. 296-320.]

2778. **Tracey, Hugh.** *Native dancing—a wasted asset.* Nada [Bulawayo], no. 17, 1940, 28-34, ill.

2779. —— *The poetry of the Bachopi ballet.* Nada [Bulawayo], no. 21, 1944, 6-18, ill.

2781. —— 1952. *African dances of the Witwatersrand gold mines.* Pp. (0), 156, ill., maps as end-papers. Johannesburg: African Music Society.

2783. **Vedder, H.** *Die Bergdama.* Abh. Hamburg. Univ. Reihe B, v7, VI, pp. 92-95, 1923.

2784. **Waterhouse, Gilbert.** 1932. *Simon van der Stel's journal of his expedition into Namaqualand, 1685-86.* Pp. 46-47, 133-4. Dublin: U.P. [Reed dances.]

2785. **Winkelman, Franz von.** *Reisaantekeningen (1788-89).* Godee-Molsbergen, E. C. (*ed.*), Reizen in Zuid Afrika (Linschoten-Vereeniging Werken, 36). 1932, 81-84. Amsterdam: . . . .

See also 1430, 1434.

SOUTHERN RHODESIA (DANCE)

2786. **Carnegie, D.** 1894. *Among the Matabele.* Pp. – . London . . . .

2787. **Depelchin, H.,** and **C. Croonenberghs.** *Trois Ans dans l'Afrique Australe, 1879-1881.* 2 vols. Brussels: . . . . [An account of the first fruits dances.]

2788. **Hole, H. M.** *The rise of the Matabele.* Proc. Rhodesia scientific assoc., **12**, 1913, 135.

2788a. **Hughes, A. J. B.,** and **J. van Velsen.** 1954. *The Ndebele.* Pp. 41–129, bibl. London: International African Institute. [Ethnographic Survey of Africa, Southern Africa, Part 4.]

2788b. **Taylor, Guy A.** *Some Mashona songs and dances.* N.A.D.A., **4,** 1926, 38–42.

SPANISH GUINEA (DANCE)

2789. **Gonzáles Echegaray, Carlos.** *Magia y poesia de la Ivanga.* Africa [Madrid], **11,** 145, Enero 1954, 21–23, ill.

2790. —— *Cómo se prepara una ivanga.* Africa [Madrid], 151, July 1954, 11–14, ill.

2791. **Manfredi Cano, Domingo.** *Fiesta en un poblado bubi.* Africa [Madrid], **8,** 114, June, 1951, 23–25, ill.

2792. **Mangua, Carlos.** *La ceremonia del so: escenas de miedo en la noche para probar el valor de los jovenes Fang.* Guinea espa., **59,** 1560, Sept. 1962, 272–4.

2793. **Ndongo Mba, Marcelo A.** *El tam tam: mientras la tumba brama en su selvatica canción.* Guinea espa, **56,** 1528, Jan. 1960, 13–15 [in continuation].

2794. **Tican, Michel.** 1928. *La Danza de los Caníbales: Narración de un viaje a travérs de la Guine.* Pp. 224, ill. Barcelona: Editorial Lux.

SUDAN (DANCE)

2795. **Beaton, A. C.** *The poetry of the Bari dance.* Sudan notes and records, **21** (1), 1938, 105–22.

2796. **Beaton, A. C.** *Fur dance songs.* Sudan notes and records, **23** (2), 1940, 305–29, ill.

2798. **Browne, W. G.** 1799. *Travels in Africa, Egypt and Syria from . . . 1792–1798.* Pp. xxxviii + 496, ill., maps. London: T. Cadell. [Pp. 291–2.]

2799. **Crowder, Michael.** *Islam on the Upper Nile.* Geog. mag., **31** (5), 1958, 222–35, ill., map.

2800. *Dance of the skeletons in the Sudan.* Travel, **68,** 1937, 26–27, ill.

2801. **Evans-Pritchard, E. E.** *The dance (Azande).* Africa, **1,** 4, Oct. 1928, 446–62, ill.

2802. **Giorgetti, F.** *La danza nel culto.* Nigrizia, 1954, 9–11.

2803. **Nebel, A.** *Dinka Lieder.* Arch. f. Völkerde., **15,** 1960, 34–47.

2804. **Oyler, D. S.** *Shilluk notes: some ceremonies connected with electric storms.* Sudan notes and records, **9,** 1926, 57–68. [Dance initiation.]

2805. **Tescaroli, Cirillo.** *Tersicore africana (Azande).* Nigrizia, **2,** 1963, 33–35, ill.

2806. **Titherington, G. W.** *The Raik Dinka of the Bahr El Ghazal Province.* Sudan notes and records, **10,** 1927, 192–5, ill.

2807. **Tucker, Archibald Norman.** 1933. *Tribal music and dancing in South Sudan at social and ceremonial gatherings.* Pp. 57, ill. London: W. Reeves.

See also 1484, 1532.

SWAZILAND (DANCE)

2807a. **Carter, G. H.** and **P. A.** *The Incwala festival in Swaziland.* Geog. mag., **30,** 1957–8, 263–72, ill.

2807b. **Twala, Regina G.** *Umblanga (Reed) Ceremony of the Swazi maidens.* Afr. stud., **11,** 1952, 93–104.

TANGANYIKA (DANCE)

2808. **Hall, R. de Z.** *The dance societies of the Wasukuma, as seen in the Maswa district.* Tanganyika notes and records, **1,** 1936, 94–96.

2809. **Hollis, A. C.** *Dance of Sagara women, Tanganyika Territory.* Man, **24,** 4, 1924, 5–6, ill.

2810. **Johnson, V. Eugene.** *African harvest dance (Turu).* Tanganyika notes and records, **37,** July 1954, 138–42, ill.

2810a. **Kohl-Larsen, L.** 1958. *Wildbeuter in Ostafrika—Die Tindiga.* Pp. 165, ill. Berlin: Reimer.

2811. **Mattea, A.** *Danze Kihehe.* Miss d. Consolata, 1944, 11–12.

2812. **Pakenham, R. H. W.** *Two Zanzibar ngomas (Tumbatu dances).* Tanganyika notes and records, **52,** Mar. 1959, 111–16.

2813. **Skene, R.** *Arab and Swahili dances and ceremonies,* J. roy anthrop. inst., **47,** 1917, 413–34.

See also 1544, 1977.

TOGOLAND (DANCE)

2814. **Froelich, J. C.** 1954. *La tribu Konkomba du Nord Togo.* Pp. 253, bibl., ill., maps. Dakar: I.F.A.N. [Mém. de l'I.F.A.N., no. 37.] [Dance, p. 87; music, p. 98.]

2815. **Sassoon, D. V.** *The Cabrais of Togoland.* Geog. mag., **23,** 1950–1, 339–41, ill., map.

See also 1597.

UGANDA (DANCE)

2816. **Bere, R. M.** *Acholi dances (Myel).* Uganda J., **1,** 1, Jan. 1934, 64–65.

2817. **Clark, Doris.** *Memorial service for an ox in Karamoja.* Uganda J., **16,** 1, Mar. 1952, 69–71.

2818. **Edel, May M.** 1957. *The Chiga of western Uganda.* Pp. (6) + 200, map. London: Int. African Inst.

2819. **Ingrams, William Harold.** 1960. *Uganda.* Pp. xvi + 365, bibl., ill., maps. London: H.M.S.O.

2820. **Middleton, John.** *The Yakan or Allah water cult among the Lugbara.* J. roy. anthrop. inst., **93** (1), 1963, 80–108, bibl., map. [See p. 95 for description of the ceremonial dance.]

2820a. **Wachsmann, K. P.** *Curator's report, 1955. The Uganda Museum report for the years 1954–55.* Trustees of the Uganda Museum, 1956. [Pl. 1, Dance map of Uganda.]

2821. **Winter, Edward H.** 1956. *Bwamba.* Pp. ix + 264, ill., map. Cambridge: Heffer. [Pp. 168–9.]

See also 1632, 1642.

VOLTAIC REPUBLIC (DANCE)

2822. **Delobsom, A. A. Dim.** *Les danses mossies et leur signification.* Rev. anthrop., **42,** 1932, 169–73.

2823. **Mangin, E.** *Les Mossi.* Anthropos, **9,** 1914, 98–124, 477–93, 705–36; **10/11,** 1915–1916, 187–217, 323–31.

WEST AFRICA (DANCE)
(General)

2823a. **Béart, Charles.** 1955. *Jeux et jouets de l'Ouest Africain.* Vol. 2, chaps. 27 and 29. Dakar: I.F.A.N.

2824. **Darbois, Dominique,** and **V. Vasut.** 1963. *Afrika tanzt (Guinée, Dahomey, Niger, Côte d'Ivoire).* Pp. 132 + 150, ill. Prague: Artia. Hanau: Dausien.

2825. —— 1963. *African dance.* Ill. London: Paul Hamlyn.

2825a. **Gorer, G.** 1938. *Africa Dances.* Pp. 254, ill., map. London: Lehmann. (Revised edition, 1949.)

2826. **Helfritz, H.** *Musica y danzas con mascaras en Africa occidental.* Revista musical Chilena, **14,** 1960, n. 73 (90–93); n. 74 (97–100), ill.

See also 1691.

ZAMBIA (DANCE)
(Formerly Northern Rhodesia)

2827. **Anley, V. R.** *Some dances (ancient and modern) of the Bakaonde tribe of Northern Rhodesia.* Nada [Bulawayo], **4,** 1926, 83–85.

2828. **Brelsford, W. V.** *History and customs of the Basala.* J. roy. anthrop. inst., **65,** 1935, 214–15.

2829. —— 1948. *African dances of Northern Rhodesia.* Pp. 26, ill. Livingstone: Rhodes-Livingstone Museum, Occasional Papers, no. 2.

2830. —— *Tribal dancing on the Copperbelt: European influences on old customs.* Times Brit. colonies rev., **10**, Summer 1953, p. 31, ill.

2831. **Ellenberger, D. F.** *Sur les danses de masques Mbunda (Haut-Zambeze).* L'Anthropologie, **40**, 1930, 112–15.

2832. **Jones, A. M.** *African music: the Mganda dance.* Afr. stud., **4** (4), 1945, 180–8.

2833. —— and **L. Kombe.** 1952. *The Icila dance—old style (a description of the drum and dance rhythm).* Pp. 49. Capetown: Longmans, Green, for the African Music Society.

2834. **Leenhardt, Maurice.** *La danse Makishi.* Documents [Paris], **2** (8), 1931, 52–54.

2835. **Melland, Frank Hulme.** 1923. *In witch-bound Africa.* Pp. 316, ill., map. London: Seeley Service.

2836. **Mitchell, J. Clyde.** *The Kalela dance.* Pp. viii + 52, bibl., ill. Manchester: Published on behalf of the Rhodes-Livingstone Inst. by the Manchester Univ. Press. [The Rhodes-Livingstone papers, no. 27.]

2836a. **Njungu, Agrippa.** *Dances in Barotseland.* Afr. mus. soc., **2** (4), 1961, 77–80.

2837. **Turner, V. W.** 1953. *Lunda rites and ceremonies.* Pp. 56, ill. Livingstone: Rhodes Livingstone Museum. [Occ. papers of the Rhodes/Livingstone Museum, no. 10.]

2838. **Young, Cullen.** 1931. *Notes on the customs and folklore of the Tumbuka-Kamanga peoples.* Pp. 284– . Livingstonia: Mission Press.

ZANZIBAR (DANCE)

See Tanganyika.

CATALOGUES

2839. **Angola: Luanda: Museu de Angola.** 1955. *Coleccão Etnografica.* Pp. 101, ill. Luanda: Imprensa Nacional. [With French and English summaries.]

2839a. —— 1964. *Expozição Ethnografica de Instrumentos Musicais e Máscaras dos Povos de Angola.* Pp. 34. Luanda: Museu de Angola.

2840. **Balout, L.** 1959. *Collections ethnographiques.* Album no. 1, 'Touareg Ahaggar'. S.P. 76 pl. with descriptive text. Tunis: Musée d'Ethnographie et de Préhistoire du Bardo [Tunis].

2841. **Bruxelles: Discothèque de l'Institut National de Radio-diffusion.** [s.d.]. *Catalogue de musique populaire, folklorique et ethnique* [3 vols.]. Vol. 1, Afrique, pp. 9–103 [ronéo].

2842. **Fraser, Norman** (ed.). 1954. *The international catalogue of recorded folk music* [English and French]. Pp. xii + 201. London: Oxford Univ. Press for Unesco (International Folk Music Council. Archives of recorded music, series C: Ethnographical and folk music, **4**).
See also 2875.

2843. **Gretschel, E.** *Die Buschmannsammlung Hannemann.* Jb. S. Mus. Völkerkunde [Leipzig], **5**, 1911–12, 110–12, ill.

2844. **International Commission on Folk Arts and Folklore.** 1952. *Collection Musée de l'Homme, Paris.* Pp. 74. Paris: UNESCO. [Archives de la musique enregistrée, ser. C, Musique ethnographique et folklorique, vol. 2.]

2845. —— *Collection phonothèque nationale, Paris.* Pp. 254. Paris: UNESCO. [Archives de la musique enregistrée, ser. C, Musique ethnographique et folklorique, vol. 1.]

2846. **International Folk Music Council.** 1954. *International catalogue of recorded folk music.* Pp. 201. London: Oxford Univ. Press. [Archives of recorded music, ser. C, Ethnographical and folk music, vol. 4.]

2847. **Brown, Mary Elizabeth,** and **William Adams.** 1888. *Musical instruments and their homes.* Pp. 227–72, ill. New York: Dodd, Mead.

2848. **de Amorim, Fernando Bayolo Pacheco,** and **Maria Helena Xavier de Morais.** 1955. *Catálogo-Inventário do Museu de Etnografia do Ultramar do Instituto de Antropologia da Universidade de Coimbra.* Anais Junta Investigacões Ultramar, **10** (1), Estudos de Ethnologia. Pp. 581, ill. Lisbon: Ethnographical Museum, University of Coimbra. [Music, 214–25; Africa, 1–495.]

2849. **Densmore, Frances.** 1927. *Handbook of the collection of musical instruments in the U.S.A. National Museum.* Pp. iii + 164, ill. Washington: U.S. Nat. Museum.

2850. **Ethnographie Malgache: Arts et techniques.** *Exhibition catalogue at Tananarive, including musical instruments.* Rev. Madagascar, **24**, 1955, 9–18, ill.

2851. **Farmer, H. G.** 1945. *The Glen collection of musical instruments.* Pp. 7, ill. London: Hinrichsen.

2852. **Hickmann, Hans.** 1949. *Catalogue générale des antiquités égyptiennes du Musée du Caire—instruments de musique.* Pp. iv + 213, ill. Cairo: Imprimerie de l'Institut Français d'Archéologie Orientale.

2853. **Hintermann, H.** 1932. *Eine Führung durch die Sammlung für Völkerkunde der Universität, Zürich. Abt. Afrika u. Südsee.* Pp. 168, ill., map. Zürich: Grethlein & Co. [Afrikanische Musikinstrumente, 12–18.]

2854. **Jenkins, Jean.** 1958. *Musical instruments* (*some African*). Pp. 109, bibl., ill., maps. London: Horniman Museum.

2855. **Lampreia, José D.** 1962. *Catálogo-Inventário da Secção de Etnografia do Museu da Guiné Portuguesa.* Pp. 91 + 17, ill. Lisbon: Junta de Investigações do Ultramar.

2856. **Leipzig: Karl-Marx-Universität.** 1955. *Führer durch das Musikinstrumenten-Museum.*

2857. **Maesen, A.,** and **Others.** 1950. *Les arts au Congo belge et au Ruanda-Urundi.* Pp. 98, ill. Brussels: Centre d'Information et de Documentation. [Exposition Vaticane.]

2858. **Mahillon, Victor.** *Catalogue descriptif et analytique du Musée instrumental du Conservatoire Royal de Musique de Bruxelles* [5 vols.]. Vol. 1, 1893, pp. 535. Vol. 2, 1909, pp. 521. Vol. 3, 1900, pp. 524. Vol. 4, 1912, pp. 508. Vol. 5, 1922, pp. 237. 1893–1922, ill. Gand: Huste.

2859. **Mercier, P.,** and **J. Lombard.** 1959. *Guide du Musée d'Abomey.* Pp. 40, ill. Dakar: I.F.A.N. [Études Dah., I.F.A.N.]

2860. **Meslé, d'E.** *Les Musées de l'I.F.A.N. au Cameroun.* Études Cam., special no. (1956), 1–55, bibl., ill.

2861. **Montandon, Georges.** *Catalogue raisonné des instruments de musique du Musée ethnographique de Genève au Parc Mon-Repos.* Archives suisses d'anthrop. générale, **3** (3), 1919, 95–118.

2862. **Museums and Art Galleries. Great Britain:** 1956. *Museums and galleries in Great Britain and Northern Ireland.* Pp. 48, ill. London: Index Publishers.

2863. **New York: Metropolitan Museum of Art.** 1907. *Handbook no. 13. Catalogue of the Crosby Brown collection of musical instruments of all nations.* Vol. 1, no. 3, pt. 1, Africa.

2864. **Osorio de Oliveira, José.** *Le musée d'une culture africaine* (*Musée de Dundo*). Congo-Tervuren, **2** (3–4), 1956, 55–59, ill.

2865. **Philadelphia: Commercial Museum.** 1961. *A handbook of the musical instrument collection . . . by J. Barone.* Pp. 63 [Africa, 37–48], ill. Philadelphia: Commercial Museum.

2866. **Puccioni, Nello.** *Les instruments de musique du Musée national d'Anthropologie.* Archivio Antr. p. Etnol., **36**, 1906.

2866a. **Rome: Museo Preistorico-Etnografico 'Luigi Pigorini'.** *Gli instrumenti musicali Africani del . . . Museo.* [A catalogue by Pietro Scotti, with plates, 1940.] Archivio antrop. and etnol., **70** (1–4), 1871.

2867. **Schlosser, Julius.** 1920. *Die Sammlung alter Musikinstrumente.* Pp. 143, ill. Vienna: Anton Schroll.

2868. **Scotti, Pietro.** *Gli strumenti musicali africani del R. Museo Pigorini* (*Rome*). Archivio p. Antr. & Etnol., **70**, 1–4, 1940, 5–60, ill.

2869. **Spannaus, Gunther.** 1954. *Musik und Musikinstrumente.* Führer durch die Schausammlungen des Instituts für Völkerkunde, Universität Göttingen, pp. 91–99.

2870. **Thomas, E. S.** 1924. *Catalogue of the Ethnographical Museum of the Royal Geographical Society of Egypt.* Pp. 1–17, Music. Cairo: Royal Geographical Society.

2871. **Tracey, Hugh.** *African music research: transcription library of gramophone records. Handbook for librarians* (*with classified catalogues of Bantu and non-Bantu languages*). 1948. Pp. 77, ill., map. Johannesburg: Gallo (Africa) Ltd.

2872. —— *Catalogue, July 1951. Gramophone records of African music and semi-African music, recorded in many different territories on the continent of Africa by African Music Research.* Pp. 34, ill. Johannesburg: Gallo (Africa) Ltd.

2872a. —— 1952. Pp. 54. (2nd Edition.)

2873. —— 1963. *The 'Sound of Africa' series of long-playing records, collected and classified with card index for . . . all students of the indigenous arts of central and southern Africa by the International Library of African Music* (*Msaho, Box 138, Roodepoort, Transvaal*). Pp. 36.

2874. **Vienna: Museum für Völkerkunde.** *Aussereuropäische Musikinstrumente. Vienna, 1961.* 8vo. Pp. 89, ill. [By Alfred Janata.]

2875. **Wachsmann, Klaus P.** (*ed.*). *An international catalogue of published records of folk music: a selected list of records of authentic folk music by traditional performers (compiled on behalf of the International Folk Music Council).* Bull. Brit. inst. recorded sound, **17/18**, 1960, pp. iii + 37.

2875a. **Zürich: Switzerland, Museum Rietberg.** 1963. *Afrikanische Skulpturen: Beschreibender Katalog* (*Widmung zum 80. Geburtstag von Dr. Edouard von der Heydt*). [By E. Leuzinger.] Pp. 326, bibl., ill., map. Zürich: Atlantis Verlag. [German and English in parallel columns.]

BIBLIOGRAPHIES

BIBLIOGRAPHIES OF MUSIC AND DANCING IN AFRICA

BIBLIOGRAPHY PART 1

2876. **African Music Society.** *The international library of African music.* Afr. mus. soc., 1 (1), 1954, 71–73; 2 (1), 1958, 63–64.

2877. **Anon.** 1930. *A bibliography relating to indigenous art in tropical Africa: notes on African music and exhibitions of African art.* Typescript of (11 pp.) R.C.S.

2878. **Barblan, Guglielmo.** 1941. *Musiche e strumenti musicali dell' Africa orientale Italiana.* Pp. 147, bibl., ill. Naples: Edizioni della Triennale d'Oltremare.

2879. **Carl Gregor, Duke of Mecklenburg.** 1962. *Bibliographie einiger Grenzgebiete der Musikwissenschaft.* Pp. 197. Baden-Baden: Bibliotheca Bibliographica Aureliana, vol. 6. [Over 3,500 entries.]

2880. **Daugherty, D. N.** 1940. *A bibliography of periodical literature in musicology and allied fields and a record of graduate theses accepted.* Washington: American Council of Learned Societies.

2881. **George, Zelma Watson.** 1953. *A guide to negro music. An annotated bibliography of negro folk music and art music by negro composers or based on negro thematic material.* Ann Arbor University. [Microfilms publ. no. 8021.]

2882. **Hambly, Wilfrid D.** 1937. *Source book for African anthropology* [2 vols.]. Vol. 2, Bibliography music and dancing, pp. 613–46. Chicago: Field Museum. [Supplement to Source Book 'Bibliography' 1937–49. Publications of the Field Museum of Natural History: Anthropological Series.]

2883. **Hutson, Jean Blackwell.** *African materials in the Schomburg collection of negro literature and history.* Afr. Stud. Bull., 3, no. 11, 1960, 1–4.

2884. **Johannesburg: Public Library.** 1944. *Catalogue of music in the Strange collection of Africana.* Pp. 118. Johannesburg: Public Library. [Supplement issued 1945.]

2885. **Jolly, David.** *Bibliography and the arts of Africa.* Afr. Stud. Bull., 3 (1), 1960, 4–9.

2886. **Jones, A. M.** *Sound of Africa series (International Library of African Music, Johannesburg, Director Hugh Tracey).* Africa, 30, 1, Jan. 1960, 98–99.

2886a. **Kunst, Jaap.** 1959. *Ethnomusicology.* Pp. x + 303. The Hague: Nijhoff. [3rd ed.]

2887. —— 1960. *Supplement to the third edition.* Pp. vii + 45. The Hague: Nijhoff.

2888. **Kurath, Gertrude Prokosch.** *Panorama of dance ethnology.* Current anthropology, 1 (3), May 1960, 233–54, bibl.

2889. **McCrindell, Jane M.** *The scope of the African Music Research Library, Johannesburg.* S. Afr. Libr., 17, 3, Jan. 1950, 133–4.

2890. **Merriam, Alan P.** *An annotated bibliography of African and African derived music since 1936.* Africa, 21, 1951, 319–29, bibl.

2891. —— *A bibliography of jazz.* American folklore Soc. (bibliographical series), vol. 4, 1954, 145 pp.

2892. —— *An annotated bibliography of theses and dissertations in ethnomusicology and folk music accepted at American universities.* Ethnomusicology, 4, 1960, 21–39.

2893. —— *African music (bibliography).* Afr. Stud. Bull., 5, 2, May 1962, 35–40.

2894. **Nettl, Bruno.** 1961. *Reference materials in ethnomusicology.* Pp. 46 (2), bibl. Detroit: Information Service Inc. [Detroit studies in music bibliography, 1.]

2895. **Sachs, Curt.** 1929. *Geist und Werden der Musikinstrumente.* Pp. xii + 282, bibl., ill. Berlin: Reimer. [Included here for the bibliography.]

2896. **Sammelbände zur vergleichenden Musikwissenschaft, 1.** Munich, 1922.

2897. **Thieme, Darius L.** *A selected bibliography of periodical articles on the music of the native peoples of sub-Saharan Africa.* Afr. music, 3, 1, 1962, 103–10.

2898. —— 1964. *African music: a briefly annotated bibliography.* Pp. xxvi + 55, map. Washington: Library of Congress (Ref. Dept., Music Div.).

2899. **Valle, Rafael Heliodoro.** *Para la Bibliografíá Afroamericana.* Ortiz, Fernando, Miscelanea de Estudios dedicados a Fernando Ortiz, vol. 3, 1957, 1427–65.

2900. **Varley, D. H.** 1936. *African native music: an annotated bibliography.* Pp. 116. London: The Royal Empire Society.

2901. **Van der Merwe, F. Z.** 1958. *Suid-Afrikaanse Musiekbibliografie, 1787–1952.* Pp. iii + 407. Pretoria: Van Schaik. [Aanhangsel: Muziek van 1953, p. 410.]

BIBLIOGRAPHY PART 2

BIBLIOGRAPHIES OF AFRICANA LIKELY TO BE OF USE TO THE STUDENT

2902. *Africana Newsletter.*

2903. *African Abstracts.*

2904. *African Studies.* Bull, New York.

2905. *African Studies,* London.

2906. **Balandier, G., Middleton, J. F. M., and Others.** *International bibliography of social and cultural anthropology.* Vol. 1 (1955), pub. 1958, 259. Vol. 2 (1956), pub. 1959, 391. Vol. 3 (1957), pub. 1959, 410. Paris: UNESCO.

2907. **Banks, A.** 1960. *An African book-list.* London: . . . .

2908. **Belgium: Ministère des Colonies.** 1913. *Catalogue de la bibliothèque: 1 Afrique.*

2909. **Blaudin de Thé, Bernard.** 1960. *Essai de bibliographie du Sahara français et des régions avoisinantes.* Pp. 258. Paris: Arts et Métiers Graphiques. [Addresses of some of the French periodicals mentioned in the bibliography.]

2909a. *Boletim Bibliografico do Centro de Documentação Científica Ultramarina.* Lisbon: In progress.

2910. **Breuil, Henri.** *Publications on Africa.* J. soc. africanistes, 32, 1962, 75–89, map.

2911. **Collison, R. L.** *Bibliographical services throughout the world* [Africa, pp. 8–19]. 4th ann. rep., 1954/55, 145. Paris: UNESCO.

2912. —— 1950. *The cataloguing, arrangement and filing of special material in special libraries.* Pp. iv + 76. London: A.S.L.I.B.

2912a. **Conover, Helen F.** 1960. *A list of references on libraries, archives and book production in Africa.* Pp. 54. Washington: Library of Congress.

2912b. —— 1961. *Serials for African studies.* Pp. viii + 163. Washington: Library of Congress. [Introductory list of bibliographies, 1861, p. 7.]

2912c. —— 1962. *African libraries, book production and archives.* Pp. vi + 64. Washington: Library of Congress.

2913. —— 1959. *The bibliography of newly developing areas.* Library trends [Urbana, Ill.], 8 (2), 1959, 322–41.

2914. **Dahlberg, Richard E., and B. E. Thomas.** *An analysis and bibliography of recent African atlases.* Afr. Stud. Bull., 5, no. 3, 1962, 23–33.

2915. *Encyclopédie de l'Afrique française.* *Algérie–Sahara* [2 vols.]. Tunisie. Maroc. *Afrique occidentale française* [2 vols.]. Afrique équatoriale française. Cameroun-Togo, 1951. Madagascar-Réunion [2 vols.]. [Ed. by Eugène Guernier.] Editions de l'Union Francaise.

2916. *Ethnographic survey of Africa.* [Ed. by C. D. Forde.]

2917. *Ethnologischer Anzeiger.* 1926–1944. [4 vols.].

2918. *Ethnology and sociology.* Quarterly list of ethnology (and) sociology. An international index of current books, monographs, brochures and separates. Vol. 2, no. 1. 1951– .

2919. **Evanston: North Western University.** 1962. *Catalog of the African collection (21,500 vols.) [2 vols.].* Vol. 1, A–K, pp. 698. Vol. 2, L–Z, pp. 652. Boston, Mass.: G. K. Hall.

2920. **Fontán Lobé, Juan.** 1946. *Bibliografia colonial: contribución a un indice de publicaciones africanas.* Pp. 669. Madrid: Dirección general de Marruecos y Colonias.

2921. **Forde, C. D.** N.D. *Select annotated bibliography of tropical Africa.* Pp. 504. London: International African Institute, 20th Century Fund, New York.

2922. **Fraser, Douglas.** *African architecture (bibliography).* Afr. Stud. Bull., **5**, no. 2, 1962, 47–49.

2923. **Freer, P.** (ed.). 1952. *Catalogue of Union periodicals.* Vol. 2, The humanities. Pp. 806. Pretoria: National Council of Social Research.

2924. **Geiger, P.,** and **R. Wildhaber.** 1949, 1950. *Bibliographie internationale des arts et des traditions populaires, 1939–41, 1942–47.* Pp. 273, 482. Paris: Commission Int. des Arts et Traditions Populaires (C I A P).

2925. **Gray, T.** 1875. *Bibliographie des ouvvrages relatifs à l'Afrique et a l'Arabie: catalogue méthodique de tous les ouvrages français et des principaux en langues etrangères traitant de la géographie, de l'histoire, du commerce, des lettres et des arts de l'Afrique et de l'Arabie.* San Remo Paris: . . . .

2926. **Haden, J. W.** 1958. *Bibliographical contributions.* No. 16, Africa. Pp. 97. Geneva: Int. Labour Office.

2927. **Hambly, Wilfrid D.** 1937. *Source book for African anthropology.* Pp. 404, 953, 292, bibl., ill., maps. Pt. 2, 728–866. Chicago: Field Museum of Natural History (Anthropological Series), vol. 26. [Supplement in Fieldiana (anthropology), **37**, 1952, 155–292.]

2927a. **Hewitt, A. R.** 1958. *Guide to resources for Commonwealth studies in London.* Pp. – . Oxford: . . . .

2928. **Holdsworth, Mary.** *Afrikakunde in der Sovjetunion.* Osteurapa [Stuttgart], 7–8, 1959, 442–51.

2929. **Hodgkin, Thomas.** *Soviet Africanists.* West Afr., **2209**, 1959, 801; **2210**, 1959, 829–30; **2211**, 1959, 857–8.

2930. **Hughes, H. G. A.** *The bibliography of British Africa and the co-ordination of African studies.* Afr. affairs, **48** (190), 1949, 63–72.

2931. **Italiaander, Rolf.** 1961. *Africana: selected bibliography of readings in African history and civilisation.* Pp. 6 + 103. Hope College, Holland, Michigan.

2932. **Jones, Ruth** (Africa Bibliography Series). 1958. *West Africa.* Pp. 116. London: Int. Afr. Inst.

2933. —— 1959. *N.E. Africa.* Pp. 51. London: Int. Afr. Inst.

2934. —— 1960. *East Africa.* Pp. 62. London: Int. Afr. Inst.

2935. —— 1961. *S. E. Central Africa.* Pp. 53. Int. Afr. Inst.

2936. **Keesing, F. M.** 1953. *Culture change: an analysis and bibliography of anthropological sources.* Pp. i, ix + 242. Stanford, Calif.: Stamford Univ. Press.

2937. **King, P. S.,** and **P. L. Theimer.** 1956. *Tropical Africa: administrative division (map and list).* Pp. 5. Stanford, Calif.: Stanford Univ. Press. [Stanford University Ford Research Institute, California, U.S.A.]

2938. **Lavanoux, Maurice.** *A selected, annotated bibliography on Africa.* Liturgical arts [N.Y.], **26**, 3/4 (suppl.), Apr. 1959, 3–39.

2939. **Levi-Strauss, C.** 1956. *French bibliographical digest: Anthropology 1—Physical anthropology and prehistoric archaeology; 2—Ethnology and social anthropology.* Pp. 63 and 88, ill. New York: Cultural Division of the French Embassy.

2940. **von Luschan, Felix.** *Die Bibliographie Felix von Luschan.* Zeit f. Ethnol., **83**, 1958, 285–95, ill.

2941. **McKay, V.,** and **Others.** *American library resources for African studies.* Afr. Stud. Bull. [N.Y.], **2** (1), 1959, 21.

2942. **Michigan State University.** 1958. *Michigan State University: Institute of Research and Overseas programmes. The international progress of American universities: an inventory and analysis.*

2943. **Mylius, Norbert.** 1952. *Afrika bibliographie, 1943–1951.* Pp. vi + 237. Vienna: Museum für Völkerkunde.

2944. **New York: Metropolitan Museum of Art.** 1960. *Library catalog.* Vols. 1–25, A–Z. Boston: G. K. Hall.

2945. **Paris: Comité du Film.** *Ethnographique catalogue des filmes ethnographiques français.* UNESCO: Cah. Centr. Documen., **15**, 1955, 72.

2946. **Paulitschke, P.** 1882. *Die Afrika-l'teratur in der Zeit von 1500 bis 1750 B.C.* Pp. v + 122. Vienna: – .

2947. **Porter, D. P.** (ed.). 1958. *A catalogue of the African collection in the Moorland Foundation, Howard University Library.* Pp. 398. Washington: Howard Univ. Press.

2948. **Ragatz, L. J.** 1943. *A bibliography for the study of African history in the 19th and 20th centuries.* Pp. 47. Washington: Paul Pearlman.

2949. **Robinson, A. M. L.** 1955. *A bibliography of African bibliographies.* Pp. 169. Cape Town: S. African Library. [Grey bibliographies, no. 6.]

2950. **Sieber, Roy.** *African art (bibliography).* Afr. Stud. Bull., **5**, no. 2, 1962, 40–44.

2951. **Spain.** 1947. *Exposition de libros espanoles sobre historia de Africa.* Pp. 100.

2952. **Streit, P. Robert,** and **P. Johannes Dindinger.** 1951–4. *Bibliotheca Missionum* [6 vols.]. [Afrikansiche Missionsliteratur.] Band 15, 1053–1599, nos. 1–2217. Band 16, 1600–99, nos. 2218–5151. Band 17, 1700–1879, nos. 5152–7723. Band 18, 1880–1909, nos. 7724–9753. Band 19, 1910–40, nos. 9754–9843. Band 20, 1910–40, nos. 9844–10818. Freiburg: Herder.

2953. **Tenri Central Library: Tenri, Japan.** 1960. *Catalogue of books relating to Africa.* Tenri Central Library, series no 24. Pp. 431, ill.

2953a. —— 1964. *Catalogue of books relating to Africa.* Tenri Central Library, series no. 27. Pp. 283, ill.

2954. **Ternaux-Compans, Henri.** 1841. (1–2). *Bibliotheque asiatique et africaine ou catalogue des ouvrages relatifs à l'Asie et à l'Afrique qui ont parus depuis la découverte de l'imprimerie jusqu'en 1700.* Pp.: vi + 347. Paris: . . . .

2955. **University of London: School of Oriental and African Studies.** 1963. *Library catalogue.* Vol. 15. Subject-catalogue Africa. Boston, Mass.: G. K. Hall.

2956. **U.S.A. Dept. of State: Office of Intelligence.** *Africa.* External research list no. 13.6. April 1956, 12.

2957. **Washington: Library of Congress [European Affairs Division].** 1952. *Introduction to Africa: a select guide to background reading.* Pp. x + 237. Washington: Univ. Press.

2959. **Wieschoff, H. A.** 1948. *Anthropological bibliography of negro Africa (up to 1942).* Pp. xi + 461. New Haven, Conn.: Amer. Orient. Soc. Amer. Orient Series, vol. 23.

2960. **Work, Monroe Nathan.** 1928. *A bibliography of the negro in Africa and America.* Pp. 21, 698. New York: H. W. Wilson.

NORTH AFRICA

2961. **Bauer, Y.,** and **Ignacio Landauer.** 1922. *Apuntes para una bibliografia de Marruecos.* Pp. xvi + 1023. Madrid: Editorial Ibero-Africano-Americana.

2962. **Conover, H. F.** 1957. *North and North-East Africa: a selected, annotated list of writings 1951–57.* Pp. 182. Washington: Library of Congress.

2963. **C.O.W.A. Surveys and Bibliographies.** *North-West*

Africa, no. 1. 1958. Cambridge, Mass.: Council for Old World Archaeology.

2964. **de Centival, Pierre,** and **Others.** n.d. *Bibliographie marocaine, 1923–1933.* Pp. 606. Paris: Larose.

2965. **Hill, R. W.** 1959. *A bibliography of Libya.* Pp. 100. Durham: Durham Colleges in the University of Durham: Dept. of Geography, Research papers series no. 1.

2966. **Ibrahim Hilmi, Prince.** *The literature of Egypt and the Soudan from the earliest times to . . . 1885* [2 vols.].

2966a. **Jones, Ruth.** 1959. *North-East Africa.* Pp. iii + 51. London: Int. African Inst. [Africa bibliography series.]

2967. **Lacoste, Camille.** 1962. *Bibliographie ethnologique de la Grande Kabylie.* Pp. 103. Paris and The Hague: Mouton & Co.

2968. **el Nasri, Abdel Rahman.** 1962. *A bibliography of the Sudan, 1938–58.* Pp. x + 171. London: Oxford Univ. Press.

2969. **Pearson, J. D.** 1958. *Index Islamicus, 1906–55.* Pp. xxxvi + 897. Cambridge: Heffer.

2970. —— 1962. *Supplement to Index Islamicus, 1956–60.* Pp. xxviii + 316. Cambridge: Heffer.

2971. **Rabat: Institut des Hautes Études Marocaines.** *Publications de l'institut des hautes études marocaines, 1915–35.* Tables et Index-supplement à 'Hespéris', 1936, p. 81. Rochfort-sur-Mer: Institut des Hautes Études Marocaines.

2972. **Tetuán: Bibliotheca General del Protectorado.** 1946. *Catálogo de Autores.* Pp. 677, ill. Tetuán: Librería Escola.

CENTRAL AFRICA

2973. **Baxter, J. W.** *The preservation of archives with particular reference to Central Africa.* Human problems, British Central Africa, 8, 1949, 57–66.

2974. **Santandrea, S.** 1948. *Bibliografia di studi africani della missione dell' Africa Centrale (Verona Mission).* Pp. xxviii + 167, map. Verona: Istituto Missioni Africani. [Museum Combonianum, no. 1.]

2975. **University of Sydney: Anthrop. Dept.** *Ethnography of Central Africa. Select bibliography revised to February 1958.* 1958, 16.

CONGO

2976. **Belgium.** 1957. *Office de l'information pour le Congo belge et le Ruanda-Urundi. Liste des sociétés et institutions coloniales.* Pp. 80.

2977. **Berlage, J.** 1955. *Répertoire de la presse du Congo belge (1884–1954) et du Ruanda-Urundi (1920–1954).* Pp. 64. Brussels: Min Colonies (Bibl. Belgica, 10).

2978. **Boone, Olga.** *Bibliographie ethnographique du Congo belge et des regions avoisinantes.* 1925– . [In progress (1963).]

2979. **C.E.P.S.I.** *Centre d'Étude des Problèmes Sociaux Indigènes.* 1948. *Catalogue de la bibliothèque.* Pp. 103. Elisabethville: C.E.P.S.I.

2980. **de Rop, E. P. A.** 1956. *Bibliografie over de Mongo.* Pp. 101, map. Brussels: Acad. roy. des Sci. Col. Classe des Sci. Mor. & Polit. Mem. in 80, N.S. tome 8, fasc. 2.

2981. **Heyse, Théodore.** 1948. *Bibliographie du Congo belge et du Ruanda-Urundi (1939–47).* Pp. 32. Brussels: Cahiers Belges et Congolais, no. 6.

2982. —— 1950. *Bibliographie du Congo belge et du Ruanda-Urundi, 1939–1949.* Pp. 46, ill. Brussels: Cahiers Belges et Congolais, no. 11.

2983. —— 1951. *Bibliographie du Congo belge et du Ruanda-Urundi (1939–50).* Pp. 51. Brussels: G. van Campenhout.

2984. **Inbocol.** 1, 7, 1937, Placard 99. *Index bibliographique colonial Congo belge & Ruanda Urundi div.,* by Th. Heyse. Placard 99–101, Art indigène. Placard 131–3, Arts indigènes, arts plastiques et métiers.

2985. **Kellermann, L.** 1953. *Catalogue de la bibliothèque de l'I.É.C. (Suppl. no. 1.)* Pp. 234. Brazzaville: Inst. d'études Centrafricaines.

2986. **Lambert, J.** 1951. *Catalogue de la bibliothèque de l'I.É.C. (matières, auteurs et périodiques).* Pp. 153. Brazzaville: Institut d'études Centrafricaines (Mém. no. 4).

2987. **Simar, Th.** 1912. *Bibliographie congolaise de 1895 à 1910.* Pp. – . Brussels: . . . .

2988. **Tervuren: Musée Royale du Congo Belge.** *Bibliographie ethnographique du Congo belge et des regions avoisinantes. See 2978.*

2989. **Walraet, M.** *Bibliographie du Katanga.* Fasc. 1, 1824– . Fasc. 2, 1900–24. Fasc. 3, 1925–9. A.R.S.C. (sciences morales), **32,** 14 and 23, 1954–60, 136, 234, 280, maps.

2990. **Wauters, A. J.** 1895. *Bibliographie du Congo, 1880–1895. Catalogue methodique de 3800 ouvrages et brochures relatifs au Congo.* Brussels, 354.

2991. **Wauters, G.** 1949. *L'Esoterie des noirs devoilée.* Pp. 384, ill. Brussels: Éditions Éuropeennes.

EAST AFRICA

2992. **Brantschen, Anastas.** *Die ethnographische Literatur über den Ulaga-Distrikt, Tanganyika Territorium.* Acta Tropica: Separatum, vol. 10, no. 2, 1953, 150–85.

2992a. **C.O.W.A. Surveys and Bibliographies.** *East Africa,* no. 1. 1958. Cambridge, Mass.: Council for Old World Archaeology.

2993. **Gillman, C.** *A bibliography of Kilimanjaro.* Tanganyika notes and records, **18,** 1944, 60–68.

2993a. **Jones, Ruth.** 1960. *East Africa.* Pp. iii + 62. London: Int. African Inst. [Africa bibliography series.]

2994. **Whiteley, W. H.,** and **A. E. Gutkind.** 1954. *A linguistic bibliography of East Africa.* Pp. 61. Kampala: Government Printer.

WEST AFRICA

2995. **Brasseur, Paule.** *Bibliographie générale du Mali (Anciens Soudan français et Haut-Sénégal-Niger.* Pp. 461, map. Dakar: I.F.A.N. [Catalogues et documents, no. 16.]

2996. **Bruel, Georges.** 1914. *Bibliographie de l'Afrique équatoriale française.* Pp. iv + 326. Paris: E. Larose.

2997. **Cardinall, A. W.** 1932. *A bibliography of the Gold Coast.* Pp. 384. Accra: Government Printing Office.

2998. **Clozel, M.** 1891. *Bibliographie des ouvrages relatifs à la Sénégambia et au Soudan occidental.* Pp. 60. Paris: Institut Géographique de Paris. [Ex. La revue de géographie.]

2999. **Conover, H. F.** 1959. *Nigerian official publications, 1869–1959: a guide.* Pp. xii + 153. Washington: Library of Congress.

3000. —— 1960. *Official publications of French West Africa, 1946–58: a guide.* Pp. 88. Washington: Library of Congress.

3000a. **C.O.W.A. Surveys and Bibliographies.** *Equatorial Africa,* no. 1. 1958. Cambridge, Mass.: Council for Old World Archaeology.

3000b. —— *West Africa,* no. 1–99. 1958–99. Cambridge, Mass.: Council for Old World Archaeology.

3001. **Gamble, David Percy.** 1958. *Bibliography of the Gambia.* Pp. 36. London: Colonial Office Research Department.

3002. **Harris, J.** 1959. *Books about Nigeria: a select reading list.* Pp. 39. Ibadan: Univ. Press.

3002a. **Jones, Ruth.** 1958. *West Africa.* Pp. v + 116. London: Int. African Inst. [Africa bibliography series].

3003. **Joucla, E.,** and **Others.** 1937. *Bibliographie de l'Afrique occidentale Française.* Pp. 704. Paris: Société d'Éditions Géographiques, Maritimes et Coloniales. [2nd ed.]

3004. **Junta de Investigacões do Ultramar.** *Centro de Documentacão Científica Ultramarina.* Bibliografia Científica da Junta de Investigacões do Ultramar. Vol. 1 (1958), pp. 371. Lisbon: Junta de Investigacões do Ultramar.

3005. **Lebeuf, Jean-Paul.** *Bibliographie Saô et Kotoko (A.O.F.)* Bull. Études Cam., 1948.

3006. **Lopes Cardoso, Carlos.** *Contribuição para a Bibliografia dos Bochimanes de Angola.* Boletim do Instituto de Angola, no. 14, 1960, 21, map.

3007. **Luke, Harry Charles.** 1910. *A bibliography of Sierra Leone.* Pp. 144, maps. Oxford: Clarendon Press.

3008. **Pitcher, G. M.** 1960. *Bibliography of Ghana, 1957–1959.* Pp. 177. Kumasi: Kumasi College of Technology.

3009. **Portugal: Junta de Investigacões do Ultramar.** 1959. *Periódicos Portugueses de interesse ultramarino (actualmente em publicacão).* Pp. 89. Lisbon: Centro de Documentacão Cientifica Ultramarina.

3010. **Sanner, P.** 1949. *Bibliographie ethnographique de l'Afrique équatoriale française, 1914–48.* Pp. 107. Paris: Imprimerie Nationale.

SOUTH AFRICA

3011. **Boone, Olga** (ed.). 1962. *Bibliographie ethnographique de l'Afrique Sud-Saharienne to 1960.* Pp. (6) 444. Tervuren: Musée Royal de l'Afrique Centrale.

3012. **Brett, Edwin A.** N.D. *Tentative list of books and pamphlets on southern Africa, published in the U.S.A. and Canada.* Pp. iii + 48. Johannesburg: Public Library.

3013. **Brown, J. Cudd.** 1959. *A reading list on Africa south of the Sahara.* Pp. 21. Stanford, Calif.: Hoover Inst. on War, Revolution and Peace.

3014. **Cape Town: South African Public Library.** 1948. *A bibliography of African bibliographies.* Grey bibliographies, no. 2. Pp. 52.

3015. —— 1951. *Classified list of South African annual publications as at March 1951.*

3016. —— 1951. *Handlist of South African periodicals current in December 1951.*

3017. —— 1952. *South Africa in print: catalogue of an exhibition of books atlases and maps in the . . . Library, 1 March to 5 April 1952.*

3018. —— *Africana Nova: a quarterly bibliography.* No. 1 (1958), 20. Cape Town: S.A. Public Library.

3019. **Carpenter, Olive.** 1946. *The development of Southern Rhodesia from the earliest times to 1900: a bibliography.* s.p. Cape Town: University School of Librarianship.

3020. **Conover, H. F.** 1957. *Africa south of the Sahara: a selected, annotated list of writings, 1951–56.* Pp. 269. Washington: Library of Congress.

3021. **Costa, Mário.** 1946. *Bibliografia geral de Moçambique.* Pp. 359. Lisbon: Agência Geral das Colónias.

3021a. **C.O.W.A. Surveys and Bibliographies.** *South Africa,* no. 1. 1958. Cambridge, Mass.: Council for Old World Archaeology.

3022. **de Almeida de Eca, Filipe Gastão.** 1949. *Bibliografia de Mocambique.* Pp. 134. Lisbon: Agência Geral das Colónias.

3023. **Grandidier, Alfred** and **Guillaume.** 1904–28. *Ethnographique de Madagascar.* Tom. 1, 2 and 3 (1908–17), ill., maps.

3025. **Grandidier, G.,** and **E. Joucla.** 1935 and 1957. *Bibliographie de Madagascar, 1904–33. Bibliographie de Madagascar, 1934–35.* Pp. viii + 1350; viii + 1351–1910, ill. Paris: Société d'Éditions Geographiques, Maritimes et Coloniales. Tananarive: Institut de Récherche Scientifique de Madagascar.

3026. **Johannesburg: Public Library.** 1959. *Tentative list of books and pamphlets on Southern Africa published in the United States and Canada.* [Compiled by A. E. Brett.] Pp. iii + 48. Johannesburg: Public Library.

3026a. **Jones, Ruth.** 1961. *South-East Central Africa and Madagascar.* Pp. iii + 53. London: Int. African Inst. [Africa bibliography series.]

3027. **Kelley, Douglas C.** 1960. *Africa in Paperbacks:* 199 paperbound books on Africa south of the Sahara, in print May 1960. Pp. 37. East Lansing: Michigan State Univ.

3028. **Klein, H.** *Afrika südlich der Sahara: Ethnologische Veröffentlichungen, 1945–50.* Paiduma, 5, 1951, 138–50.

3029. **Mendelssohn, S.** 1910. *Mendelssohn's South African bibliography* [2 vols.]. Vol. 1, lxxii + 1008. Vol. 2, (6) + 1139. London: Kegan Paul.

3030. **Musiker, R.** (ed.). 1958. *Guide to South African reference books.* Rondebosch, P.O. 59 for Univ. of Cape Town.

3031. **Rita-Ferreira, A.** 1962. *Bibliografia Etnologica de Mocambique (Das origens a 1954).* Pp. xiii + 254. Lisbon: Junta de Investigações do Ultramar.

3032. **Schapera, Isaac.** 1941. *Select bibliography of South African native life and problems.* Pp. xii + 249. London: Oxford Univ. Press. [Supplement to above by A. Holden and A. Jacoby, 1950. Pp. 32. Cape Town Univ.]

3033. **Sherlock, J.** 1963. *The Zambezi: a bibliography.* Pp. iv + 20. Cape Town: Univ. of Cape Town (School of Librarianship).

3034. **South Africa: University.** 1958. *List of dissertations and theses accepted by the University of South Africa 1919–1958.* Pp. 96. Pretoria: Communications of the University of S. Africa.

3035. **Spohr, O. H.** 1949. *Photographic service points in libraries, archives and museums in South Africa.* Pp. 18. Cape Town: Univ. Library.

3036. **Stevens, Pamela.** 1947. *Bibliography of Bechuanaland.* Pp. —.

3037. **Van den Berghe, L.,** and **L. de Heusch.** *Rencontres internationales: le cinéma et l'Afrique au sud du Sahara.* Expos. Univ. et Internat. [Brussels], 24–26 July, 1958, 130.

3038. **Van Warmelo, N. J.** 1952. *Language map of Africa.* Pp. 20, map. Pretoria: Department of Native Affairs. [Ethnol. pubn., no. 27.]

3039. **Welch, Floretta J.** 1946. *South West Africa: a bibliography.* Pp. v + 88. Cape Town: University School of Librarianship.

3040. **Worthington, E. B.** (ed.). 1954. *Recherches relatives aux sciences humaines en Afrique au Sud du Sahara.* [In French and English]. Pp. 75. Bukavu, C. B.: CSA, BP, 5175 (pubn. no. 7.)

PERIODICALS

PERIODICALS CONCERNED SPECIFICALLY WITH MUSIC OR DANCING

3041. *African Music Society Newsletter*. Vol. I, no. 1, June 1948. Pp. 33. Johannesburg, P.O. Box 2616.

3042. *African Music*. Journal of the African Music Society. Vol. 1. 1954.

3043. **Collaer, Paul** (ed.). *Colloques de Wégimont: cercle international d'études ethno-musicologiques*. Brussels: Vol. 1. 1954.

3044. *English Folk Dance and Song Society*. 1936. Vol. 1. London: The Society.

3045. *Ethnomusicology*. Journal of the Society for Ethnomusicology. Vol. 1. 1953. Middletown, Conn.

3046. *The Folklore and Folk Music Archivist*. Bloomington, Ind. 1958.

3046a. *International Folk Music Council*. Journal. Vol. 1. 1949. London: Cambridge Univ. Press.

3047. *Jahrbuch für Musikalische Volks und Völkerkunde*. Vol. 1. 1963.

3048. *Journal of the Galpin Society*. Vol. 1. 1948.

3049. *The Music Index*. Vol. 1. 1949. Publishers Information Service Inc., 10 W. Warren, Detroit 1, Michigan.

3050. **Tracey, Hugh.** *The African music society*. Ethnomusicology Newsletter, XI, 1957, 16–18.

3051. *Zeitschrift für Vergleichende Musikwissenschaft* [Gesellschaft zur Erforschung der Musik des Orients]. Berlin: V, 1–3, 1933–35.

OTHER PERIODICALS CONSULTED

Numbers in brackets refer to entries extracted from the periodicals consulted.

A

3051a. *Abhandlungen zur Anthropologie, Ethnologie und Urgeschichte* (1782).

3051b. *Abhandlungen des Hamburgischen Kolonial Instituts* (1547), (1572).

3052. *Acadèmie Royale des Sciences Coloniales (Sciences Morales) Mém.* [Brussels]. (1845), (2558), (2558a), (2587).

3053. *Acta Musicologica* (240), (244), (732), (2387), (2443), (2458).

3054. *Aequatoria* (268), (491), (504a), (557), (559), (2133), (2589).

3055. *Africa* [London] (167), (178), (363), (1197), (1712), (1775), (2089), (2096), (2100), (2681), (2801), (2890).

3056. *Africa* [Madrid] (1045), (1064–5), (1268), (1467), (1470), (1473), (1482), (1972), (2262), (2704), (2789), (2791).

3057. *Africa* [Rome] (216), (529), (2273).

3057a. *Africa-Christo* (2297).

3058. *Africa-Tervuren* (581), (1287), (1905).

3059. *African Abstracts* (2903).

3060. *African Affairs* (176), (258), (1184), (2930).

3061. *African Language Studies* (180a).

3062. *African Drum* (2311).

3062a. *African Music Society Newsletter* [afterwards *African Music*] (126), (128), (139), (172), (179), (180), (213), (222), (259), (260–1), (263), (266), (272), (329), (330), (341), (504), (527), (575), (582), (612), (689), (698–9), (848), (859), (860), (874), (935), (1006), (1110), (1125), (1150–1), (1171), (1173–4), (1178), (1179), (1181), (1183), (1355), (1398), (1402), (1409), (1424–5), (1428), (1462), (1464), (1488), (1535), (1570), (1658), (1709–10), (1728), (1727), (1730), (1734), (1739), (1812), (1880), (1889), (1890), (1987), (2007), (2017), (2060–1a), (2068), (2081), (2088), (2118), (2119), (2121), (2139), (2160), (2162), (2196), (2233), (2266), (2323), (2418), (2489), (2494), (2520), (2687), (2748), (2781), (2836a), (2876), (2897).

3063. *African Studies* (67), (828), (2156–7), (2317), (2501), (2581), (2807b), (2832), (2905).

3063a. *African Studies Bulletin* (2519), (2883), (2885), (2893), (2904), (2914), (2922), (2941), (2950).

3063b. *African World* (1400), (2123).

3064. *Africana* (1505), (1975).

3064a. *African Newsletter* (2902).

3065. *Africanae Fraternae Ephemerides Romanae* (349), (824), (2582).

3066. *Afrika Rundschau* (2209).

3067. *Afrika und Übersee* [formerly *Zeitschrift für Eingeborenen-Sprachen*] (371), (381), (901), (1577), (2431).

3068. *Algéria* (281).

3069. *Allgemeine Musikalische Zeitung* [Leipzig] (87), (1214), (1430).

3070. *Alumni* (2641).

3071. *American Anthropologist* (37), (41), (69), (80), (111), (296), (1810), (2016), (2185), (2309), (2411), (2425), (2508).

3072. *American Journal of Archaeology* (2439).

3073. *Annales de Notre Dame du Sacré Coeur* (651).

3074. *Annales des Pères du Saint Esprit* (302), (2303), (2591), (2630).

3074a. *Annales du Service des Antiquités de l'Égypte* (1866–8), (2019–20), (2022), (2215), (2372), (2374–8) (2383), (2385), (2463).

3075. *Annali Lateranensi* (1291), (1941b), (2276).

3076. *Annals of the Natal Museum* (1124).

3077. *Annals of the South African Museum* (2756).

3078. *L'Anthropologie* (34), (470), (926), (958), (1683), (1893), (2097), (2336), (2414), (2502), (2537), (2596), (2831).

3079. *Anthropology Quarterly* (91), (1360), (1566).

3080. *Anthropos* (21), (187), (432), (611), (631), (902), (976), (1286), (1288), (1292), (1544), (1554), (1569), (1602), (1645), (1752), (2011), (2105), (2172), (2223), (2299), (2325), (2331), (2351), (2404), (2775), (2823).

3081. *Anuario Musical* [Barcelona] (1274–5).

3081a. *Apollon* (818).

3081b. *Archiv für Anthropologie* (286), (367), (1751).

3082. *Archiv für Musikforschung* (122), (239), (1656).

3083. *Archiv für Musikwissenschaft* (749), (1611).

3083a. *Archiv Orientálni* (2380).

3084. *Archiv für Vergleichende Phonetik* (891).

3084a. *Archiv für Völkerkunde* [Wien] (2291), (2488), (2803).

3085. *Nouvelles Archives des Missions Scientifiques* (923).

3086. *Archives Suisses d'Anthropologie Générale* (832), (1719), (1786), (2109), (2861).

3086a. *Archivio per l'Antropologia e la Etnologia* [Florence] (2449), (2866), (2866a), (2868).

3087. *Archivos del Instituto de Estudios Africanos* (1469).

3089. *Artisan et Arts Liturgiques* (1364).

3089a. *Arts et Métiers Indigènes* (607).

3090. *Atlantic Monthly* (1167), (2269).

3090a. *Atlantis* (1280), (1282), (1758), (2143), (2195), (2734).

3091. *Atlas* (1071).

3091a. *Atti della Societa Romana di Antropologia* (76), (1755).

3092. *Auftakt, Der* (194), (1241).

3093. *Ausland*.

3094. *Avenir Coloniale Belge* (563), (2249).

B

3095. *Baessler-Archiv* (40), (284), (375), (1489), (1545), (1558), (1578), (1976a), (2183), (2332).

3096. *Band* (516), (528), (2576), (2593).

3097. *Bantu Studies* (287), (328), (1089), (1118), (1122), (1390–1), (1955), (2006), (2098), (2232), (2314), (2395), (2397–8), (2434), (2754).

3098. *Beaux-Arts* (615), (1843), (2409), (2724).

3099. *Beiträge zur Kolonialpolitik* [Frankfurt] (400).

3099a. *Beiträge zur Kolonial-Forschung* (2210).

3100. *Belgian Congo of To-day* (630), (2141), (2226), (2349), (2574), (2602).

3101. *Belgique d'Outremer* (2573).

3101a. *Berliner Missions Berichte* (2557).

3102. *Bibliotheca Africana* [Innsbruck] (1938).

3103. *Black Orpheus* (2231).

3104. *Blythswood Review* (1792), (2394).

3105. *Boletim Cultural da Guiné Portuguesa* (1284).

3106. *Boletim do Instituto de Investigacão, Cientifico de Moçambique* (1101).

3107. *Boletim da Sociedad de Geographia de Lisboa* (282), (1816).

3108. *Boletim da Sociedade de Estudos da Colonia de Moçambique* (1091), (1111).

3109. *Boletim Museu Nampula* (1087), (2669).

3110. *Bolletino della Reale Società Geografica Italiana* (1341–2), (1621).

3110a. *British Association for the Advancement of Science—Reports, South Africa* (1946).

3111. *British Journal of Psychology* (88), (941).

3112. *British Museum Quarterly* (2150), (2180–1).

3113. *Brousse* [Brussels] (358), (505), (540), (1009), (2044), (2201), (2481).

3114. *Bulletin de l'Académie des Sciences, Cracovie* (1554a).

3115. *Bulletin de l'Académie Malgache* (2652), (2655).

3116. *Bulletin de l'Agence Générale des Colonies* (1192).

3117. *Bulletin des Amis d'Art Indigène du Katanga* (2278), (2410), (2586), (2594).

3118. *Bulletins et Mémoires de la Société d'Anthropologie de Paris* (110), (380), (438), (1322), (2427), (2709).

3118a. *Bulletin de la Société d'Anthropologie de Bruxelles* (1556).

3118a. *Bulletin British Institute of Recorded Sound* (1410).

3119. *Bulletin de la Société d'Archéologie Copte* (2024), (2371).

3120. *Bulletin de la Société des Études Camerounaises* [afterwards *Études Camerounaises*].
See under Études (3169).

3121. *Bulletin de l'Institut d'Études Centrafricaines* [Brazzaville] (448), (1791).

3122. *Bulletin de Comité d'Études Historiques et Scientifiques de l'Afrique Occidentale Française* (468), (670a), (1285a), (1764), (2189), (2243), (2280), (2643).

3123. *Bulletin de l'Enseignement de l'Afrique Occidentale* (230).

3124. *Bulletin de l'Enseignement Publique du Maroc* (1051).

3125. *Bulletin de l'Institut d'Égypte* (728–728a), (737), (2025), (2216), (2217), (2386).

3125a. *Bulletin de l'Institut Français d'Afrique Noire*, I.F.A.N. (1898), (2482).

3125b. *Bulletin de l'Institut des Hautes Études Marocaines* (1069).

3126. *Bulletin d'Information et de Documentation* [Brazzaville] (483).

3127. *Bulletin des Juridictions Indigènes et du Droit Coutumier Congolais* (350), (532).

3128. *Bulletin du Musée d'Ethnographie du Trocadéro* [Paris] (2245), (2504).

3128a. *Bulletin de la Société des Amis de l'Art Copte* (2027).

3129. *Bulletin de la Société Royale Belge de Géographie* (5), (512), (535–7), (539), (554), (567), (644–6), (650), (1828).

3130. *Bulletin de la Société des Recherches Congolaises* (481), (524), (525), (2578).

3131. *Bulletin de la Société de Géographie d'Alger* (1239), (1246).

3132. *Bulletin de la Société Neuchâteloise de Géographie* (306), (307), (798), (884), (1093), (1952), (1963), (2108), (2672).

3133. *Bulletin de la Société des Récherches Soudanaises* (1022).

3133. *Bulletin Touring Club, Congo Belge* (2597).

3134. *Bulletin de l'Union des Femmes Coloniales* (572).

3134a. *Bulletin de la Société 'Union Musicologique'* (72).

C

3135. *Cahiers d'Études Africains* (676).

3136. *Cahiers Belges et Congolais* [Brussels].

3137. *Cahiers d'Histoire Égyptiennes* (726), (1871), (2621).

3137a. *Cahiers Musicaux* (577).

3138. *Cahiers d'Outre-Mer* [Bordeaux] (456).

3139. *Central Africa* (442).

3139a. *Century Magazine* (2579).

3140. *Chronique d'Égypte* (2460), (2465).

3141. *Les Colloques de Wégimont* (47), (99), (231), (235), (542), (576), (1278), (1289), (1433), (2335).

3142. *Comité de l'Afrique Française* (435).

3143. *Congo* (521), (610), (1839), (2013), (2106), (2146), (2244), (2284), (2318), (2606–7), (2609).

3144. *Congo Illustré* (492), (647), (1485), (2130), (2306), (2355), (2612).

3145. *Congo Namur* (2560).

3146. *Congo-Tervuren* (531), (2062), (2864).

3146a. *The Consort* (1060).

3147. *Courier de l'Unesco* (2129), (2523).

D

3147a. *Daily Graphic* (1787), (2270).

3147b. *Dakar: Bulletin Information et Renseignement* (821).

3148. *Dance Observer* (2517).

3149. *Dancing Times* (2615), (2723), (2753), (2765).

3150. *De Wereld der Muziek* (2048).

3151. *Der Alte Orient* (1875).

3151a. *Der Kolonialdeutsche* (1331).

3152. *Der Monat* (174).

3153. *Deutsche Kolonialzeitung* (163), (1438), (1592), (1757).

3153a. *Die Instrumentenbau Zeitung* [Berlin] (2236).

3154. *Die Musik* (1584).

3155. *Die Musikforschung* (694), (1169), (2094a), (2095), (2377), (2379), (2455), (2459), (2498).

3156. *Die Welt des Orients*.

3156a. *Discovery* (164), (2617).

3157. *Documents Algériens* (277).

3158. *Documents* [Paris] (2834).

E

3159. *East African Annual* (2617a), (2643a).

3160. *Eastern Anthropologist* [Lucknow] (2532).

3160a. *L'Education Afrique* (2126).

3161. *Der Erdball* (2543), (2559), (2628).

3162. *Estudos Coloniais* (298). Continued as Estudos Ultramarinos, q.v.

3163. *Estudos sobre a Etnologia do Ultramar Português* (2330).

3163a. *Estudos Ultramarinos*.

3164. *Ethnologica*.

3165. *Ethnologisches Notizblatt* [Berlin] (377), (1754), (2212), (2327).

3166. *Ethnology* (190–1).

3167. *Ethnomusicology* (6), (131), (211), (249), (344), (425), (708), (892), (1670), (1702), (1708), (2149), (2478).

3167a. *Ethnomusicology: News Letter* (18), (92).

3168. *Ethnos* [Sweden] (1337), (1851), (2004), (2250), (2302), (2499), (2645).

3168a. *Étude* (558), (1405).

3169. *Études Camerounaises* (386), (388), (2202), (2565), (2860).

3170. *Études Dahoméennes* (659), 1860–1), (2190).

3171. *Études Guinéennes* (907), (1882), (2636), (2638), (2639).

3172. *Études Historiques et Scientifiques*.

3172a. *Expansion Belge* (545), (1838).

3173. *Exploration* (2132).

F

3174. *The Field* (2038a).

3175. *Field Musuem of Natural History* [Anthropological series] (1912), (2213), (2882).

3176. *Folk* (2720).
3177. *Folklore* (385), (653), (2625), (2712).
3177a. *Forschungen u. Fortschritte* (1612), (2065).
3178. *France d'Outre-Mer* (232), (234).
3178a. *France-Maroc* (1213).

G

3179. *Garcia de Orta* [Lisbon] (1904a), (2115–6), (2566c), (2668).
3180. *Geographical Magazine* (464), (1678), (1878), (2562), (2631), (2656), (2722), (2799), (2807a), (2815).
3180a. *Geographical Journal.* *See* Journal of the Royal Geographical Society.
3181. *Globus* (76), (200), (895), (1432), (1435–6), (1548), (1555), (1563), (1597), (1600), (2179), (2241), (2256), (2275).
3182. *Gold Coast Review* (896).
3182a. *Gold Coast Teachers' Journal* (2274).
3183. *Grands Lacs* [Namur] (355), (639).
3184. *Guide Musical* (Brussels) (4), (1780), (2441).
3185. *Guinea Española* (1973), (2792–3).

H

3186. *Hésperis* (afterwards *Hésperis Tamuda*] (408), (1271).
3187. *Het Missiewerk* (171), (2572a).
3188. *Hinrichsens Musical Year Book* (1401).

I

3189. *Ibadan* (1201), (2684).
3190. *Illustrated London News* (1940).
3191. *Illustration Congolaise* (585), (1840), (1848).
3192. *Illustrierte Zeitung* [Berlin] (2328).
3193. *Império* (2667b), (2670).
3194. *Information Coloniale* (275).
3195. *Institut des Belles Lettres Arabes* (1265).
3196. *Institut royal Colonial Belge (Sciences Morales) Bulletins et Mémoires* (502), (636), (637), (1847), (2159), (2599).
3197. *Internationales Archiv für Ethnographie* (948).

J

3198. *Jahrbuch des Bernischen Historischen Museums* (2295).
3199. *Jahrbuch des Städtischen Museums für Völkerkunde* (Leipzig] (1058), (2178), (2194), (2843).
3200. *Jahresbericht Geographisch-Ethnographischen, Gesellschaft* [Zurich] (790).
3201. *Jahresbericht des Vereins für Erdkunde* [Dresden] (1302).
3201a. *Jahresbericht des Vereins für Handelsgeographie* [Stuttgart] (2184).
3202. *Jeune Afrique* (203), (352), (357), (1407), (2230), (2279), (2590a).
3203. *Journal of the (Royal) African Society* (215), (324), (755), (944), (1000), (1154), (1200), (1207), (1260), (1336), (1643–4), (1729), (1821a), (1885), (1919), (1923), (2090), (2171), (2182), (2288), (2294), (2338), (2437), (2496), (2700), (2702).
3204. *Journal of African Languages* (677).
3205. *Journal of American Folk-lore* (205), (2477), (2891).
3206. *Journal of the American Musicological Society* (49), (93), (94), (101), (130), (507), (508), (751), (2050).
3206a. *Journal of the American Oriental Society* (1976).
3207. *Journal Asiatique* (763), (1216), (1220), (1237), (2475).
3208. *Journal of the Royal Anthropological Institute* (335), (623–6), (654), (1002), (1004), (1202), (1203), (1376), (1495), (1524), (1531), (1649), (1667), (1675), (1913), (2056), (2205), (2333–4), (2346), (2469), (2644), (2682), (2813), (2820), (2828).
3208a. *Journal of the Royal Asiatic Society* (1818), (2018), (2177), (2360), (2361–2), (2452).

3209. *Journal of the Galpin Society* (1869).
3209a. *Journal of the Royal Geographical Society* (962), (1932), (2601), (2683), (2742).
3210. *Journal of the Historical Society of Nigeria* (2076).
3211. *Journal of Human Relations* (194a), (209).
3212. *Journal of the International Folk Music Council* (50), (75), (106), (177), (204), (210), (578), (875), (1112), (1140), (1397), (1411), (1668), (1671), (2430), (2464), (2540), (2623).
3212a. *Journal of the Manchester Geographical Society* (867), (1701).
3213. *Journal Mensuel de la Féderation Nationale des Jeunesses Musicales de Belgique.*
3214. *Journal of the Royal Society of Arts* (148), (2164).
3215. *Journal de la Société des Africanistes* (373), (1028), (1768), (1825), (2034), (2042), (2300), (2368–9), (2435), (2483), (2662), (2718), (2910).
3217. *Journal de la Société Internationale de Musicologie* (986), (2728).

K

3217a. *Kêmi: Revue de Philologie et Archéologie Egyptiennes et Coptes* (2021a), (2384).
3218. *Koloniale Rundschau* [Berlin] (2491a).
3219. *Kongo-Overzee* (579), (1846), (2228–9).
3220. *Kongress-Bericht der International Gesellschaft für Musikwissenschaft* [Basle].
3221. *Kosmos* [Stuttgart] (1767), (2367).
3222. *Kultuurpatronen* (Patterns of Culture) [Bulletin of the Delft Ethnographical Museum] (15), (1771), (2051), (2174).
3223. *Kush* (2446).

L

3224. *La Belgique Coloniale* (493–4), (588), (617), (2542).
3225. *La Géographie* (1609).
3226. *L'Homme* (675).
3227. *La Lettura* (796).
3228. *La Nature.*
3228a. *Lantern* (121).
3228b. *La Revue Musicale* (132).
3229. *La Revue Sincère* (616).
3231. *La Tribune des Nations* (1257).
3234. *Le Ménestrel* (250), (683), (997), (1048), (1050), (1080), (1209), (1262), (2707).
3235. *Le Monde Colonial Illustré* (1034), (2539).
3235a. *Le Petit Messager des Missions Évangeliques* (990).
3235b. *Les Lettres Françaises* (1263).
3236. *Lesotho* (2087).
3236a. *L'Humanité Nouvelle* (1295).
3237. *Liaison* [Brazzaville] (189), (472), (2572).
3237a. *Liberia Bulletin* (950).
3237b. *Life* (1500).
3237c. *Liturgical Arts* (2938).

M

3238. *Man* (23), (255), (606), (619), (621), (633), (1175), (1326), (1461), (1530), (1690), (2005), (2008), (2009), (2033), (2034a), (2036), (2045), (2063), (2071), (2077), (2078), (2085), (2086), (2206), (2254), (2259), (2292), (2301), (2307), (2312), (2444), (2445), (2448), (2468), (2470), (2495), (2647), (2737), (2738), (2740), (2809).
3238a. *Marco Polo* [Paris] (2654).
3239. *Mauritania* (1062).
3239a. *Mededelingen van het Afrika Instituut* [Rotterdam] (2721).
3240. *Memoirs of the Manchester Literary Society* (2467).
3241. *Mensario Administrativo* (144), (292), (2260).
3242. *Mercure Musicale* (279).
3243. *The Metronome* (2169).

3243a. *Micro-Magazine* (573).

3244. *Midwest Folklore* (1188).

3245. *Minotaure* (568), (1139), (2031), (2660), (2665).

3245a. *Miroir du Monde* (1074).

3247. *Missions Catholiques* (2127).

3248. *Missiones Catolicas* [Barcelona] (685).

3249. *Missions Peres Blancs* (597).

3249a. *Missionswissenschaft und Religionswissenschaft* (33).

3250. *Mitteilungen der Anthropologischen Gesellschaft in Wien* (10), (497), (1833), (1977), (1990), (2432).

3251. *Mitteilungen der Institut für Auslandsbeziehungen* [Stuttgart] (734).

3252. *Mitteilungen aus den Deutschen Schutzgebieten* (370), (378), (404), (704), (1553), (1557), (1587), (1595), (1953), (2144), (2771).

3253. *Mitteilungen der Geographischen Gesellschaft* [Hamburg] (933).

3254. *Mitteilungen des Seminars für Orientalische Sprachen: Afrikanische Studien* (1580), (1981), (2265), (2326).

3255. *Moçambique* (1082–3), (1105–6), (2072).

3255a. *Monthly Musical Record* (35), (746).

3256. *Mouvements Sociologiques Internationaux* (551).

3257. *Musées de Genève* [Annual Reports] (2010), (2354).

3258. *Musée Vivant* (827).

3259. *Museum Journal* [Philadelphia] (1854), (2203–4).

3259a. *Music Courier* (1686).

3260. *Music Journal* (245), (1165), (1427).

3260a. *Music and Dance* (105a).

3261. *Music and Letters* (36).

3262. *Music and Youth* (887), (1196).

3263. *Music Educators Journal* (1907).

3264. *Music News* (885).

3264a. *Music Student* (593).

3264b. *Music Times.*

3265. *Musica* (712), (724), (964), (1870).

3265a. *Musica d'Oggi* (1332a).

3265b. *Musical America* (1687), (2059).

3266. *Musical Antiquary* (90).

3267. *Musical Quarterly* (39), (81a), (181), (772), (1072), (1233), (1247), (1419).

3268. *Musical Standard* (1223).

3269. *Musikalisches Wochenblatt* [Leipzig] (1430), (1534).

3270. *Musik-Forschung* (170).

3270a. *Mutter Erde* (2188).

N

3271. *Nada* [Bulawayo] (192), (253), (1459–60), (1463), (1811), (1939), (2120), (2308), (2778–79), (2827).

3272. *National Geographic Magazine* (1081), (1660).

3273. *Natural History* (25), (499), (1132), (1648), (2163), (2199).

3274. *Nature* (2429).

3275. *Negro History Bulletin* (2627).

3276. *Neues Afrika* (183), (184), (185).

3277. *Nieuw Afrika* (555), (2321), (2603).

3278. *Nigeria* [afterwards *Nigeria Magazine*] (1152–3), (1155–6), (1161), (1198), (1206), (1915–16), (1925), (2140), (2240), (2246), (2673), (2674), (2676), (2676a), (2677), (2679–80), (2685), (2689), (2693–8), (2701).

3279. *Nigerian Field* (1166), (1168), (1208), (1908), (1917), (2690).

3280. *Nigerian Teacher* (1933), (2699).

3281. *Nigrizia* (779), (1261), (1344), (1504), (2198), (2802), (2805).

3282. *Notes Africaines, Institut Français d'Afrique Noire* [I.F.A.N.] (119), (665), (813), (841), (915), (1032), (1756), (1858–9), (2083), (2124), (2155), (2170), (2261), (2263), (2356), (2635), (2640), (2663), (2730).

3283. *Nyasaland Journal* (2657).

O

3284. *Occasional Papers of the Rhodes-Livingstone Museum* (1725–6), (1740a), (2829), (2836–7).

3284a. *Occasional Papers—Uganda Museum* (1669).

3285. *Odu* (878), (2247), (2675).

3285a. *Ontwakend Afrika* (2211).

3286. *Onze Kongo* (2405).

3287. *Opinion* (2667).

3288. *Optima* (264).

3289. *Outre-Mer* (1049), (1075), (1217).

3289a. *Outward Bound* (1001).

3289b. *Oversea Education* (899).

P

3289c. *Pages Congolaises* (2726).

3289d. *Pall Mall Magazine* (1129).

3290. *Petermanns Mitteilungen* (945), (1456), (1522), (1571).

3291. *Phylon* (2131), (2168).

3292. *Picture Post* (1109).

3293. *Portugal em Afrika* (302), (1085).

3294. *Prace Ethnologiczne* (2012).

3295. *Presence Africaine* (137), (147), (223), (446), (452), (1033), (1296), (1705), (1777), (2639b).

3296. *Problèmes d'Afrique Centrale* (13), (152), (157), (166), (347), (429), (433), (451), (484), (574), (629), (819), (825), (2600).

3296a. *Proceedings of the Society for Biblical Archaeology* (1877).

3297. *Proceedings of the Musical Association* (186), (1387), (1795).

3298. *Prometheus* (2365).

3299. *Psychological Bulletin* [Lancaster, Pa.].

R

3300. *Rassegna di Studi Etiopici* (767).

3301. *Reclams Universum* (1814).

3301a. *Reflets du Monde* (570).

3302. *Renseignements Coloniaux* [Paris] (436), (440), (947).

3303. *Revista de Estudios Musicales* (687).

3304–3305. *Revista del Instituto de Etnologia* [Universidad Nacional de Tucumán] (2402).

3306. *Revue d'Afrique* (991), (1077).

3307. *Revue d'Anthropologie* (834), (2822).

3308. *Revue de la Raza* (1044).

3309. *Revue de la Société Belge de Musicologie.*

3309a. *Revue Coloniale Belge* (2524).

3310. *Revue Congolaise* (495), (506), (533), (2064), (2255b).

3310a. *Revue Congolaise Illustré* (2324).

3311. *Revue d'Ethnographie* [Paris] (426), (476), (666), (1298), (1317), (1944).

3312. *Revue d'Ethnographie et des Traditions Populaires* (473), (912), (2282), (2642).

3313. *Revue d'Études Ethnographiques et Sociologiques* [Paris] (919), (920), (922), (1135), (1679).

3314. *Revue de Madagascar* (974–5), (980), (992), (2651), (2850).

3315. *Revue du Monde Noir.* (434).

3316. *Revue de Musicologie* [Paris] (723), (911), (1707).

3317. *Revue Méditerranée* (1059).

3318. *Revue Musicale* (462), (830), (1046), (1145), (1253–4), (1804), (1817a), (1895), (1994), (2039), (2073), (2281).

3319. *Revue Nationale* (Brussels] (143).

3320. *Revue de Psychologie des Peuples* (145).

3321. *Revue Questions Scientifiques* (2253).

3321a. *Revue Romande* (198), (1568).

3322. *Rivista di Etnografia* [Naples].

3322a. *Rivista Musicale Italiana* (886).

S

3323. *The Sackbut* (1418).
3324. *Sammelbände der Internationalen Musikgesellschaft,* vol. 11, 1909–10 (1238).
       Sammelbände für vergleichende Musikwissenschaft [Munich], vols. 1–4, 1922–3 [vol. 2 never published] (22), (1610).
3324a. *Saturday Review* (2688).
3325. *Schweizerische Zeitschrift für Instrumentalmusik* (759–60).
3326. *Sciences et Voyages* (638), (2604), (2664).
3326a. *Selection* [Paris] (598).
3327. *Semaine Missiologie* [Louvain] (351), (2584), (2592), (2727).
3328. *Sénégal* (1313).
3329. *Sierra Leone Studies* (2733).
3330. *Société International de Musicologie* [Paris].
3331. *Sociologus* (97).
3331a. *Somalia d'Oggi* (1343).
3332. *South African Archaeological Bulletin* (182), (1947), (2079), (2080), (2082), (2084), (2486), (2490–1), (2493).
3333. *South African Association for the Advancement of Science* (327). (Reports.)
3334. *South African Journal of Science* (30), (68), (214), (326), (1367), (1384), (1385), (1389), (1957), (2029), (2237), (2293), (2396), (2471).
3335. *South African Museums Bulletin* (1958), (2239).
3336. *South African Outlook* (1348–9).
3337. *South African Panorama* (1363).
3338. *South African Railways and Harbours Magazine* (1386).
3338a. *Southern Folklore Quarterly* (2322).
3339. *Southern Workman* (133), (134), (1115), (1778), 1834).
3340. *'Sphynx'* (2030).
3340a. *Studies in Ethnomusicology* (114).
3341. *Sudan Notes and Records* (1506), (1517), (1518), (1519), (1525), (1623), (2058), (2795), (2796), (2804), (2806).
3342. *Svensk Tidskrift for Musikforskning* (115).

T

3342a. *Table Ronde* (1039).
3343. *Tanganyika Notes and Records* (1583), (1978), (2224), (2659), (2808), (2810), (2812), (2993).
3343a. *Der Tanz* (2710).
3343b. *Teacher's Journal* [Gold Coast] (120).
3343c. *Times British Colonies Review* (2830).
3344. *Togo-Cameroun* (372), (396), (1589).
3344a. *Toren* (515).
3345. *Tour du Monde* (656).
3346. *Transactions of the Ethnological Society* [London] (829).
3346a. *Transactions: Glasgow University Oriental Society* (1864).
3347. *Transactions Gold Coast and Togoland Historical Society* (890).
3348. *Travel* (2661), (2768), (2800).

3348a. *Tribus* (241).
3349. *Tropiques* (2111), (2518), (2571).

U

3350. *Uganda Journal* (124), (1618), (1625–6), (1659), (1663), (1983), (2252), (2450–1), (2816), (2817).
3350a. *Uganda Teachers' Journal* (1634).
3351. *Unesco Courier* (406).
3352. *United Empire* (256), (1713).
3353. *Universitas* [Accra] (873), (876–7), (880).

V

3354. *Verhandlungen der Naturforscher Gesellschaft in Basel* (865), (2255).
3354a. *Verhandlungen des Vereins für Naturwissenschaftliche* Unterhaltung zu Hamburg (2510).
3354b. *Veröffentlichungen des Städtischen Völkermuseums* [Frankfurt a/M].
3354c. *Voix du Congolaise* (28), (595), (2225).
3355. *Vox* [Hamburg] (463), (934).

W

3356. *West Africa* (123), (900), (1688), (2732), (2929).
3357. *West African Review* (153), (858), (1324), (1700), (1711), (2191–3), (2289), (2632–3), (2650), (2698a).
3357a. *West African Students Union* (1327).
3358. *Westermanns Monatshefte* [Brunswick] (1146), (2342).
3358a. *Wissen Berlin* (118).
3359. *Word* (2214).

XYZ

3360. *Ymer* (667).
3361. *Zaire* (188), (248), (353), (648), (2067), (2298), (2598).
3362. *Zambesi Mission Record* (1458).
3362a. *Zeitschrift für Aegyptische Sprache und Altertumskunde* (2021), (2421).
3363. *Zeitschrift Gesellschaft für Erdkunde* [Berlin] (150).
3364. *Zeitschrift für Eingeborenen-Sprachen* [afterwards *Afrika und Übersee*] (1164), (2207).
3365. *Zeitschrift fur Ethnologie* (19), (117), (237), (238), (339), (365), (402), (474), (1266), (1450), (1511), (1575), (1579), (1749–50), (1776), (2038), (2052), (2094), (2406), (2940).
3366. *Zeitschrift für Instrumentenbau* (1061), (2026).
3367. *Zeitschrift der Internationalen Musikgesellschaft* (20), (1796).
3368. *Zeitschrift für Musikwissenschaft* (965), (1258), (1339), (1509), (1874).
3369. *Zeitschrift für Vergleichende Musikwissenschaft* [Berlin] (669), (784), (1052–3), (1235–6), (1273), (1817).
3370. *Zeitschrift für Völkerpsychologie und Sprachwissenschaft* (53).

ABBREVIATIONS

A

Abh. Hamburger. Kol. Inst. *Abhandlungen des Hamburgischen Kolonial-Instituts.*

Abh. zur Anthr. Ethn. Urgesch. *Abhandlungen zur Anthropologie, Ethnologie und Urgeschichte.*

Acta Musicol. *Acta musicologica.*

A.E.F. *Afrique Equatoriale Franciase.*

Aegyptol. stud. *Aegyptologische Studien.*

Africain: Alm. des missions africains. *Africain: Almanach des Missions Africains* [Lyon].

AFER. *Africanae Fraternae Ephemerides Romanae.*

Afr. affairs. *African Affairs.*

Afr. mus. soc. *African Music Society Newsletter* [later *Journal*].

Afr.-RDSCH. *Afrika Rundschau.*

Afr. stud. *African Studies.*

Afr. stud. bull. *African Studies Bulletin.*

Afr. u. Übersee. *Afrika und Übersee.*

Allg. Musik. Zeit. *Allgemeine Musikalische Zeitung* [Leipzig].

A.M.E. *Algemene Muziek Encyclopedie.*

Amer. anthrop. *American Anthropologist.*

Amer. J. of arch. *American Journal of Archaeology.*

Annali Lat. *Annali Lateranensi.*

Ann. Pères Saint Esprit. *Annales des Pères du Saint Esprit.*

Ann. de N.D. du Sacre Coeur. *Annales de Notre Dame du Sacre Coeur.*

Ann. service, antiq. Égypte. *Annales du Service des Antiquités de l'Égypte.*

Ann. S. African Museum. *Annals of the South African Museum.*

Anthrop. quart. *Anthropology Quarterly.*

A.O.F. *Afrique Occidentale Française.*

Archiv f. Anthrop. *Archiv für Anthropologie.*

Arch. f. Musikfors. *Archiv für Musikforschung.*

Archiv. f. Musikw. *Archiv für Musikwissenschaft.*

Archiv. suisses anthrop. générale. *Archives Suisses d'Anthropologie Générale.*

Archiv f. vergl. Phonetik. *Archiv für vergleichende Phonetik.*

Arch. f. Völkerkunde. *Archiv für Völkerkunde* [Wien].

Archivio antrop. & ethnol. *Archivio per l'Antropologia e la Etnologia* [Florence].

Arch. inst. est. afr. *Archivos del Instituto de Estudios Africanos.*

Arch. folk Cubano. *Archivos de Foklore Cubano.*

Arch. orientalni. *Archiv Orientalni.*

Arch. Venezolanos folk. *Archivos Venezolanos de Folklore.*

A.R.S.C. *Acadèmie Royale des Sciences Coloniales (Sciences Morales). Mém.* [Brussels].

Art & arch. *Art and Archaeology.*

Atti della suc. Roma d'antrop. *Atti della Societa Roma d'Antropologia.*

Avenir Col. Belge. *Avenir Coloniale Belge.*

B

Bantu stud. *Bantu Studies.*

Beitr. Kol. Forschung. *Beitrage zur Kolonial-Forschung.*

Beitr. Kol. Polit. *Beiträge zur Kolonialpolitik* [Frankfurt].

Belg. Col. *La Belgique Coloniale.*

Bibl. *Bibliography.*

Bibl. Afr. *Bibliotheca Africana* [Innsbruck].

Bol. cultural da Guiné Portuguesa. *Boletim Cultural da Guiné Portuguesa.*

Bol. inst. invest. cient. Mocambique. *Boletim do Instituto de Investigação Cientifico de Mocambique.*

Bol. soc. estud. Moc. *Boletin da Sociedade de Estudios da Colonia de Mocambique.*

Bol. soc. geog. Lisbon. *Boletim da Sociedad Geografia de Lisboa.*

Bol. mus. Nampula. *Boletim Museu Nampula.*

B.R. soc. geog. Ital. *Bollettino della reale Società Geografica Italiana.*

Brit. J. of psychol. *British Journal of Psychology.*

B.M.Q. *British Museum Quarterly.*

Bull. acad. sci. Cracovie. *Bulletin de l'Académie de Sciences Cracovie.*

Bull. acad. Malg. *Bulletin de l'Académie Malgache.*

Bull. ag. génl. col. *Bulletin de l'Agence Générale des Colonies* [Paris].

Bull. amis. art. indig. Katanga. *Bulletin des Amis de l'Art indigène du Katanga.*

Bull. B.R.S. *Bulletin British Institute of Recorded Sound.*

Bull. com. étude A.O.F. *Bulletin du Comité d'Études Historiques et Scientifiques de l'Afrique Occidentale, Francaise* [Paris].

Bull. enseign. A.O.F. *Bulletin de l'Enseignement de l'Afrique Occidentale.*

Bull. enseign. pub. Maroc. *Bulletin de l'Enseignement publique du Maroc.*

Bull. Ethnog. Museum, Delft. *Bulletin Ethnographical Museum, Delft.*

Bull. mus. ethnog. Troc. *Bulletin du Musée d'Ethnographie du Trocadéro* [Paris].

Bull. Folk-song Soc. of the Northeast. *Bulletin Folk-song Society of the Northeast.*

Bull. inform. haut commissariat de la republique A.E.F. *Bulletin d'Information, Haut Commissariat de la République A.E.F.*

Bull. inform. et docum [Brazzaville]. *Bulletin d'Information et de Documentation* [Brazzaville].

Bull. inst. ét. centrafricaines. *Bulletin de l'Institut des études Centrafricaines* [Brazzaville].

Bull. de l'inst. d'Égypte. *Bulletin de l'Institut d'Égypte.*

Bull. inst. hautes études Marocaines. *Bulletin de l'Institut des Hautes Études Marocaines.*

Bull. jurid. indig. *Bulletin des Juridictions Indigènes et du Droit Coutumier Congolais.*

Bull. rech. soudanaises. *Bulletin de la société des Recherches Soudanaises.*

Bull. soc. amis de l'art Copte. *Bulletin de la Société des Amis de l'Art Copte.*

Bull. soc. anthrop. [Paris]. *Bulletins et Mémoires de la Société d'Anthropologie de Paris.*

Bull. soc. anthrop. Brux. *Bulletin de la Société d'Anthropologie de Bruxelles.*

Bull. soc. Neuchât géog. *Bulletin de la Société Neuchâteloise de Géographie.*

Bull. soc. d'archéol. Copte. *Bulletin de la Société d'Archéologie Copte.*

Bull. soc. géog. d'Alger. *Bulletin de la Société de Géographie d'Alger.*

Bull. soc. rech. Congol. *Bulletin de la Société des Recherches Congolaises.*

Bull. soc. roy. Belge. géog. *Bulletin de la Société Royale Belge de Géographie.*

Bull. union femmes colon. *Bulletin Union Femmes Coloniales.*

Bull. union musicol. *Bulletin de la Société 'Union Musicologique'.*

C

Cah. d'ét. afr. *Cahiers d'Études Africaines.*

Cah. hist. Égyptienne. *Cahiers d'Histoire Égyptiennes.*

CEPSI. *Bulletin du Centre d'Étude des Problémes Sociaux Indigènes.*

Com. Afr. franc. *Comité de l'Afrique Française.*

C.R. sommaires séances inst. franc. anthrop. *Compte-rendues Sommaires des Séances de l'Institut Français d'Anthropologie.*

Conf. int. Africanistas ocid. *Conferencia Internacional dos Africanistas Ocidentais.*

Congo illus. *Congo Illustré.*

Congr. int. sci. anthrop. et ethnol. *Congrès Internationale des Sciences Anthropologiques et Ethnologiques.*

Courier [Unesco]. *Le Courier de l'Unesco.*

D

Deut. Kol. Zeitg.   *Deutsche Kolonialzeitung.*
D. Instrbauztg.   *Die Instrumentenbau Zeitung.*

E

E. Afr. ann.   *East African Annual.*
L.Educ. afr.   *Education Africaine.*
Ergän.   *Ergänzungsheft.*
Est. Etnol. Ultramar Portug.   *Estudos Sobre a Etnologia do Ultramar Português.*
Est. Ultramarinos.   *Estudos Ultramarinos.*
Ethnol. Notizbl.   *Ethnologisches Notizblatt* [Berlin].
Études Cam.   *Études Camerounaises.*
Études Dah.   *Études Dahoméennes.*
Études Guin.   *Études Guinéennes.*

F

Forsch. u. Fortschritte.   *Forschungen und Fortschritte.*

G

Geog. J.   *Journal of the Royal Geographical Society.*
Geog. Mag.   *Geographical Magazine.*
Gold Coast rev.   *Gold Coast Review.*
Guinea Españ.   *Guinea Española.*

H

Human probl. Brit. Central Afr.   *Human Problems in British Central Africa.*

I

I.B.L.A.   *Institut des Belles Lettres Arabes.*
I.F.A.N.   *Institut Français d'Afrique Noire Bulletins and Memoires.*
Ill.   *Illustrations.*
Illustr. congol.   *Illustration Congolaise.*
I.L.N.   *Illustrated London News.*
Illus. Deut. Monatshefte.   *Illustrierte Deutsche Monatshefte.*
Illus. Zeitung [Berlin].   *Illustrierte Zeitung* [Berlin].
Inst. intern. bibliog.   Institut International de Bibliographie [Brussels].
I.R.C.B.   Institut Royale Coloniale Belge.
Int. archiv. ethnog.   *Internationales Archiv für Ethnographie.*
Int. Afr. Inst.   International African Institute.
Int. Ges. f. Musikwiss.   *Internationale Gesellschaft für Musikwissenschaft.*

J

Jb. bern. Hist. Mus.   *Jahrbuch des Bernischen Historischen Museums.*
Jahresber. Geog. Gesells in Bern.   *Jahresbericht der Geographischen Gesellschaft von Bern.*
Jahresber. Verh. Erdk. Dres.   *Jahresbericht des Vereins dür Erdkunde* [Dresden].
Jahresber. Ver. Handersgeogr.   *Jahresbericht des Vereins für Handelsgeographie* [Stuttgart].
Jahresber. Geog.-Ethnog. Gesell [Zurich].   *Jahresbericht Geographischen-Ethnographischen Gesellschaft* [Zurich].
Jb. S. Mus. Völkerkunde [Leipzig].   *Jarhbuch des Städtischen Museums für Völkerkunde* [Leipzig].
Jb. f. Musikalische Volks- u. Völkerkunde.   *Jahrbuch für musikalische Volks- und Völkerkunde.*
Jeune Afr.   *Jeune Afrique.*

J. Afr. soc.   *Journal of the African Society* [afterwards *Royal African Society*].
J. soc. Africanistes.   *Journal de la Société des Africanistes.*
J. Afr. languages.   *Journal of African Languages.*
J. Amer. Folklore.   *Journal of American Folklore.*
J. Amer. mus. soc.   *Journal of the American Musicological Society.*
J. roy. soc. arts.   *Journal of the Royal Society of Arts.*
J. roy. Asiat. soc.   *Journal of the Royal Asiatic Society.*
J. roy. geog. soc.   *Journal of the Royal Geographical Society.*
J. roy. anthrop. inst.   *Journal of the Royal Anthropological Institute.*
J. Manch. geog. soc.   *Journal of the Manchester Geographical Society.*
J. int. folk music council.   *Journal of the International Folk Music Council.*
J. men. Jeunesses musicales.   *Journal Mensuel de la Fèderation Nationale des Jeunesses Musicales de Belgique.*
J. soc. intern. de musicologie.   *Journal de la Société Internationale de Musicologie* [Paris].
J. hist. soc. Nigeria.   *Journal of the Historical Society of Nigeria.*

K

Kêmi.   *Revue de Philologie et d'Archéologie Égyptiennes et Coptes.*
Kol. Rund.   *Koloniale Rundschau* [Berlin].
Kongressbericht.   *International Gesellschaft für Musikwissenschaft,* Utrecht.

L

La géog.   *La Géographie.*
Le Maroc. cath.   *Le Marocco Catholique.*
Liberia bull.   *Liberia Bulletin.*

M

Meded. Afrika Inst. [Rotterdam].   *Mededelingen van het Afrika Instituut* [Rotterdam].
Mém. I.F.A.N.   *Mémoires de l'Institut Français d'Afrique Noire.*
Mem. Manchester Lit. Soc.   *Memoirs of the Manchester Literary Society.*
Mensario admin.   *Mensario Administrativo.*
Missionswiss. u. Religionswiss. [Münster].   *Missionswissenschaft und Religionswissenschaft.*
Mitt. Anthrop. Gesell. Wien.   *Mitteilungen der Anthropologischen Gesellschaft in Wien.*
Mitt. Deutschen Archaeol. Inst. abt. Kairo.   *Mitteilungen des Deutschen Archaeologischen Instituts, Abteilung Kairo.*
Mitt. D. Inst. f. Auslandsbeziehungen.   *Mitteilungen der Institut für Auslandsbeziehungen.*
Mitt. Geog. Gesell. [Hamburg].   *Mitteilungen der Geographischen Gesellschaft* [Hamburg].
Mitt. Schutz.   *Mitteilungen aus den deutschen Schutzgebieten.*
Mitt. Sem. Orient. Sprach. Afr. Stud.   *Mitteilungen des Seminars für Orientalische Sprachen: Afrikanische Studien* [Berlin].
Mouvements soc. intern.   *Mouvements Sociologiques Internationaux.*
Mus. J. Phil.   *Museum Journal Philadelphia.*
Musik. Wochenbl.   *Musikalisches Wochenblatt* [Leipzig].
Mus. quart.   *Musical Quarterly.*
Mus. roy. Afr. centr.   *Musée Royal de l'Afrique Centrale.*

N

Nat. geog. mag.   *National Geographic Magazine.*
Nat. hist.   *Natural History* [New York].
Neue Z. Missionswiss. [Switzerland].   *Neue Zeitschrift für Missionswissenschaften.*
Neues Afr.   *Neues Afrika.*
Notes Afr. I.F.A.N.   *Notes Africaines, Institut Français d'Afrique Noire.*

O–P

P. or pp. Page or pages.
Portugal em Afr. *Portugal em Africa.*
Probl. Afr. Centr. *Problèmes d'Afrique Centrale.*
Proc. mus. assoc. *Proceedings of the Musical Association.*
Proc. soc. biblical arch. *Proceedings of the Society of Biblical Archaeology.*

R

Rass. studi Etiopici. *Rassegna di Studi Etiopici.*
Rens. col. *Renseignements Coloniaux* [Paris].
Rep. Brit. ass. *Reports of the British Association for the Advancement of Science.*
Rev. est. musicales. *Revista de Estudios Musicales.*
Rev. afr. *Revue Africaine.*
Rev. anthrop. *Revue d'Anthropologie.*
Rev. col. belge. *Revue Coloniale Belge.*
Rev. cong. *Revue Congolaise.*
Rev. congol. ill. *Revue Congolaise Illustré.*
Rev. d'Afrique. *Revue d'Afrique.*
Rev. de la soc. belge de musicol. *Revue de la Société Belge de Music-ologie.*
Rev. ethnog. *Revue d'Ethnographie.*
Rev. ethnog. trad. pop. *Revue d'Ethnographie et des Traditions Popu-laires.*
Rev. étud. ethnog. sociol. *Revue d'Études Ethnographiques et Sociol-ogiques* [Paris].
Rev. Madagascar. *Revue de Madagascar.*
Rev. musicale. *Revue Musicale.*
Rev. quest. scientif. *Revue Questions Scientifiques.*
Rev. de sci. missionaire. *Revue de Science Missionnaire.*
Rev. Psychol. des peuples. *Revue de Psychologie des Peuples.*
Riv. col. Ital. *Revista delle Coloniale Italiane.*
Riv. di etnog. *Rivista di Etnografia* [Naples].
Riv. musicale Italiana. *Revista Musicale Italiana.*

S

S.A.M.B. *South African Museums Bulletin.*
Sammel. f. vergl. Musikw. *Sammelbände für vergleichende Musik-wissenschaft.*
Sci. et voyage. *Sciences et Voyages* [Paris].
Sem. missiologie. *Semaine Missiologie* [Louvain].
Sér. Série.
S.I.M. Société International de Musicologie [Paris[.
Soc. rech. Congo. *Bulletin de la Société des Récherches Congolaises.*
Soc. miss. evan. *Société des Missions Evangèliques.*
Soc. Rom. anthrop. *Atti della Società Romana di Antropologia* [Rome].
Soc. roy. belge. géog. *Bulletin de la Société Royale Belge de Géographie.*
S. Afr. archaeol. bull. *South African Archaeological Bulletin.*

S. Afr. assoc. adv. science. *South African Association for the Advancement of Science.*
S. Afr. J. of science. *South African Journal of Science.*
S. Afr. libr. *South African Libraries.*
S. Afr. rlwys & harbours mag. *South African Railways and Harbours Magazine.*

T

Tom. Tome or volume.
Trans. ethnol. soc. *Transactions of the Ethnological Society.*
Trans. Gold Coast & Togoland hist. soc. *Transactions of the Gold Coast and Togoland Historical Society.*

U

Uganda J. *Uganda Journal.*
U. Empire. *United Empire.*

V

Verhand. Naturf. Gesell. in Basel. *Verhandlungen der Naturforscher Gesellschaft in Basel.*
Verhandl. des Vereins für Naturwiss. [Unterhaltung zu Hamburg, **9**, 1896]. *Verhandlungen des Vereins für Naturwissenschaftliche Unter-haltung zu Hamburg.*
Veröff. Städt. Völker-mus. [Frankfurt a/M.]. *Veröffentlichungen des städtischen Völkermuseums* [Frankfurt-am-Main].
Vol. Volume or volumes.

W

WASU. *Magazine of the West African Students Union of Great Britain.*
West Afr. *West Africa.*
W.A.R. *West African Review.*

XYZ

Zambesi Mission rec. *Zambesi Mission Record.*
Z. f. ägypt. Sprache u. Altertumskunde. *Zeitschrift für Aegyptische Sprache und Altertumskunde.*
Z. f. Ethnol. *Zeitschrift für Ethnologie.*
Z. Ges. Erdkunde. *Zeitschrift Gesellschaft für Erdkunde* [Berlin].
Z. f. Eingeb. Sprachen. *Zeitschrift für Eingeborenen-Sprachen.*
Z. f. Instrumentenbau. *Zeitschrift für Instrumentenbau.*
Z. Intern. Musikgesell. *Zeitschrift der Internationalen Musikgesellschaft.*
Z. f. Musikw. *Zeitschrift für Musikwissenschaft.*
Z. f. Vergleich. Musikwiss. *Zeitschrift fur Vergleichende Musik-wissenschaft* [Berlin].
Z. f. Völkerpsychol. u. Sprachwissens. *Zeitschrift für Völkerpsychologie und Sprachwissenschaft.*

INDEX OF AUTHORS

Tican, M., 2794
Tidjani, S., 2571
Tiersot, J., 250-2, 682-3, 837, 997, 1080, 1262
Tilkens, E., 617
Titherington, G. W., 2806
Tongue, H., 1421
Tönjes, H., 315, 1446, 2117
Tonnoir, R., 2600
Torday, E., 618-22, 1833, 2601
— with T. A. Joyce, 623-8
Törnberg, G., 2004, 2035
Torrend, J., 1422, 1738, 2777
Toutain, L., 1317
Tracey, A., 2118-19
Tracey, H. T., 105a, 253-64, 329-31, 341, 629-30, 698-700, 1006, 1105-12, 1131a-2, 1423-7, 1460-4, 1583, 1739, 1811, 2072, 2120-1, 2778-81, 2871-3
Traoré, M., 2640
Tremearne, A. J. N., 1203-5, 2738-9
Trilles, H., 631-2, 838-9, 2073
Tripe, W. B., 2312
Trowell, M., and K. P. Wachsmann, 1991
Tsala, Th., 2313
Tsamas, S., 2572
Tshibangu, 2602
Tucker, A. N., 1530-2, 2314, 2807
Tucker, J. T., 2315
Turnbull, C. M., 265, 633-4
Turner, V. W., 1740, 2837
Twala, Regina G., 2807b

U

Ukeje, L. O., 2701
Ullendorf, E., 810
Underwood, Leon, 2316
University of London: School of Oriental and African studies, Library catalogue, 2955
University of Sydney: Anthrop. Dept., 2975
Urpsrung, Otto, 1278a
U.S.A. Dept. of State: Office of Intelligence, 2956

V

Valdez, F. T., 316, 1993
Valentyn, Francois, 2428
Valle, R. H., 2899
van Bulck, G., 637

Vancoillie, G., 2317
Van den Bergh, Leonard John, 635
Van den Berghe, L., and L. de Heusch, 3037
Vanden Plas, J., 1533, 2319
van der Burgt, J. M. M., 359-60
van der Elsken, Eduard, 454a
van der Kerken, G., 636
van der Merwe, F. Z., 2901
van Goethem, L., 2318
Van Hoepen, A. E., 2320
van Loo, E., 638, 2604
van Mol, D., 639, 2606-7
van Overbergh, C., 640
— with E. de Jonghe, 641-3
Van Riet Lowe, C., 2493
Van Saefthingen, W., 2321
Vansina, J., 2608
van Valen, L., 2322
van Warmelo, N. J., 1607, 3038
Van Wing, J., 2609-10
Varley, D. H., 2900
Vaughan, J., 2086
Vedder, H., 1447, 1968, 2783
Vedy, Dr., 644-5
Veenstra, A. J. F., 2494
Vela, D., 2074
Verbeken, A. L., 646, 2322a-4
Vereyecken, 647
Verger, P., 930, 2552
— See Adandé, A., and P. Verger
Vergiat, A. M., 455
Verneuil, V., 1319
Verwilghen, L. A., 361, 648-9
Viaene, E. and B., 650
Vianney, J. J., 1343
Vienna: Museum f. Völkerkunde, 2874
Vignato, A., 1344
Vilheno, J. de, 1812
Villault, Le Sieur, 1714-15
Villoteau, G. A., 756-7a
Vincent, F., 1813
Vischer, H., 1932
Vista, T. de, 317
Vivaldi, Le R. P., 1345
von Francois, H., 1448
von Rosen, E., 1941
Vortisch, H., 895

W

Wachsmann, K. P., 106-7, 266-6a, 701, 1346, 1428, 1663-74a,

1862, 1980, 2429-30, 2495, 2820a, 2875
— See Trowell, M., and K. P. Wachsmann
Wallaschek, R., 108, 2432
Wallis, B., 962
Walraet, M., 2989
Walschap, A., 268, 651
Walton, J., 1969, 2036, 2087
Wangemann, H. T., 1970
Wängler, H. H., 267, 2431
Ward, H., 652, 1855-6
Ward, W. E. F., 269, 896-9
Washington: Library of Congress, 2957
Wassing, R. S., 2721
Waterhouse, G., 2784
Watternberg, B., and R. L. Smith, 2553
Wauters, A. J., 1856a, 2990
Wauters, G., 2991
Wayland, E. J., 1675
Webb, M., 1429
Weber, W., 270, 1584, 1814
Webster, W. H. B., 2433
Weeks, J. H., 653-4, 1857, 2513, 2611
Weiss, M., 1585, 1676
Welch, Floretta J., 3039
Wellesz, E., 74, 758, 811
Weman, H., 271
Werner, A., 944, 1007, 1008, 2122, 2338, 2434, 2496
Werner, H., 1450
Werth, E., 702, 1586
Wessmann, R., 2123
West African Review, 2650
Westcott, J. A., and P. M. Williams, 1206
Westermann, D., 963, 1981, 2325-6
Westphal, E. O. J., 272, 1451
Weule, K., 703, 704, 1587-8, 2327-8
Wheeler, A. J., 2037
White, C. M. N., 1740a
Whitehouse, A. A., 1207
Whiteley, W. H., and A. E. Gutkind, 2994
Whyte, E. T., 1877
Whyte, Harcourt, 1208
Widdicombe, J., 1821b, 1971
Widenmann, A., 945, 1588a, 2497
Wiegrabe, P., 901
Wieschhoff, Heinz, 2329
Wieschhoff, Heinrich A., 2959

Williams, C., 1347
Williams, H. C. N., and J. N. Maselwa, 273
Williams, P. M. See Westcott, J. A., and P. M. Williams
Wilson, C. T., and R. W. Felkin, 1677
Wilson, W. A. A., 2330
Wilson-Haffenden, J. R., 2702
Wilverth, Lieut., 2612
Winkelman, F. von, 2785
Winter, E. H., 2821
Winterbottom, T. M., 1332
Wintersgill, H. G., 1834
Wiora, W., 75
Wissmann, H., 2434a, 2514
— and Ludwig, Wolf, 1835
Witte, F., 902
Witte, P. A., and W. Schmidt, 1602, 2331
Wolf, Ludwig. See Wissmann, H., and L. Wolf
Wolfson, F., 903, 2634
Wollaston, A. F. R., 655
Work, Munroe, Nathan, 2960
Work, T. H., 2722
Worthington, E. B., 3040

X

Y

Yafil, E., and J. Rouanet, 1279
Yale University: Human Relations Area Files, 54a
Yeatman, W. B., 1933
Young, C., 2723, 2838

Z

Zaba, Z., 2515
Zahan, D., 1037
Zeller, R., 2332
Zemp, H., 930a
Zenker, G., 404
Zerries, O., 2516
Zerrouki, M., 281, 1263-5
Zerwick, W., 2557
Ziéglè, H., 456
Zintgrafe, E., 405
Zöhrer, L. G. A., 1266
Zöllner, H., 1534
Zurich: Museum Rietberg, 2875a
Zuure, B., 362-3

GEOGRAPHICAL AND ETHNIC INDEX

For consistency English versions of the names of all countries have been given.
Spelling of vernacular names follows that of the author of the book or paper concerned.

Numbers quoted here refer to the sections "Music", "Musical Instruments" and "Dance" as well as the individual entries.

Khartoum, 2150

Khassonké, 1026

Kikuyu. *See* Akikuyu

Kipsigis, 942

Les Kissi, 918, 958

Konkomba, 1591

The Korana, 411; musical instruments, 1955

Kouroumba, 2034, 2300

Les Kuku, 2319

Kwango River, 569, 628

L

Lambas of Northern Rhodesia, 1721

Lango, 1624

Les Lesa, 495, 650

Liberia: music, 946; dance, instruments, 1891; dance, 2648

Libya: music, 964; musical instruments, 1215

Lokele, 2156

Lozi of N. W. Rhodesia, 1740

Luba, 2154

Lunda-Lovale, 318

Lur, 560

M–N

Madagascar: music, 974; musical instruments, 1892, 1894; dance, 2651

Makidi, the Hausa drummer, 2240

Makraka, 560

Malawi (formerly Nyasaland): music, 998; musical instruments, 1000; dance, 2657

Mali (formerly Soudan Français): music, 1009; musical instruments, 1896; dance, 2659b

Mandara, 374

Mandingas of Portuguese Guinea, 1283, 1313

Les Mandjia, 439

Les Mangbetu (Congo Belge), 643

Marghi of Nigeria, 2086

Masai, 939

Mashonas, 1458–9

Mauritania: music, 1038; musical instruments, 1898; dance, *see* N. Africa

Les Mayombe, 642

Mbae, 2007

Mbagani, 2317

Mboum du Nord-Cameroun, 373

Les Minianka, 919, 1679

Mofu du Massif de Durum, 388

Mongo, 636

Mongo of Sankuru, 532

Morocco: music, 1044; musical

instruments, 1899; dance, *see* N. Africa

Mossi, 2255a, 2822–3

Les Moundans, 2578

Les Mousserongos, 512

Mozambique: music, 1081; musical instruments, 1904a; dance, 2667b

Le Muhaya, 346

Natal: music, 1113; musical instruments, 1965

Ndebele (Southern Rhodesia), 1455

Ndiki tribe, 369

Ngbandi, 613–14

Niger (formerly part of A.O.F.): music, 1133; musical instruments, 1904b; dance, 2671

Nigeria: music, 1142; musical instruments, 1905; dance, 2673

Les Nkundo, 505

Nkundu (Belgian Congo) Dances, 2581

North Africa: music, 1209; dance, 2703

North African Music in relation to that of the Iberian Peninsula, 1267–9

Nsenga (Northern Rhodesia) music, 2088–9

Nyamwezi, 1576

N'Zérékoré, circle of (including Guerzé, Kono, Manon), 907

O–Q

Ogowe-Congo Mission to French Equatorial Africa, 2567–8

Ost-Mbamlandes, 376

Ovamboland, 2117, 2213

Ovimbundu, 295–7

Les Pahouins, 470, 480–1, 486

Païennes du Nord-Cameroun et de l'Adamaoua, 383

The Pangwe, 478, 834

Pende, 2062

Les Peulhs, 1012, 2671

Phonogram Archiv, Berlin, 40, 169

Pilapila of Dahomey, 2190

Les Pomo, 426

Portuguese Guinea, 1280

R

Rongo (Sudan), 2058

Royal Anthropological Institute, 116

Rwanda (formerly part of Rwanda-Urundi): music, 1286; musical instruments, 1941a; dance, 2724

S

Sandawe of Tanganyika: musical instruments, 1978

São Tomé, 1293

Sara-Kaba, 463

Senegal: music, 1294; musical instruments, 1942; dance, 2728

Senoufo (Ivory Coast), 922, 924, 1135, 1138

Sherbro River, 1143

Shilluk, 1512

Shona, 1455

Sierra Leone: music, 1320; dance, 273

Siwah and El Garah, 968

Soga, 1984

Sokoto Province, Nigeria, 1913

Somalia (including former British Somaliland): music, 1332a; dance, 2740

South Africa: music, 1348, musical instruments, 1946, 1956; dance, 2742

Southern Rhodesia: music, 1452; musical instruments, 1937; dance, 2786

South-West Africa: music, 1431; musical instruments, 1946

Spain, 2951

Spanish Guinea: music, 1465; musical instruments, 1972; dance, 2789

Spanish West Africa, 1472

Sudan (formerly Anglo-Egyptian Sudan): music, 1484; musical instruments, 1974; dance, 2795

Swaziland: music, 1535; musical instruments, 1956; dance, 2807a

T

Tambou kunyu (Soudan Français), 2155

Tanganyika: music, 1539; musical instruments, 1976a; dance, 2808

Teda of Tibesti, 460, 465, 468

Timbuctoo, 1023, 1070

Tiv, 1142, 1169, 1178, 2147

Togo: music, 1589; musical instruments, 1981, 2212; dance, 2814

Les Tomas, 947, 958, 2189

Transvaal: music, 1603; musical instruments, 1604, 1956; dance, *see* S. Africa

Tschokwe, 284, 575

Tsopi tribe, 2098

Tuareg, 278a–b, 1019

Tunisia: music, 1608; musical instruments, 1982, dance, *see* N. Africa

Les Tyèblenké (masked dancers), 2662

U–V

Uganda: music, 1617; musical instruments, 1983, 1991; dance, 2816

Usuku, 1983

Valenge women (Portuguese East Africa), 1089–90

Va-Nyaneka, 301

Voltaic Republic (formerly Haute Volta, A.O.F.): musical instruments, 1992; dance, 2822

W X Y Z

Wagogo, 1545

Wa-Luguru, 2303

Wambuti pigmies, 2105

Les Wangata, 544

Waniaturu, 1578

Wanyamwezi, 1554, 1579–80

Wapangwa, 1977

Wapogoro (Tanganyika), 1548, 1566, 2179

Wapokomo of Tana Valley, 944

Les Warega, 538, 567, 2585

Les Warembas, 535

Les Warundi and les Wahoro-horo, 536

Les Wasamba, 568, 1139

Die Waschamba: musical instruments, 1976a

Wasiba, 1553

Les Wasongola du Sud, 537

Wasukuma, 1554a

Wayao of Nyasaland, 1003

West Africa (General): music, 1684; musical instruments, 1993; dance, 2823a

Whistle language in Canary Islands, 406, 408

Die Wute, 1826

Yorubas: songs, 1149; folk operas, 1150; music, 1151–2, 1162, 1170, 1171–3, 1193, 1914, 2137, 2139, 2231, 2246–7

Zambia (formerly Northern Rhodesia): music, 1716; musical instruments, 1722, 2033; dance, 2827

Zanzibar: music, 1741; musical instruments, 1994; dance, *see* 2812

Zulus, 1122, 1131a–2, 2237